Risk, Death, and Well-Being

POPULATION-LEVEL BIOETHICS

Ethics and the Public's Health

VOLUMES IN THE SERIES

Inequalities in Health: Concepts, Measures, and Ethics
Edited by Nir Eyal, Samia A. Hurst, Ole F. Norheim, and Dan Wikler

Valuing Health: Well-Being, Freedom, and Suffering
Daniel M. Hausman

Identified versus Statistical Lives: An Interdisciplinary Perspective
Edited by I. Glenn Cohen, Norman Daniels, and Nir Eyal

Saving People from the Harm of Death
Edited by Espen Gamlund and Carl Tollef Solberg
Foreword by Jeff McMahan

Measuring the Global Burden of Disease
Edited by Nir Eyal, Samia A. Hurst, Christopher J. L. Murray, S. Andrew Schroeder, and Daniel Wikler

How Health Care Can Be Cost-Effective and Fair
Daniel M. Hausman

Risk, Death, and Well-Being: The Ethical Foundations of Fatality Risk Regulation
Matthew D. Adler

Risk, Death, and Well-Being

The Ethical Foundations of Fatality Risk Regulation

MATTHEW D. ADLER

OXFORD
UNIVERSITY PRESS

OXFORD
UNIVERSITY PRESS

Oxford University Press is a department of the University of Oxford.
It furthers the University's objective of excellence in research, scholarship,
and education by publishing worldwide. Oxford is a registered trade mark of
Oxford University Press in the UK and in certain other countries.

Published in the United States of America by Oxford University Press
198 Madison Avenue, New York, NY 10016, United States of America.

CIP data is on file at the Library of Congress

ISBN 9780197505953

DOI: 10.1093/9780197505984.001.0001

Printed by Marquis Book Printing, Canada

The manufacturer's authorized representative in the EU for product safety is
Oxford University Press España S.A., Parque Empresarial San Fernando de Henares,
Avenida de Castilla, 2 – 28830 Madrid (www.oup.es/en).

MIX
Paper | Supporting responsible forestry
FSC® C103567

For my grandparents and great-aunt, Helen Adler, Irving Adler, Beatrice Spiegler, Jack Spiegler, and Jeanne Spiegler

Contents

Acknowledgments

Many people helped me write this book. I am deeply grateful for their help (with the normal disclaimer: I'm alone responsible for the book's flaws). For their comments on drafts or presentations, or for answering my questions during the research process, thanks to Gustaf Arrhenius, Danae Arroyos-Calvera, Geir Asheim, Gabrielle Badano, Oren Bar-Gill, Jacob Barrett, SJ Beard, Christopher Belshaw, Juliana Bidadanure, Joseph Blocher, Greg Bognar, Walter Bossert, Jamie Boyle, Ben Bradley, Richard Bradley, Campbell Brown, Mark Budolfson, Susanne Burri, Krister Bykvist, Tim Campbell, Susumu Cato, Caroline Cecot, Daniel Cole, Richard Cookson, Victor Crespo, Roger Crisp, Nir Eyal, Maddalena Ferranna, Chico Ferreira, Marc Fleurbaey, Susan Griffin, Jim Hammitt, Daniel Hemel, Anders Herlitz, Iwao Hirose, Nils Holtug, Kohei Kamaga, Tom Kniesner, Carl Knight, Christoph Lakner, Michael Livermore, Doug MacKay, Anna Mahtani, Jonathan Masur, Joseph Millum, Kaname Miyagishima, Jake Nebel, Ole Norheim, Jennifer Nou, Kieran Oberman, Michael Otsuka, Dalia Patino-Echeverri, Christian Piller, Lisa Robinson, Veronica Root Martinez, Arden Rowell, Itai Sher, Ieva Skarda, Walter Sinnott-Armstrong, Dean Spears, Katie Steele, Orri Stefánsson, Cass Sunstein, Nicolas Treich, Alex Voorhoeve, Kate Vredenburgh, Jonathan Wiener, Emmett Witchel, Tony Zhou, Stéphane Zuber; to two anonymous referees for Oxford University Press; and to others who participated in book manuscript workshops at Cambridge University, Duke University, the Institute for Futures Studies, LSE, Oxford University, and the University of York. Many thanks to Anders Herlitz, SJ Beard, Richard Cookson, and Alex Voorhoeve for organizing these workshops.

I am deeply grateful, too, to Dean Kerry Abrams of the Duke Law School for extremely generous research funding and institutional support without which this book could not have been written; to Leanna Doty for incredible administrative support; and to Jennifer Bahnson, Jennifer Behrens, and Wick Shreve for terrific library research.

I am very pleased that Nir Eyal and Dan Wikler included this book in their series on *Population-Level Bioethics*. Special thanks are owed to them; to my editor at Oxford University Press, Lucy Randall; to Chelsea Hogue, who oversaw production; and to others at OUP and Newgen who helped bring the book to fruition, including Gopinath Anbalagan and Patterson Lamb.

Love and thanks to my wife, sons, and parents—Julia, Jonathan, Spencer, Jack, and Judy—who have always sustained me with their affection, care, and curiosity, and did so while I was laboring on *Risk, Death, and Well-Being*.

Symbols and Abbreviations

This list of symbols and abbreviations is intended to remind the reader of the meaning of the main symbols and abbreviations used in Chapters 1–3 and 5–8. Those that are specific to the chapter appendices or to Chapter 4 (a more technical chapter) are not included here. Symbols may be followed by one or more asterisks, primes, or plusses to indicate an item of the relevant type. For example, d is used to indicate a world, but so are d^*, d^{**}, d^+, and d'. Symbols may have subscripts or superscripts, the former normally to indicate an individual, the latter a time. For example, R_i is the preference of individual i; b_j^t is the bundle of individual j at time t;

A	age
b	attribute bundle
d	possible world
$(d; i)$	the history of individual i in world d
$\mathbf{D}$	set of worlds
$E(P)$	ethical value assigned to policy P by an uncertainty module
$g(\cdot)$	prioritarian transformation function
γ	Atkinson-prioritarian priority parameter
h	history
$\mathbf{H}$	set of histories
i, j	individual
$\mathbf{I}$	set of individuals (population)
$\mathbf{I}^{\mathbf{Mod}}$	set of notional individuals (model population)
l	lifespan, longevity
N	number of individuals
$\mathbf{O}$	set of outcomes
Ω	non-existence
p	survival probability
$\rho_{P,i}(b)$	probability with policy P that individual i receives bundle b
$\pi_P(x)$	probability of outcome x given policy P
P	policy
$\mathbf{P}$	set of policies
R	preference
t	time
T	maximum possible lifespan
$u(\cdot)$	utility function
μ_i^t	probability that individual i lives exactly t periods

w, W	well-being number
$w(\cdot)$	well-being measure
$w^p(\cdot)$	period well-being measure
$\mathbf{w}$	well-being vector
x, y	outcome
$\succcurlyeq$	a ranking (quasiordering). Can be read to mean "at least as good" or "at least as large."
$\succcurlyeq^E$	an ethical ranking of worlds, outcomes, or well-being vectors
$\succcurlyeq^{E\text{-}P}$	an ethical ranking of policies, as per an SWF's uncertainty module
$\succcurlyeq^L$	a ranking of well-being levels
$\succcurlyeq^D$	a ranking of well-being differences
iff	if and only if
CBA	cost-benefit analysis
EDE	equally distributed equivalent. Used in "expected EDE prioritarianism."
ME	monetary equivalent
MU	marginal utility
OHP	ordinary human person. See Section 1.1.3 for definition.
SVRR	social value of risk reduction. $SVRR^{SU}$, $SVRR^{EPP}$, and $SVRR^{EAP}$ indicate, respectively, the utilitarian, ex-post-prioritarian, and ex-ante-prioritarian SVRRs
SWF	social welfare function
vNM	von Neumann-Morgenstern
VSL	value of statistical life
VSLY	value of statistical life year

Introduction

This book aims to provide a rigorous philosophical treatment of the ethical foundations of fatality risk regulation. Specifically, it will develop a welfare-consequentialist ("welfarist") account of those foundations. The book's expository strategy will be to work within welfarism—to take as given the basic structure of ethical assessment that welfarism sets forth—and to elaborate, in detail, what welfarism has to say about fatality risk regulation.

By "fatality risk regulation," I mean governmental policies that seek to reduce the risk to humans of premature death—a risk that arises from toxic substances, radiation, viruses, bacteria, hazardous human artifacts or structures, dangerous human activities, natural disasters, and other sources. Risk regulation, thus described, encompasses a wide range of regulatory programs characteristic of the modern state, including those addressing air, water, and soil pollution; food ingredients and contaminants; cigarettes; alcohol and recreational drugs; firearms; drinking water; consumer product safety; motor vehicle design and manufacture; aircraft design and manufacture; accidents and toxins in the workplace; building construction; energy production (e.g., nuclear power); the design and operation of transportation systems; and programs to mitigate the effects of natural disasters. Another example of fatality risk regulation has recently taken center stage: *pandemic policies*, which aim to control the spread of highly transmissible pathogens and to mitigate their lethality on those infected (the recent pandemic, of course, being the worldwide spread of COVID-19 disease).[1]

Welfarism is a class of ethical views that includes utilitarianism. Utilitarianism has played a central role in ethical thinking and debates for more than two

[1] One metric of the significance of fatality risk regulation as a component of modern governance is its economic impact. The US Office of Management and Budget (OMB) has routinely noted that the largest benefits from major federal regulations (those required by executive order to undergo cost-benefit analysis and OMB review) are associated with regulations that reduce fatality risks. See, e.g., US Office of Management and Budget (2017, p. 11; 2016, p. 12; 2015, p. 13). Daniel Hemel specifically examined the largest federal regulations between 2001 and 2018, those with over $1 billion in costs, and found that the main benefits of many consisted in mortality and morbidity reduction (Hemel 2022, pp. 665–70). An OECD report observes: "Policies and projects in the environmental, transport, energy, food safety and health sectors all involve changes in public mortality risks. When assessed in economic terms, the value of these changes tend[s] to dominate estimates of the benefits of environmental and other policies" (OECD 2012, p. 18, citing sources).

hundred years, since Bentham's writings.[2] This role continues: many contemporary moral philosophers reject utilitarianism, to be sure, but a vibrant utilitarian sub-literature within moral philosophy works to defend and refine the view.[3] Utilitarianism also has had, and continues to have, a large role in shaping normative scholarship outside of philosophy—e.g., in welfare economics[4] or in legal scholarship.[5]

But welfarism outstrips utilitarianism. It is the genus of which utilitarianism is the best-known species. "Welfarism," again, is used here as a synonym for *welfare-consequentialism.* A "goodness ranking" of the set of possible worlds is a comparison structure whereby any given world is ranked as ethically better than, worse than, equally good as, or incomparably good as every other world. An ethical view is consequentialist if it posits a goodness ranking of possible worlds and then derives its ethical assessment of *actions* from the goodness ranking of worlds. An ethical view is *welfarist* if the goodness ranking of worlds is determined by individual well-being (and not also by non-welfare features of worlds).[6]

Utilitarianism ranks worlds according to the simple sum total of well-being. One of the major developments within consequentialist ethics over the last several decades has been the development of plausible welfarist alternatives to utilitarianism, in particular prioritarianism;[7] sufficientism;[8] and egalitarianism.[9]

Yet despite the importance (on the one hand) of fatality risk regulation to contemporary governance, and (on the other) of welfarism to ethical thought, there has been no systematic attempt to *apply* welfarism to this policy domain: to

[2] See Eggleston and Miller (2014).

[3] Leading modern defenses of utilitarianism include Brandt (1979), Broome (1991), Goodin (1995), Hare (1981), Harsanyi (1977), Singer (2011), Smart (in Smart and Williams 1973), and Tännsjö (1998). For more recent book-length defenses, see Forcehimes and Semrau (2019) and Woodard (2019). Utilitarianism plays a dominant role in current philosophical debates about population ethics. See Greaves (2017). See also Adler and Holtug (2019), reviewing utilitarian scholarship in critiques of prioritarianism.

[4] Utilitarian social welfare functions (SWFs) figure centrally both in the theoretical literature on welfare economics, see sources cited Chapter 1, note 37, and in applied literatures where SWFs are used, such as optimal tax theory (see Kaplow [2008];Tuomala [2016]) and climate economics (see Botzen and van den Bergh [2014]).

[5] See, e.g., Kaplow and Shavell (2002).

[6] See Chapter 1.

[7] The seminal defense of prioritarianism is Parfit (2000). I have written extensively in defense of prioritarianism, as has Nils Holtug. See Adler (2012, 2019b, 2022b); Holtug (2010, 2017, 2019); Adler and Holtug (2019). Other philosophers who have defended prioritarianism are cited in Adler and Holtug (2019).

[8] For examples of sufficientism specified as a variant of welfarism, see Crisp (2003); Huseby (2010). See Hirose (2014, ch. 5) for an overview.

[9] The view that well-being inequality is a bad-making feature of outcomes ("telic egalitarianism") is discussed, although not endorsed, by Parfit (2000). See Hirose (2014) for an overview of different forms of egalitarianism, including telic egalitarianism. Scholars who elaborate and endorse this view (modified to take account of considerations of responsibility) include Otsuka and Voorhoeve (2018); Segall (2016); and Temkin (1993).

provide a careful philosophical analysis of how fatality-risk policies are to be assessed in light of welfarism. My ambition, in this book, is to fill this gap.

To be sure, there is a significant *non-consequentialist* philosophical literature regarding lifesaving and risk-imposition, including monographs by Frances Kamm, Jeff McMahan, and John Oberdiek,[10] and many journal articles.[11] However, the only book that even partly addresses these topics from a welfarist perspective is John Broome's *Weighing Lives.*[12] Broome's book is a model of rigor and insight, to which I am indebted. But the scope of the current work is quite different from that of *Weighing Lives.* Broome seeks to explain how the pattern of individuals' well-being at particular times is aggregated—across times within an individual's life, and across individuals—so as to determine the goodness ranking of worlds. The problem of *uncertainty*—namely, how a non-omniscient decisionmaker should assess their choices in light of the world- ranking—is not a focus of Broome's analysis. Moreover, Broome adopts a utilitarian world-ranking. By contrast, the ambition of the book now at hand is to cover utilitarianism as one part of a broader welfarist examination: to investigate how *both* utilitarianism *and* other welfarist views (here placing special emphasis on prioritarianism) give guidance with respect to fatality risk policies.

Why haven't philosophers in the welfarist tradition paid more attention to the topic of fatality risks? Certainly not because the question has escaped philosophical notice. As just noted, there is plenty of non-consequentialist scholarship (in particular, deontological and contractarian scholarship) regarding death, killing, and risk-imposition.

A different answer, perhaps, is that many consequentialists have seen their main task to be specifying the ethical *criterion of rightness* for actions[13] and have placed to one side the problem of specifying an ethically appropriate decision procedure. A criterion of rightness ignores the epistemic position of the actor. Such a criterion states how the features of a given action within an actor's choice set determine the ethical status of that action, with "ethical status" here understood to be independent of the actor's information, knowledge, or beliefs. In the case of consequentialism, the task of specifying the criterion of rightness is trivial once the world-ranking has been established. Act *a* is ethically better than act *b* if and only if ("iff") the world that would result, were *a* to be chosen, is better than the world that would result, if *b* were to be chosen; the two acts are equally good

[10] Kamm (1993, 1996); McMahan (2002); Oberdiek (2017).

[11] See, e.g., Fei (2019); Frick (2015); Kumar (2015); Lazar (2019); Lenman (2008); Otsuka (2015); Reibetanz (1998); Voorhoeve (2014); Walen (2020). Further contributions to this non-consequentialist literature are cited in Horton (2020).

[12] Broome (2004).

[13] See, e.g., Holtug (2019); Sinnott-Armstrong (2023).

iff those two worlds are equally good; the two are incomparable iff those two worlds are incomparable.

But for anyone who aims to use an ethical theory as a source of human *guidance*—as a basis for making recommendations, to human decisionmakers, about the actions they should choose—the consequentialist criterion of rightness is woefully incomplete. A human decisionmaker can't store in their brain a description of a complete possible world, let alone the set of all such descriptions. Nor can any computers that now exist. Moreover, even if humans *could* cognize whole possible worlds, a human decisionmaker (by virtue of being nonomniscient) would often not know for sure *which* world would result from each of the actions available to them. Thus the goodness ranking, for them, would not be a source of action-guidance.

In short, consequentialism and, specifically, welfarism needs a *decision procedure.* The best-developed welfarist decision procedure, appropriate for the assessment of large-scale governmental choices such as fatality risk policies—a decision procedure that I have written about at length elsewhere—is the "social welfare function" (SWF) framework.[14] One of the main analytic tasks of this book is to show how welfarism can be operationalized via the SWF decision procedure so as to assess risk-regulation policies.

Chapter 1 sets out the building blocks. It introduces the concepts, assumptions, and methods that will undergird the book's analysis of fatality risk regulation. One fundamental assumption concerns the "ethical population." Any welfarist theory identifies some such population, namely, the beings whose welfare drives the world-ranking. This book (until Chapter 8, the concluding chapter) assumes that the ethical population is a fixed and finite population of "ordinary human persons" (OHPs). OHPs are human beings who, after birth, undergo the typical processes of human brain development so that they eventually acquire the array of psychological properties that are sufficient for personhood; and who retain these properties, without breaks in intertemporal psychological continuity, until death. The collection of OHPs comprising the ethical population is assumed to be a *fixed* and *finite* group of human beings: fixed in the sense that each OHP in the population exists in all of the worlds being ranked; finite in the sense that the number of OHPs in a given world is finite. I use the term "the Focal Case" to denote this package of premises: that the ethical population consists of a fixed and finite group of OHPs.

A second basic assumption concerns the temporal structure of welfarism. I posit that the world-ranking is determined by the *lifetime well-being* of the

[14] See Adler (2012, 2019b, 2022b); Adler and Fleurbaey (2016); Adler and Norheim (2022); Blackorby, Bossert, and Donaldson (2002; 2005, chs. 2-4); Boadway and Bruce (1984, ch. 5); Bossert and Weymark (2004); d'Aspremont and Gevers (2002); Mongin and d'Aspremont (1998); Weymark (2016).

humans in the ethical population—not their momentary well-being or their well-being during some life-stage. In short, the analytic setup for this book is *lifetime welfarism*, as opposed to momentary welfarism or stage welfarism. Lifetime welfarism can be expressed axiomatically, via the axiom of Lifetime Pareto Indifference as well as related axioms. *Lifetime Pareto Indifference*: If each individual (that is, each OHP in the ethical population) has the same level of lifetime well-being in world d that they do in world d^*, then d and d^* are equally ethically good.

Chapter 1 sets out the components of welfarism, namely, an ethical population and a world-ranking in light of the well-being of the individuals in that population. It explains the Focal Case (the assumption that the ethical population consists of a fixed and finite population of OHPs) and the structure of lifetime welfarism (as captured in the axiom of Lifetime Pareto Indifference and related axioms). Chapter 1 also reviews theories of well-being: *experientialist* theories (well-being depends upon pains and pleasures or other types of mental states); *preferentialist* theories (an individual is better off if their preferences are more fully satisfied); and *objective-good theories* (well-being depends upon objective goods, which are not reducible either to experiential states or to preference-satisfaction). The book is agnostic as between experientialist, preferentialist, and objective-good accounts of welfare. Its analysis of risk regulation applies to all three types of accounts, and to others as well.

Chapter 1 then discusses the main lifetime-welfarist world-rankings: utilitarianism, prioritarianism, sufficientism, leximin, and egalitarianism. Finally, Chapter 1 introduces the SWF framework, as configured so as to operationalize lifetime welfarism. A "policy," abbreviated as *P*, is some course of action by government: enacting a particular regulation or statute, building infrastructure, disseminating information, deploying personnel, etc. The SWF methodology includes various components, which are brought together so as to yield choice guidance with respect to any set of policies **P**. These components are a model population $\mathbf{I}^{\text{Mod}}$; the outcome set **O**; a lifetime well-being measure $w(\cdot)$, which converts a given outcome x into a "vector" (list) of lifetime well-being numbers, one for each person in the population; the SWF proper, which is a rule for ranking well-being vectors; and an uncertainty module for the SWF, which ranks policies understood as probability distributions across outcomes (each such outcome corresponding to a well-being vector).

An outcome is a simplified and, thus, cognitively tractable representation of a whole possible world. An outcome is characterized with respect to *some* of the features of a world that are relevant to individuals' well-being. Outcomes are generally abbreviated in this book with the symbols x or y or variations on these symbols. $\mathbf{O} = \{x, y, \ldots\}$ is the set of outcomes that will be used to determine the ranking of the policy set **P**. **O** is a cognitively tractable *model* of the set of possible worlds; the ranking of O achieved by an SWF is a model of the world-ranking; and a given policy *P* is associated with a probability distribution across O. All of this implements the consequentialist idea that the ethical evaluation of choices (policies) is grounded in the world- ranking.

Chapter 2 provides a substantive defense of lifetime welfarism as against momentary and stage welfarism. Momentary and stage welfarism are each species of time-slice welfarism. In the Focal Case, time-slice welfarism takes the form of dividing each OHP's life into a series of "slices" shorter than an entire lifetime; the world-ranking is, then, a function of the pattern of time-slice well-being in each world across the population of OHPs. For momentary welfarists, each moment of time is its own time-slice, whereas stage welfarists identify slices as "stages," namely, temporal segments longer than moments but shorter than entire lifetimes. Chapter 2 clarifies the difference between lifetime welfarism and time-slice welfarism. It then critiques, in turn, momentary and stage welfarism. Momentary welfarism faces a serious indeterminacy problem. On many theories of human well-being, momentary well-being is not well-defined; rather, well-being accrues to a whole lifetime or to non-momentary time-slices, in virtue of the features of the human's life that are spread out over multiple moments. Moreover, for purposes of any version of non-utilitarian welfarism that is concerned about the *fair distribution* of welfare between persons (for example, prioritarianism), momentary welfarism involves a problematic picture of the temporal scope of fair distribution. Stage welfarism also faces this fair-distribution critique; it may face the indeterminacy critique, if stages are short; and it runs up against the problem of arbitrariness. How are we to arrive at a non-arbitrary segmentation of an OHP's life into a series of non-momentary stages?

Chapter 3 brings death into the picture. Specifically, it clarifies how lifetime welfarism conceptualizes the ethical significance of death at the level of worlds. The answer (not surprisingly) is that death is ethically significant just insofar as death affects lifetime well-being. Consider any two worlds which are such that some individual *i* dies earlier in the second world than the first, producing some change (Δ_i) in their lifetime well-being and perhaps some changes (Δ_j, Δ_k, . . .) in the lifetime well-being of other persons (individuals *j*, *k*, . . .). The ethical impact of individual *i*'s death on the second world's position in the world-ranking is exactly the same as if they had not died earlier but their lifetime well-being had changed by Δ_i and the other persons' lifetime well-being by Δ_j, Δ_k. . . .

Next, Chapter 3 discusses the voluminous philosophical literature regarding the "badness"/"harmfulness" of death. It explains how the lifetime-welfarist account of the ethical significance of death relates to this literature. Finally, Chapter 3 discusses a range of questions regarding *how* death impacts lifetime well-being. Is death a non-compensable welfare-setback? Is life-extension always a benefit? Can the risk of death itself be a setback to lifetime well-being? Can posthumous events change lifetime well-being?

Chapter 4 turns from the world-ranking (the focus of Chapters 2 and 3) to the SWF methodology. The methodology uses outcomes (simplified models of possible worlds) that are built up from individual attribute bundles. In a given outcome x, each individual i is assigned a bundle of attributes, $b_i(x)$. The types of attributes in a bundle are *some* of the individual attributes (properties) that constitute or causally contribute to well-being. The attribute bundles are *lifetime bundles*: they describe the individual's attributes over their entire lifetime. For example, if income is included as an attribute, a bundle will specify the individual's income for each period they are alive. If health is included as an attribute, the bundle will describe their health in each period.

Thus a given outcome x corresponds to a list of lifetime bundles: one for each person in the population. Our well-being measure $w(\cdot)$ maps bundles onto lifetime well-being numbers. Outcomes are converted into well-being vectors via the mapping from bundles to lifetime well-being numbers.

Chapter 4 discusses the content of attribute bundles. It then reviews the construction of the well-being measure $w(\cdot)$. Here, Chapter 4 provides a fully generic methodology for building a well-being measure—one that is agnostic as between different theories of well-being. Next, it discusses the specific form that well-being measurement takes in the case of a preference-based account. Finally, Chapter 4 addresses temporal additivity, both in general and in the case of a preference-based account.

Chapter 5 is the centerpiece of the book. It shows, in detail, how both utilitarian and prioritarian specifications of lifetime welfarism can be brought to bear to evaluate risk-regulation policies, via the SWF methodology. A lifetime-utilitarian world-ranking orders worlds according to the sum total of lifetime well-being. A lifetime-prioritarian world-ranking employs a concave transformation function and orders worlds according to the sum total of transformed lifetime well-being. This has the effect of giving extra weight (priority) to well-being changes affecting those at lower levels of lifetime well-being.

Why utilitarianism? My own views are prioritarian, not utilitarian. But utilitarianism was for hundreds of years the *only* version of welfarism figuring in philosophical discourse; more recently, notwithstanding the development of non-utilitarian forms of welfarism, utilitarianism continues to be supported by many welfarists. A philosophical exploration of welfarism with respect to some policy domain (in this book, risk regulation) surely should not ignore or downplay utilitarianism. Rather, the strategy I pursue in Chapter 5 is to elaborate *utilitarian* and *non-utilitarian welfarist* guidance with respect to risk regulation in tandem—here focusing on prioritarianism as (I believe) the most attractive variant of non-utilitarian welfarism. Seeing the similarities and differences between utilitarianism and prioritarianism brings insight into both approaches—insight that we would not gain in a book solely devoted to analyzing risk regulation from a prioritarian perspective or from a utilitarian one.

Why prioritarianism? Although the book does not wholly ignore non-utilitarian views other than prioritarianism, these are given much less space than prioritarianism. I have elsewhere argued at length in favor of prioritarianism.[15] In light of those arguments, prioritarianism plays a starring role in this book's analysis of risk regulation, while egalitarianism, sufficientism, and leximin appear much more briefly (see Chapter 7). Utilitarianism is marred by its insensitivity to the fair distribution of well-being. Prioritarianism repairs this defect. It satisfies the Pigou-Dalton axiom (the axiomatic expression of a concern for the fair distribution of well-being), while utilitarianism does not. Sufficientism does not fully satisfy Pigou-Dalton. Leximin and egalitarianism do, but have other difficulties. Leximin gives absolute priority to every worse-off individual over every better-off one. Finally, egalitarianism has no axiomatic advantage over prioritarianism at the level of the world-ranking, and a serious disadvantage when operationalized to provide decisional guidance via the SWF methodology. This disadvantage relates to the SWF-level axiom of "Policy Separability," which is discussed in Chapter 5 and again in Chapter 7.

Chapter 5 (the application of utilitarianism and prioritarianism to risk regulation) proceeds as follows. A given SWF has multiple uncertainty modules—an uncertainty module being a formula for ranking policies understood as probability distributions over outcomes (each outcome corresponding to a well-being vector), as already noted. Chapter 5 focuses on what I take to be the best-justified modules for utilitarianism and prioritarianism, respectively: *simple utilitarianism* (the expected sum of individual well-being or, equivalently, the sum of individuals' expected well-being) and *ex post prioritarianism* (the expected sum of individual transformed well-being or, equivalently, the sum of individuals' expected transformed well-being.) Simple utilitarianism and ex post prioritarianism each satisfy the axiom of Policy Separability. If an uncertainty module satisfies this axiom, the process of assessing risk-regulation policies becomes *much* more tractable. A policy can, now, be conceptualized as an array of lotteries over lifetime bundles, one for each affected person in the population. Explicitly characterizing each policy as a lottery over whole outcomes (each outcome describing the bundle attained by everyone in the population) is no longer necessary.

Chapter 5 then explains how risk-regulation policies are modeled as lotteries over lifetime bundles for the various members of the population. Lifetimes are divided into periods (e.g., years), with T the maximum number of periods that

[15] See Adler (2012, 2019b, 2022b); Adler and Holtug (2019).

an individual can live. A given lifetime bundle *b* consists of a realized longevity $l \leq T$, i.e., the number of periods that the individual lives; and a series of period bundles, one for each period from the first period until *l*. Each individual *i* has a current age A_i (the number of periods they have survived until now). A given policy *P* endows the individual with a *risk profile* (a probability of surviving until the end of each period, conditional on being alive at the start) and an *attribute profile* (the period bundle that they receive in each period, conditional on surviving until its end). An individual's age and policy-specific risk profile and attribute profile define the lottery over lifetime bundles that they face with the policy.

Using the well-being measure $w(\cdot)$ as constructed in Chapter 4, simple utilitarianism calculates the expected lifetime well-being associated with each individual's lottery; while ex post prioritarianism calculates the expected *transformed* lifetime well-being associated with each individual's lottery. The overall ethical value that simple utilitarianism assigns to a given policy *P* is the sum of individuals' expected lifetime well-being; while the overall ethical value that ex post prioritarianism assigns to *P* is the sum of individuals' expected transformed lifetime well-being. Moreover (in light of the Policy Separability axiom), unaffected individuals—those whose risk and attribute profiles are not changed by any of the policies under consideration, e.g., prior generations—can be dropped from the analysis without changing simple-utilitarian and ex-post-prioritarian policy recommendations.

Chapter 5 illustrates these methods and valuations via a simulation model based on US data. It also introduces a concept that captures how the ethical value of policies (as per simple utilitarianism or ex post prioritarianism) depends upon fatality risk. This concept is the social value of risk reduction (SVRR).[16] SVRR_i^{SU} is the increase in simple-utilitarian ethical value, per unit of current risk reduction to individual *i*, as evaluated for a marginal risk reduction relative to individual *i*'s baseline risk profile and attribute profile. Similarly, SVRR_i^{EPP} is the increase in ex-post-prioritarian ethical value, per unit of current risk reduction to individual *i*, as evaluated for a marginal risk reduction relative to individual *i*'s baseline risk profile and attribute profile. The pattern of variation of SVRR_i^{SU} and SVRR_i^{EPP} across the population captures how simple utilitarianism and ex post prioritarianism value risk reduction as a function of individual age and other characteristics. Moreover, comparing SVRR_i^{SU} to SVRR_i^{EPP} crystallizes the similarities and differences between simple utilitarianism and ex post prioritarianism as frameworks for assessing risk policies. Chapter 5 both

[16] See Adler, Ferranna, Hammitt, and Treich (2021); Adler, Hammitt, and Treich (2014); Ferranna, Hammitt, and Adler (2023); Ferranna, Sevilla, and Bloom (2022); Hammitt and Treich (2022).

illustrates the SVRR concept using the simulation model and presents theoretical findings regarding SVRR.

Chapter 6 discusses cost-benefit analysis (CBA). CBA is, at present, the dominant economic methodology for evaluating governmental policies and, specifically, risk-regulation policies.[17] Although CBA is sometimes seen as applied utilitarianism, this view of CBA is quite misleading. Utilitarianism ranks worlds according to the sum total of well-being. The SWF methodology implements utilitarianism via outcomes (models of worlds) translated into well-being vectors with an interpersonally comparable well-being measure $w(\cdot)$. The simple-utilitarian uncertainty module assigns each policy P an overall value equaling the sum of individuals' expected well-being—as calculated with $w(\cdot)$. By contrast, CBA does not require the assignment of interpersonally comparable well-being numbers. Instead, the well-being impact of a policy on some individual is expressed in terms of a monetary equivalent relative to baseline. The overall CBA value of a policy is the sum of monetary equivalents.

The key concept in applying CBA to risk regulation is the so-called value of statistical life (VSL). VSL_i is a conversion factor that translates risk reductions into monetary equivalents. If individual *i*'s current fatality risk is reduced by Δp, the monetary equivalent is $\Delta p \times VSL_i$. As Chapter 6 explains, VSL is the CBA analogue to the SVRR concept discussed in Chapter 5. However, the pattern of variation of VSL_i by age and other individual characteristics is quite different from that of $SVRR_i^{SU}$, let alone $SVRR_i^{EPP}$. As a consequence of the SVRR/VSL divergence, and more generally as a result of CBA's use of monetary equivalents rather than well-being or transformed well-being as its measuring scale, CBA yields recommendations for risk-regulation policies that can be quite different from those of simple utilitarianism, let alone ex post prioritarianism.

Chapter 7 reviews welfarist methodologies for assessing risk regulation other than the two discussed in detail in Chapter 5. Simple utilitarianism is the dominant method for applying the utilitarian SWF under uncertainty; it has no widely defended competitors. By contrast, how to apply a prioritarian SWF under uncertainty *is* seriously contested. *Ex ante prioritarianism* and *expected*

[17] Cost-effectiveness analysis (CEA) with the "quality-adjusted life year" (QALY) as the measure of policy effectiveness (see generally Pinto-Prades, Herrerro, and Abellán [2016]) can also, in principle, be employed to assess fatality risk policies. QALY-based CEA is not a widely used technique in the US government. (See US Office of Management and Budget [2023, pp. 4–7], generally disfavoring CEA as compared to CBA for purposes of regulatory analysis.) It *is* widely used in the UK and some other governments for assessing certain types of policies that affect health and fatality risks, e.g., allocating the public health budget. Even in those governments, however, CBA may instead be used for valuing other types of risk-reducing policies, e.g., the regulation of transport safety or pollution. (See HM Treasury [2022, ch. 6], discussing both CBA and QALYs as tools for measuring fatality risk and health impacts.)

I have elsewhere discussed the differences between CEA and the SWF framework. See Adler (2012, pp. 148–53; 2020a). Space constraints preclude a comparison here.

equally distributed equivalent (EDE) prioritarianism are two major competitors to ex post prioritarianism. Chapter 7 discusses the axiomatic trade-offs in choosing an uncertainty module. In light of these trade-offs, it argues in favor of ex post prioritarianism over competing prioritarian modules. Then, Chapter 7 considers how ex ante prioritarianism and expected EDE prioritarianism would apply to risk-regulation policies. Finally, Chapter 7 shifts focus away from utilitarianism and prioritarianism and addresses how egalitarianism, sufficientism, and leximin would be applied to the risk-policy domain.

Chapter 8 moves beyond the Focal Case: the assumption of a fixed and finite population of OHPs. Normative inquiry, such as that attempted in this book, invariably faces a trade-off between generality and depth. By narrowing the field of inquiry in Chapters 1 through 7 to the Focal Case, I have been able to sideline a slew of tricky questions that arise once the ethical population expands beyond OHPs, and thereby (I hope) to arrive at a reasonably thorough understanding of the utilitarian and prioritarian approach to risk regulation in this more limited case. Chapter 8 widens the lens. It considers three ways in which the premises that define the Focal Case might be relaxed—each such alteration yielding a broader definition of the ethical population.

First, the population of OHPs might be *variable* rather than fixed—that is, policy analysis might account for the possibility that the identity and number of existing individuals might vary across worlds. The flourishing philosophical literature on population ethics grapples with this possibility. In this part of the chapter, I show that the risk-regulation frameworks that are the centerpiece of the book (simple utilitarianism and ex post prioritarianism) smoothly generalize to handle variable population.

Second, Chapter 8 addresses infant deaths. Third, Chapter 8 addresses psychological impairments (e.g., Alzheimer's disease) and breaks in psychological continuity. Neither a human being who dies in infancy nor an adult who experiences a sufficiently severe psychological impairment or a break in psychological continuity is an OHP. How should the well-being of such humans figure into welfarist ethics—via their lifetime well-being, or in some other way? On the issues of infant deaths and psychological impairments and breaks, as with the question of variable population, I don't purport to provide definitive answers. Rather, my (less ambitious) aim in Chapter 8 is to show how the lifetime-welfarist account set forth in earlier chapters is *plausibly extended* to address these issues.

A different and very important topic—how a population of OHPs should be broadened to encompass non-human animals—is not attempted in Chapter 8. This is, admittedly, a major limitation of the analytic framework of the book; no welfarist can plausibly deny that the well-being of sentient non-human animals has ethical weight. How to account ethically for the lifetime well-being of OHPs *and* the (lifetime? momentary?) well-being of different species of non-human animals, with a range of psychological capacities, is well beyond what the book can address—even in a sketchy way. Here, I can only state—emphatically—that the limitation of the book's analytic focus to humans is a major incompleteness.

The book's aim, again, is to develop a philosophically rigorous, welfarist account of the ethical foundations of fatality risk regulation. In doing so, the book works at two levels, as the reader can see from the preceding chapter summaries. First, the book elaborates the account *at the level of possible worlds.* How should worlds be ranked in light of individual well-being, and how does death figure into this ranking? This is the topic addressed, in great detail, in Chapters 1 through 3 and again (moving beyond the Focal Case) in Chapter 8. Second, the book elaborates the account *at the level of a policy-evaluation methodology* by which to implement a welfarist world-ranking—specifically, the SWF framework. This is accomplished in Chapters 4, 5, and 7 as well as Chapter 8 (moving beyond the Focal Case). Chapter 6 also subserves this second aim, in showing that the methodology defended is significantly different from the currently dominant tool for assessing risk regulation, namely, CBA.

It is well beyond the scope of the book to *defend* welfarism. Utilitarianism has been debated for centuries, and there is also now a flourishing philosophical literature debating non-utilitarian specifications of welfarism (prioritarianism, sufficientism, egalitarianism, etc.). The contribution of this book, instead, is to improve our understanding of welfarism by specifying its content with respect to a major domain of governmental action: fatality risk regulation. The reader might wonder why the boundaries of the domain should be delineated this way. Fatality risk regulation is a natural delineation, I believe, for two major reasons. First, death has a distinctive impact on well-being: the loss in lifetime well-being that occurs by virtue of reduced lifespan. (That death is distinctive in this way is evidenced by the voluminous philosophical literature on the badness of death, discussed in Chapter 3.) Second, at the assessment level, incorporating changes in fatality risk into policy evaluation raises distinctive issues. The risk-and-attribute-profile apparatus set forth in Chapter 5, and the key concept of the SVRR, would not be applicable to other policy domains (as evidenced already by the fact that CBA has developed its own distinctive construct for handling fatality risk policies, VSL).

It is also beyond the scope of the book to compare the picture presented here with what non-consequentialists (in particular, contractualists and deontologists) would say about the ethics of fatality risk regulation.[18] Such comparison is very important, I believe, but must be left for future research. (To do so sketchily adds little; to do so in the appropriate detail would make an already long book much longer.) Nor do I consider non-welfarist consequentialism.

[18] See sources cited in notes 10–11.

One significant family of such ethical views is fairly close to welfarism. Here, I am thinking of a consequentialism that attends both to individuals' welfare and to their desert, opportunity, or responsibility.[19] It *may* be the case that the world-ranking and policy evaluation framework set forth here can integrate individuals' desert, opportunity, or responsibility without major modification. Whether this is true must, again, be left as a question for future inquiry.

A clarificatory comment: Policies that aim to reduce fatality risks may also have other objectives. In particular, while the various sources of fatality risk described in the second paragraph of this Introduction (toxic substances, radiation, viruses, bacteria, hazardous human artifacts or structures, dangerous activities, etc.) *may* cause immediate death, they also frequently cause an injury or illness that leads over time but not instantaneously to death. In short, these risk sources frequently have morbidity as well as mortality impacts; and policies targeted at these sources will naturally be intended to mitigate both sorts of impacts. The modeling apparatus set out in Chapter 5 (the risk-and-attribute-profile apparatus) readily captures *both* the health improvements *and* the fatality risk reductions that flow from governmental interventions. More generally, *any* change in individuals' attributes (whether health, income, leisure, happiness, etc.) that results from a policy can be modeled, using this apparatus, as a delta to individuals' attribute profiles.[20]

A word on presentation: Some parts of this book's content cannot be accurately explained without a certain degree of mathematical formalism. That is especially true of the parts discussing the SWF framework—which is built upon mathematical constructs (functions, measures, vectors) and indeed owes the precision and sensitivity of its guidance to these tools. That said, in the main text of the book I try not to use too much formalism, recognizing that some readers may well find it a hindrance rather than aid to understanding. To the extent that complicated mathematical formulas are used in the main text, I accompany them with a verbal explanation.

The one part of the main text that *is* quite formal is Sections 4.2–4.4, discussing the construction of the well-being measure. The reader if they wish can skip these sections; nothing in the rest of the book assumes a close engagement with them.

Readers who *are* mathematically inclined will find backup for the main text in chapter appendices accompanying some of the chapters; in footnotes; and in

[19] See, e.g., Arneson (2000, 2007); Feldman (1995); Ferreira and Peragine (2016); Kagan (2012b); Segall (2016); Temkin (1993).

[20] Chapter 5 also discusses a generalization of the risk-and-attribute-profile apparatus to allow for stochastic attributes. This gives added flexibility in handling the morbidity-reduction benefits of policies. See Section 5.5. That said, the simulation model presented in Chapter 5 to illustrate the risk-and-attribute-profile apparatus ignores morbidity; the policies simulated reduce fatality risk, at a cost in income, and have no other impact.

cited sources. Chapter appendices are intended for readers who are comfortable with formalism.

Finally, a note on cross-referencing. "Section" means a portion of a chapter. A section is cited by its number, the first number indicating the chapter. For example, Section 5.1 and Section 5.3.2 are both portions of Chapter 5. An appendix section begins with the chapter number and then "A." For example, Section 5.A.2 is part of the appendix to Chapter 5.

1
Ethical Foundations
Welfarism

This book provides a *welfarist* account of the ethical foundations of fatality risk regulation. "Welfarism," here and throughout the book, is used as shorthand for "welfare consequentialism." That is, "welfarist" ethical theories (in my usage) are a subset of consequentialist ethical theories.[1]

An ethical theory is *consequentialist* if its guidance, for any given decisionmaker, is grounded upon a ranking of the possible consequences of the decisionmaker's choices. More precisely, ethical guidance is grounded upon a ranking of possible worlds. For any two worlds, this ranking specifies whether the first world is ethically better than the second, worse than the second, equally good as the second, or incomparable with the second.

The world-ranking is *nonrelative*. A consequentialist theory (as I'll interpret the concept of "consequentialism") posits a single world-ranking that applies to all agents at all times, rather than a multiplicity of world-rankings that are agent-relative and/or time-relative.[2]

An ethical theory is not merely consequentialist but, more specifically, *welfarist* if it links the ranking of possible worlds to the *well-being* of some population of welfare-subjects. Welfare-subjects are the kinds of beings that possess welfare. A being ("Xavier") is a welfare-subject if it is meaningful to ascribe welfare to Xavier and to compare worlds, choices, and other items in light of Xavier's welfare. Humans are paradigmatic welfare-subjects. But it is also widely supposed by philosophers of well-being that sentient non-human animals also possess welfare.

The nature of well-being has long been philosophically contested and remains so.[3] One school of thought, dating back to Jeremy Bentham, adopts a hedonic view of well-being. Welfare consists in experiencing pleasures (positive sensations) and avoiding pains (negative sensations). A different, older view,

[1] On consequentialism, see generally Portmore (2020); sources cited in Horta, O'Brien, and Teran (2022, p. 384). On welfare-consequentialism, see Adler (2012, pp. 32–56); Holtug (2010, ch. 6).

[2] Consequentialism is often understood to involve a single, non-relative ranking of worlds (or of "consequences" understood in some other sense) but sometimes instead to allow for relativized rankings. See Hammerton (2020); Horta, O'Brien, and Teran (2022, p. 372). The first, non-relative view is more perspicuous, I believe, because it sharply brings into focus how consequentialism and deontology are distinctive approaches to morality. For other arguments against the relativized view, see Broome (2004, pp. 68–74); Hammerton (2020, pp. 59–64).

[3] See sources cited note 21.

Risk, Death, and Well-Being. Matthew D. Adler, Oxford University Press. © Oxford University Press 2025.
DOI: 10.1093/9780197505984.003.0001

running all the way back to Aristotle, analyzes welfare in terms of various "objective goods." A third type of account, dominant in economics and endorsed by some philosophers, links well-being and preferences. On this approach, a subject is better off just insofar as their preferences are more fully satisfied.

Welfarist ethical views therefore vary along multiple dimensions. In order to arrive at a fully fleshed out welfarist view, we need to (1) specify an *ethical population*, the welfare-subjects whose well-being drives the world-ranking; (2) specify an *account of well-being*, be it based upon hedonic states, objective goods, preferences, or some mixture; and (3) specify a *world-ranking*, namely, the rule by which worlds are compared as better or worse in light of the well-being (accorded to the stipulated account) of members of the population.

As regards (1), the ethical population, this book ignores non-human animals. The population is assumed to consist only of human beings. Moreover, until the end of the book (Chapter 8), I adopt a yet more restrictive assumption: that the human beings in the ethical population are "ordinary human persons" (OHPs), namely, human beings who, after birth, undergo the typical processes of brain development that lead to their acquiring an array of psychological properties that are jointly sufficient for personhood, properties that are typically possessed by adult humans; and who retain these properties, without breaks in intertemporal psychological continuity, until death.

My reasons for restricting the ethical population in this manner are inquiry-based (reasons that concern the structure of ethical inquiry), not substantive. Many species of non-human animals (plausibly, all species of sentient animals) do possess a well-being, as do human beings who are not OHPs. To deny that their well-being lacks ethical weight is highly implausible. Rather, I exclude non-human animals from the ethical population, and also human beings who are not OHPs (until Chapter 8), because the task of developing a comprehensive world-ranking that is sensitive to the interests of both OHPs and all other types of welfare subjects raises many difficult problems—problems that philosophy has barely begun to confront. Rather than address these problems, this book sets itself the more tractable task of applying the extant literature on welfarism (largely limited to OHPs) to the specific domain of fatality risk regulation.

I will use the term "Focal Case" to denote the restriction of the ethical population to OHPs. In short, what this book mainly provides is a welfarist theory of fatality risk regulation for the Focal Case.

As regards (2), the nature of well-being, the book is completely agnostic. I will adopt certain assumptions about the formal structure of well-being comparisons; but these formal assumptions are consistent with the full range of plausible views regarding the content of well-being, including hedonic, objective-good, and preferentialist views as well as others.

As regards (3), the world-ranking, I assume (until Chapter 8) that this ranking is some species of *lifetime welfarism*. Roughly speaking, what drives the ranking is the lifetime well-being of members of the population—not their momentary well-being or their well-being during some life-stage (a non-momentary fraction of a whole lifetime).

The first three sections of this chapter discuss, in greater detail, these three components of welfarism. Section 1.1 covers the ethical population. It elaborates upon my rationale for excluding non-human animals from this group and then discusses the nature of human persons. Because this book focuses on OHPs, it is important to say something at the outset about the properties of such beings and how they endure over time.

Section 1.2 briefly surveys different extant views regarding the content of well-being, and it then explains the formal structure of well-being comparisons.

Section 1.3 discusses the world-ranking. It makes precise the concept of lifetime welfarism. And it surveys the main species of lifetime welfarism, in particular lifetime utilitarianism and lifetime prioritarianism, as well as others (lifetime leximin, lifetime sufficientism, lifetime egalitarianism).

The topic of lifetime welfare is further pursued in Chapter 2, which argues in favor of lifetime welfarism (in the Focal Case, for a population of OHPs) rather than non-lifetime welfarism. My aim in the current chapter is simply to get clear about the structure of welfarism—about the population, well-being, and the world-ranking—and so I postpone making the substantive case for lifetime welfarism until Chapter 2.

I have said nothing thus far about how a welfarist ethical view provides guidance to a decisionmaker. The world-ranking itself does not do so. A possible world is a complete description of a possible history of the universe, from start to finish. It tells us "what might happen" in full detail. The description is complete in the sense that every possible fact is either included within the description or precluded by it. (So, for example, a possible world will specify either that Matt Adler is awake at 6 a.m. on July 1, 2024, or that it is not the case that Matt Adler is awake then.) A human and hence cognitively bounded decisionmaker cannot hold in consciousness a possible world, let alone the set of all possible worlds. Although Maria, a cognitively bounded decisionmaker, can *think about* the world-ranking (she can deliberate about which features of a given world determine its location in the world-ranking), Maria can't directly *use* the world-ranking as a decisional tool.

In short, a welfarist ethical account—in order to serve up choice-guidance to cognitively bounded decisionmakers—needs to incorporate a decision-procedure of some sort. This procedure will tell Maria how to rank a given choice set (a set of choices available to her) in light of the population, well-being account, and world-ranking.

By far the most systematic and rigorous decision-procedure for welfarism is the SWF framework. This framework is a linchpin of the book. Section 1.4 introduces the SWF framework.

1.1 The Population

A welfarist ethical theory includes, as one component, an "ethical population": the welfare subjects whose well-being is given weight by the theory. I assume throughout the book that the ethical population excludes non-human animals. Section 1.1.1 explains why. Indeed, until the last chapter (Chapter 8), I assume that it includes only ordinary human persons (OHPs). The characteristics of persons, intertemporal psychological continuity, the metaphysics of persons, and the further restriction of the ethical population to OHPs, are discussed in Sections 1.1.2 through 1.1.5.

1.1.1 Humans, Not Animals

Many species of non-human animals are sentient, i.e., capable of feeling pleasure and pain. This includes, as far as we know, all mammals and many non-mammalian species as well.[4]

The proposition that all sentient non-humans are welfare subjects seems very plausible.[5] This is surely plausible if one adopts a hedonic account of human well-being; nor need the proposition be undercut by a non-hedonic view of *human* well-being. Causing serious pain to a non-human animal is, intuitively, bad for that animal. And one truism of the philosophical literature on welfare is the conceptual connection between welfare and what is good or bad *for* a being. If a state of affairs is good or bad *for* the being, then it affects the being's welfare. Causing severe pain to Rick the cow (or Rick the cat, Rick the frog, Rick the rat, ...)—let alone Rick the chimpanzee—is bad *for* Rick. Rick is a locus of various attributes, including perceptions and sensations; these are perceived and felt *by* Rick; and it is bad *for* Rick when, among those perceptions and sensations, there occurs a severe pain. Thus, severe pain lowers Rick's welfare.

Does the welfarist theorist have good grounds for rejecting the ethical standing of a given non-human species even if the theorist accepts that animals within this species are welfare subjects? It seems not. To deny these beings ethical standing merely because they belong to a particular species (and not because

[4] See, e.g., DeGrazia (1996); Varner (2012).
[5] Kagan (2019); Singer (2011).

of the nature of their welfare) is parochial. To deny them ethical standing because their welfare is different in kind from humans' (if it is) is not parochial, but remains problematic. Let two worlds be identical with respect to well-being, except that in the second Rick (a sentient non-human animal) experiences severe, ongoing pain. Then surely the second world is ethically worse than the first—regardless of the differences between Rick's welfare and human welfare.

In short, a version of welfarism that excludes all non-human animals from the ethical population is not substantively plausible. This book works within the framework of human-centered welfarism for inquiry-based reasons—because doing so advances our understanding of welfarism—and not because I deny ethical standing to non-human animals.

How to specify welfarism with an ethical population of all welfare subjects (an "inclusive" population), both humans and sentient non-human animals, poses difficult questions that the philosophical literature has barely grappled with. These difficulties are of three kinds. (1) A human being is aware of itself as existing over time. This temporal self-awareness—"autonoetic consciousness," to use Gary Varner's term[6]—is in turn one key component of the argument for lifetime welfarism in the case of humans. Events that impinge upon the life of a particular human being at different ages are integrated into their lifetime well-being; and it is the pattern of lifetime well-being, rather than stage or momentary well-being, that should drive ethical assessment insofar as humans are concerned—or so I shall argue below.[7] But many species of sentient non-human animals lack autonoetic consciousness. Defending lifetime welfarism for such animals is much harder. Specifying welfarism with an inclusive population therefore means balancing the lifetime well-being of certain welfare subjects against the stage or momentary well-being of others. Philosophers have barely addressed how to do this.

(2) Some plausible theories of human well-being rely upon psychological capacities that are not possessed by some sentient non-human animals. For any such theory, how to make well-being comparisons between humans and animals lacking the relevant capacities poses a difficulty. For example, a preference theory of well-being may (a) appeal to individuals' "global" preferences, preferences over whole lives; and/or (b) appeal to preferences that satisfy various "idealization" conditions, such as being well-informed, formally rational, or fully deliberated. But a sentient animal species may lack preferences entirely; or, if it has preferences, may lack global preferences or preferences meeting the idealization conditions. Preference accounts of well-being, or a subset thereof, will

[6] Varner (2012, p. 160).
[7] See Chapter 2.

therefore face serious difficulties in comparing the welfare of such animals with human welfare.

(3) Much recent writing in welfarist ethics has worked to develop non-utilitarian criteria of ethical goodness—specifically criteria that take account of equity considerations, in some way. For example, egalitarian welfarists argue that the inequality of well-being has intrinsic ethical relevance alongside the sum total of well-being. Prioritarian welfarists argue that a given increment to the well-being of someone who is worse off has greater ethical weight than the very same increment to the well-being of someone who is better off. Sufficientists reject priority if the worse-off one is above a threshold, but they conversely argue for absolute priority if the worse-off one is below a threshold and the better-off one is above. Extending these non-utilitarian views to non-human animals poses serious challenges[8] and has been little discussed.

These three issues cry out for philosophical attention. But doing so is well beyond the scope of a single book—let alone a single book that seeks to apply welfarism to a particular policy domain, here fatality risk regulation. Rather than trying to tackle the issues in depth as a prolegomenon to an account of risk regulation that posits an inclusive ethical population, I simply ignore them—and do so by excluding non-human animals from the ethical population. What this yields is a *partial* welfarist account of the policy domain: an account that explores what welfarism recommends with respect to risk regulation insofar as human beings are concerned.

1.1.2 Human Persons: Psychological Characteristics

A human being, as they develop from a fertilized ovum, to a fetus, then infant, child, and adult, typically acquires an array of psychological characteristics, described immediately below. The timing of the acquisition of the attributes varies. By OHP, I mean a human being who will live long enough to acquire all of these characteristics; after acquiring them, will retain those characteristics until the being dies; and never experiences a break in intertemporal psychological continuity (on psychological continuity, see Section 1.1.3).

When they are old enough to have acquired all of these characteristics, the OHP is a full *person*. The characteristics that follow are, collectively, *sufficient* for personhood. Not all may be *necessary* for personhood. Philosophers have articulated a wide range of accounts of personhood, identifying one or another subset of these characteristics as constitutive of personhood—individually necessary

[8] See Holtug (2007); Kagan (2019); Vallentyne (2007). See also Korsgaard (2018).

and jointly sufficient.[9] I don't need to adjudicate between such accounts here. There is no doubt that a being with *all* of these characteristics is a person. The welfare-relevance of the various characteristics will depend upon the theory of well-being adopted.

The psychological characteristics of OHPs, jointly sufficient for personhood, are these:

(1) *Phenomenal Consciousness/Sentience.* By "phenomenal consciousness" (I'll use "sentience" as a synonym), I mean being the subject of some form of mental life. To quote Gary Varner:

> Phenomenal consciousness is the subjective "feel" of our lives as we experience them. . . . Phenomenal consciousness is simultaneously extremely important and deeply mysterious. It is deeply mysterious because it is so hard to define or characterize clearly. We use mysterious expressions like "the subjective 'feel' of our lives or experiences" to describe it, and, in a phrase made famous by Thomas Nagel, we say that for a phenomenally conscious being "there is something it is like to be that being." At the same time, phenomenal consciousness is extremely important, because we each value our own lives in large measure as a function of the positive (and negative) phenomenally conscious experiences they contain. This is illustrated by the fact that most of us would be indifferent to the option of going on living for many years, even if we behaved in complicated ways, if we were to do so as "zombies," stripped of phenomenal consciousness.[10]

(2) *Perceptions.* Ordinary human beings experience a range of visual, auditory, and tactile perceptions. (3) *Pains, Pleasures and Feelings.* Ordinary humans experience "pains" and "pleasures" meaning, in the first case, a type of negative sensation; and, in the second, a type of positive sensation. Ordinary human beings also experience other types of positive and negative sensations.

(4) *Beliefs and Desires.* Beliefs and desires (preferences) are the two central cases of propositional attitudes. A belief is a propositional attitude with a "mind to world" direction of fit; a desire is a propositional attitude with a "world to mind" direction of fit. Ordinary human beings come to possess both.

(5) *Concepts.* A concept is a mental representation of some aspect of the world (an entity, a property, a fact, etc.). Presumably having beliefs and desires requires

[9] On the nature of persons, see, e.g., DeGrazia (1996); Frankfurt (1971); Millum (2019); Singer (2011); Varner (2012); Warren (1973).

[10] Varner (2012, pp. 107–8).

at least rudimentary concepts. In any event, having concepts is part of the mental equipment that ordinary humans eventually acquire.

(6) *Self-Consciousness.* A being is self-conscious if it has a concept of itself. This is the concept expressed, in English, with the words "I" or "me." Note that a being might be sentient/phenomenally conscious without possessing self-consciousness. Indeed, a being might be sentient *and* have perceptions, feelings, beliefs, desires, and concepts without being self-conscious. But, of course, ordinary humans do come to acquire a self-concept. Further, while the constitutive connection between personhood and some of the other properties listed here can be disputed, that connection can't plausibly be disputed for *this* property. If a being isn't self-conscious, it isn't a person.

(7) *Autonoetic Consciousness.* Gary Varner uses "autonoetic consciousness" to mean a being's having a robust, conscious sense of its own past and future.[11] To be "autonoetically conscious," a being needs to have a self-concept *and* (a) the concept of itself existing over time; (b) memories, i.e., perception-like mental states that the being conceptualizes as a record of its past experiences; and (c) the ability to imagine itself in future situations. Autonoetic consciousness implies self-consciousness, but not vice versa.

(8) *Language Use.* Ordinary humans, as they develop, learn one or more languages (expressed in words, writings, and/or other signs) to communicate their beliefs and other aspects of their mental states.

(9). *Autonomy.* Definitions of personhood often see autonomy, *in some sense*, as a constitutive feature of persons. Plausible aspects of autonomy include the following. (a) *Theoretical and practical reasoning.* Humans can reason about what to believe and what to do. (b) *Higher-order preferences.* Human preferences are not fixed; nor is the source of preference change, when it occurs, necessarily exogenous. Humans have higher-order preferences—preferences about what to want. One way that lower-order preferences change is by coming into alignment with higher-order preferences. (c) *Intentions.* An intention is a commitment to act. Sometimes, human action occurs without an intention—e.g., flowing directly from beliefs and desires. But ordinary humans are also capable of formulating an intention (e.g., as the upshot of practical reasoning) and then acting in accordance with that intention. (d) *Norms.* Humans can adopt norms governing action, desire, and belief—such as ethical norms, norms of rationality, or epistemic norms—and aim to come into conformity with such norms.

[11] Varner (2012, p. 160).

1.1.3 Human Persons: Intertemporal Psychological Continuity

Not merely is it the case that ordinary human beings come to acquire the many and varied psychological attributes just enumerated. Further, and critically, ordinary humans have a psychological makeup that is *intertemporally continuous*. Imagine that Felicia wakes up on Wednesday, June 20, 1973 remembering nothing of what occurred on Tuesday, June 19, 1973 or any previous day; and having desires and beliefs, but quite different desires and beliefs than on that Tuesday. This would be unusual!

The philosophical literature on psychological identity has grappled with how to specify intertemporal psychological continuity. Consider Mary, an ordinary human who dies at the age of 70, and never experiences any kind of psychological disease or abnormality (no dementia, amnesia, brain damage, etc.). Mary at 70 is psychologically continuous with Mary at earlier ages *in some sense*—but what sense is that? It's surely not the case that Mary at 70 has the very same mental states as Mary at 69, let alone Mary at 50, 40, or 30. Indeed, Mary on February 2, 2020, will not have the very same mental states as Mary on February 3, 2020—because, for example, Mary will have new perceptions on the second day, and her perceptions on the first day will leave traces as memories on the second (which she didn't have on the first).

A more plausible proposal, following Derek Parfit, is to analyze psychological continuity in terms of *direct connections* between mental states.[12] This is a looser concept than *identity* of mental state. Certainly, if Mary believes P on February 2 and believes P on February 3, then her belief state on the second day is directly connected to (because identical with) her belief state on the first. Ditto if Mary on February 2 has a desire for D and on February 3 also has a desire for D. However, in the case where Mary on February 2 has a perception and then on February 3 has a memory of that perception, the memory on the second day is (per Parfit) directly connected to the perception on the first even though not identical to it.

Parfit, next, defines two momentary clusters of mental states as *strongly connected* if there are a sufficient number of direct connections between the clusters. Mary on February 3, 2020, is strongly connected with Mary on February 2, 2020. *Psychological continuity*, in turn, is analyzed as "overlapping chains of strong connectedness."[13] Mary's cluster of mental states on a given day in her life at age 70 may not be strongly connected to a cluster of mental states on a given day at age 50; and her cluster of mental states on that age-50 day may not be strongly connected to a cluster of mental states on a given age-30 day. But her

[12] Parfit (1987, pt. 3).
[13] Parfit (1987, p. 207).

age-30 day's mental states will be strongly connected to the next day's, and that day's to the following, and so forth—so that there is an overlapping chain of day-to-day connections from the age-30 day to the age-50 day. Similarly, there is an overlapping chain of strong day-to-day connections from the age-50 day to the age-70 day. By virtue of these overlapping chains, Mary is psychologically continuous throughout her life.

Parfit's account of intertemporal psychological continuity is a prominent one in the literature on personal identity, and I'll rely on it here.[14] An OHP, as I define that term, is a human being who (1) will live long enough to acquire the full array of psychological characteristics set forth in Section 1.1.2 (the characteristics of typical adult humans that are jointly sufficient for personhood); (2) having acquired the characteristics, will retain them until the being dies; *and* (3) is psychologically continuous, over their entire lifetime, in Parfit's sense (this human being's psychological states at any moment of their life are linked, via an overlapping chain of strong moment-to-moment connections, to their psychological states at any other moment).

It is important to stress that "OHP" ("ordinary human person"), as that term is used in this book, is a term of art. Humans who are atypical in some way but meet the definition immediately above—they live long enough to acquire the full array of *psychological* characteristics sufficient for personhood—are OHPs. For example, a human being with substantial physical impairments, whose physical body has atypical functional capacities, might be described as "not ordinary" in the colloquial sense; but these physical features of that person are irrelevant to their status as OHP. Moreover, an individual might be psychologically atypical but still meet the definition of OHP, in virtue of having the full suite of attributes set forth in Section 1.1.2.[15]

Whether a human is an OHP takes account of that individual's entire life history. In one possible world, Juanita suffers serious brain damage at age 60 and ceases to be a person; in a second possible world, she lives a normal life. In the second world Juanita is an OHP while in the first she is not. It is indeterminate whether a given human is an OHP (since one of the life histories of that human may be that of an OHP, while a second may not be). It may also be indeterminate whether a given human with a partial life history specified up until time *t* is an OHP (since one continuation of that partial history may be an OHP's, while a second not). What *is* determinate is whether a given human *in a given world d* is an OHP (since *d* will include a full specification of a possible life history of that human, which will either be that of an OHP or not).

[14] That literature is cited in Olson (2023).
[15] For discussion of psychological impairments and OHPs, see Section 8.3.

This leads to a second way in which the term "OHP" is a term of art. Assume that some human is indeed an OHP in some world *d*. That human will not be a person at all times in *d*; at birth, and during some stretch of time thereafter, they will not have all the properties necessary for personhood (whatever exactly they are). Still, I will say that this human *is* an OHP in *d*. That individual *is* an OHP in *d* in virtue of *becoming* a person in *d* (and then remaining a psychologically continuous person until death).

1.1.4 Human Persons: Metaphysics

A substantial philosophical literature has arisen concerning the ontology or "metaphysics" of human persons.[16] Consider the case of Matt Adler, who is an ordinary human being, born from particular parents, at a particular time, with particular DNA. Matt has all the psychological attributes of persons, and his psychological makeup is continuous over time. Julie Smith is an ordinary human being, with a different body from Matt's, born to different parents, at a different time, with different DNA. Julie has all the psychological attributes of persons, and her psychological makeup is continuous over time. Matt and Julie are distinct beings. This is a matter of common sense, and the scholars writing in the literature just mentioned would generally agree (on the facts presented). To use the philosophical jargon, Matt is "numerically identical" (one and the same particular being) to Matt, and not to Julie. Julie is numerically identical to Julie, and not to Matt.

The thorny question is how best to analyze the facts of numerical identity in this commonplace case, and, relatedly, to determine what the facts would be in more esoteric cases. A general premise in the literature on the ontology of human persons (one I have no reason to dispute) is that each individual being (and specifically each human person) is characterized by certain *persistence conditions* (also referred to as "essential properties"). The persistence conditions for a being are the properties it retains at all times that it exists. It can't begin existence until it has those properties. And, in losing any of them, the being goes out of existence; either it becomes a different (numerically distinct) being, or no being at all.

The properties of a being that are not among its persistence conditions are merely contingent. For example, having long hair is (obviously) a contingent property of human persons. One particular human being might have short hair, then let it grow long, and after that cut it short, yet remain numerically the same being throughout this sequence.

[16] See, e.g., Baker (2000); Blatti and Snowdon (2016); DeGrazia (2005); McMahan (2002, ch. 1); Olson (2007, 2014); Parfit (2012); Shoemaker (2011).

The disputed question is this: what *are* the persistence conditions of human persons? In particular, is being a person among the persistence conditions of a human person? Is being human among those persistence conditions?

One main position in this dispute, "Animalism," says that the persistence conditions of a human person are just the *persistence conditions of a human animal.* Human-animal persistence conditions are a cluster of biological properties. What exactly these biological properties are is a matter for further discussion, but surely they include the properties of being a living organism and being of the species Homo sapiens; and they may also include properties such as having a body that develops continuously over time, and having the same DNA over time or at least a DNA that does not change radically. Crucially, however, according to Animalists, the persistence conditions of human animals do *not* include being a person.

Human beings may, of course, be persons; but on the Animalist view, personhood is a merely contingent property of human persons. Animalists assert that, for example, one individual being might for some time be a human animal but not a person (at these times, lacking the attributes characteristic of persons); then acquire those attributes, hence become a person; then lose those attributes, and hence cease to be a person—and yet remain one and the same being throughout. On this view, because personhood is merely a contingent property of human persons, a human person may be numerically identical to a non-person.

Consider the case of Doug, the human being, who comes into existence no later than live birth; becomes a person, let's assume, by age 8; and remains a person until Doug suffers a terrible accident at age 40, placing him in a permanent vegetative state—in which state he remains until he dies at 50. According to Animalists, Doug is the same particular being from live birth until his death at 50, even though he only falls into the category person between ages 8 and 40. The human person Doug is (according to Animalists) numerically identical to the human animal Doug between the ages 8 and 40, during which time that animal has the contingent property of personhood; *and* numerically identical to the human animal Doug before the age of 8 and after the age of 40, during which time that animal lacks the contingent property of personhood.

The main competing position in the dispute, Personalism, asserts that personhood *is* among the persistence conditions for human persons. A human person necessarily has the status, "person," for as long as they exist. They come into existence only when they have the attributes of personhood, and they cease to exist once they lose them. In the "Doug" case just described, Personalists take the view that the human person Doug is *not* numerically identical to the human animal Doug before the age of 8 and after the age of 40. This follows from the core premise of Personalism, that personhood is among the persistence conditions of human persons: Since Doug before the age of 8 and after the age of 40 lacks the property of personhood, no human person (Doug between the ages of 8 and 40, or any other human person) can be numerically identical to that being.[17]

Each side can point to unappetizing implications of the contending view. Personalists note that Animalism's account of transplant cases is counterintuitive. Assume that Anne, a human being, undergoes an unusual series of medical procedures. Anne's cerebrum is removed from her body and placed in a machine that keeps it functioning, where it remains for some time. Then, Billy (another human being) has his cerebrum removed and replaced with Anne's. Anne, prior to the procedures, has all the psychological attributes of a person (those attributes arising from physical states in her cerebrum). Anne's cerebrum, let's suppose, continues to give rise to the full range of psychological states characteristic of persons—both when in the machine and, later, when placed in Billy's body. Moreover, there is psychological continuity (overlapping chains of strong connectedness) between all of the cerebrum's momentary clusters of psychological states—whether the cerebrum is in Anne's body, in the machine, or in Billy's body.

It seems very plausible that the three beings described here—Anne before the operation, the cerebrum in the machine, and Billy with Anne's cerebrum—are, each, persons. The first and third beings are human persons; the second being is a non-human entity (a machine-plus-cerebrum) with sufficient psychological properties to be a person. Moreover, it seems that these persons are numerically identical. Insofar as persons are concerned, there are not three distinct beings but three stages of the same particular person. Anne, the machine-cerebrum hybrid, and Billy with Anne's cerebrum are psychologically continuous with each other, and indeed their psychological attributes have a common physical basis (the cerebrum). However, Animalists are forced to conclude that Anne, the machine-cerebrum hybrid, and Billy with Anne's cerebrum are three different—numerically distinct—persons. Again, Animalists assert that human persons

[17] How to specify the persistence conditions of human persons is a matter for debate within the Personalist camp. Personalists generally deny that being *human* is among the persistence conditions of human persons. In particular, they generally agree that numerical identity would be preserved if a human person's cerebrum were removed from their body and placed in a machine that supports the cerebrum's functioning. (See the Anne/Billy case in the text following this note.) If the human person associated with the cerebrum while in a human body is indeed one and the same being as the non-human person associated with the cerebrum in the machine (a cerebrum in a machine is not a human animal), being human is not among the persistence conditions of human persons.

What remains open for debate within the Personalist camp is how to specify the persistence conditions of human persons consistent with the core premise that personhood is among those conditions and the generally held further premise that being human is not. One much-discussed issue is how to handle cases in which psychological continuity between a human person A and a person B (human or not) is produced by esoteric means. To illustrate: Imagine that Anne's brain is removed from her body and its contents perfectly transferred to a computer with all the capacities of a human brain. Anne's brain is destroyed, and the computer is then implanted as the control system for a robot. Assuming the robot is a person, is the human person Anne numerically identical to it?

have human-animal persistence conditions. On this view, Anne cannot be the same being as the machine-cerebrum hybrid, because the latter is not a human being. Nor can she be the same being as Billy with her transplanted cerebrum, since the two are distinct human animals.

Animalists argue that Personalism faces a dilemma in enumerating thinking beings. Call this the "How Many Thinkers?" question. Consider Zeke, a human person. Zeke, right now, is sitting in his desk chair. How many thinking individuals are in the chair? One such individual, according to Personalism, is Zeke. But there is also a human being in the chair. Surely Personalists can't deny that human beings *are* beings. Let's use "Zeke" to refer to the person, and "Mo" to refer to the human being. Zeke is thinking, but what about Mo? Personalists, here, *might* answer "no." Zeke thinks while Mo doesn't. Yet this is odd: Mo's body includes a well-functioning cerebrum that supports thinking; indeed, it is by virtue of this cerebrum that *Zeke* thinks. So why can Zeke think but not Mo? Alternatively, personalists might answer "yes." If so, there are two different thinking beings in the very same place. This too is odd: There's no esoteric physical or psychological feature of the case that would multiply beings. (Mo and Zeke have the same cerebrum and think the same thoughts.)

Further, a "yes" answer gives rise to an epistemic difficulty. Mo, according to Personalists, is a being that is not a person. Zeke, according to Personalists, is a distinct being who is a person. If both beings think, then Zeke cannot have good reason to believe that he is a person. Whatever thoughts (perceptions, beliefs, intentions, etc.) Zeke might be having, those thoughts cannot be a reliable basis for Zeke to conclude that he is a person—since Mo is having the very same thoughts, and yet isn't a person. In short, a "yes" answer yields skepticism about personhood: No individual person should believe that they are a person.

The approach taken in this book will be Animalist, not Personalist. I don't believe that the arguments adduced by Animalists have shown Personalism to be so deeply problematic as to be incoherent or unworkable, nor that Animalism is free of flaws. (It isn't; again, it is at the very least counterintuitive in transplant cases.) However, I believe that Animalism is on balance the better approach here.

How we individuate beings is relative to our purposes. There is not a single, uniquely correct scheme of individuation. The individual entities that exist for purposes of physics, say, are not the same entities that exist for purposes of biology—which in turn are not the same entities that exist for purposes of ordinary life. At the level of reality engaged by physics, individual entities are atoms, subatomic particles, and the like. At the level of reality engaged by biology, individual entities include living organisms. At the level of reality of ordinary human life, entities include inanimate macroscopic entities (chairs, houses, ships, etc.) that neither physicists nor biologists would recognize as distinct, individual things.

The position that each human being is a distinct being, with human-animal persistence conditions, is a coherent view. Personalists haven't shown otherwise, and indeed (as just mentioned) this would be a natural position for purposes of biology. To be sure, difficulties will arise in making precise human-animal type persistence conditions—but there are difficulties in making precise *any* scheme of individuation. Moreover, for the purposes of the ethical theory adopted in this book—a welfarist account grounded in the well-being of a population of humans—Animalism is preferable to Personalism because the latter is overly complicated and also constrains the structure of ethical assessment in a problematic way.

Ceteris paribus, simpler conceptual schemes are preferable (Occam's razor). Animalism is simpler than Personalism (for purposes of this book) because it involves fewer types of beings. Consider any population of OHPs. According to Animalism, each such population involves a single type of being: human animals. According to Personalism, it involves two: human animals and persons. For example, consider the (humdrum) case of the OHP Alice who is born; develops normally; acquires all of the characteristics of a person by age 8; and dies at age 80. Animalism asserts that there is a single being in this scenario: a human animal (call her Alice*), who comes into existence whenever human animals do (at some point between conception and birth), and lives until age 80. Personalism asserts that there are two beings: Alice* as well as a separate being, the person Alice**, who pops into existence when Alice* acquires the characteristics of a person and ceases to exist when Alice* dies.[18]

[18] At this juncture, I should note the distinction between "endurantist" and "perdurantist" accounts of intertemporal identity—a distinction that is interwoven into the philosophical literature on human personhood. Endurantists deny, while perdurantists affirm, that beings have temporal parts. Perdurantists see beings as four-dimensional spacetime "worms," with a part located at each spacetime point where the being exists. See, e.g., Hawley (2014). The endurantism/perdurantism dichotomy is orthogonal to the Animalism/Personalism debate: Animalism can be specified in either an endurantist or a perdurantist fashion, as can Personalism. Perdurantism allows for multiple beings to occupy the very same spatial region and have the same properties at that time. (According to perdurantism, this can readily occur, since one being can have a time-*t* temporal part that coincides spatially and in terms of time-*t* properties with a time-*t* temporal part of a second being, and yet be distinct from that second being—since such overlap doesn't occur at all times.) Endurantism has difficulty explaining how multiple beings can occupy the very same spatial region and have the same properties at some time.

In the case under discussion, perdurantist Personalism will identify two beings: the human animal Alice* and a person Alice**. For concreteness, assume that Alice* is born on January 1, 1990; becomes a person on her 8th birthday, January 1, 1998; and dies at age 80 on January 1, 2070. According to the perdurantist Personalist, the human animal Alice* is a spacetime "worm" with her initial temporal part on January 1, 1990 and her final temporal part on January 1, 2070. The person Alice** is a spacetime "worm" with her initial temporal part on January 1, 1998, and her final temporal part on January 1, 2070. At all these times Alice** occupies the very same spatial regions as Alice* and has the same properties.

In the text to which this note is attached, I state: "Personalism asserts that there are two beings: Alice* as well as a separate being, the person Alice**, who pops into existence when Alice* acquires the characteristics of a person and ceases to exist when Alice* dies." That statement assumes *perdurantist* Personalism. By contrast, *endurantist* Personalism will identify two beings in a different

The additional complexity of Personalism might be a cost worth incurring *if* it were useful—if Personalism's doubling of the types of beings (humans *and* persons) bore fruit in conceptual resources that Animalism lacks. But the extra complexity isn't useful. Animalism, not Personalism, is the more supple conceptual framework for purposes of welfarism. Animalism is consistent with (and agnostic as between) a number of different versions of welfarism, including both lifetime welfarism (each human animal is assigned a lifetime well-being that subsumes everything in the human's life from the time it comes into existence until it dies); and a modified version of lifetime welfarism whereby events in a human animal's life prior to a threshold age (the "age of integration") are not included in lifetime well-being. By contrast, Personalism *precludes* straight lifetime welfarism, or a modified lifetime welfarism with the age of integration set below the age of personhood. See Sections 2.5, 8.2, and 8.3 for a fuller discussion of these points.[19]

To sum up: The humans that figure in this book, both humans who are OHPs, and humans who are not OHPs (Chapter 8), are taken to have the persistence conditions given by the Animalist account. Each such human is a single being that comes into existence at some point between conception and live birth and that remains one and the same being until its death. These beings may acquire the psychological characteristics of persons (as do OHPs), but since these psychological attributes are only contingent rather than essential properties of humans, such acquisition does not give rise to a new being.

way: the human animal Alice* who comes into existence on January 1, 1990, and ceases existence on January 1, 1998; and the person Alice**, who comes into existence on January 1, 1998, and ceases existence on January 1, 2070.

By contrast, both *perdurantist* and *endurantist* Animalism will identify a single being: the human animal Alice* who comes into existence on January 1, 1990, and ceases existence on January 1, 2070.

[19] Animalism is also consistent with both endurantism and perdurantism. See note 18. Nothing in this book requires my taking a position on that issue.

The proponent of Personalism might object that the true advantages of Personalism emerge not in the Focal Case (all humans are OHPs), or in the extensions discussed in Chapter 8 (infant deaths, psychological impairments and breaks), but in more esoteric cases *not* discussed in Chapter 8—specifically, cases in which the mental contents of the brain of a human being ("Jia") are transferred to a location outside that human's body (e.g., via a brain transplant to a different human), with psychological continuity maintained. Animalists are seemingly precluded from counting post-transfer events as components of Jia's well-being even though Jia's mind persists through the transfer.

I believe that Animalism has the resources to handle this sort of case; note, here, that the lifetime well-being of the human animal Jia can depend on events that occur after that animal's death (see Section 3.4.4). Even if Animalism *does* handle the Jia-type case more awkwardly than Personalism, I believe that its advantages over Personalism in the Focal Case and the less esoteric extensions discussed in Chapter 8 outweigh any disadvantages.

1.1.5 The Focal Case

We are now in position to give a clear statement of the Focal Case, the analytic setup that will structure the inquiry for most of the book (until Chapter 8).

The Focal Case is a stipulation regarding the ethical population: that it includes only OHPs. A moment's reflection will reveal that such stipulation creates a puzzle. A given human being, Leila, might develop to adulthood in one world, acquiring all of the typical psychological attributes of humans, and retaining them continuously until death; but die in infancy in a second world. So Leila is an OHP in the first world but not the second.

I'll handle this issue by restricting the *set of worlds* that are being ranked. Observe that the development of a welfarist ethical theory might start by explaining how it yields a ranking of some *subset* of the set of all possible worlds. Although any welfarist theory worth its salt will *ultimately* explain how the set of all possible worlds is ranked, the theorist need not do so at the outset. They might begin the difficult task of theory-elaboration by specifying the theory's ranking of a subset D of the grand set of *all* possible worlds—with a promise of ultimately extending the ranking to the grand set.

With this observation in hand, the Focal Case can now be described with precision. The Focal Case means explaining how a welfarist ethical theory will rank any set D of possible worlds (D some subset of the set of all possible worlds) such that (1) for each world in D, any human who exists in that world is an OHP in that world; and (2) the ethical population is defined to be the set of all humans each of whom exists in at least one of the worlds in D.

Two further stipulations will also be adopted. (3) The ethical population is *fixed*. That is, the very same humans exist in all of the worlds in D.[20] (Each human who exists in any of the worlds in D exists in all of them.) (4) The population is *finite*. (A finite number of humans exist in each of the worlds in D.) Adopting stipulation (3) allows us to avoid the difficult problems of a variable population. Those problems are postponed until Chapter 8. Adopting stipulation (4) avoids the equally difficult task of specifying welfarism for an infinite population—a problem ignored in this book.

[20] To say that the ethical population is *fixed* in the sense here—the very same humans exist in all of the worlds in D—does not imply, of course, that the number of humans who exist at any particular time *t* is fixed. It's standard practice both among philosophers and as a matter of common sense to posit that a human exists at times when they are alive, not before birth or after death. By saying that a human "exists" in a world *d*, I mean that they exist *at some times* in *d*: they are born in *d* and, at a later point, die.

The posit of a fixed ethical population, thus, means that each human in that population is born in each of the worlds in D. It *doesn't* mean that each of those humans exists at the very same times in each of those worlds.

The Focal Case involves premises (1) through (4). As a shorthand, we might say that the Focal Case assumes an ethical population consisting of a fixed and finite group of OHPs. But this is merely shorthand for the more precise description of the case given by those four premises.

1.2 Well-Being

1.2.1 Accounts of Well-Being

A variety of accounts of well-being have been developed in the philosophical literature.[21] Although the book is agnostic as between them, it will be useful to have some sense of their contours.

I will present the accounts by describing what they say about lifetime well-being. The accounts also may analyze momentary or stage well-being. But since the version of welfarism deployed in this book will be lifetime welfarism, not a welfarism of moments or stages, it will be simplest to present the accounts via their analyses of well-being over a whole lifetime.

The accounts are generally focused on the well-being of human persons. They implicitly or explicitly train their attention on what makes the life of a human person better or worse for that individual. In particular, then, the accounts tell us what constitutes the lifetime well-being of an OHP. In what follows, and for the remainder of the chapter, I will (unless otherwise noted) be using the terms "human," "person," and "individual" as synonyms for "OHP."[22]

Hedonic accounts of well-being analyze an individual's well-being in terms of their hedonic states: their positive sensations (pleasures) and negative sensations (pains). Whether a person is better or worse off in world d^* as compared to world d depend upon the pleasures and pains they experience over their lifetime in the two worlds. Hedonic accounts fall into a more general class of welfare theories—"experientialist" theories. An experientialist theory identifies one or more types of mental states and then posits that an individual's well-being in d^* as compared to d depends upon the mental states, of the stipulated type(s), that they experience over their lifetime in the two worlds. The mental states picked out by the

[21] For overviews of this literature or of specific families of accounts, see Adler (2012, ch. 3); Arneson (1999, 2006); Bradley (2015); Bykvist (2016); Fletcher (2016b); Griffin (1986); Haybron (2016); Hurka (2016); Lin (2022a,2022b); Scanlon (1998, ch. 3); Sumner (1996).

[22] A well-being account, if comprehensive, will also tell us what constitutes the lifetime well-being of a human person who is not an OHP—for example, someone who succumbs to serious Alzheimer's or suffers a psychological break. What the account says in this case may be the same as for an OHP (this would be true, for example, of a hedonic account) or it may not. In any event, in what follows I present the accounts as they apply to OHPs.

theory might be pains and pleasures, feelings of satisfaction, feelings of happiness, a sense of purpose, perceptions, memories, etc.

What experientialist theories have in common is that they satisfy an experientialist restriction: If a person's mental states are identical in two worlds, then the person is equally well off in the two. This is not true of the other two main types of welfare theories. The disagreement here concerns whether a person's welfare is or is not reducible to what occurs "in their head."

Objective-good theories set forth various lists of goods. According to a given objective-good theory, a person's well-being in d^* as compared to d depends upon how their life fares with respect to the goods on that theory's list in d^* and how it fares in d. For example, John Finnis proposes this list of goods: life, knowledge, play, aesthetic experience, sociability, practical reasonableness, religion.[23] James Griffin proposes accomplishment, "the components of human existence" (roughly, autonomy and physical integrity), understanding, enjoyment, deep personal relations.[24] Guy Fletcher suggests achievement, friendship, happiness, pleasure, self-respect, virtue.[25] George Sher endorses this list: moral goodness, rational activity, development of abilities, having children and being a good parent, knowledge, awareness of true beauty.[26] Richard Kraut proposes "the exercise of cognitive, social, affective, and physical skills."[27]

An objective-good account may include some type(s) of experience on its list, but the goods aren't *all* reducible to experiences—hence the account doesn't satisfy the experientialist restriction. Individual preferences may enter into some of the goods, but the goods aren't generally reducible to preferences—hence an account of this sort is not a preference theory.

A preference theory defers to an individual's preferences over lifetimes in determining how worlds compare for the well-being of that individual. The individual is better off in d^* as compared to d just in case they prefer their life in d^* to that in d. This type of view of well-being is (implicitly if not explicitly) adopted in much of welfare economics, and it's also endorsed by some philosophers.[28]

A preference with respect to a whole lifetime—a "global" preference—is a constructed object. Since Gabriel (a given human being) is cognitively bounded

[23] Finnis (1998, ch. 4).
[24] Griffin (1996, pp. 29–30).
[25] Fletcher (2016a, p. 149).
[26] Sher (1997, p. 201).
[27] Kraut (2007, p. 145).
[28] "On the question of how good an entire life would be for a person, there are two main ways a desire approach might go: it can sum the values of all the instances of desire satisfaction and frustration *within* that life; or it can look to the person's desires *about* that whole life and hold that the best life is the one the person most wants to lead." Heathwood (2016, p. 135.) See also Parfit (1987, p. 497), discussing "global preferences"; Hausman (2012, ch. 4), arguing that "total subjective comparative evaluation" is the notion of preference in economics and decision theory; Rawls (1999, pp. 358–72), defining an individual's good with reference to a rational life-plan.

and hence can't literally think about everything that occurs in his life in worlds d^* and d, Gabriel's preference as between the two worlds must be inferred from his more circumscribed preferences.

Preference theories can build in various idealization conditions. For example, in determining Gabriel's lifetime well-being, we might appeal to what Gabriel would prefer were he to satisfy formal rationality criteria and to be sufficiently well-informed.[29]

This trichotomy of well-being theories—experientialist, objective-good, and preference-based theories—is a rough map of the landscape of philosophical work on well-being. It's an introductory guide to the territory—nothing more. Note that there can be hybrid theories that don't fall into any of the three categories just delineated.[30]

1.2.2 The Structure of Lifetime Well-Being

Lifetime welfarism depends upon a comparison of lifetime well-being levels. It requires an account of well-being that licenses statements such as the following: Felicia is at a higher level of lifetime well-being in world d than in world d^*; Henry is at the same level of lifetime well-being in d as in d^*; Keith is at a higher level of lifetime well-being in world d than Livia is in world d^*; Max's level of lifetime well-being in d is the same as Nate's in d^*.

Moreover, many if not all of the plausible versions of lifetime welfarism also depend upon a comparison of well-being differences with respect to lifetime well-being.

I'll express how a given theory of well-being makes comparisons of levels and differences of lifetime well-being via the following formal structure.[31] The

[29] An account of lifetime well-being that appeals to global preferences should be distinguished from one that analyzes lifetime well-being in terms of the satisfaction of local preferences (sometimes termed "desires"). What this latter sort of account says, very roughly, is this. Let S be the hybrid state of affairs of i preferring that some state of affairs A obtain (as compared to A not obtaining), and A. World d is pro tanto better for individual i than world d^* iff there is some S that is part of d but not d^*.

The literature on well-being certainly does include local-preference as well as global-preference accounts. My discussion in the text focuses on global-preference accounts, because I take them to be more plausible than local-preference accounts. That said, this book's analysis applies to local-preference accounts, just as it does to experientialist accounts, objective-good accounts, and global-preference accounts—and to hybrids (see note 30). The lifetime well-being comparison structure (see Section 1.2.2), world-ranking (Section 1.3), and SWF framework (Section 1.4) are compatible with all of these.

[30] A theory of well-being might hybridize goods and experiences (for example, stipulating that well-being is a matter of attaining goods and experiencing pleasure as a result); it might hybridize goods and preferences (stipulating that well-being is a matter of attaining those goods that the individual prefers to attain); or it might hybridize experiences and preferences (well-being is a matter of experiencing preferred mental states).

[31] This structure for formalizing well-being levels and differences is set forth in Adler (2016b).

structure is fully generic: It is consistent with experientialist theories of well-being, objective-good theories, preferentialist theories, and hybrids. (The structure is presented here without all the technical details, and more rigorously in the chapter appendix.)

Let D, as above, be the set of worlds being ranked; and let I be the set of individuals (OHPs) who exist in those worlds (that is, the ethical population). A "history" is a pairing of a world and an individual. A given history h takes the form $h = (d; i)$, with d some world in D and i some person in I. Then the set H of histories consists in all possible such pairings.

Comparisons of levels of lifetime well-being can now be represented as a ranking of the set of histories. I'll use the symbol "$\succcurlyeq^L$" to denote this ranking. "$(d; i) \succcurlyeq^L (d^*; j)$" means that the first history is at least as good for lifetime well-being as the second. $\succcurlyeq^L$ is assumed to be a quasiordering (a reflexive, transitive, binary relation). Relations of equally-good-for-lifetime-well-being and better-for-lifetime-well-being can be derived from $\succcurlyeq^L$.

Intra- and interpersonal comparisons of levels of lifetime well-being are grounded in $\succcurlyeq^L$ in a straightforward way. Individual i in d is at least as well off as individual i in d^* iff $(d; i) \succcurlyeq^L (d^*; i)$: an intrapersonal comparison. Now, let i and j be distinct individuals. Then individual i in d is at least as well off as j in d^+ iff $(d; i) \succcurlyeq^L (d^+; j)$: an interpersonal comparison.

The "history" formalism not only unifies intra- and interpersonal comparisons but is quite flexible in two ways. First, it allows for *incompleteness* in well-being level comparisons. There could well be cases in which someone's life in one world is incomparable with their life in another world, or with someone else's life—and the formalism here allows for this, since $\succcurlyeq^L$ is a quasiordering, which need not be complete. Second, the formal structure is wholly agnostic about the *content* of lifetime well-being. This is why it can be meshed with any account of lifetime well-being, be it experientialist, preference-based, objective-good, etc. Any account of well-being will specify *certain* well-being-relevant attributes as the basis for well-being comparisons. But note that a given history $h = (d; i)$ specifies *everything* about the individual i in world d (all of their properties), and all the properties of everyone else too, since it specifies the entire world d. Thus all the information that an account could count as relevant to an individual's well-being in a world is included in the corresponding history. Any given such account will then focus on a portion of this information.

The "history" construct can also be used to formalize comparisons of *differences* in lifetime well-being. H × H is the product set of H with itself. Each member of H × H is an ordered pair (h, h^*), such that h is some history in H and h^* also is some history in H. Difference comparisons can now be expressed as a ranking (quasiordering) of the set H × H, with this ranking denoted as $\succcurlyeq^D$. $((d; i), (d^*; j)) \succcurlyeq^D ((d^+; k), (d^{++}; l))$ indicates that the difference in lifetime well-being between history (d; i) and history (d^*; j) is at least as large as the difference in lifetime well-being between history (d^+; k) and history (d^{++}; l). This ranking, $\succcurlyeq^D$, grounds intra- and interpersonal difference comparisons in a straightforward way. Further, it is flexible in the same way that $\succcurlyeq^L$ is. The fact that $\succcurlyeq^D$ is a quasiordering allows for incomparability in difference comparisons; and it can be meshed with any account of well-being.

For short, let's call the ranking of histories and differences associated with a given well-being account (that is, $\succcurlyeq^L$ and $\succcurlyeq^D$) a "lifetime well-being comparison structure."[32]

1.3 The World-Ranking

A welfarist ethical theory includes, as a core component, a *world-ranking* for every set **D** of possible worlds. The world-ranking is a comparison structure with respect to **D**. I will assume that this comparison structure is a quasiordering (again: a reflexive, transitive, binary relation), and will denote it as $\succcurlyeq^E$. The superscript "*E*" stands for "ethical": Worlds are being ranked as better or worse for purposes of a theory that provides *ethical* guidance: "$d \succcurlyeq^E d^*$" should be read: "world d is at least as good as world d^*."

As I stated at the beginning of the chapter, the world-ranking is a *single* ranking of **D**, which applies to all agents (decisionmakers) and at all times. The premise of a single ethical-goodness ranking is a core element of consequentialism, as traditionally understood. Although it is possible to develop a revisionary consequentialism that drops this premise, this book will work within the confines of traditional consequentialism.[33]

Different accounts of the determinants of this world-ranking can be offered. Roughly speaking, lifetime welfarism supposes that $\succcurlyeq^E$ is determined by the patterns of lifetime well-being in the worlds under comparison. This is by contrast with a momentary-welfarist or stage-welfarist world-ranking, which depend upon the patterns of momentary or stage well-being in the worlds, respectively; and with a non-welfarist world-ranking, which takes account of non-well-being facts.

In what follows, I provide a more precise statement of lifetime welfarism and then review the dominant versions thereof: utilitarianism, prioritarianism, sufficientism, leximin, and egalitarianism.

[32] For purposes of constructing a well-being measure, it is also useful to posit that the lifetime well-being comparison structure includes a ranking of lotteries over histories. See chapter appendix, Section 1.A.2.

[33] See note 2.

At the outset, it's important to head off one potential misunderstanding about the terms "lifetime well-being" and "lifetime welfarism." An individual's "lifetime well-being" in a given world takes account of *everything* about the world that makes it better or worse for them, according to the well-being theory adopted. All of these sources of well-being are reflected in the lifetime well-being comparison structure ($\succcurlyeq^L$ and $\succcurlyeq^D$). In particular, $(d; i) \succcurlyeq^L (d^*; i)$ iff world d is at least as good for i as world d^*. The lifetime-welfarist world-ranking $\succcurlyeq^E$ is in turn keyed to the lifetime well-being comparison structure, in a manner to be discussed momentarily.

The misunderstanding to be avoided is this: The determinants of an individual's lifetime well-being may *not* be limited to events that occur during their lifetime. Some well-being theories posit that welfare may be affected by posthumous events.[34] On such a theory, posthumous events are inputs into "lifetime well-being," as I intend that term. The well-being rankings of histories and history differences, $\succcurlyeq^L$ and $\succcurlyeq^D$, take account of *everything* about the histories that make them better or worse for the individuals involved—including, potentially, posthumous (or prenatal!) events. Think of "lifetime well-being" as a maximally temporally inclusive rubric, covering all the time-slices during the individual's life, and all the time-slices afterward and before as well.

To be sure, a welfare theory may well insist that posthumous or prenatal events *don't* figure into an individual's well-being. If so, lifetime well-being is determined by what occurs when the individual is alive. But this will be a substantive conclusion of the theory; it is not a conceptual entailment, since the concept of "lifetime well-being" uses the widest possible temporal lens and thus (odd as this may sound) allows for someone's "lifetime well-being" to take account of what occurs after they die or before they are born.

1.3.1 Lifetime Welfarism

I will make precise the concept of "lifetime welfarism" via three axioms: Lifetime Pareto Indifference, Lifetime Anonymity, and Lifetime Strong Pareto. A world-ranking is lifetime welfarist if, and only if, it satisfies these three axioms—or so I'll posit. The axioms are stated as applicable to the Focal Case. The very same OHPs, a finite number, exist in all of the worlds being compared; the ethical population is the collection of these OHPs.

The *Lifetime Pareto Indifference* axiom requires this: If each individual (that is, each OHP in the ethical population) has the same level of lifetime well-being in d as they do in d^*, then d and d^* are equally good.

[34] See Section 3.4.4.

Imagine a case in which Lifetime Pareto Indifference is violated. Suppose that each person is equally well off, in terms of lifetime well-being, in the two worlds *d* and *d**. And yet the worlds are *not* ranked equally good. What is producing the ethical inequality between the two worlds? Not any difference in individuals' lifetime well-being. By hypothesis, there is no such difference for any one of the individuals. So the ethical inequality between the worlds must be arising by virtue of (1) some difference between *d* and *d** with respect to the momentary well-being of the individuals; (2) some difference with respect to their stage well-being; (3) some difference with respect to the well-being of non-human animals; and/or (4) some non-welfare feature of the worlds. But to explain the ethical inequality between the worlds in any one of these four ways is to bring into play something other than lifetime well-being as a determinant of the world-ranking. And that is precisely what lifetime welfarism precludes.

It might be thought that the axiom of Lifetime Pareto Indifference is sufficient to define lifetime welfarism. To see why it isn't, consider the following. There are three individuals: Amy, Barry, Casey. Let L_1, L_2, and L_3 denote, respectively, the lifetime well-being levels of Amy, Barry, and Casey in world *d*, these being three *different* levels of well-being. In world *d** we permute the levels, so that Amy is at L_2 in world *d**, Barry at L_3, and Casey at L_1. Imagine, now, that the two worlds are *not* ranked equally good.

Note that such a ranking does not violate Lifetime Pareto Indifference. And yet it still seems to be in tension with lifetime welfarism. The pattern of lifetime well-being in *d* is the same as the pattern of lifetime well-being in *d**. In each world we have one of the three levels L_1, L_2, L_3, assigned to one of the three individuals. What is driving the ranking of the worlds, then, is not a difference in *which* lifetime well-being levels are instantiated in the two worlds, but rather a difference in *which* individuals are assigned to the various lifetime well-being levels. But that is a kind of non-welfare fact.

To handle this kind of case, we can require that the world-ranking must satisfy Lifetime Anonymity: If the arrangement of well-being levels in *d* is a permutation of the arrangement in *d**, then the two worlds are equally good.

Note that Lifetime Anonymity implies Lifetime Pareto Indifference, so—strictly speaking—we don't need to posit that a world-ranking must satisfy both. I keep them separate because doing so highlights the minimal requirement that Lifetime Pareto Indifference imposes (at the very minimum, a world-ranking must satisfy *this* axiom in order to be lifetime-welfarist) and the more robust requirement that Lifetime Anonymity does.

The anonymity axiom is often seen not as a defining feature of welfarism but as an axiom expressing ethical impartiality. On this view of things, a world-ranking satisfying Pareto indifference but not anonymity would constitute a non-impartial welfarism.[35] As just explained, I think it's very plausible to see anonymity as flowing *from* welfarism, understood informally as the idea that the world-ranking is determined by the pattern of well-being. For this reason, I include Lifetime Anonymity along with Lifetime Pareto Indifference as a component of lifetime welfarism.

Finally, Lifetime Strong Pareto requires: If each person has either the same or a higher level of lifetime well-being in d^* as they do in d, and at least one person has a strictly higher level, then d^* is better than d.

The strong Pareto axiom, generically, says: It is an ethical improvement to make some people strictly better off and ensure that everyone is at least as well off. This axiom (in whatever specific form is relevant to the context at hand) is very widely accepted in welfare economics and among welfarist philosophers—but it is usually seen as a compelling *substantive* axiom rather than as part of the definition of welfarism. As with anonymity, so with strong Pareto: I think it's very plausible to view this axiom as a component of welfarism.

Lifetime welfarism, specifically, says that the ethical comparison of two worlds is determined by the pattern of lifetime well-being. There are two aspects (I suggest) to this notion of "determined by": first, that differences between the worlds other than lifetime well-being do not give rise to an ethical difference between the worlds; and, second, that differences with respect to lifetime well-being *do* generate an ethical difference. The first aspect is covered by Lifetime Pareto Indifference and Lifetime Anonymity; the second, by Lifetime Strong Pareto. Well-being is what is *good* for an individual, not what is bad for them; thus, if improvements in well-being make an ethical difference, surely this must be a positive difference. If some have a higher level of lifetime well-being in d^* than d, and none vice versa, then all the well-being improvements make an ethical difference in favor of d^*. And this is just what Lifetime Strong Pareto says.

So again: I take lifetime welfarism to be the combination of Lifetime Pareto Indifference, Lifetime Anonymity, and Lifetime Strong Pareto, and the analysis in this book works within lifetime welfarism thus understood. That said, the analysis is fully consistent with a "thinner" definition of "lifetime welfarism" to mean just Lifetime Pareto Indifference, with the other two axioms understood as constraints that rule out non-impartial or non-Paretian variants thereof.[36]

[35] Consider, for example, the weighted-utilitarian ranking in which individuals' well-being numbers are multiplied by individual-specific fixed weights, not all equal, and then added up.

[36] In the literature on social welfare functions (SWFs), welfarism is typically understood to mean not merely Pareto indifference but also the supposition that outcomes are ranked according to their corresponding well-being vectors *and* that the ranking of well-being vectors is accomplished via a single, "profile-independent" SWF that does not depend upon *which* well-being measure is mapping outcomes to vectors. See Bossert and Weymark (2004); Weymark (2016).

The SWF framework, as used in this book, does conform to welfarism in this sense (a profile-independent SWF). Moreover, to the extent that well-being is measurable, the world-ranking should plausibly satisfy a kind of profile independence too. See chapter appendix, Section 1.A.4.1. That

1.3.2 The Main Versions of Lifetime Welfarism

Five versions of welfarism are most widely discussed in theoretical welfare economics and philosophy: utilitarianism, prioritarianism, leximin, sufficientism, egalitarianism.[37] Each translates to a lifetime-welfarist world-ranking (or a family of such rankings) for a given **D**, that is, a world-ranking that satisfies the axioms of Lifetime Pareto Indifference, Lifetime Anonymity, and Lifetime Strong Pareto.

Expressing these rankings is a bit tricky. One difficulty is that the lifetime well-being comparison structure (that is, $\succcurlyeq^L$ and $\succcurlyeq^D$) may not be *measurable*. By "measurable," I mean that there exists a well-being measure $w(\cdot)$, which assigns well-being numbers to histories so as to represent the ranking of levels and differences.

An assumption of *measurability* is certainly useful in thinking about welfarism. And, as we'll see below, it's an essential component of the SWF decision-procedure, which adopts this assumption so as to facilitate decisionmaking. But there's no good reason to think that any plausible account of welfare, in order to *be* a plausible such account, must satisfy measurability. In particular, it's perfectly plausible to believe that there can be *incomparability* with respect to well-being levels or differences. Sara might be neither better off in d than d^*, nor worse off, nor equally well off. I've therefore defined $\succcurlyeq^L$ and $\succcurlyeq^D$ to allow for incomparability. But incomparability in the well-being comparison structure precludes measurability.[38]

A second difficulty is that the world-ranking might not be complete. That is, $\succcurlyeq^E$ itself might contain incomparabilities at the level of worlds: World d is

said, I will not incorporate profile-independence, a concept that presupposes well-being measurability, into the very definition of lifetime welfarism (which, as I've defined it, does not presuppose measurability).

[37] For overviews of welfarism as developed in theoretical welfare economics, see Adler (2012, 2019b); Blackorby, Bossert, and Donaldson (2002; 2005, chs. 2–4); Boadway and Bruce (1984, ch. 5); Bossert and Weymark (2004); d'Aspremont and Gevers (2002); Mongin and d'Aspremont (1998); Weymark (2016). Citations to contemporary philosophical discussions of utilitarianism, prioritarianism, egalitarianism, and sufficientism are provided above in the Introduction, notes 3,7–9. Leximin is less prominent in philosophy than in welfare economics (but see Tännsjö [2019]).

[38] Measurability means, to be precise, that there exists a real-valued well-being measure $w(\cdot)$ such that (1) for any two histories h and h^*, $w(h) \geq w(h^*)$ iff $h \succcurlyeq^{L\text{-}D} h^*$; and (2) for any four histories h, h^*, h^+, h^{++}, $w(h) - w(h^*) \geq w(h^+) - w(h^{++})$ iff $(h, h^*) \succcurlyeq^{D\text{-}D} (h^+, h^{++})$. See chapter appendix, Section 1.A.4. Incomparability with respect to well-being levels occurs if there are two histories h, h^* such that neither $h \succcurlyeq^{L\text{-}D} h^*$ nor $h^* \succcurlyeq^{L\text{-}D} h$. Incomparability with respect to well-being differences occurs if there are four histories h, h^*, h^+, h^{++} such that neither $(h, h^*) \succcurlyeq^{D\text{-}D} (h^+, h^{++})$ nor $(h^+, h^{++}) \succcurlyeq^{D\text{-}D} (h, h^*)$. From the definition of measurability and the nature of real numbers (one number is either greater than, less than, or equal to a second), it can be seen that both sorts of incomparability are precluded by measurability.

neither better than, nor worse than, nor equally good as world d^*. This could arise by virtue of incomparability in well-being, or independently.

In what follows, I set forth the lifetime utilitarian, prioritarian, leximin, sufficientist, and egalitarian world-rankings for the simplest case in which well-being *is* measurable and the world-ranking *is* complete. How to generalize these definitions beyond that case is discussed in the chapter appendix.

If the lifetime well-being comparison structure is measurable, then a given world d corresponds to a well-being vector. d corresponds to $(\mathbf{w}_1(d), \ldots, \mathbf{w}_N(d))$, with $\mathbf{w}_i(d)$ the well-being number of i in d, and N the number of individuals in the ethical population. If we further assume that the world-ranking is complete, then lifetime utilitarianism, prioritarianism, leximin, sufficientism, and egalitarianism take the following forms. (In what follows, "$d \succcurlyeq^E d^*$" should be read as "world d is ethically at least as good as world d^*.")

(1) Utilitarianism. Lifetime utilitarianism ranks worlds according to the rule: $d \succcurlyeq^E d^*$ iff $\sum_{i=1}^{N} \mathbf{w}_i(d) \geq \sum_{i=1}^{N} \mathbf{w}_i(d^*)$. That is, worlds are ranked according to the sum of individual well-being.

(2) Prioritarianism. Lifetime prioritarianism is a family of rankings, each of which uses some strictly increasing, strictly concave, and continuous transformation function $g(\cdot)$,[39] as displayed in Figure 1.1. While utilitarianism adds up well-being, prioritarianism adds up transformed well-being. That is, a prioritarian world-ranking orders worlds according to the rule:

$$d \succcurlyeq^E d^* \text{ iff} \sum_{i=1}^{N} g(\mathbf{w}_i(d)) \geq \sum_{i=1}^{N} g(\mathbf{w}_i(d^*)).$$

(3) Leximin. Lifetime leximin compares world d to world d^* according to the well-being levels of the worst-off individuals in $\mathbf{w}(d)$ and $\mathbf{w}(d^*)$, with d ranked higher/lower if the worst-off individual in $\mathbf{w}(d)$ is better off/worse off than the worst-off individual in $\mathbf{w}(d^*)$; and if the levels of the worst-off individuals are equal, then according to the well-being levels of the second-worst-off individuals; and if *those* are equal, then according to the well-being levels of the third-worst-off, fourth-worst-off, etc.

[39] (1) To say that $g(\cdot)$ is "strictly increasing" means that larger inputs yield larger outputs. That is, if $w^* > w$, then $g(w^*) > g(w)$. (2) To say that $g(\cdot)$ is "strictly concave" means that its slope diminishes with larger inputs. The standard definition of strict concavity is this: for all α, $0 < \alpha < 1$, and for all w, w^* with $w \neq w^*$, $\alpha g(w) + (1 - \alpha)g(w^*) < g(\alpha w + (1 - \alpha)w^*)$. Strict concavity, thus defined, is equivalent to requiring that $g(\cdot)$ have diminishing slope: if $w < w^* < w^{**}$, $(g(w^{**}) - g(w^*))/(w^{**} - w^*) < (g(w^*) - g(w))/(w^* - w)$. (3) To say that $g(\cdot)$ is "continuous" means that it doesn't have "jumps": the limit of $g(w)$ as w approaches w^* is $g(w^*)$. If the domain of $g(\cdot)$ is an open interval, continuity follows automatically from the strict concavity of $g(\cdot)$.

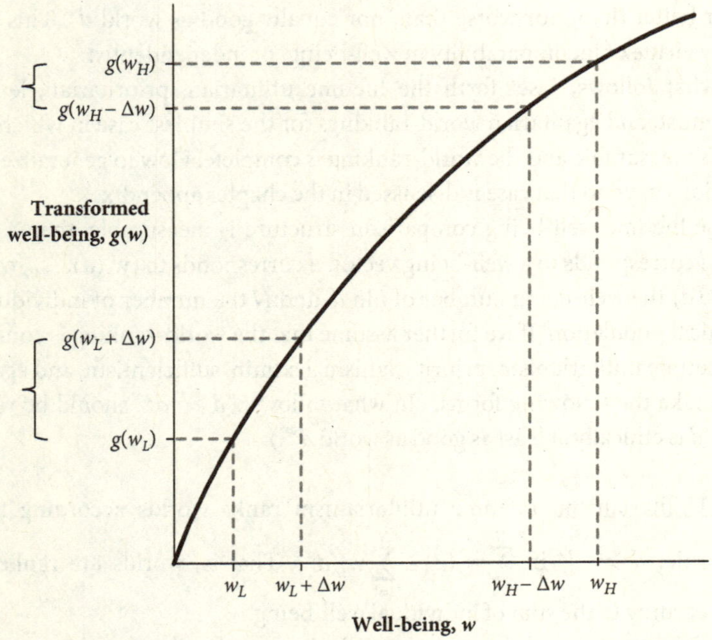

Figure 1.1 A Prioritarian Transformation Function

Explanation: This figure displays a strictly increasing, strictly concave, and continuous transformation function $g(\cdot)$. The figure also illustrates that a pure, gap-diminishing transfer of Δw units of well-being from a better-off individual (at higher well-being level w_H) to a worse-off individual (at lower well-being level w_L), with everyone else unaffected, increases the sum of transformed well-being.

Leximin is absolutist. Imagine that in world *d*, one individual (Karl) is worse off than everyone in some group of individuals. In *d** Karl is worse off than he is in *d*; everyone in the group is better off than they are in *d*; no one else is affected. Then leximin counts *d* as better than *d**, regardless of the size of Karl's loss (however small), regardless of the size of the gains to each member of the group (however large those gains may be), and regardless of the number of the individuals in the group.

(4) Sufficientism. Sufficientism is a mixture of utilitarianism, prioritarianism, and leximin. It posits a well-being threshold. Absolute priority is given to individuals below the threshold, as against individuals above. (This is the sense in which sufficientism borrows from leximin.) A prioritarian rule is used to balance the well-being losses and gains of individuals below the threshold; and a utilitarian rule is used to balance the well-being losses and gains of individuals above the threshold. Applying this approach to lifetime well-being numbers, we have lifetime sufficientism.[40]

[40] Sufficientism (also known as "sufficientarianism") covers a wide range of views in distributive ethics. See Shields (2020). The version stated here and formalized in the chapter appendix, Section 1.A.4, is welfarist and, specifically, follows the account set forth in Roger Crisp's (2003) influential presentation. For a similar formalization, see Bossert, Cato, and Kamaga (2022).

(5) Egalitarianism. Let $I(\cdot)$ be an inequality metric (a function that measures the degree of inequality, assigning a higher value to well-being distributions that are more unequal). Then the ranking of two worlds, d and d^*, depends upon two factors: how they compare with respect to the sum total of lifetime well-being (that is, $\sum_{i=1}^{N} \mathbf{w}_i(d)$ as compared to $\sum_{i=1}^{N} \mathbf{w}_i(d^*)$) and how they compare with respect to inequality (that is, $I(\mathbf{w}_1(d), \ldots, \mathbf{w}_N(d))$ as compared with $I(\mathbf{w}_1(d^*), \ldots, \mathbf{w}_N(d^*))$). Ceteris paribus, an increase in the sum total of lifetime well-being is an ethical improvement; ceteris paribus, a reduction in the degree of inequality is. Moreover, these two factors are balanced against each other so that the world-ranking (a) satisfies Lifetime Strong Pareto[41] and (b) violates an axiom of Separability.[42]

In prior books and articles, I have argued at substantial length in favor of prioritarianism.[43] Repeating those arguments in detail here is unnecessary (the reader can consult those works) and would distract from the aim of *this* book, which is to apply welfarism to risk regulation. So I'll just mention some key points.

Prioritarianism embodies a concern for the equitable distribution of well-being. This can be expressed via the Pigou-Dalton axiom. Stated in terms of lifetime well-being, the Pigou-Dalton axiom says this. Let two worlds d and d^* be as follows. (a) In world d, one individual ("Ahmed") is at a higher level of lifetime well-being than a second ("Bogart"). (b) In d^*, Ahmed's level of lifetime well-being is lower than in d, while Bogart's is higher than in d, and the difference in Ahmed's lifetime well-being between d and d^* is equal to the difference in Bogart's lifetime well-being between d^* and d. (Thus the transfer of lifetime well-being is "pure"; Bogart's gain in lifetime well-being exactly equals Ahmed's loss.) (c) The magnitude of the difference ("gap") between Ahmed's lifetime well-being in d^* and Bogart's lifetime

[41] To be sure, some egalitarian world-rankings violate Lifetime Strong Pareto. This would be true of an egalitarian world-ranking that focused solely on the degree of inequality (such a ranking violates Lifetime Strong Pareto in "leveling down" cases, where equality is increased by reducing the well-being levels of better-off individuals); or that balanced equality against overall well-being, but doing so in a manner that violates Lifetime Strong Pareto. But what is being described, here, are the different versions of lifetime welfarism. If an egalitarian ranking falls within the category of lifetime welfarism, it must satisfy Lifetime Strong Pareto.

[42] The Separability axiom is stated below. Why insist that an egalitarian ranking must violate this axiom? (a) A ranking that balances equality against overall well-being in a manner that is lifetime welfarist (as defined here) *and* satisfies Separability plus an additional continuity axiom will end up being equivalent to some prioritarian ranking. See Adler (2019b, pp. 95–106, 276–77). In order to distinguish egalitarianism from prioritarianism, we should stipulate that the former violates Separability. (b) More substantively: a ranking of worlds *just* in terms of inequality necessarily violates Separability. It *could* be the case that, by introducing the second factor of overall well-being, the ranking ends up satisfying Separability. But why this *would* be the case is hard to explain. See Adler (2019b, pp. 148–52).

[43] Adler (2012, 2019b, 2022b); Adler and Holtug (2019).

well-being in d^* is less than the gap between Ahmed's lifetime well-being in d and Bogart's lifetime well-being in d. (d) Everyone else is equally well off, in terms of lifetime well-being, in the two worlds. *Then*: world d^* is better than world d. See Figure 1.2 (and see Section 1.A.5 for a precise statement of the axiom).

In short, the Pigou-Dalton axiom states that a pure, gap-diminishing transfer of lifetime well-being from a better- to a worse-off individual that leaves everyone else unaffected is an ethical improvement.

There are strong grounds to adopt the Pigou-Dalton axiom—or so I have argued. Let L_A and L_A^* denote Ahmed's levels of lifetime well-being in d and d^*, respectively; and let L_B and L_B^* denote Bogart's levels of lifetime well-being in d and d^*, respectively. There are, then, two competing ethical considerations governing the ranking of the two worlds. One consideration is the increase in Ahmed's lifetime well-being from L_A^* to L_A (this consideration favors world d); the second consideration is the increase in Bogart's lifetime well-being from L_B to L_B^* (this consideration favors world d^*). Which consideration is stronger? Surely the second. In assigning ethical weight to a change in someone's well-being, we should give *some* weight to the levels of well-being involved; we should not *wholly* ignore the levels and focus just on the magnitude of the change. But in the case at hand, the changes are equal, while the levels are not. The increase in Ahmed's lifetime well-being from L_A^* to L_A has less ethical weight than the increase in Bogart's from L_B to L_B^*, because the well-being differences are the same (the L_A/L_A^* difference equals the L_B^*/L_B difference), while the levels are not (L_B is less than L_A^*). Again, see Figure 1.2.

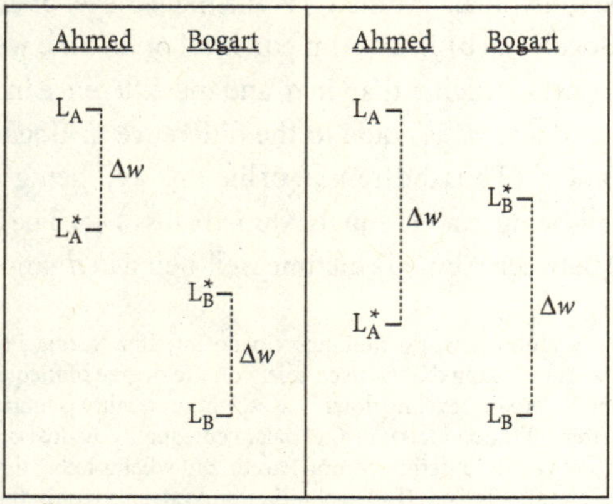

Figure 1.2 The Pigou-Dalton Axiom

Explanation: This figure illustrates the two types of gap-diminishing pure transfers of lifetime well-being. In each case, one individual starts out at a higher level of lifetime well-being (here, Ahmed at level L_A) than a second individual (here, Bogart at level L_B). The better-off one's lifetime well-being is reduced by $\Delta w > 0$, while the worse-off one's is increased by the same amount (a "pure transfer"). The transfer is gap-diminishing in that the magnitude of the difference between the individuals' ending points (here, between L_A^* and L_B^*) is less than the magnitude of the difference between the individuals' starting points (here, between L_A and L_B).

In one case (on the left of the figure), the transfer is rank-preserving: the individual who starts out better off (Ahmed) remains at least as well off as the second individual. In the second case, the transfer is rank-switching but still gap-diminishing. Note that, in either case, the individual initially better off ends up at a level of lifetime well-being (here, L_A^*) that is higher than the starting point level of the individual initially worse off (here, L_B).

Prioritarianism satisfies the Pigou-Dalton axiom (as can be seen from Figure 1.1), while utilitarianism does not. If I am right that there are strong ethical grounds to endorse the Pigou-Dalton axiom, then the failure of utilitarianism to satisfy this axiom is a serious flaw.

Consider any two worlds d^+ and d^{++} such that one person is better off in d^{++} than d^+, a second in d^+ than d^{++}, and everyone else is unaffected. In this two-person case, utilitarianism compares the worlds by comparing the magnitudes of the two well-being differences. World d^{++} is better than/worse than/equally good as world d^+ iff the first person's gain from d^{++} is larger than/smaller than/equal to the second person's loss. Because utilitarianism resolves two-person cases in this manner, it violates the Pigou-Dalton axiom.[44]

Utilitarianism has a second flaw (which, like the violation of Pigou-Dalton, flows directly from the utilitarian approach to two-person cases). Imagine that the two worlds are as follows: Carlos is better off than Danny in d^+; Carlos in d^{++} is better off than he is in d^+, while Danny is worse off than he is in d^+; the magnitude of Carlos' well-being difference between the two worlds is larger than the magnitude of Danny's; and everyone else is unaffected. Then utilitarianism considers d^{++} to be the better world. This is true even if the magnitude of Carlos's well-being difference is only slightly larger than Danny's, and even if Carlos is *much* better off than Danny in both worlds.[45]

Leximin, like prioritarianism, satisfies the Pigou-Dalton axiom. But the absolutist feature of leximin (see immediately above) is troubling. Whether Karl's loss ethically outweighs the gains to the group should—it seems—take account of the magnitude of that loss, the size of the group, and the magnitude of their gains. Leximin does not do so, while prioritarianism does. How precisely well-being changes for better- and worse-off individuals are balanced is a matter for further deliberation, within the general framework of prioritarianism. While leximin is a specific world-ranking, prioritarianism is a family of such rankings—each one defined by a particular transformation function $g(\cdot)$. A more concave such function means more priority for the worse-off. Prioritarianism approaches leximin at the limit, as $g(\cdot)$ becomes increasingly concave.

Sufficientism does not fully satisfy the Pigou-Dalton principle. It fails to do so as applied to pure, gap-diminishing well-being transfers between individuals above the well-being threshold. But it's hard to see why the case for the Pigou-Dalton principle disappears above the threshold. Further, sufficientism replicates the dubious absolutism of leximin with respect to trade-offs across the threshold. Consider once more the "Karl" case—now imagining that Karl is slightly below

[44] In the Pigou-Dalton case, the two individuals' well-being differences are equal.

[45] This second feature of utilitarianism—ranking the worlds in two-person cases with unequal well-being differences according to the comparative magnitude of those differences, without reference to well-being levels—is not logically the same as violating Pigou-Dalton. Consider a two-step rule that prefers d to d^* if the sum total of well-being in d is greater and uses a Pigou-Dalton-respecting rule to rank the worlds if the sum totals are equal; this approach has the second feature of utilitarianism just mentioned but *satisfies* Pigou-Dalton. Prioritarianism, however, both satisfies Pigou-Dalton *and* does not have the second feature.

the threshold and the group of better-off individuals slightly above. Sufficientism prefers to avoid the loss to Karl over achieving the gains for the group, regardless of the size of that group, the size of those gains, and the size of Karl's loss.[46]

Egalitarianism satisfies the Pigou-Dalton axiom, and it avoids the absolutism of leximin. In these two respects, egalitarians and prioritarians are alike. But egalitarianism has a substantial shortcoming, as compared to prioritarianism. Prioritarianism satisfies, while egalitarianism fails, an axiom of Separability.

> Separability: Let d and d^* be such that one or more individuals has the same level of lifetime well-being in the two worlds. Then the d/d^* ranking is invariant to the lifetime well-being levels of these individuals.

The case for the Separability axiom is pragmatic. The fact that a world-ranking satisfies Separability is advantageous when it comes to operationalize that world-ranking as a decision-procedure. To be precise, Separability at the level of the world-ranking is a necessary condition for a companion axiom at the level of the decision-procedure ("Policy Separability"). Policy Separability says: If a decision is predicted to affect only a subset of the population, the decisionmaker can focus just on those effects and ignore the well-being levels of the unaffected.[47] The meaning and pragmatic advantages of Policy Separability will become clear as we discuss the evaluation of risk-regulation policies—here contrasting procedures that satisfy Policy Separability with those that do not.[48]

1.4 The SWF Framework

The SWF framework is a decision-procedure for welfarism. It is a rigorous methodology for *operationalizing* a welfarist world-ranking (be it utilitarian, prioritarian, egalitarian, sufficientist, leximin, or some other).

[46] A modification to sufficientism, which I've elsewhere referred to as "prioritarianism with a lexical threshold," does fully satisfy the Pigou-Dalton principle. But it is still absolutist with respect to across-threshold trade-offs. See Adler (2012, pp. 374–77; 2019b, pp. 144–47).

[47] See Chapters 5, 7.

[48] In prior work, I have developed a second, more substantive argument against egalitarianism. The outcome ranking can be seen as arising from individual "claims across outcomes." See Adler (2012, ch. 5; 2018; 2022a; 2025); see also Adler and Holtug (2019). This mode of justification is attractive because it provides a unified rationale for the axioms of strong Pareto, anonymity, and Pigou-Dalton; explains the "justificatory priority" of the strong Pareto axiom; and respects the separateness of persons. If well-being is measurable, the claims framework also implies the pro tanto person-affecting principle: world d is not better than world d^* in any respect unless better for at least one person. Ranking outcomes by balancing overall well-being against equality is a *different* and incompatible mode of justification—one that fails to explain the justificatory priority of the strong Pareto axiom and that rejects the pro tanto person-affecting principle.

I have written at great length elsewhere about this methodology.[49] One of the chief tasks of the present book is to explore how the methodology can be brought to bear in assessing risk-regulation policies.

The SWF framework is a kind of act-consequentialist decision-procedure.[50] Describing and engaging the debate between act- and rule-consequentialists is beyond the scope of this book.[51] Instead, the book elaborates a welfarist approach to risk regulation via the SWF approach and thus takes act-consequentialism as given.

What follows is a capsule summary of the SWF methodology. I'll summarize the methodology as it would be applied in the Focal Case and as it would be used in that case to operationalize lifetime welfarism.

The SWF framework gives guidance in ranking any set of policies $\mathbf{P} = \{P, P^*, P^{**}, \ldots\}$. A policy P is some course of action by government: enacting a particular regulation or statute, building infrastructure of some type, deploying personnel, etc. At a given point in time, some governmental decisionmaker or body is deliberating about which policy to adopt. **P** is the set of possible policies that the decisionmaker or body is considering.

The methodology includes a number of key components, which are brought together so as to yield choice guidance with respect to any set **P**. These components are a model population $\mathbf{I}^{\mathbf{Mod}}$; the outcome set **O**; a lifetime well-being measure $w(\cdot)$; the SWF proper, which is a rule for ranking well-being vectors; and an uncertainty module for the SWF, which ranks policies understood as probability distributions across well-being vectors.

The model population $\mathbf{I}^{\mathbf{Mod}}$ is a set of notional individuals, N in total. $\mathbf{I}^{\mathbf{Mod}} = \{1, 2, \ldots, N\}$. Each such individual is denoted by a unique designator—for simplicity, in my presentation, by one of the N numbers.[52] Individual 1 is a particular notional individual, individual 2 another one, etc. These individuals are "notional"

[49] Adler (2012, 2019b, 2022b). See also Adler and Fleurbaey (2016); Adler and Norheim (2022); Blackorby, Bossert and Donaldson (2002; 2005, chs. 2–4); Boadway and Bruce (1984, ch. 5); Bossert and Weymark (2004); d'Aspremont and Gevers (2002); Mongin and d'Aspremont (1998); Weymark (2016).

[50] As will be explained in what follows, the framework advises the decisionmaker to choose among the actions (policies) available to them by conceptualizing each as a probability distribution over outcomes (simplified models of worlds) and to rank such distributions via a formula that is grounded in the world-ranking. By contrast, a rule-consequentialist decision-procedure would have a two-step structure: first, identify that ethical code (collection of ethical rules) which, if generally complied with by actors, best effectuates the world-ranking; second, choose any action that is permissible under this code.

[51] See sources cited in Adler (2012, pp. 25–29).

[52] It is typically assumed in the SWF literature that $N \geq 3$—an assumption adopted for reasons having to do with the logical relations between standard axioms. (In particular, with $N = 2$, the Separability axiom is implied by the Pareto axioms rather than being logically distinct.) That said, the SWF framework *can* be used with a population of two or even one individual. In later chapters, I sometimes use tables with $N = 2$; such tables are always meant as simple illustrations of features of the SWF framework that generalize to the case of $N \geq 3$.

or "fictional" in the sense that they are representations of OHPs. Individual 1 is *not* an actual OHP, with "1" the designator that refers to this actual human being. Rather, the population $\mathbf{I}^{\mathbf{Mod}}$ is a theoretical construct that functions as a model of a population of actual OHPs, and "individual 1," "individual 2," etc. are the members of this made-up population.

An outcome is a simplified representation of a whole possible world. Outcomes are generally abbreviated in this book with the symbols x or y or variations on these symbols (x^*, x^+, etc.). $\mathbf{O} = \{x, y, \ldots\}$ is the set of outcomes that will be used to determine the ranking of the policy set **P**. **O** is a *model* of the set of possible worlds **D**; the ranking of **O** achieved by an SWF is a model of the world-ranking; and a given policy P is associated with a probability distribution across **O**. All of this implements the consequentialist idea that the ethical evaluation of choices (policies) is grounded in the world-ranking.

Because we are here implementing the Focal Case (a *fixed* and finite population of OHPs), it is assumed that the very same individuals exist in each outcome in **O**, namely, the members of the model population $\mathbf{I}^{\mathbf{Mod}}$. Individual 1 exists in each outcome in **O**, individual 2 exists in each outcome in **O**, etc.

When I say that an outcome is a simplified representation of a possible world, this means that an outcome is characterized with respect to *some* of the features of a world that are relevant to individuals' well-being. In particular, in a given outcome x, each individual i is assigned a bundle of attributes $b_i(x)$. The types of attributes in a bundle are *some* of the individual attributes (properties) that constitute or causally contribute to well-being. The attribute bundles are *lifetime* bundles; they describe the individual's attributes over their entire lifetime. For example, if income is included as an attribute, a bundle will specify individual i's income for each period (e.g., year) that they are alive. If health is included as an attribute, the bundle will describe individual i's health in each period (year).

Thus, a given outcome x corresponds to a list of lifetime bundles: one for each person in the population. The list of bundles associated with x is: $(b_1(x), \ldots, b_i(x), \ldots, b_N(x))$. See Chapter 4 for a detailed discussion of the internal structure of lifetime bundles and how to select the types of attributes included within them.

The lifetime bundle is the device that the SWF framework uses to represent individual *histories.* Recall that a "history" is a pairing of a world and an individual. So a world is composed of a series of histories, one for each person in the ethical population. Within the SWF methodology, the composition of worlds by histories is mirrored by seeing outcomes (world-models) as composed of a series of bundles (history-models).

Recall, too, that I have imposed a generic, formal structure on any account of well-being: a lifetime well-being comparison structure. This is a ranking $\succcurlyeq^L$ of the set of histories and a ranking $\succcurlyeq^D$ of the set of history pairs. Within the SWF framework, the lifetime well-being comparison structure is operationalized via a well-being measure $w(\cdot)$ that operates on bundles. (Again, a *bundle* is the framework's simplified representation of a *history*; and so what the account says at the level of histories is captured, within the methodology, by rankings of *bundles* and the assignment of numbers to *bundles*).

$w(\cdot)$ maps each bundle onto a real number. These numbers track the well-being ranking of bundles and bundle differences. Bundle b is at least as good for well-being as bundle b^* iff $w(b) \geq w(b^*)$. The well-being difference between bundles b and b^* is at least as large as the well-being difference between bundles b^+ and b^{++} iff $w(b) - w(b^*) \geq w(b^+) - w(b^{++})$. How to construct $w(\cdot)$ is the topic of Chapter 4.

Note that the SWF framework's device of modeling a lifetime well-being comparison structure via well-being measure $w(\cdot)$ involves a double simplification. First, bundles are sparser descriptions of individuals' lives than histories. A history $(d; i)$ is a pairing of a world, d, and an individual, i. It is a complete description of one possible life for the individual—the life that the individual lives in that world. By contrast, a bundle describes only *some* of the features of an individual's life, indeed only *some* of the well-being-relevant features. Sparser descriptions are easier to use in policy analysis, although of course produce a less accurate picture of the sources of well-being.[53] Second, the lifetime well-being comparison structure need not be complete: Recall that $\succcurlyeq^L$ and $\succcurlyeq^D$ need not be complete. But the SWF framework streamlines matters by assuming completeness. It does so because of the very great decisional advantages of well-being measurability. The existence of a well-being measure $w(\cdot)$ means that all of our theory's verdicts regarding well-being levels and differences—whatever these may be—can be captured in an assignment of well-being numbers to bundles. But measurability implies completeness.[54]

With $w(\cdot)$ in hand, each outcome is mapped onto a well-being vector. Bundle $b_i(x)$, the bundle of individual i in outcome x, is assigned the well-being number $w(b_i(x))$. Thus the whole outcome x is mapped onto a vector (list) of N well-being numbers, one for each of the N individuals in the model population. x becomes the well-being vector $(w(b_1(x)), \ldots, w(b_N(x)))$.

The lifetime-welfarist world-ranking is captured within the SWF framework as a rule for ranking well-being vectors (the SWF proper). Let $\mathbf{w}$ denote a well-being vector, with $\mathbf{w}_i$ the well-being number of individual i. Then the utilitarian SWF is the following vector-ranking rule: Vector $\mathbf{w}$ at least as good as vector $\mathbf{w}^*$ iff $\sum_{i=1}^{N} \mathbf{w}_i \geq \sum_{i=1}^{N} \mathbf{w}_i^*$. There are a family of prioritarian SWFs, each defined by

[53] See Section 4.1.2 regarding this trade-off between tractability and accuracy.
[54] See note 38.

some strictly increasing, strictly concave, and continuous transformation function $g(\cdot)$. These rules are as follows: Vector **w** at least as good as vector **w*** iff $\sum_{i=1}^{N} g(\mathbf{w}_i) \geq \sum_{i=1}^{N} g(\mathbf{w}_i^*)$. There are also leximin, sufficientist, and egalitarian SWFs, corresponding to those world-rankings.

For any given SWF, we can immediately rank the set **O** of outcomes using the following formula:

> Outcome x at least as good as outcome y iff $(w(b_1(x)), \ldots, w(b_N(x)))$ is ranked by the SWF at least as good as $(w(b_1(y)), \ldots, w(b_N(y)))$.

However, this formula doesn't tell us how to rank *policies*. A policy is a possible course of action by the decisionmaker. An omniscient decisionmaker would *know* what the outcome of a given policy choice on their part would be; but a real-world decisionmaker may well lack this knowledge.

The SWF framework captures the decisionmaker's uncertainty about policy outcomes—and functions to give guidance to non-omniscient decisionmakers—by conceptualizing a given policy P as a (finite)[55] probability distribution across outcomes. Let $\pi_P(x)$ be the probability of outcome x given the choice of policy P. $\pi_P(x)$ is a notional *epistemic* probability. It is the decisionmaker's notional degree of belief that were policy P to be chosen, outcome x would occur.[56]

The term $\pi_P(x)$—the probability of outcome x given the choice of policy P—can be specified along the lines of so-called "causal" decision theory,

[55] Throughout the book, I assume finite lotteries, i.e., there are a finite number of outcomes x such that $\pi_P(x) > 0$. This is a standard assumption in the literature on SWFs under uncertainty.

[56] $\pi_P(x)$ is a *notional* degree of belief—not an actual degree of belief. It is tempting to think of an outcome x as a set of possible worlds (a subset of the set **D** of possible worlds), and $\pi_P(x)$ as the decisionmaker's actual degree of belief that, were policy P to be chosen, outcome x would occur. But this tempting thought must be rejected. As already explained, the model population is a set of fictional individuals; and an outcome assigns an attribute bundle to each such individual. If $\pi_P(x)$ were an actual degree of belief, then the decisionmaker would also hold the actual degree of belief that—were P to be chosen—individual i would exist and have a particular bundle, $b_i(x)$. But the decisionmaker doesn't believe *to the slightest degree* that i exists; i is a *representation* of a person, not an actual person, and x is a representation of a world, not an actual set of worlds.

How these notional degrees of belief are assigned depends (1) on the types of attributes included in the description of outcomes and (2) on which aspects of the decisionmaker's *actual* uncertainty are being modeled. The notional degrees of beliefs are *representations* of the decisionmaker's epistemic probabilities, and are derived from *actual* probabilistic data regarding the link between policies and the modeled attributes—the data that undergird the decisionmaker's actual epistemic probabilities.

Section 5.2 illustrates this modeling of probabilities for purposes of applying the SWF framework to fatality-risk-regulation policies. Each fictional individual i has a current age. A given policy P endows each such individual with a lottery over possible lifespans (longevities) and with a lifetime bundle of attributes (period-by-period income, health, etc.) that the individual will attain if they live

or instead along the lines of so-called "evidential" decision theory.[57] If the former, $\pi_P(x)$ is the cumulative probability of those "states of nature" which, together with policy P, lead to outcome x. (Each "state of nature" is a possible background condition that is causally independent of any choice by the decisionmaker and that, together with any choice by the decisionmaker, yields some outcome.) Although I am sympathetic to causal decision theory, and in some previous work have relied upon that theory and the state-of-nature construct to set forth the SWF framework,[58] the presentation here is more general.[59] Everything in this section and in the remainder of the book is consistent with both causal and evidential decision theory; thus the state-of-nature construct is not used.[60]

We now turn to the final component of the SWF framework—the "uncertainty module." Any given SWF (be it the utilitarian SWF, a prioritarian SWF, an egalitarian SWF, etc.) is associated with *multiple* uncertainty modules. An uncertainty module ranks policies as a function of the probability distribution over outcomes associated with each policy, via the well-being vector corresponding to each outcome.

I will use the symbol $\succcurlyeq^{E\text{-}P}$ to denote an uncertainty module ("*E*" indicating ethical and "P" that what's being ranked is the set of policies). "$P \succcurlyeq^{E\text{-}P} P^*$" indicates that policy P is ranked at least as good as policy P^* by the module.

I've just noted that a given SWF has multiple uncertainty modules. For example, three distinct uncertainty modules for a prioritarian SWF, widely discussed in the literature, are so-called ex post prioritarianism, ex ante prioritarianism, and expected equally distributed equivalent (EDE) prioritarianism. Each of these modules assigns a score to each policy and then ranks policies in the order of these scores; but the scores are calculated in different ways.

A prioritarian SWF, recall, is specified by choosing a transformation function $g(\cdot)$. The ex-post-prioritarian module assigns each policy a score by calculating the expected sum of $g(\cdot)$-transformed well-being. For each possible outcome of the policy, we sum up individuals' $g(\cdot)$-transformed well-being numbers. We then discount this sum by the probability of the outcome and finally add up these discounted sums across all outcomes.

a given lifespan. The probabilities in this P-specific longevity lottery are the decisionmaker's *notional* degrees of belief that i will live a particular lifespan, if P is chosen. These notional probabilities are derived from actual data regarding the survival probabilities of different types of individuals, as a function of age, risk exposure, and attributes.

[57] On causal versus evidential decision theory, see, e.g., Jeffrey (1990); Joyce (1999); Joyce and Gibbard (1998); and the brief overview in Adler (2012, pp. 481–90).
[58] See Adler (2019b, 2022b).
[59] As was Adler (2012, ch. 6).
[60] Except in one place: see Section 7.2, introducing the state-of-nature construct to bolster the argument against expected EDE prioritarianism.

The ex-ante-prioritarian module associates each policy with a list of expected well-being numbers, one for each person in the population. The $g(\cdot)$ function is then applied to these well-being expectations. We assign each policy a score equaling the sum of individuals' $g(\cdot)$-transformed expected well-beings, and rank policies in the order of *these* scores.

Finally, expected EDE prioritarianism takes each possible outcome of a policy; associates that outcome with the "equally distributed equivalent" (if x is an outcome, the equally distributed equivalent for x is that well-being level w such that an outcome in which all individuals are at w is equally good as x, according to the $g(\cdot)$ function being used); and then calculates the expected value of these equally distributed equivalents. (EDE is an acronym for "equally distributed equivalent.")

The various uncertainty modules for a given SWF are all *consistent* with the SWF, in the following sense. For any two "degenerate" policies—a "degenerate" policy being such as to assign probability 1 to one well-being vector, and probability 0 to all others—the module ranks the policies according to the SWF. (It is not too difficult to see, for example, that the ex-ante-prioritarian, ex-post-prioritarian, and expected-EDE-prioritarian modules are all consistent with the prioritarian SWF in this sense.) The various modules for a given SWF may diverge, however, in ranking non-degenerate policies.

Utilitarianism, like prioritarianism, has multiple uncertainty modules. However, one module is by far the most widely used in the literature—what I'll term "simple utilitarianism," namely, the expected sum of well-being. Table 1.1

Table 1.1 Utilitarian and Prioritarian Uncertainty Modules

Utilitarian Modules	
Simple Utilitarianism	$\sum_x \pi_p(x) \sum_{i=1}^{N} \mathbf{w}_i(x)$
Prioritarian Modules	
Ex Post Prioritarianism	$\sum_x \pi_p(x) \sum_{i=1}^{N} g(\mathbf{w}_i(x))$
Ex Ante Prioritarianism	$\sum_{i=1}^{N} g\left(\sum_x \pi_p(x)\mathbf{w}_i(x)\right)$
Expected EDE Prioritarianism	$\sum_x \pi_p(x) g^{-1}\left(\frac{1}{N}\sum_{i=1}^{N} g(\mathbf{w}_i(x))\right)$

Explanation: Simple utilitarianism, ex post prioritarianism, ex ante prioritarianism, and expected EDE prioritarianism each use some formula for assigning scores to policies and then rank policies according to these scores. This table displays the formulas. In the case of the three prioritarian modules, these are modules for a specific prioritarian SWF, defined by some strictly increasing, strictly concave, and continuous transformation function; $g(\cdot)$ is that transformation function.

provides formulas for simple utilitarianism and for ex post, ex ante, and expected EDE prioritarianism.

I believe that ex post prioritarianism is, on balance, the best justified prioritarian module. For this reason, it figures centrally, along with simple utilitarianism, in Chapter 5—where these two approaches are deployed to evaluate risk regulation policies. Making the case for ex post prioritarianism (rather than ex ante or expected EDE prioritarianism) is one of the topics that will be addressed in Chapter 7.

Chapter 1: Appendix

1.A.1 Quasiorderings

Quasiorderings are used throughout the book and denoted generically as $\succcurlyeq$. Let $\mathbf{S} = \{r, s, t, \ldots\}$ be a set of items. A quasiordering on **S** is a binary relation that is reflexive and transitive. Reflexivity: $s \succcurlyeq s$ for every s in **S**. Transitivity: if $r \succcurlyeq s$ and $s \succcurlyeq t$, then $r \succcurlyeq t$.

A quasiordering is the formal expression of the "at least as good" relation. From a given $\succcurlyeq$, we can define two associated binary relations, $\sim$ and $\succ$, as follows. $s \sim t$ iff $s \succcurlyeq t$ and $t \succcurlyeq s$. $s \succ t$ iff $s \succcurlyeq t$ and not $t \succcurlyeq s$. $\sim$ is the formal expression of the "equally good" relation, while $\succ$ expresses the "better than" relation.

Quasiorderings may be complete. A complete quasiordering is such that, for every s and t in **S**, $s \succcurlyeq t$ or $t \succcurlyeq s$ or both. In the case of an incomplete quasiordering, there will be some pairs of items that are incomparable: neither $s \succcurlyeq t$ nor $t \succcurlyeq s$.

1.A.2 Worlds, Individuals, Histories, and the Lifetime Well-Being Comparison Structure

Let **D** be a set of worlds with a fixed and finite population of OHPs. Here and throughout the book, d and variations (d^*, d^+, etc.) denote a member of **D**, unless otherwise noted. Let $\mathbf{I} = \{1, 2, \ldots, N\}$ be the individuals (OHPs) who exist in **D**. **H**, the set of histories, is defined as follows: $\mathbf{H} = \{(d; i): d \in \mathbf{D} \text{ and } i \in \mathbf{I}\}$. Let h denote a member of **H**.

The lifetime well-being comparison structure consists of a quasiordering on **H**, the well-being level quasiordering, denoted $\succcurlyeq^{L\text{-}\mathbf{D}}$; and a quasiordering on $\mathbf{H} \times \mathbf{H}$, the well-being difference quasiordering, denoted $\succcurlyeq^{D\text{-}\mathbf{D}}$. The superscript "**D**" indicates that these are well-being level and difference quasiorderings for a particular world set **D**. In the main text, I have simplified the symbols by dropping the **D** superscripts.

These comparison structures satisfy a group of axioms meant to capture our intuitive sense of how well-being levels and differences behave. Linkage: $h \succcurlyeq^{L\text{-}D} h^*$ iff $(h, h^*) \succcurlyeq^{D\text{-}D} (h^*, h^*)$. Reversal: $(h, h^*) \succcurlyeq^{D\text{-}D} (h^+, h^{++})$ iff $(h^{++}, h^+) \succcurlyeq^{D\text{-}D} (h^*, h)$. Difference Separability: If $(h, h^+) \succcurlyeq^{D\text{-}D} (h^*, h^+)$ then $(h, h') \succcurlyeq^{D\text{-}D} (h^*, h')$; and if $(h^+, h) \succcurlyeq^{D\text{-}D} (h^+, h^*)$ then $(h', h) \succcurlyeq^{D\text{-}D} (h', h^*)$. Neutrality: $(h, h) \sim^{D\text{-}D} (h^*, h^*)$. Concatenation: If $(h, h^*) \succcurlyeq^{D\text{-}D} (h', h'')$ and $(h^*, h^{**}) \succcurlyeq^{D\text{-}D} (h'', h''')$ then $(h, h^{**}) \succcurlyeq^{D\text{-}D} (h', h''')$.[61]

It may also be useful to posit that the lifetime well-being comparison structure includes a ranking of history lotteries. Let T be the set of all lotteries over H. A lottery L is such as to assign probabilities to histories, $p_L(h)$ the probability of history h with lottery L. $0 \le p_L(h) \le 1$, $p_L(h) > 0$ for a finite number of histories, and $\sum_h p_L(h) = 1$. $\succcurlyeq^{Lott\text{-}D}$ is a quasiordering of T. Positing $\succcurlyeq^{Lott\text{-}D}$ is useful because it provides a welfare-theoretic basis at the level of worlds for the counterpart lottery ranking within the SWF framework; that counterpart lottery ranking will, in turn, offer one route for constructing a well-being measure within the SWF framework. See Section 4.2.

1.A.3 Lifetime Welfarism: Defining Axioms

$\succcurlyeq^{E\text{-}D}$, the world-ranking, is a quasiordering on D. (In the main text, I have simplified symbolism by dropping the D superscript.) A world-ranking is defined to be "lifetime welfarist" iff it satisfies the axioms of Lifetime Pareto Indifference, Lifetime Anonymity, and Lifetime Strong Pareto.

> Lifetime Pareto Indifference: Let d, d^* be such that $(d; i) \sim^{L\text{-}D} (d^*; i)$ for all i. Then $d \sim^{E\text{-}D} d^*$.
>
> Lifetime Anonymity: Let $\pi(\cdot)$ be any permutation mapping on I (a one-to-one, onto mapping from I to I). Let d, d^* be such that $(d; i) \sim^{L\text{-}D} (d^*; \pi(i))$ for all i. Then $d \sim^{E\text{-}D} d^*$.
>
> Lifetime Strong Pareto: Let d, d^* be such that $(d; i) \succcurlyeq^{L\text{-}D} (d^*; i)$ for all i; and $(d; j) \succ^{L\text{-}D} (d^*; j)$ for at least one j. Then $d \succ^{E\text{-}D} d^*$.

[61] I here describe the lifetime well-being comparison structure for a given set of worlds D. However, it is also very plausible that these structures should be consistent across different sets of worlds; how histories compare in terms of well-being levels and differences depends just on the histories being compared and not on which other histories belong to the sets at issue. Call this "World Set Well-Being Consistency." Let D and D* be two sets of worlds, each with a fixed and finite population of OHPs, the same in both cases. Then World Set Well-Being Consistency requires that (1) if histories h and h' belong to the set of histories arising from both D and D*, then $h \succcurlyeq^{L\text{-}D} h'$ iff $h \succcurlyeq^{L\text{-}D^*} h'$; and (2) if histories h, h', h'', and h''' belong to the set of histories arising from both D and D*, then $(h, h') \succcurlyeq^{D\text{-}D} (h'', h''')$ iff $(h, h') \succcurlyeq^{D\text{-}D^*} (h'', h''')$.

1.A.4 The Main Versions of Lifetime Welfarism

The lifetime well-being comparison structure on a given world-set **D** is "measurable" if there exists a well-being measure (a real-valued function $w(\cdot)$ on the set of histories **H** associated with **D**) such that $w(h) \geq w(h^*)$ iff $h \succcurlyeq^{L\text{-}\mathbf{D}} h^*$; and $w(h) - w(h^*) \geq w(h^+) - w(h^{++})$ iff $(h, h^*) \succcurlyeq^{D\text{-}\mathbf{D}} (h^+, h^{++})$. Let $\mathbf{w}(d)$ denote the N-dimensional well-being vector onto which $w(\cdot)$ maps d, namely: $\mathbf{w}_i(d) = w(d; i)$. The world-ranking on **D** is "complete" if $\succcurlyeq^{E\text{-}\mathbf{D}}$ is complete.

1.A.4.1 A Measurable Lifetime Well-Being Comparison Structure and Complete World-Ranking

Let **w** be an N-dimensional vector of well-being numbers, with $\mathbf{w}_i$ the i-th element, and **W** the set of all such vectors of well-being numbers (or all within some orthant of N-dimensional space). Let $\succcurlyeq^E$ denote a complete quasiordering of **W**. If the lifetime well-being comparison structure on set **D** is measurable and $\succcurlyeq^{E\text{-}\mathbf{D}}$ is complete, then $\succcurlyeq^{E\text{-}\mathbf{D}}$ conforms to $\succcurlyeq^E$ as follows:

$$d \succcurlyeq^{E\text{-}\mathbf{D}} d^* \text{ iff } \mathbf{w}(d) \succcurlyeq^E \mathbf{w}(d^*)$$

That is, the ranking of any two worlds in **D** corresponds to the ranking by $\succcurlyeq^E$ of the two vectors onto which the worlds are mapped by $w(\cdot)$, the well-being measure representing $\succcurlyeq^{L\text{-}\mathbf{D}}$ and $\succcurlyeq^{D\text{-}\mathbf{D}}$.[62]

The main versions of lifetime welfarism order **W** as follows:

<u>Utilitarianism</u>. $\mathbf{w} \succcurlyeq^E \mathbf{w}^*$ iff $\sum_{i=1}^{N} \mathbf{w}_i \geq \sum_{i=1}^{N} \mathbf{w}_i^*$.

<u>Prioritarianism</u>. Prioritarianism is a family of rankings of **W**. Each such ranking is defined by some strictly increasing, strictly concave, and continuous function $g(\cdot)$, and ranks well-being vectors as follows: $\mathbf{w} \succcurlyeq^E \mathbf{w}^*$ iff $\sum_{i=1}^{N} g(\mathbf{w}_i) \geq \sum_{i=1}^{N} g(\mathbf{w}_i^*)$.

<u>Leximin</u>. Let $\hat{\mathbf{w}}$ be the elements of **w** rearranged from smallest to largest. The leximin vector ranking is as follows: $\mathbf{w} \succcurlyeq^E \mathbf{w}^*$ iff **w** is a permutation of $\mathbf{w}^*$ or there exists a $j \leq N$ such that $\hat{\mathbf{w}}_k = \hat{\mathbf{w}}_k^*$ for all $k < j$ and $\hat{\mathbf{w}}_j > \hat{\mathbf{w}}_j^*$.

[62] Generating $\succcurlyeq^{E\text{-}\mathbf{D}}$ in the manner just stated yields world-rankings for each **D** with the properties of Profile Independence and World Set Ethical Consistency. I take each of these to be a plausible property for lifetime welfarism to have. (1) <u>Profile Independence</u>. This property assumes well-being measurability and is a plausible feature of $\succcurlyeq^{E\text{-}\mathbf{D}}$ in that case. It says that the ranking of $\succcurlyeq^{E\text{-}\mathbf{D}}$ conforms to a *single* ranking $\succcurlyeq^E$ of the set **W** of N-dimensional well-being vectors; $\succcurlyeq^E$ is independent of *which*

Sufficientism. Sufficientism is a family of rankings of W. Each such ranking is defined by a threshold level of well-being (a number w^{Thresh}) and some strictly increasing, strictly concave, and continuous function $g(\cdot)$. For a given vector **w**, let $\overline{\mathbf{w}}$ be the elements of **w** truncated above at w^{Thresh}; and $\underline{\mathbf{w}}$ the elements of **w** truncated below at w^{Thresh}. (That is, $\overline{\mathbf{w}}_i = \min\{\mathbf{w}_i, w^{Thresh}\}$ and $\underline{\mathbf{w}}_i = \max\{\mathbf{w}_i, w^{Thresh}\}$.)

The ranking is as follows: (1) If $\sum_{i=1}^{N} g(\overline{\mathbf{w}}_i) > \sum_{i=1}^{N} g(\overline{\mathbf{w}}_i^*)$, then $\mathbf{w} \succ^E \mathbf{w}^*$; (2) If $\sum_{i=1}^{N} g(\overline{\mathbf{w}}_i) = \sum_{i=1}^{N} g(\overline{\mathbf{w}}_i^*)$ and $\sum_{i=1}^{N} \underline{\mathbf{w}}_i > \sum_{i=1}^{N} \underline{\mathbf{w}}_i^*$, then $\mathbf{w} \succ^E \mathbf{w}^*$. (3) If $\sum_{i=1}^{N} g(\overline{\mathbf{w}}_i) = \sum_{i=1}^{N} g(\overline{\mathbf{w}}_i^*)$ and $\sum_{i=1}^{N} \underline{\mathbf{w}}_i = \sum_{i=1}^{N} \underline{\mathbf{w}}_i^*$, then $\mathbf{w} \sim^E \mathbf{w}^*$.

Egalitarianism. Egalitarianism is a family of rankings of W. Each such ranking is associated with some inequality metric $I(\cdot)$[63] and satisfies the following conditions as well as being complete:[64] (1) If $I(\mathbf{w}) < I(\mathbf{w}^*)$ and $\sum_{i=1}^{N} \mathbf{w}_i = \sum_{i=1}^{N} \mathbf{w}_i^*$, then $\mathbf{w} \succ^E \mathbf{w}^*$; (2) if $I(\mathbf{w}) = I(\mathbf{w}^*)$ and $\sum_{i=1}^{N} \mathbf{w}_i > \sum_{i=1}^{N} \mathbf{w}_i^*$, then $\mathbf{w} \succ^E \mathbf{w}^*$; and (3)

well-being measure is used to represent the well-being information in $\succcurlyeq^{L\text{-}D}$ and $\succcurlyeq^{D\text{-}D}$. (For a discussion of profile-independence for the SWF framework, see Bossert and Weymark [2004]; Weymark [2016]; and for a defense, see Adler [2012, pp. 69–71; 2019b, pp. 260–62; 2022b, pp. 93–97]. Parallel arguments support the profile-independence of $\succcurlyeq^{E\text{-}D}$.) (2) World Set Ethical Consistency. Let **D** and **D*** be two sets of worlds, each with a fixed and finite population of OHPs, the same in both cases. If d and d' belong to both **D** and **D***, then: $d \succcurlyeq^{E\text{-}D} d'$ iff $d \succcurlyeq^{E\text{-}D^*} d'$. (This axiom is analogous to World Set Well-Being Consistency. It says that the ethical ranking of a given pair of worlds should be fixed by the features of those worlds rather than varying depending on which other worlds happen to belong to the world set being ranked.)

The axiom of Profile Independence goes hand in glove with an assumption of Invariance: namely, that if there are multiple admissible well-being measures—admissible in the sense of representing all of the well-being information in $\succcurlyeq^{L\text{-}D}$ and $\succcurlyeq^{D\text{-}D}$—the rule $d \succcurlyeq^{E\text{-}D} d^*$ iff $\mathbf{w}(d) \succcurlyeq^E \mathbf{w}(d^*)$ should achieve the very same ranking of **D** for every admissible $w(\cdot)$. In the case of a prioritarian $\succcurlyeq^E$, Invariance will in turn require that the lifetime well-being comparison structure contain *more* than well-being and difference information. That additional information might consist, for example, in information about well-being ratios. On Invariance, see Adler (2019b).

[63] See Adler (2019b, p. 276), discussing the defining features of inequality metrics. $I(\cdot)$ assigns real numbers to vectors (in the application here, well-being vectors) so as to satisfy the axioms of Anonymity and Pigou-Dalton and to assign the lowest number (the lowest degree of inequality) to a perfectly equal distribution.

[64] Conditions (1) through (5) do not themselves ensure completeness.

if $I(\mathbf{w}) = I(\mathbf{w}^*)$ and $\sum_{i=1}^{N} \mathbf{w}_i = \sum_{i=1}^{N} \mathbf{w}_i^*$, then $\mathbf{w} \sim^E w^*$. Moreover (4) $\succcurlyeq^E$ satisfies Lifetime Strong Pareto[65] and (5) $\succcurlyeq^E$ violates the Separability axiom.[66]

1.A.4.2 The Lifetime Well-Being Comparison Structure Is Not Measurable or the World-Ranking Is Not Complete

For short, I'll refer to the twin assumptions of a measurable lifetime well-being comparison structure and a complete world-ranking as the "Standard Setup" and to the setup in which one or both assumptions are dropped as the "General Setup." Section 1.A.4.1 immediately above sets forth the utilitarian, prioritarian, leximin, sufficientist, and egalitarian world-rankings for the Standard Setup. How to generalize these rankings to the General Setup is a topic that, surprisingly, has been little discussed by either welfare economists or philosophers. The following remarks are necessarily somewhat tentative.

In what follows, it will be useful to think of utilitarianism, prioritarianism, etc. as providing a rule or a family of rules for arriving at a world-ranking of a given **D**, given the lifetime well-being comparison structure on **D**. A rule associates each **D** and associated structure ($\succcurlyeq^{L\text{-}\mathbf{D}}$ and $\succcurlyeq^{D\text{-}\mathbf{D}}$) with a ranking $\succcurlyeq^{E\text{-}\mathbf{D}}$.

Consider a rule *R* in the Standard Setup (be it the utilitarian rule, a prioritarian rule, etc.). *R* takes the following form: For every **D** in which the lifetime well-being comparison structure is measurable (for short, a "measurable" **D**), *R* specifies a complete ranking $\succcurlyeq^{E\text{-}\mathbf{D}}$ of **D**.

Let R^* be a "generalization" of *R* to the General Setup. R^* is such that, for *every* **D** (whether or not measurable), R^* specifies a ranking $\succcurlyeq^{E\text{-}\mathbf{D}}$, which need not be complete.

Then, presumably, the following should be true of R^*. (1) If **D** is measurable, the *R* ranking should be identical with the R^* ranking modulo incomparability.[67]

[65] Lifetime Pareto Indifference, Lifetime Anonymity, and Lifetime Strong Pareto, which are constraints on $\succcurlyeq^{E\text{-}\mathbf{D}}$ (see above), each correspond in an obvious way to constraints on $\succcurlyeq^E$ (which are denoted by the same names). A ranking $\succcurlyeq^E$ that satisfies (1), (2), (3) and (5) will satisfy Lifetime Pareto Indifference and Lifetime Anonymity but need not satisfy Lifetime Strong Pareto—hence condition (4) is inserted as a separate condition. The utilitarian, prioritarian, leximin and sufficientist rankings as stated here do satisfy all three axioms (the axioms of lifetime welfarism), hence those axioms are not stated as separate conditions in defining those rankings.

[66] See Section 1.A.5 for a statement of Separability (stated as a constraint on $\succcurlyeq^{E\text{-}\mathbf{D}}$; there is a corresponding constraint on $\succcurlyeq^E$); and see note 42 for an explanation of why a violation of Separability is built into the definition of egalitarianism.

[67] That is, if the R^* ranking says that world d^+ is better than world d, then the *R* ranking should also say that world d^+ is better than world d; and if the R^* ranking says that world d^+ and world d are equally good, then the *R* ranking should do the same. The idea here is that the R^* ranking may be incomplete (failing to rank two worlds as better, worse, or equally good), but if the R^* ranking *does* compare two worlds, it should do so the same way as the *R* ranking.

(2) Let A be any axiom that does not imply a measurable lifetime well-being comparison structure or a complete world-ranking. Assume that, in every measurable D, R yields an $\succcurlyeq^{E\text{-}D}$ that satisfies A. Then R^* should be such as to yield an $\succcurlyeq^{E\text{-}D}$ that satisfies A in *every* D.[68]

To illustrate, consider a prioritarian rule R for the Standard Setup. This rule is defined by a strictly increasing, strictly concave, and continuous $g(\cdot)$, and arrives at $\succcurlyeq^{E\text{-}D}$ for any measurable D as follows: $d \succcurlyeq^{E\text{-}D} d^*$ iff $\sum_{i=1}^{N} g(\mathbf{w}_i(d)) \geq \sum_{i=1}^{N} g(\mathbf{w}_i(d^*))$. Let R^* be such that, in every measurable D, R^* ranks D as follows, using a set F of strictly increasing, strictly concave, and continuous functions, with $g(\cdot)$ an element of F: (a) $d \succ^{E\text{-}D} d^*$ iff $\sum_{i=1}^{N} f(\mathbf{w}_i(d)) > \sum_{i=1}^{N} f(\mathbf{w}_i(d^*))$ for every $f(\cdot)$ in F; and (b) $d \sim^{E\text{-}D} d^*$ iff $\sum_{i=1}^{N} f(\mathbf{w}_i(d)) = \sum_{i=1}^{N} f(\mathbf{w}_i(d^*))$ for every $f(\cdot)$ in F. Then R^* satisfies condition (1).

Note further that R yields an $\succcurlyeq^{E\text{-}D}$ that satisfies the following axioms (among others) in every measurable D: Lifetime Pareto Indifference, Lifetime Anonymity, Lifetime Strong Pareto, Pigou-Dalton, Separability, and Continuity.[69] Continuity presupposes well-being measurability, but the other axioms presuppose neither measurability nor the completeness of the ranking. Thus R^* should be such that it yields an $\succcurlyeq^{E\text{-}D}$, in every D, which satisfies all of these axioms except Continuity.

1.A.5 The Pigou-Dalton and Separability Axioms

Pigou-Dalton: Let d and d^* be such that $(d; i) \succ^{L\text{-}D} (d; j)$ for some i and j; $((d; i), (d^*; i)) \sim^{D\text{-}D} ((d^*; j), (d; j))$, with this difference a "positive" difference, i.e., $((d; i), (d^*; i)) \succ^{D\text{-}D} ((d; i), (d; i))$; $(d^*; i) \succ^{L\text{-}D} (d; j)$; and for all $k \neq i, j$, $(d; k) \sim^{L\text{-}D} (d^*; k)$.[70] Then $d^* \succ^{E\text{-}D} d$.

Separability: Let **M** be a subset of **I**, and let $\mathbf{M}^+ = \mathbf{I} \setminus \mathbf{M}$ (all individuals not in **M**). Assume d, d^*, d^+, d^{++} are as follows. For all $i \in \mathbf{M}$, $(d; i) \sim^{L\text{-}D} (d^*; i)$ and $(d^+; i) \sim^{L\text{-}D} (d^{++}; i)$. For all $j \in \mathbf{M}^+$, $(d; j) \sim^{L\text{-}D} (d^+; j)$ and $(d^*; j) \sim^{L\text{-}D} (d^{++}; j)$. Then $d \succcurlyeq^{E\text{-}D} d^*$ iff $d^+ \succcurlyeq^{E\text{-}D} d^{++}$.

68 In addition, R^* should satisfy World Set Ethical Consistency. See note 62.

69 On the Continuity axiom, see Adler (2019b, ch. 3 and appendix F); Adler (2022b).

70 The concept of the "magnitude of the difference" or "gap" between two histories h and h^* presupposes that h and h^* are comparable, i.e., $h \succcurlyeq^{L\text{-}D} h^*$ or $h^* \succcurlyeq^{L\text{-}D} h$ or both. Intuitively, this magnitude is the difference between whichever of the histories is better and whichever is worse. More precisely, if h and h^* are comparable, then the magnitude of the difference between them can be defined as follows: (1) if $h \sim^{L\text{-}D} h^*$, this magnitude is the zero difference (the difference between any history and itself); (2) if $h \succ^{L\text{-}D} h^*$, this magnitude is (h, h^*); and (3) if $h^* \succ^{L\text{-}D} h$, this magnitude is (h^*, h). (Note that if h and h^* are noncomparable, both (h, h^*) and (h^*, h) are noncomparable with the zero difference—so indeed the concept of the magnitude of the difference between h and h^* is not well-defined.)

As regards the Pigou-Dalton axiom as stated here, the following can be demonstrated. *If* $(d^*; i)$ and $(d^*; j)$ are comparable, then: given the antecedent conditions for the Pigou-Dalton axiom except

With well-being measurable, Separability and Pigou-Dalton can be stated as follows.

Pigou-Dalton: Let d and d^* be such that $\mathbf{w}_i(d) > \mathbf{w}_j(d)$ for some i and j; $\mathbf{w}_i(d^*) = \mathbf{w}_i(d) - \Delta w$ and $\mathbf{w}_j(d^*) = \mathbf{w}_j(d) + \Delta w$, with $\Delta w > 0$; $\mathbf{w}_i(d^*) > \mathbf{w}_j(d)$ (which is equivalent, under the preceding conditions, to a gap-diminution condition, namely, $|\mathbf{w}_i(d) - \mathbf{w}_j(d)| > |\mathbf{w}_i(d^*) - \mathbf{w}_j(d^*)|$); and for all $k \neq i, j$, $\mathbf{w}_k(d) = \mathbf{w}_k(d^*)$. Then $d^* \succ^{E\text{-}D} d$.

Separability: Let $\mathbf{M}$ be a subset of $\mathbf{I}$, and let $\mathbf{M}^+ = \mathbf{I} \setminus \mathbf{M}$ (all individuals not in $\mathbf{M}$). Assume d, d^*, d^+, d^{++} are as follows. For all $i \in \mathbf{M}$, $\mathbf{w}_i(d) = \mathbf{w}_i(d^*)$ and $\mathbf{w}_i(d^+) = \mathbf{w}_i(d^{++})$. For all $j \in \mathbf{M}^+$, $\mathbf{w}_j(d) = \mathbf{w}_j(d^+)$ and $\mathbf{w}_j(d^*) = \mathbf{w}_j(d^{++})$. Then $d \succcurlyeq^{E\text{-}D} d^*$ iff $d^+ \succcurlyeq^{E\text{-}D} d^{++}$.

1.A.6 The SWF Framework

The SWF framework, in brief, includes the following components (as it would be applied in the Focal Case and used to operationalize lifetime welfarism). $\mathbf{P} = \{P, P^*, \ldots\}$ is the set of policies. $\mathbf{I}^{\mathrm{Mod}} = \{1, 2, \ldots, N\}$ is the set of notional individuals. $\mathbf{O} = \{x, y, \ldots\}$ is the set of outcomes. For each outcome in $\mathbf{O}$, the individuals who exist in that outcome are all the members of $\mathbf{I}^{\mathrm{Mod}}$. $w(\cdot)$ is a well-being measure mapping bundles of attributes onto real numbers. $b_i(x)$ is the bundle of individual i in outcome x. $\mathbf{w}(x)$ is the well-being vector corresponding to outcome x, with $\mathbf{w}_i(x) = w(b_i(x))$. $\mathbf{W}$ is the set of all N-dimensional well-being vectors (or all within some orthant of N-dimensional space).

The SWF proper is a complete quasiordering of $\mathbf{W}$, denoted here as $\succcurlyeq^E$. This vector ranking yields a corresponding ranking of the outcome set, denoted as $\succcurlyeq^{E\text{-}O}$: for any two outcomes x and y, $x \succcurlyeq^{E\text{-}O} y$ iff $\mathbf{w}(x) \succcurlyeq^E \mathbf{w}(y)$.

A given policy P is conceptualized as a probability distribution over outcomes. $\pi_P(x)$ is the probability of outcome x given policy P, $0 \leq \pi_P(x) \leq 1$; $\sum_x \pi_P(x) = 1$. Throughout the book, I avoid the complications that arise with infinite lotteries by assuming that this probability distribution is finite (has finite support): the number of outcomes x such that $\pi_P(x) \neq 0$ is finite.

In any case in the book where I sum the numerical values of an infinite set of items, the summation is stipulated to include only non-zero values. In every such case that arises in this book, there will be at most a finite number of items with non-zero values. For example, $\mathbf{O}$ might be a finite *or* infinite set of outcomes. If the latter,

the condition that $(d^*; i) \succ^{L\text{-}D} (d; j)$, that condition is equivalent to a gap-diminishing condition (namely, that the magnitude of the difference between $(d^*; i)$ and $(d^*; j)$ is less than the magnitude of the difference between $(d; i)$ and $(d; j)$).

then the summation $\sum_x \pi_P(x)$ should be read as $\sum_{x:\pi_P(x)\neq 0} \pi_P(x)$, which has only a finite number of terms because P is a finite probability distribution over outcomes (see preceding paragraph).

If an infinite set of outcomes has no items with non-zero numerical values, then (by virtue of the above stipulation) a summation over that set is an empty summation and, as is conventional, is defined to be equal to 0. For example, let $L_{P,i}(v)$, v a real number, be defined as follows: $L_{P,i}(v) = \sum_{x:\mathbf{w}_i(x)=v} \pi_P(x)$. If there are *no* outcomes with $\mathbf{w}_i(x) = v$, then this is an empty summation and equal to 0. If there are a finite number of outcomes with $\mathbf{w}_i(x) = v$, then this is an ordinary summation. If there are an infinite number of outcomes with $\mathbf{w}_i(x) = v$, then at most a finite number will be such that $\pi_P(x) \neq 0$, and the summation is the sum of those non-zero probabilities. Finally, if there are an infinite number of outcomes with $\mathbf{w}_i(x) = v$, and all of these are such that $\pi_P(x) = 0$, then the summation is an empty summation and equal to 0.

An SWF $\succcurlyeq^E$ has multiple associated "uncertainty modules." An uncertainty module for $\succcurlyeq^E$ is a formula for arriving at a ranking $\succcurlyeq^{E\text{-}P}$ of the policy set, as a function of the well-being vector associated with each outcome (given $w(\cdot)$) and the outcome probabilities. Any such module should be consistent with $\succcurlyeq^E$, in the sense of ranking "degenerate" policies (those giving rise to some well-being vector with probability 1) as would the SWF. That is, any uncertainty module for $\succcurlyeq^E$ must satisfy the following axiom:

> Module Consistency: Assume that policies P and P^* are as follows. (1) There is a well-being vector $\mathbf{w}$ such that, for every x such that $\pi_P(x) > 0$, $\mathbf{w}(x) = \mathbf{w}$; and (2) there is a well-being vector $\mathbf{w}^*$ such that, for every x such that $\pi_{P^*}(x) > 0$, $\mathbf{w}(x) = \mathbf{w}^*$. Then $P \succcurlyeq^{E\text{-}P} P^*$ iff $\mathbf{w} \succcurlyeq^E \mathbf{w}^*$.

See the main text for the main uncertainty modules for the utilitarian and prioritarian SWFs; and see Chapters 5 and 7 for more analysis of uncertainty modules.

2
Lifetime Welfarism
A Defense

This chapter provides a substantive defense of lifetime welfarism. Recall that Chapter 1 had defined lifetime welfarism in terms of the axioms of Lifetime Pareto Indifference, Lifetime Anonymity, and Lifetime Strong Pareto; had discussed lifetime-welfarist world-rankings; and had described the use of the SWF framework to implement lifetime welfarism—but had postponed making the case *for* lifetime welfarism. That case is set forth here.

Why should welfarism take a lifetime form? Many philosophers of well-being believe that it is meaningful not only to ascribe well-being to whole lives but also to ascribe it to temporal segments of lives ("time-slices").[1] The time-slices might be individual moments and/or "stages" (by which I mean temporal segments of lives that are longer than moments). To the extent that our theories of well-being indeed ascribe well-being to moments, an ethical ranking of worlds in light of momentary well-being—*momentary welfarism*—is a possibility. Similarly, to the extent that our theories of well-being ascribe it to stages, an ethical ranking of worlds in light of stage well-being—*stage welfarism*—is a possibility. Like lifetime welfarism, momentary and stage welfarism are *consequentialist* (ethical guidance for choices is grounded on a single world-ranking) and, more specifically, *welfarist* (the world-ranking is determined by individuals' well-being). So generic arguments in favor of consequentialism and, more specifically, welfarism are not themselves going to adjudicate between lifetime, momentary, and stage welfarism. Why, then favor the first rather than one of the latter two?

This chapter defends lifetime welfarism by, first, setting forth the serious flaws of time-slice welfarism; and, second, showing that critiques of lifetime welfarism can be deflected (at least to some extent) by adjusting the internal structure of lifetime well-being.

The chapter, like most of the book, works within the Focal Case. The ethical population consists of a fixed and finite group of OHPs (thus "person," "individual," and "human" are used, unless otherwise noted, to mean an OHP). Lifetime welfarism is defended for the Focal Case. Section 2.1 clarifies the

[1] There is a significant philosophical literature regarding the structure of lifetime well-being, including the relation between lifetime and time-slice well-being. See generally Bramble (2018) and sources cited therein at pp. 1–12. See also Brown (2019); Bruckner (2019); Bykvist (2024); Clark (2018); King (2020); Rosati (2013).

Risk, Death, and Well-Being. Matthew D. Adler, Oxford University Press. © Oxford University Press 2025.
DOI: 10.1093/9780197505984.003.0002

difference between lifetime welfarism and time-slice welfarism. Section 2.2 criticizes momentary welfarism. Section 2.3 criticizes stage welfarism.[2] Section 2.4 responds to two important critiques of lifetime welfarism.

A plausible refinement of lifetime welfarism stipulates that what occurs in the early years of life of an OHP, before their psychological capacities are sufficiently developed, shouldn't be counted as part of their lifetime well-being. Section 2.5 considers whether occurrences during an OHP's early years should be incorporated into their lifetime well-being or, instead, hived off.[3]

[2] A substantial body of work addresses the choice between lifetime and time-slice welfarism, including my own prior writing. See Adler (2012, ch. 6); Andrić and Herlitz (2021); Bidadanure (2021); Bramble (2018); Brink (1997); Gosseries (2003); Hirose (2005); Holtug (2010, ch. 10); Kappel (1997); Lippert-Rasmussen (2003); McKerlie (1989, 1992, 1997, 2001a, 2001b, 2007, 2013); Nagel (1979b; 1991, ch. 7); O'Brien (2019); Parfit (1986; 1987, ch. 15); Segall (2016); Temkin (1993, ch. 8). The arguments in Sections 2.2 and 2.3 build upon this literature.

[3] It will be useful for the reader to see how the arguments of this chapter line up with John Broome's *Weighing Lives* (Broome [2004], cited in what follows by page and chapter numbers). Broome speaks of "temporal" well-being; I take this to be the same as "momentary" well-being as I am using that term. (Broome assumes a discrete-time model, in which time proceeds by quantum steps, pp. 23–24; temporal well-being is well-being at one or another such time.)

As I do in the current chapter, Broome endorses lifetime welfarism—not momentary (or stage) welfarism. He endorses the weak "principle of personal good" (pp. 120–23) as well as a strong version of this principle (pp. 133–34). The weak version of this principle is equivalent to the conjunction of Lifetime Pareto Indifference and Lifetime Strong Pareto. Broome also endorses an "impartiality" axiom (p. 135) which implies Lifetime Anonymity.

However, Broome's argument for lifetime welfarism differs from mine in important respects. One component of my argument is skepticism about whether individuals have determinate levels of momentary or stage well-being such that lifetime well-being is monotonic with respect to it. I also argue that, independent of such skepticism, prioritarians have good reason to reject time-slice approaches and instead to accept lifetime prioritarianism.

By contrast, Broome is *not* skeptical about the determinacy of momentary well-being such that lifetime well-being is monotonic with respect to it. His basic setup (conceiving of alternatives as "distributions" of momentary well-being across people, times, and states of nature; see chs. 2–3) assumes well-defined momentary well-being. And he endorses the monotonicity of lifetime well-being with respect to momentary well-being (p. 120). (Although Broome acknowledges that lifetime well-being may not supervene on the pattern of momentary well-being [pp. 46–47], this possibility is placed to one side for purposes of his book.)

Moreover, Broome rejects prioritarianism (see p. 133), instead endorsing a *utilitarian* ranking of distributions that (in the fixed-population case) does so according to the sum total of individuals' lifetime well-being (ch. 9).

How, then, does Broome argue for lifetime welfarism? He does so by rejecting what he terms "the separability of times" (see ch. 7). Separability of times means that we value a two-dimensional distribution of momentary well-being across persons and times by first assigning a value to the vector of momentary well-beings at each time, and then an overall value to the distribution as a function of these time-specific values (pp. 105–6). (Note that momentary prioritarianism and momentary utilitarianism would satisfy the "separability of times.") Broome argues against the separability of times by appealing to "the value of longevity" (pp. 107–8). "Suppose some total amount of time is lived by people, at some level of [momentary] well-being. For longevity to be valuable means that, given this fixed total of time and level of [momentary] wellbeing, it is better for the time to be divided up amongst fewer lives rather than amongst more lives" (p.108).

My argument, by contrast, does not rely upon the "value of longevity." The "value of longevity" has implications for the lifetime-welfarist world-ranking beyond the Focal Case, with a variable population. In particular, if lifetime well-being is the sum total of momentary well-being, the "value of longevity" would preclude both total utilitarianism and total prioritarianism (discussed in Chapter 8 of this book). Indeed, Broome in *Weighing Lives* defends critical-level rather than total utilitarianism

2.1 Time-Slice Welfarism

Here, I define time-slice welfarism and contrast it with lifetime welfarism. This discussion is applicable to both momentary and stage welfarism (in the former case, the time-slice is a moment; in the latter case, a stage).

Consequentialism, as conceptualized throughout this book, involves a *single* world-ranking $\succcurlyeq^E$—not a plurality of agent- or time-relative rankings. Time-slice welfarism, as discussed in this chapter, is a species of consequentialism thus understood. In particular, ranking worlds from the perspective of the present time-slice is *not* the type of theory considered in this chapter. Note that this involves a plurality of time-relative rankings—a ranking for each calendar time, which becomes the operative ranking when that calendar time is the present time—rather than a single $\succcurlyeq^E$.

A given account of well-being *might* have a time-slice component along with its lifetime component. It's open to question whether various well-being accounts really do have a time-slice component, especially for momentary slices (see Section 2.2.1), but for now let's assume we're working with a well-being theory that does. The theory makes comparisons of time-slice well-being levels and differences, just as it makes comparisons of lifetime well-being levels and differences. If so, the time-slice comparisons can be expressed in terms of "histories," just as the lifetime comparisons can. A time-slice is a temporal segment of a history, and time-slice well-being comparisons (level and difference) are comparisons of these temporal segments.

An important question, of course, is how time-slice and lifetime well-being covary. A strong requirement is *temporal additivity*: a history's lifetime well-being is the sum of its time-slice well-being. Some philosophers defend temporal additivity or at least employ it as a working premise in their analyses; others reject it.[4] Even if temporal additivity fails, it's hard to believe that lifetime well-being and the well-being of time-slices can be wholly separated. A weaker requirement is *monotonicity*: (1) If two histories h and h^* have the same duration ("duration" here is used to mean the number of slices) and the level of time-slice well-being is the same at each slice, then their levels of lifetime well-being are the same. (2) If two histories h and h^* have the same duration and are such that

(pp. 200–1, 255). By contrast, the arguments I advance in this chapter defending lifetime welfarism are completely agnostic with respect to the functional form of lifetime welfarism in variable-population cases. Still, nothing in my analysis is incompatible with Broome's "value of longevity" argument for lifetime welfarism. It can be combined with, or substituted for, the arguments in this chapter.

[4] See sources cited note 1. Broome in *Weighing Lives* takes the position that there is "no solid basis for the additive value function" but adopts it as a useful working assumption (2004, p. 223).

the level of time-slice well-being is at least as high in h^* at each slice, and strictly higher in some slice(s), then h^* has a higher level of lifetime well-being.[5]

Time-slice welfarism can be defined in terms of axioms of Pareto indifference, anonymity, and strong Pareto, analogous to those for lifetime welfarism.

> Time-slice Pareto Indifference: Let two worlds d and d^* be such that each person's history has the same duration in d as in d^*. If, for each person, the well-being level at each slice in d is the same as the well-being level at that slice in d^*, the two worlds are equally good.
>
> Time-slice Anonymity: Let two worlds d and d^* be such that each person's history has the same duration in d as in d^*. If the arrangement of time-slice well-being levels in d is a permutation of the arrangement in d^*, the two worlds are equally good.
>
> Time-slice Strong Pareto: Let two worlds d and d^* be such that each person's history has the same duration in d as in d^*. If (1) for each person, the well-being level at each slice in d is at least as high as the well-being level at that slice in d^* and (2) for at least one person and slice, the well-being level at that slice is strictly higher, then world d is better than world d^*.

Time-slice welfarism is, then, a family of world-rankings (most prominently time-slice utilitarianism, prioritarianism, leximin, sufficientism, and egalitarianism) satisfying these foundational axioms.

Lifetime welfarism and time-slice welfarism are *different*. The two approaches will, in general, yield different world-rankings. Operationalized via the SWF decision procedure, they can thus be expected to result in divergent policy recommendations. One can't make much progress in developing a welfarist perspective on policy choice while remaining agnostic on the lifetime/time-slice issue.

To see how the two frameworks diverge, consider first the foundational axioms. (1a) It's possible that the *lifetime* axioms will constrain d and d^* to be ranked equally good (so that any lifetime-welfarist world-ranking will thus rank them), while the time-slice axioms impose no such constraint. This is true even if the well-being account conforms to temporal additivity, and *a fortiori* if it merely conforms to monotonicity. See Table 2.1. (1b) Conversely, it's possible that the *time-slice* axioms will constrain d and d^* to be ranked equally good (so that any time-slice-welfarist world-ranking will thus rank them), while the lifetime axioms impose no such constraint. (Again, even with temporal additivity, and *a*

[5] This is what Broome (2004, pp. 120–23), calls the "weak principle of temporal good," which he endorses.

Table 2.1 Lifetime Axioms Constrain while Time-Slice Axioms Do Not: Equal Goodness

	World d			World d^*		
	Period 1	Period 2	Lifetime	Period 1	Period 2	Lifetime
Amy	10	20	30	15	15	30
Bob	10	20	30	15	15	30
	World d^+			World d^{++}		
	Period 1	Period 2	Lifetime	Period 1	Period 2	Lifetime
Sari	30	40	70	15	15	30
Tal	10	20	30	35	35	70

Explanation: The table entries are time-slice or lifetime well-being numbers. In the top half of the table, Lifetime Pareto Indifference requires that d and d^* be ranked equally good. In the bottom half of the table, Lifetime Anonymity requires that d^+ and d^{++} be ranked equally good. In neither case do the foundational time-slice axioms constrain the ranking. Moreover, a time-slice ranking that satisfies Time-slice Pigou-Dalton along with Time-slice Pareto Indifference, Anonymity, and Strong Pareto will rank d^* better than d and d^{++} better than d^+—in violation of the foundational lifetime axioms.

Table 2.2 Time-Slice Axioms Constrain while Lifetime Axioms Do Not: Equal Goodness

	World d			World d^*		
	Period 1	Period 2	Lifetime	Period 1	Period 2	Lifetime
Mia	10	10	20	10	20	30
Jude	20	20	40	20	10	30

Explanation: Time-slice Anonymity requires that d^* be ranked equally good as d. The foundational lifetime axioms do not constrain the ranking. Moreover, a lifetime ranking that satisfies Lifetime Pigou-Dalton along with Lifetime Pareto Indifference, Anonymity, and Strong Pareto will rank d^* better than d —in violation of the foundational time-slice axioms.

fortiori only with monotonicity.) See Table 2.2. (2a) It's possible that the lifetime axioms will constrain d to be ranked better than d^*, while the time-slice axioms impose no such constraint. (Yet once more, even with temporal additivity and *a fortiori* only with monotonicity.) See Table 2.3. (2b) Conversely, it's possible that the time-slice axioms will constrain d to be ranked better than d^*, while the lifetime axioms impose no such constraint. See Table 2.4.

What we have so far is a pattern of asymmetric constraints as regards the foundational axioms. The lifetime axioms require one world to be better than/equally

Table 2.3 Lifetime Axioms Constrain while Time-Slice Axioms Do Not: Betterness

	World *d*			World *d**		
	Period 1	Period 2	Lifetime	Period 1	Period 2	Lifetime
Sarah	10	20	30	13	13	26
Trevon	10	20	30	13	13	26

Explanation: Lifetime Strong Pareto requires that *d* be ranked better than *d**. The foundational time-slice axioms do not constrain the ranking. Moreover, although Time-slice Pigou-Dalton does not *require* that *d** be ranked better than *d*, *some* of the time-slice rankings that satisfy Time-slice Pigou-Dalton along with Time-slice Pareto Indifference, Strong Pareto, and Anonymity will do so. For example, time-slice prioritarianism with a sufficient degree of priority for the worse off will rank *d** better than *d*—in violation of the foundational lifetime axioms.

Table 2.4 Time-Slice Axioms Constrain while Lifetime Axioms Do Not: Betterness

	World *d*					
	Period 1	Period 2	Lifetime			
Liang	10	13	23			
Rowan	20	20	40			
	World *d**			World *d***		
	Period 1	Period 2	Lifetime	Period 1	Period 2	Lifetime
Liang	10	10	20	10	20	30
Rowan	20	20	40	20	10	30

Explanation: The combination of Time-slice Strong Pareto and Time-slice Anonymity requires that *d* be ranked better than *d***. (Time-slice Strong Pareto requires that *d* be ranked better than *d**; Time-slice Anonymity, that *d** be ranked equally good as *d***. By the transitivity of the ranking, *d* is better than *d***.) The foundational lifetime axioms do not constrain the *d*/*d*** ranking. Moreover, although Lifetime Pigou-Dalton does not *require* that *d*** be ranked better than *d*, *some* of the lifetime rankings that satisfy Lifetime Pigou-Dalton along with Lifetime Pareto Indifference, Strong Pareto, and Anonymity will do so. For example, lifetime prioritarianism with a sufficient degree of priority for the worse off will rank *d*** better than *d*—in violation of the foundational time-slice axioms.

good as a second, while the corresponding time-slice axioms do not—or vice versa. In principle, such asymmetric constraints allow for particular versions of welfarism (utilitarian, prioritarian, etc.) to arrive at identical world-rankings whether specified in a lifetime or time-slice manner.

But this doesn't happen either—at least not for utilitarianism or prioritarianism. Lifetime prioritarianism can diverge from time-slice prioritarianism—even if the well-being account conforms to temporal additivity, and *a fortiori* if it merely conforms to monotonicity. Perhaps surprisingly, lifetime utilitarianism can also diverge from time-slice utilitarianism—again, even with temporal additivity.[6]

2.2 Against Momentary Welfarism

Momentary welfarism faces two serious objections. The first concerns the temporal scope of welfare constituents; the second, the temporal scope of distributional equity.

2.2.1 The Temporal Scope of Welfare Constituents

It's very plausible to adopt what the literature terms "internalism" about time-slice well-being. An individual's well-being at a time-slice in a given world depends only on the features of the world at that time and is independent of its

[6] Let **w** be a vector representing the well-being of each of the N individuals in the population in each of the slices during which the individual is alive. Assuming well-being measurability, any given world corresponds to such a vector. T_i is the duration of individual i's life (which may vary between vectors); $\mathbf{w}_i^t$ is the well-being of individual i during slice t. (In general, it need not be the case that an individual's well-being during a slice when they are not alive is 0—see Section 4.4.1; but for simplicity I am assuming as much here.)

Consider first a set of vectors such that the duration of a given individual's life is the same in all vectors. Assume that the world-ranking is complete. If so, lifetime prioritarianism, time-slice prioritarianism, lifetime utilitarianism, and time-slice utilitarianism are all score-based: they rank a given set of vectors in the order of scores assigned each vector. In the case at hand, assuming temporal additivity, the lifetime-prioritarian score is $\sum_{i=1}^{N} g\left(\sum_{t=1}^{T_i} \mathbf{w}_i^t\right)$. The timeslice-prioritarian score is $\sum_{i=1}^{N}\sum_{t=1}^{T_i} g(\mathbf{w}_i^t)$. Clearly these two rankings need not be the same. By contrast, assuming temporal additivity, the lifetime and time-slice *utilitarian* rankings *are* the same. The lifetime utilitarian score is $\sum_{i=1}^{N}\left(\sum_{t=1}^{T_i} \mathbf{w}_i^t\right)$. This equals the time-slice-utilitarian score, namely, $\sum_{i=1}^{N}\sum_{t=1}^{T_i} \mathbf{w}_i^t$.

But consider a set of vectors in which the duration of individual lives may vary. In that case, there are different versions of time-slice utilitarianism (analogous to the different versions of lifetime utilitarianism in the variable-population case; see Section 8.1). Let $w^{t\text{-}crit}$ be the time-slice critical level. Then critical-level time-slice utilitarianism uses the following score: $\sum_{i=1}^{N}\sum_{t=1}^{T_i} (\mathbf{w}_i^t - w^{t\text{-}crit})$. The ranking of the vectors according to this score *can* deviate from the lifetime ranking, which continues to use the score $\sum_{i=1}^{N}\left(\sum_{t=1}^{T_i} \mathbf{w}_i^t\right)$.

features at other times. John Broome articulates internalism thus: "How well off a person is at a time depends only on how things are for her at that time."[7] Douglas Portmore expresses internalism about momentary well-being, specifically, as follows: "Momentary well-being is the welfare value that some momentary segment of one's life would have if that segment existed alone, apart from any relationship it has with other segments of one's life."[8] Internalism about time-slice well-being is widely (if not universally) endorsed.[9]

Until now, I've been supposing that a given well-being account will assign well-being to time-slices (moments or stages). This premise has been adopted for the sake of defining time-slice welfarism and exploring its divergence from lifetime welfarism. In fact, however, internalism substantially undermines the very ascription of well-being to moments. On a variety of plausible welfare views, comparisons of levels and differences of momentary well-being become indeterminate.[10]

Consider first objective-good views. The goods of achievement/accomplishment, knowledge, and having deep relationships with other people (or with certain other people, as with lists that specify the goods of friendship or parenthood), figure repeatedly in the philosophical literature on well-being. But these goods aren't reducible to occurrences at a moment.

Achievement/accomplishment, for example, involves adopting a goal; then, at later times, working toward the goal; then, at yet later times, realizing the goal. Imagine that, at a particular moment *t* in world *d*, Ahmed is adopting goal *G*; at the same moment in world *d**, Ahmed is working toward a different goal, goal *H*; and there are no other goals that Ahmed is adopting, working toward, or realizing at *t* in either world. How does Ahmed's momentary well-being in the two worlds at time *t* compare with respect to the good of achievement/accomplishment? Is Ahmed at moment *t* better off in *d* than *d** with respect to that good; worse off in *d* than *d** with respect to that good; equally well off with respect to that good; or perhaps incomparably well off with respect to that good?

I suggest that these questions have no determinate answer, *if* internalism about time-slice well-being is true. *If* internalism about time-slice well-being is true, then comparing the two worlds at *t* with respect to Ahmed's achievement/accomplishment reduces to this comparison: (1) Ahmed is adopting goal *G* and not adopting, working toward, or realizing any other goal (the momentary facts in *d*) *as compared* to (2) Ahmed is working toward goal *H* and not adopting, working toward, or realizing any other goal (the momentary facts in *d**). But

[7] Broome (2004, p. 101).
[8] Portmore (2007, p. 21).
[9] See Bramble (2018, pp. 33–37). Dorsey (2013) argues against internalism.
[10] The argument advanced here is similar to that presented in Bramble (2018, pp. 29–40) and Brink (1997).

it is *indeterminate* whether the facts specified in (1) leave him better off, worse off, equally well off, or incomparably well off with respect to achievement/accomplishment than the facts specified in (2). If the facts in (1) and (2) are supplemented in one way (by adding possible facts about what occurs at times *other* than *t* in the two worlds), Ahmed in the first scenario will be better off with respect to achievement/accomplishment than in the second; if those facts are supplemented in a different way (by adding *different* possible facts about what occurs at times other than *t* in the two worlds), Ahmed in the first scenario will be worse off with respect to achievement/accomplishment than in the second.[11]

Consider this analogy. A sentence asserting that some individual has some property will be true or false. "Richard Nixon was elected President in 1968" is true. A sentence fragment will be neither true nor false. The truth of "Richard Nixon . . ." is indeterminate. That sentence fragment doesn't say enough to determine a truth value. Similarly, telling us that in one scenario Ahmed is adopting goal *G* and that in another he is working toward goal *H* doesn't give us enough information to determine how the scenarios compare with respect to the good of accomplishment/achievement.

A parallel analysis can be given for any *temporally extended* objective good: a good whose realization is grounded in facts that occur over a stretch of time longer than a moment.[12] Knowledge and personal relationships, like achievement/accomplishment, are temporally extended goods. Thus, *if* internalism about time-slice well-being is true, comparisons of moments with respect to the realization of the good of knowledge or the good of deep personal relations are also indeterminate.

Consider, now, any objective-good theory of well-being that includes at least one temporally extended good. *If* internalism about time-slice well-being is true, comparisons of momentary well-being, in light of this theory, will be indeterminate—or so my argument suggests.

I've been discussing the indeterminacy that occurs for momentary well-being within the context of an objective-good theory that includes temporally extended goods such as achievement/accomplishment, personal relationships, or knowledge. But indeterminacy arises in a similar way for preference-based theories. Consider, specifically, theories that analyze well-being in terms of global preferences. A global preference is a ranking of possible lives. It takes as

[11] For example, if we add to (1) the fact that Ahmed works toward *G* and realizes *G*, and add to (2) the fact that Ahmed adopts *H* but does not realize *H*, then Ahmed in the first scenario is better off with respect to achievement/accomplishment than in the second. Conversely, if we add to (1) the fact that Ahmed does not work toward *G* and does not realize *G*, and add to (2) the fact that Ahmed adopts *H* and realizes *H*, then Ahmed in the second scenario is better off with respect to achievement/accomplishment than in the first.

[12] Equivalently, specifying only facts about a single moment in any two worlds does not suffice to determine whether the good is more fully realized in one or the other world, ceteris paribus.

its object life-histories (or simplified representations of such histories, which the person holding the preference uses to think about their strength of preference for different lives). A life is a temporally extended object. Annie, let's say, has a global preference. The preference is more fully realized by her history in d^* than in d. But it's indeterminate, for any moment t, whether that momentary slice of her history in d^* more fully satisfies Annie's global preference than the momentary slice of her history in d. Thus, internalism about well-being plus a global-preference account of well-being makes momentary well-being indeterminate.

This analysis clearly generalizes beyond global-preference theories to *any* preference theory of well-being that includes[13] preferences with temporally extended objects (a preference R such that the ranking of worlds with respect to R depends upon what occurs over a stretch of time longer than a moment).

It might be thought that experientialism about well-being, at least, avoids the indeterminacy objection. This *is* true for an experientialist theory that defines well-being wholly in terms of momentary experiential goods: features of someone's mental life that occur at a particular moment. Pains and pleasures are the paradigmatic such goods: one can say, at any moment (or at least for each short stretch of time), whether the person is feeling pain or pleasure. But an experientialist theory might also include temporally extended goods—for example, the sequence of mental states that constitutes the "enjoyment" derived from listening to a song, watching a movie, reading a book, etc. If so, the indeterminacy problem arises here in the same manner as it does for the goods posited by objective-good accounts.

In short: If one adopts internalism about momentary well-being, comparisons of momentary well-being become indeterminate for a wide range of plausible welfare theories: objective-good theories that include temporally extended goods; global-preference theories or other theories that include preferences with temporally extended objects; experientialist theories that include temporally extended experiential goods. But *momentary welfarism* (the ethical view under consideration in this section) can't be coupled with an account of well-being that makes momentary well-being pervasively indeterminate. Momentary welfarism requires the world-ranking to comply with the foundational axioms—Momentary Pareto Indifference, Momentary Anonymity, and Momentary Strong Pareto—and these in turn presuppose *determinate* comparisons of momentary well-being, at least in general. Thus, momentary welfarism requires the rejection of a wide range of plausible welfare accounts. Conversely, anyone espousing one of these accounts should reject momentary welfarism.

[13] By "includes preferences," I mean that the theory recognizes the satisfaction of such preferences as contributing to well-being.

One objection to my analysis here runs as follows: Given internalism about momentary well-being, comparisons of momentary well-being are *not* indeterminate with respect to temporally extended goods or preferences with temporally extended objects. Rather, such goods and preferences are simply *inapplicable* in making comparisons of momentary well-being. Let us say that a "momentary" as opposed to temporally extended good is a good whose realization is grounded in facts that occur within a single moment.[14] One might then argue as follow: Comparisons of momentary well-being with respect to a given welfare theory are undertaken using only the momentary goods, or preferences with momentary objects, included in that theory.[15]

This is certainly a possible way to handle the issue I have been exploring, but it breaks down in the case of welfare theories that include no momentary goods or preferences with momentary objects.[16] As for welfare theories that include both momentary and temporally extended goods, or preferences with both momentary and temporally extended objects, momentary welfarism can now be criticized for having a world-ranking that ignores some sources of well-being. The momentary-welfarist $\succcurlyeq^E$ compares worlds in light of the pattern of momentary well-being—a dependency crystallized in the axioms of Momentary Pareto Indifference, Momentary Anonymity, and Momentary Strong Pareto—but this pattern, now, doesn't reflect temporally extended goods and/or preferences with temporally extended objects.[17]

[14] Equivalently, specifying only facts about a single moment in any two worlds *does* suffice to determine whether the good is more fully realized in one or the other world, ceteris paribus.

[15] This is the approach suggested by Bykvist (2024). Note how this approach yields determinacy, *if* a welfare theory includes at least one momentary good and/or includes preferences with momentary objects. If a good is a momentary good, then facts about a given person *i* in any two worlds at a moment *t* will suffice to determine how the two compare with respect to *i*'s well-being at *t*. The same is true for preferences with momentary objects. Thus, if a theory includes at least one momentary good and/or preferences with momentary objects, comparisons of momentary well-being that are grounded *only* in those components of the theory—and that ignore temporally extended goods and preferences with temporally extended objects—will be determinate.

Note that, if we followed this approach, there would be no basis for supposing that lifetime well-being satisfies a monotonicity constraint with respect to momentary well-being, let alone additivity. See Section 2.1. See Broome (2004, p. 216), noting that goods that do not appear in the sequence of an individual's temporal well-beings are ruled out by the principle of temporal good (monotonicity). Thus, the divergence between momentary and lifetime welfarism described in Section 2.1 given additivity or monotonicity could occur yet more easily.

[16] In that case, we would have to conclude either that momentary well-being comparisons are indeterminate (since there are no well-being goods applicable to such comparisons), or perhaps that everyone at every moment in every world is equally well off, or incomparably well off, as everyone at every moment in every other world (since there are no well-being goods that would ground a betterness or worseness determination).

[17] A third possibility is to suppose that momentary well-being with respect to a temporally extended good or a preference with a temporally extended object summarizes the *contribution* of the momentary facts to lifetime well-being. Call this the "contributory" view of momentary well-being. The idea is that, in a given world *d*, we go from (1) facts that occur at a given moment *t* to (2) a level of momentary well-being at *t* for a given individual *i*, depending only on those facts. This is a

The discussion, up to this point, has assumed internalism about time-slice well-being. Dropping internalism allows for all welfare goods and welfare-relevant preferences to be reflected in momentary well-being. Why? With internalism dropped, we can assign well-being to a moment as a function of facts both at that moment and at other times.

To illustrate, return to the case in which Ahmed at moment *t* in world *d* adopts goal *G*; at the same moment in world *d**, Ahmed is working toward a different goal, goal *H*; and there are no other goals that Ahmed is adopting, working toward, or realizing at *t* in either world. Facts about world *d* at times other than *t*, together with the time-*t* facts, will enable us to determine whether a temporally extended process that instantiates the good of achievement/accomplishment has occurred with respect to goal *G*—and similarly for world *d** and goal *H*. These non-momentary features of the two worlds can then show up in a comparison of Ahmed's *momentary* well-being at *t*, since internalism has been dropped. For example, if Ahmed in *d* at times after *t* works toward *G* and then realizes *G*, but at no times in *d** after *t* realizes *H*, and the two worlds are otherwise identical with respect to his achievement/accomplishment, we can say: Ahmed *at moment t* is at a higher level of momentary well-being in *d* than *d** with respect to the good of achievement/accomplishment.

However, dropping internalism about time-slice well-being is very counterintuitive. As David Velleman observes:

> We think of a person's current well-being as a fact intrinsic to the present, not as a relation that he currently bears to his future. We don't say, of a person who dies in harness, that he fares progressively worse toward the end, simply because he

"contributory" level of momentary well-being, in the sense that (3) *i*'s lifetime well-being in *d* in turn supervenes on the pattern of momentary well-being over time in *d*.

Such an approach runs into difficulties once we allow for interactions between facts at different moments in producing lifetime well-being. To illustrate, assume that the good of accomplishment/achievement consists in adopting, realizing, and working toward either goal *G* or goal *H*. The set of possible momentary facts at a given moment is {Adopting*G*, Working*G*, Realizing*G*, Adopting*H*, Working*H*, Realizing*H*, None}. Assume that the contributory view holds and (for simplicity) that levels with respect to contributory momentary well-being are captured in a measure $w^t(\cdot)$; $w^t(\cdot)$ assigns a number to each of the possible momentary facts, such that the value for lifetime well-being of a sequence of those facts is captured in the sequence of $w^t(\cdot)$ values.

But assume that the momentary facts interact over time in the following way. (I) The three-moment sequences (Adopting*G*, Working*G*, Realizing*G*) and (Adopting*H*, Working*H*, Realizing*H*) are equally good for lifetime well-being, and better than (None, None, None). (II) All other sequences are equally good for lifetime well-being as (None, None, None). (That is, what contributes to lifetime well-being is to adopt, then work toward, then realize one of the goals; absent such a sequence, there is no increment to lifetime well-being.) If we assume the monotonicity of lifetime well-being in $w^t(\cdot)$ values, there is no way to assign $w^t(\cdot)$ values to the momentary facts so as to satisfy I and II. Conversely, adopting the contributory view but dropping monotonicity is unattractive; absent monotonicity, the axiom of Momentary Strong Pareto seems hard to defend (on the contributory view). See generally Velleman (1991), denying that lifetime well-being is reducible to the pattern of momentary well-being; and Broome (2004, p. 46), agreeing on this point.

was acquiring more and more ambitions that would go unfulfilled. Nor do we say, of a person raised in adversity, that his youth wasn't so bad, after all, simply because his youthful hopes were eventually fulfilled later in life. We might say that such a person's adulthood compensated for an unfortunate youth; but we wouldn't say that it made his youth any better.[18]

Similarly, Ben Bradley writes:

> Suppose Kate is a pianist, and will be giving a big performance at the end of September. She practices hard, making many sacrifices, during September; as a result, she gives a spectacular performance, and this is a very good thing for her . . . . During the concert we might well say that *all her hard work is paying off now*; we might say that it is good that she worked so hard before, or more stiltedly, that her previous hard work had *instrumental* value as a result of what is now happening. It is much stranger that to say that her current performance is *paying off her past self*, in the sense that it is retroactively making her better off in the past. If Kate's performance made it the case that she was well-off while she was practicing over the previous month, it would be hard to see her practicing as involving a sacrifice of current well-being for future well-being, since her "sacrifice" would have been beneficial to her at the very time she was practicing.[19]

Moreover, dropping internalism about time-slice well-being makes it hard for the proponent of momentary welfarism to draw a line between that approach and lifetime welfarism. Assume that the comparison of Jane's well-being at a given moment t in two worlds can reflect facts in those worlds other than the facts at t. Then why would certain non-t moments have a privileged role in determining this comparison, as opposed to other non-t moments? And, absent such privileging (which seems hard to justify), it would seem that the comparison of Jane's momentary well-being at t in the two worlds reduces to a comparison of her lifetime well-being in the two worlds.

2.2.2 The Temporal Scope of Fair Distribution

The second objection to momentary welfarism arises within the context of prioritarianism. It transposes to other non-utilitarian world-rankings—but because I favor prioritarianism I'll frame the objection in those terms.

[18] Velleman (1991, pp. 56–57).
[19] Bradley (2009, pp. 20–21).

A recurrent idea in the philosophical literature on distributive justice is that of the "separateness of persons."[20] The "separateness of persons" is a high-level criterion—a criterion for evaluating ethical theories themselves—and as such is not as precise as some other components of ethics (for example, an axiom regarding the outcome ranking, e.g., Strong Pareto). Still, imprecise ideas can be persuasive and if so can be important in guiding our deliberation about ethical theories. The separateness-of-persons idea (I take it) is that there is a difference between the distribution of costs and benefits within a single life, which isn't a matter of distributive justice, and the distribution of costs and benefits among different persons, which is. Each person has their own life to lead. An ethical theory should recognize the distinction between intra- and interpersonal distribution and should decline to impose a cost on one person for the sake of benefiting a second if doing so is unfair—if it contravenes the separateness of persons by unfairly sacrificing one person's welfare for the sake of a second's.

Rawls famously criticized utilitarianism for violating the separateness of persons.[21] How it does so can be seen as follows. For utilitarians, a gain to one person ethically outweighs a loss to another as long as the gain is larger than the loss. This is true despite the fact that the improvement in well-being from the gain benefits a *different person* than the one who is made worse off by the loss (these are not losses and gains within a single life), and regardless of the comparative well-being levels of the one-who-gains and the one-who-loses.

Prioritarianism is primed to respect the separateness of persons.[22] For prioritarians, it is *not* true that a gain to one person ethically outweighs a loss to another as long as the gain is larger than the loss. Still, *momentary* prioritarianism ends up violating the separateness of persons—or so it can be argued. Why?

To see the issue, imagine three worlds d, d^*, and d^+, related as follows. In world d at time t, Keith is at level w_1 of momentary well-being; Jarrell at t is at level w_2; and Keith at a different time s is also at level w_2.

In world d^*, Keith's momentary well-being at time t has been reduced by amount Δw, and Jarrell's momentary well-being at time t has increased by amount $\Delta w'$. Keith's and Jarrell's momentary well-being at other times

[20] See, e.g., Nagel (1979b,1991), Rawls (1999), and Scanlon (1998), discussed in Adler (2012, pp. 314–17).

[21] Rawls (1999).

[22] Michael Otsuka and Alex Voorhoeve have famously argued that prioritarianism fails to respect the separateness of persons under uncertainty. Otsuka and Voorhoeve (2009). The problem here, as I see it, is that *any* non-utilitarian world-ranking, if applied under uncertainty so as to respect dominance axioms that are required by consequentialism, will violate the ex ante Pareto axioms. See Adler (2012, ch. 7); Adler (2019b, chs. 3–4); Adler and Holtug (2019). If one takes the ex ante Pareto axioms to be an aspect of the separateness of persons, then one might say that even lifetime prioritarianism fails to fully respect the separateness of persons. That said, lifetime prioritarianism *does* respect the separateness of persons at the level of the world-ranking, as contrasted with momentary prioritarianism—or so this section argues.

is the same as in d, and everyone else's momentary well-being at all times is the same.

In world d^+, the same well-being transfer has occurred—but now between different times in Keith's life. In d^+, his momentary well-being at time t has been reduced relative to d by amount Δw. His momentary well-being at time s has been increased by amount $\Delta w'$. His momentary well-being at all other times is the same as in d, and everyone else's momentary well-being is the same at all times.

Momentary prioritarianism necessarily ranks d^* and d^+ as equally good.[23] It is structured so as to treat a given interpersonal transfer of momentary well-being (at time t, Keith goes from w_1 to $w_1 - \Delta w$ and Jarrell goes from w_2 to $w_2 + \Delta w'$) identically to an intrapersonal transfer involving the same momentary levels and differences (at time t, Keith goes from w_1 to $w_1 - \Delta w$; at time s, Keith goes from w_2 to $w_2 + \Delta w'$). Momentary prioritarianism thereby fails to differentiate between within-person and across-person redistributions of well-being. By contrast, lifetime prioritarianism will evaluate d^* and d^+ quite differently; the lifetime prioritarian is certainly *not* committed to counting them as equally good. The intrapersonal transfer will be seen as ethically beneficial iff it increases Keith's lifetime well-being; the interpersonal transfer will be evaluated by comparing the reduction in Keith's transformed lifetime well-being to the increase in Jarrell's.

The same example can be used to articulate a second separateness-of-persons critique of momentary prioritarianism. The objection, here, is that momentary prioritarianism evaluates an interpersonal shift of momentary well-being by ignoring unaffected moments. It therefore ignores information that is critical to assessing the fairness of this transfer.

[23] In the example at hand, each person's history has the same duration in d, d^*, and d^+. This is true both for Keith and Jarrell, and for other individuals (who are unaffected as between the three worlds). An antecedent condition for Momentary Pareto Indifference, Momentary Anonymity, and Momentary Strong Pareto (see Section 2.1) is that the worlds under comparison are such that each person's history has the same duration in the worlds. These foundational axioms therefore apply to the comparison of the three worlds here. In particular, Momentary Anonymity requires that d^* and d^+ be ranked equally good: in d^*, Jarrell has $w_2 + \Delta w'$ at time t and Keith has w_2 at time s; in d^+, Jarrell has w_2 at time t and Keith has $w_2 + \Delta w'$ at time s; momentary well-being at every moment is otherwise the same as between the two worlds.

The example at hand assumes that momentary well-being is measurable. If so and if the world-ranking is complete, momentary prioritarianism—in comparing worlds without history-duration changes—ranks them according to the formula $\sum_{i=1}^{N} \sum_{t=1}^{T_i} g(\mathbf{w}_i^t)$, with T_i the number of moments in individual i's life. See note 6. This formula respects Momentary Anonymity and will count d^* and d^+ as equally good. Moreover, *however* momentary prioritarianism is specified for the case in which the world-ranking is not complete or well-being is not measurable, it will respect Momentary Anonymity (we're working here within momentary welfarism, and momentary prioritarianism understood as some variant thereof must respect Momentary Anonymity).

Consider again the *d*/*d** comparison. For momentary prioritarianism, this comparison depends solely on Keith's and Jarrell's well-being at *t*. It is fully determined by the initial momentary well-being levels (w_1 for Keith, w_2 for Jarrell), the changes in momentary well-being (Δw and $\Delta w'$), and whatever transformation function is being applied to momentary well-being.[24] In other words, the momentary-prioritarian *d*/*d** comparison is independent of the features of the two individuals at earlier and later times. But surely these non-momentary features *should* matter, because they bear upon the fairness of a well-being transfer between them. For example, imagine that in *d* Keith has a much higher level of lifetime well-being than Jarrell (in virtue of what occurs at moments before and after *t*), and generally a much higher level of momentary well-being. Then this counts strongly in favor of the transfer being fair. Conversely, were it to be the case that Keith in *d* has a much lower level of lifetime well-being than Jarrell, and generally a much lower level of momentary well-being, then this would count strongly against the fairness of the transfer.

By contrast, lifetime prioritarianism evaluates the Keith-to-Jarrell transfer by taking account of the two individuals' features at all times, not merely the time of the transfer.

2.2.3 OHPs and Lifetime Welfarism

Momentary welfarism may be plausible for certain welfare subjects. Imagine beings that possess phenomenal consciousness and the capacity to feel pains and pleasures but lack many of the other psychological characteristics of OHPs (for short, "merely sentient" beings).[25] Momentary utilitarianism seems a reasonable framework for ranking worlds with respect to the well-being (pains and pleasures) of a population of such beings. If so, why not for OHPs?

[24] If momentary well-being is measurable and the world-ranking is complete, momentary prioritarianism will compare *d* and *d** using the formula $\sum_{i=1}^{N}\sum_{t=1}^{T_i} g(\mathbf{w}_i^t)$. See note 6. This formula satisfies an axiom of moment separability analogous to the Separability axiom of lifetime welfarism (see Section 1.3.2): the ranking of worlds is invariant to the level of momentary well-being at slices that have the same momentary well-being in the two worlds. In the *d*/*d** comparison, the only time-slices with a momentary well-being that varies between the two worlds are Keith's time-slice at *t* and Jarrell's at *t*. To see this invariance more concretely, note that the difference between the momentary-prioritarian score for *d** and for *d* equals $(g(w_1 - \Delta w) + g(w_2 + \Delta w')) - (g(w_1) + g(w_2))$; this difference depends just on w_1, w_2, Δw, and $\Delta w'$.

However momentary prioritarianism is specified for the case of an incomplete world-ranking, it should presumably satisfy moment separability.

[25] The term "merely sentient" is taken from Varner (2012, pp. 21–22).

The two arguments against momentary welfarism set forth above—the arguments regarding the temporal scope of welfare constituents and the temporal scope of fair distribution—are arguments against momentary welfarism *for OHPs* (for the Focal Case, with an ethical population of OHPs). These arguments can be seen to be grounded in certain of the psychological attributes that *differentiate* OHPs from merely sentient beings.

One such attribute, surely, is autonoetic consciousness.[26] Recall that self-consciousness means having an "I" concept. Autonoetic consciousness means having a robust, conscious sense of one's own past and future. Autonoetic consciousness implies self-consciousness, but not vice versa.

The argument from the temporal scope of welfare constituents observed that various putative objective goods are temporally extended (occur over time)—such as the goods of achievement/accomplishment, knowledge, and personal relationships. Autonoetic consciousness is interwoven with this part of the argument, because temporally extended goods are plausible only for beings with an intertemporal "I" concept. A being without a sense of itself as existing over time cannot accomplish a goal, pursue knowledge, or develop personal relationships.

A different part of this argument pointed out that the satisfaction of a global preference—a preference regarding an entire life—is also a temporally extended matter. The object of a global preference is an entire life history. Note, now, that a being without autonoetic consciousness can't possess a global preference. Preference-based accounts anchored on such preferences are suitable only for beings with an intertemporal "I."[27]

Other characteristics that differentiate OHPs from merely sentient beings also buttress the welfare-constituents argument against momentary welfarism. First, the various temporally extended goods presuppose beings who possess some of these characteristics. Beings without beliefs, desires, and intentions couldn't pursue goals or knowledge. It's not plausible that beings without emotions would benefit (or benefit much) from deep personal relationships. Second, preference-based accounts of well-being often require, plausibly, that the preferences satisfy various idealization criteria: What matters is not what the subject prefers, but what they would prefer if sufficiently informed, rational, and deliberative. Preference theories with an idealization component are most plausible for *autonomous* subjects—subjects who can reflect upon, and revise, their own preferences.

[26] Varner (2012, p. 160) cites a number of philosophers who place moral significance on autonoetic consciousness.

[27] Whether preference accounts that include *any* preferences with temporally extended objects (not merely global preferences) presuppose beings with autonoetic consciousness is less clear.

Turn now to the *second* argument against momentary welfarism for OHPs: the argument from the temporal scope of fair distribution, grounded in the "separateness of persons." The very term, "separateness of persons," suggests that this criterion is thought applicable to the ethics of interpersonal distribution only because the beings involved are persons. Imagine beings that persist over time but are merely sentient. We could determine the lifetime well-being of such beings (as the sum of momentary well-being arising from pains and pleasures). Lifetime prioritarianism applied to a population of such creatures would respect their separateness; it would distinguish between an inter-being transfer of momentary well-being, and an intra-being transfer of the same amount from one moment in a being's life to another. But is there a persuasive case that the ethics of merely sentient beings should make this distinction?

Cows (as far as we can tell) are sentient but lack autonoetic consciousness and language capacity.[28] Imagine that cow food is scarce. In case one, Farmer Lee lacks enough food to feed his cow, Harry, both this week and next. If Harry is not fed for a week, he will not die, but will feel serious discomfort from hunger. Lee has to choose between feeding Harry now and feeding Harry later. In case two, Lee has two cows, Harry and Iris, and has enough now only to feed one now. (Both cows will be fed next week.) Imagine, further, that in this second case Harry has always been adequately fed in the past, while Iris has not been—thus Harry's sum total of momentary well-being to date is greater than Iris'.

The first case involves the distribution of discomfort within the life of a single cow, Harry. The second case involves the distribution of discomfort between two cows, Harry and Iris. Should Farmer Lee think differently about the two cases? Should Lee judge that, in the first case, it is matter of indifference whether Harry feels hungry now or later; while, in the second, it would be unfair to Iris to make her hungry now so that Harry can be fed, because Iris has suffered more in the past? Intuitively, Farmer Lee should *not* treat the cases differently. In the second case, either Iris feels discomfort now, or Harry does—that is the choice facing Lee. The fact that Harry has fared better in the past than Iris wouldn't compensate Harry for any present discomfort because Harry can't possibly recognize such compensation. Harry (lacking autonoetic consciousness) cannot see his prior pains and pleasures as "my" experiences; Harry (lacking language) cannot reason that these experiences compensate him for present discomfort.

[28] The evidence suggests that cows *do* have a significant range of psychological capacities. Marino and Allen (2017). The discussion that follows hinges specifically on their lack of autonoetic consciousness and language.

2.3 Against Stage Welfarism

A "stage" is some stretch of time considerably longer than a moment—a year, a decade, etc. Stage welfarism is time-slice welfarism with the slices defined as stages. Stage welfarism might be thought to be an attractive alternative to momentary welfarism because it avoids the two objections to the momentary view: the temporal scope of welfare constituents and the temporal scope of fair distribution. In fact, however, stage welfarism may also be vulnerable to those objections and in any event engenders new ones.

One new objection is that the specification of stages risks being arbitrary. Our attention is trained on the Focal Case, where all the humans in the world being ranked are OHPs. Consider, by contrast, the human Laurent, who develops normally and acquires all of the psychological properties of persons; on his 35th birthday, Laurent is in a car crash that causes profound amnesia and a profound change in the kind of person that Laurent is (desires, dispositions, etc.); at age 80, he dies. Here, it's straightforward to identify birth to age 35 as the first stage of Laurent's life, and age 35 to 80 as the second. OHPs, however, do not undergo this sort of break in psychological continuity and thus we can't appeal to such a break to specify the stages of an OHP's life.

Perhaps the arbitrariness objection can be addressed, even for OHPs. Here is one proposal: A stage is the longest consecutive stretch of time such that all moments in that stretch are strongly psychologically connected to each other. Imagine that Felicia's memories, preferences, beliefs, etc. are such that every moment in her life from age 21 to age 25 has a strong direct connection (in Parfit's sense)[29] to every other moment in this stretch of time. The normal psychological changes over time in early adulthood mean that her moments in the year after she turns 26 remain psychologically connected to the moments in the years from age 22 to 25 but not to the moments in the year she is age 21. Thus, the stretch of time from age 21 to 25 would be a stage, but not the stretch of time from age 21 to 26.

Let's call this the direct-connection strategy for specifying stages. It will suffice to illustrate that even if stage welfarism can circumvent the arbitrariness challenge, further problems arise.

First, there is the problem of overlapping stages.[30] Imagine that, as it happens, the changes in Felicia's psychology over her adult life are sufficiently smooth that every five-year stretch is a direct-connection stage. So there is a stage from age 21 to 25, 26 to 30, 31 to 35, etc. However, there is also a stage from age 22 to 26, 27

[29] See Section 1.1.3.

[30] See also Brink (1997), discussing the difficulties that arise in seeing overlapping person-stages (he terms them "person-segments") as agents.

to 31, 32 to 36, etc. And from age 23 to 27, 28 to 32, 33 to 37, etc. Why is the first division of Felicia's life into stages more appropriate than the second or the third?

Second, the objections to momentary welfarism will also apply to stage welfarism, to some extent. These objections may be significant if stages are short. Direct-connection stages, for example, would normally not be very long for OHPs—normally a matter of years, not decades. Let's continue, for the sake of illustration, with five-year stages. The temporal-scope-of-welfare-constituents objection still does apply, albeit with attenuated force. The comparison of some five-year stages with respect to temporally extended objective goods will be indeterminate. The comparison of five-year stages with respect to global preferences (preferences over whole lifetimes), or preferences with temporally extended objects longer than five years, will be indeterminate.[31]

The temporal-scope-of-fair-distribution objection applies with nearly full force to five-year stages. Stage prioritarianism treats transfers between two five-year stages of the same person the same way as transfers from one person to a second. But whether to reduce Keith's current-stage well-being for the sake of increasing his well-being at a future stage is not a question of distributive justice; whether to reduce Keith's current-stage well-being for the sake of increasing Jarrell's *is*. It is problematic for an ethical theory to be structured so that its answers to the two questions are necessarily the same. Further, in assessing an interpersonal transfer, stage prioritarianism ignores everything about the persons except the affected stages. But whether to reduce Keith's welfare during a five-year snapshot of his life, for the sake of Jarrell's benefit during a five-year snapshot of *his* life, should surely not be invariant to how Keith and Jarrell have fared and will fare at all other times.

2.4 Criticisms of Lifetime Welfarism

Philosophers of distributive justice often take the position that its temporal scope is to whole lifetimes—that distributive justice concerns the fair distribution of lifetime well-being, or the fair distribution of the resources that individuals have over their entire lives.[32] But this position has also been criticized. Because I take prioritarianism to be the most attractive version of non-utilitarian welfarism, I'll articulate and respond to the critiques as they apply to the choice between lifetime and time-slice prioritarianism.

[31] The indeterminacy problem assumes internalism about time-slice well-being. "Solving" the problem by dropping internalism will not be an attractive strategy for the stage welfarist, just as it isn't for the momentary welfarist. See Section 2.2.1.

[32] See Bou-Habib (2011, p. 286, n. 2), citing examples; Bidadanure (2021, p. 23), noting that a complete-lives view is "the default approach endorsed by most theorists of justice."

The two most important critiques of lifetime prioritarianism are, I believe, that (1) the attenuation of psychological connections between time-slices of an individual's life undermines lifetime prioritarianism, and that (2) there is significant intuitive support for time-slice prioritarianism. I suggest that both critiques can be answered, to some extent, via the structure of lifetime well-being, and in any event are not sufficiently powerful to make an on-balance case for time-slice prioritarianism—given the serious flaws of time-slice welfarism described above.

2.4.1 Attenuation of Psychological Connections over a Lifetime

Assume that Higher and Lower are, respectively, at higher and lower levels of lifetime well-being. Lifetime prioritarianism may endorse a reduction in Higher's lifetime well-being for the sake of an increase in Lower's lifetime well-being. At the very least, lifetime prioritarianism *will* endorse this Higher-to-Lower transfer of lifetime well-being if doing so is required by the Pigou-Dalton axiom, applied to lifetime well-being (Lower gains what Higher loses, the gap between them shrinks, and no one else is affected). And, depending on the concavity of the prioritarian transformation function, lifetime prioritarianism may endorse this transfer even if what Lower gains is *less* than what Higher loses.

Note that the loss for Higher and benefit for Lower *may* occur at a time when Higher is actually worse off (in terms of time-slice well-being) than Lower. The lifetime prioritarian will justify the transfer in this case by pointing to the facts about Higher *at other times* that put him at a higher level of lifetime well-being, all-times-considered. But—and here's the objection—Higher at the time of the transfer may have weak psychological connection to those other times. Although Higher is, metaphysically, the very same being as Higher at those other times, he is (in a manner of speaking) a "different person" because of the psychological slack. And so Higher's well-being at other times doesn't genuinely compensate him at transfer time.

For short, call this the attenuation objection. The objection is suggested by Derek Parfit's well-known discussion of the temporal scope of distributive principles in *Reasons and Persons.* Parfit considers the case in which a burden is imposed on a child for the sake of a benefit that the child will receive as an adult, and writes:

> If we are Reductionists [namely, reducing an individual's identity over time to psychological and/or physical connections], we may compare the weakening of the connections between the child and his adult self to the absence of connections between different people. We shall give more weight to the fact that, in this example, this child does not care what will happen to his adult self.

That it will be *he* who receives the benefit may thus seem to us less important. We might say, "It will not be *he* who benefits. It will only be his adult self.[33]

Lifetime prioritarianism has several responses to the attenuation objection. The first is to carefully unpack the wedge between *objective compensation* and *perceived compensation* upon which the objection rests. To add detail to the Higher/Lower case, assume that the transfer of lifetime well-being from Higher to Lower operates by decreasing Higher's current time-slice well-being and increasing Lower's; that Higher is, in fact, at a lower level of current time-slice well-being than Lower; but that Higher is at a higher level of lifetime well-being in virtue of past good times (a happy childhood, wonderful college years, . . .) to which Higher, now, has only weak psychological connections. Higher is *objectively compensated* by the prior good times; those are events within the life of a single persisting being, the human animal Higher, that contribute to a higher level of lifetime welfare for him. The worry behind the attenuation objection is that Higher will not *perceive* these events as compensation, in virtue of the weak psychological links, and thus the events will not be *genuinely* compensatory.

Let's concede that there is some nexus between perceived and genuine compensation. Even so, it seems implausibly strong to argue that a given person is never compensated by some feature of their life unless they perceive the feature as compensatory. A weaker, more plausible, claim is that a feature which *can't be perceived* as compensatory isn't genuinely compensatory. But if this is the nexus between perceived and genuine compensation, the weakness of Higher's psychological links to the good times in his past doesn't undercut genuine compensation. Higher is *capable* of seeing those times as compensatory. He *might* reason: "I am the same being, the same human animal, from birth to death, and those prior times are times in *my* life, even though I feel and think very differently now than I did then."

A second response to the attenuation objection is that the weakening of psychological connections over time might itself reduce lifetime well-being. An account of lifetime well-being could, in principle, give a premium to a psychologically unified life and discount to a disunified one. The more seriously we're bothered by the attenuation objection, the more we'll be motivated to adopt such an account.

An interesting question is whether time-relative consequentialism offers useful strategies for handling the attenuation objection that are not available to non-relativized consequentialists. Perhaps so. Consider a version of time-relative lifetime prioritarianism which says that (a) an individual's lifetime well-being relative to a given time t takes account of their characteristics at all

[33] Parfit (1987, p. 333).

times, as adjusted for the strength of psychological connections between those times and time *t*; (b) the prioritarian ranking of worlds relative to a given time *t* is the sum of *t*-relative lifetime well-being, inputted into a concave transformation function; and (c) decisionmakers should choose policies at any time in light of the prioritarian world-ranking relative to that time. Such an approach would endorse a policy at time *t* that imposes a contemporaneous (at *t*) loss on one person for the sake of another's contemporaneous equal gain only if the first person is better off over their lifetime than the second—discounting for the two individuals' degrees of psychological connection between other times in their lives and time *t*.

However, time-relative lifetime prioritarianism and other versions of relativized consequentialism are off the table; this book works within the confines of non-relativized consequentialism. Lifetime prioritarianism and time-slice prioritarianism (both momentary prioritarianism and stage prioritarianism) are variants of the non-relativized approach. There is a single world-ranking rather than a series of time-relative rankings—a single ranking that could be driven by the pattern of individuals' lifetime well-being or instead by the pattern of their time-slice well-being. The question under consideration in this section is whether the attenuation objection, on balance, justifies endorsing (non-relative) time-slice prioritarianism as opposed to (non-relative) lifetime prioritarianism. I believe that the answer is "no." In considering *that* question, it's important to see that (non-relative) lifetime prioritarianism *does* have some resources to defang the attenuation objection—namely, by adjusting each individual's lifetime well-being in a given world for the degree of psychological unity between all the different times at which the individual is alive.

2.4.2 Intuitive Support for Time-Slice Prioritarianism

In a series of articles on the temporal scope of justice, Dennis McKerlie describes cases in which there is intuitive support for giving extra weight to changes in time-slice well-being that occur at a low level of time-slice well-being.[34] The proponent of time-slice prioritarianism might point to these sorts of cases as strengthening the argument for that view.

McKerlie describes cases of intrapersonal priority to worse-off times. "We should . . . be able to say, thinking about a single person, that a benefit will be more important if it is experienced when that person is badly off. A person might think that it is more important to relieve pain when he is suffering intensely than to bring about a larger reduction in milder suffering at some other point in his

[34] McKerlie (2001a; 2001b; 2007; 2013, ch. 5).

Table 2.5 Lifetime Prioritarianism, Time-Slice Priority, and the Marginal Impact of the Sources of Lifetime Well-Being

	World *d*				World *d**		
	Period 1	Period 2	Lifetime		Period 1	Period 2	Lifetime
Kim				*Kim*			
attribute *a*	9	9		attribute *a*	9	**19**	
attribute *b*	144	144		attribute *b*	144	144	
well-being	15	15	30	well-being	15	**16.36**	**31.36**
Leia				*Leia*			
attribute *a*	25	25		attribute *a*	25	25	
attribute *b*	100	100		attribute *b*	100	100	
well-being	15	15	30	well-being	15	15	30

	World d^+		
	Period 1	Period 2	Lifetime
Kim			
attribute *a*	9	9	
attribute *b*	144	144	
well-being	15	15	30
Leia			
attribute *a*	25	**40**	
attribute *b*	100	100	
well-being	15	**16.32**	**31.32**

Explanation: This table illustrates how lifetime prioritarianism might accord a kind of priority to those who are worse off in some period with respect to one of the components of well-being. In particular, if the component has a diminishing marginal impact on time-slice well-being (and hence lifetime well-being, if lifetime well-being is additive in time-slice well-being), the lifetime prioritarian might prefer to give a *smaller* increase in the component to someone with less, as opposed to a *larger* increase to someone with more.

In this table, time-slice well-being is the sum of the square root of two different attributes, and lifetime well-being is the sum of time-slice well-being. In world *d*, Kim is at a lower level of attribute *a* than Leia in both periods. In world *d**, Kim's level of attribute *a* in period 2 increases by 10 units (from 9 to 19). The resultant increase in her lifetime well-being is from 30 to 31.36.

In world d^+, Leia's level of attribute *a* in period 2 increases by 15 rather than 10 units (from 25 to 40). But this yields a smaller increase in her lifetime well-being (from 30 to 31.32). Lifetime prioritarianism ranks *d** over d^+ (note that the combination of Lifetime Anonymity and Lifetime Strong Pareto requires this preference).

life."[35] He also describes interpersonal cases. He considers an example in which immigrants own stores in impoverished neighborhoods, populated by native-born residents who are now poorer than the immigrants.

> [The immigrants may have] suffered greatly in their countries of origin, experiencing the deep poverty of less-developed countries. Now they are modestly well off, and they can expect even better lives for their children. If we think about lifetimes, the complete life of [such an immigrant] might well be worse than the complete life of [the neighborhood resident]. Nevertheless, the special concern with poverty applies to the [neighborhood resident] who *is* living in poverty, not to the [immigrant] who is not. It supplies one reason to support a policy that would help [the former] even if it might be possible to help [the latter] more.[36]

As I have discussed at length elsewhere, these kinds of cases can—at least to some extent—be handled by lifetime prioritarianism, if coupled with a lifetime well-being account that accords non-constant marginal well-being impact to various sources of lifetime well-being.[37] See Table 2.5. For example, the effect of pain on lifetime well-being need not be linear. If pain is measured on some scale other than the scale of well-being itself (for example, some scale of psychological intensity), it is fully possible to make the function from pain to lifetime well-being a concave one—so that a unit reduction of pain produces a larger well-being increase if the reduction benefits someone at a higher level of pain. It is conventionally supposed that material resources exhibit diminishing marginal well-being impact. Thus, in McKerlie's second example here, the lifetime prioritarian could well favor a policy that delivers fewer resources to the neighborhood residents, as opposed to a policy that delivers more to the immigrants.

2.5 The Early Years of an OHP: Are They Part of Their Lifetime Well-Being?

Mei, as an infant, broke her legs and was in bad pain for months. Mei's pediatrician prescribed only low doses of pain relievers, worrying that the drugs could harm the baby. Mei's legs did heal, and she grew to adulthood. The pain *was* bad, but it didn't cause lasting trauma or inhibit her psychological development. Mei, now an adult, doesn't remember the pain. She will live to 75.

[35] McKerlie (2001a, p. 284).
[36] McKerlie (2001b, pp. 164–65).
[37] See Adler (2012, pp. 454–75).

Is Mei's lifetime well-being lower in the actual world, as compared to a counterfactual world in which she didn't break her leg and experience protracted pain as an infant, but had the same life afterward? There are plausible arguments both for and against the position that events during infancy contribute to lifetime well-being. On the one hand, even infants do have some day-to-day psychological connectedness. Moreover, although Mei as an infant lacked autonoetic consciousness, Mei later on—once she comes to possess that capacity—can reflect on the pain episode and think about it as something that happened "to me." Further, although Mei as an infant lacked the capacity to form global preferences, preferences over how her life should go, Mei later on—once she comes to possess that capacity—can reflect on the episode and prefer that her life not have included it.[38]

On the other hand, Mei's day-to-day psychological connectedness was much weaker as an infant than now, in her adulthood. (There are certain types of psychological states that an infant can't yet instantiate, and thus these types of states can't be a component of day-to-day connectedness.) Moreover, on an objective-good view of well-being, Mei's capacity as an infant to contribute to her lifetime well-being was limited. To the extent that goods are achieved via active pursuit, infant Mei was unable to contribute to the realization of the goods.

When precisely human life begins is a controversial question, of course, but it's uncontroversial that this occurs at some time during or at the end points of the interval that starts with conception and ends with live birth. In short, a human animal and, specifically, an OHP comes into existence at some point between conception and birth. An OHP's "age" at a given point in its development is the length of time that's elapsed since coming into existence.

I'll use the term "age of integration" to denote the age of an OHP such that, prior to this age, events in an OHP's life do not contribute (negatively or positively) to their lifetime well-being. These early-in-life events are not *integrated* into the overall goodness of their life.

For the reasons sketched four paragraphs above, it's reasonable to suppose that the age of integration for an OHP is zero: everything that occurs once they come into being figures into their lifetime well-being. But, as suggested three paragraphs above, it's also reasonable to posit a non-zero age of integration. The weight of the reasons to do so will depend upon the theory of well-being (hedonists will feel less motivated to adopt a non-zero age of integration than objective-good theorists); the specific stage of psychological development identified as this threshold, if adopted, will also depend on the theory.

[38] On the psychological capacities of infants, see generally Bremner and Wachs (2010).

It might be argued that the age of integration *must* be zero, by the very meaning of the term "lifetime well-being." A well-being ranking of the histories of a population of OHPs that ignores what occurs before the age of integration is not a *lifetime*-well-being ranking—since well-being sources during a portion of their human lifetimes (up to the age of integration) are being screened off. Post-integration well-being is not "*lifetime* well-being" but rather "*long-term* well-being." This is true, but to simplify the terminology I will refer to long-term well-being that takes account of everything within an OHP's life *except* pre-integration events as a version of "lifetime well-being."

Adopting a non-zero age of integration requires a modification to lifetime welfarism, even for the Focal Case. In the Focal Case, by definition, in all the worlds being ranked, each individual in the population lives long enough to develop all of the psychological attributes sufficient for personhood and characteristic of adult humans; retains those until death; and is psychologically continuous over their lifetime. Still, even in this case, a non-zero age of integration requires modifying the fundamental axioms of lifetime welfarism. Consider Lifetime Pareto Indifference. In world d, Mei before the age of integration breaks her legs and suffers protracted pain. In world d^*, this doesn't occur to Mei. Mei's lifetime well-being (taking account of everything after the age of integration) is the same in both worlds, as is everyone else's. Lifetime Pareto Indifference thus kicks in, requiring that d and d^* be ranked equally good. But surely the welfarist should deny that the two worlds are equally good. Mei as an infant was a sentient human being, capable of suffering welfare setbacks, and indeed did experience such a setback in world d by virtue of the pain. Thus d is worse than d^* by welfarist lights.

The solution, for lifetime welfarists positing a non-zero age of integration, is to modify the fundamental axioms so that they hold *conditional* on all human beings experiencing no well-being difference prior to the age of integration.

My analysis of the Focal Case in subsequent chapters will assume a zero age of integration. This simplifies the presentation; adding a proviso about pre-integration well-being would make the text wordier. Moreover, with respect to the issues discussed in these chapters, the choice between a zero and non-zero integration age makes no substantive difference. For example (Chapter 3), death has ethical significance in the case of OHPs by changing lifetime well-being. If the age of integration is zero: all welfare changes in the life of an OHP *are* changes in their lifetime well-being. If the age of integration is non-zero: an OHP's death occurs *after* that age and so changes their lifetime well-being, not their pre-integration welfare.

Similarly, the methodology for measuring lifetime well-being set forth in Chapter 4 is the same in both cases. An individual's life is divided into periods, during which they have attributes. A lifetime well-being measure $w(\cdot)$ assigns them a lifetime well-being, depending on their attributes in each period. If the age of integration is zero, the periods begin when the individual is born. If the age of integration is non-zero, the periods begin starting with that age.

The issue *does* have considerable substantive significance in evaluating policies that prevent infant death, an issue addressed in Chapter 8. At that juncture, I'll reopen the possibility of a non-zero age of integration. Until then, it will be assumed to be zero.

3

Death and Lifetime Welfarism

This chapter brings death into the picture. Like other chapters (except Chapter 8), it works within the Focal Case: a fixed and finite population of OHPs.[1]

Section 3.1 makes some brush-clearing comments regarding the nature of birth and death for human beings.

Section 3.2 analyzes the ethical significance of death as understood by lifetime welfarism. In a nutshell (and this should hardly be surprising), death is ethically significant, at the level of worlds, just insofar as it affects lifetime well-being. Consider any two worlds which are such that some individual *i* dies earlier in the second world than the first, producing some change (Δ_i) in their lifetime well-being and perhaps some changes (Δ_j, Δ_k, . . .) in the lifetime well-being of other persons (*j*, *k*, . . .). The ethical impact of their death on the second world's position in the world-ranking is exactly the same as if they had not died earlier but their lifetime well-being had changed by Δ_i and the other persons' lifetime well-being by Δ_j, Δ_k, ...

Section 3.3 situates the lifetime-welfarist account of the ethical significance of death relative to the large philosophical literature on the "badness"/"harmfulness" of death.

Section 3.4 discusses a range of questions regarding *how* death impacts lifetime well-being. The analysis of the ethical significance of death in Section 3.2 presumes that longevity does not have "lexical priority" in determining lifetime well-being—that later- and earlier-death histories can be equally good for someone's lifetime well-being. Section 3.4 elaborates on this premise and discusses the related question whether life-extension is always a benefit. It then engages scholarship regarding the harmfulness of risk and regarding posthumous harm. Can the risk of death itself be a setback to lifetime well-being? Can posthumous events change lifetime well-being?

[1] In this chapter, except in Section 3.1—which discusses human beings in general (not limited to OHPs)—the terms "individual," "person," and "human" mean an OHP.

Risk, Death, and Well-Being. Matthew D. Adler, Oxford University Press.
DOI: 10.1093/9780197505984.003.0003

3.1 Birth and Death

OHPs are essentially human beings and only contingently persons. This is the "Animalist" view of the metaphysics of persons—and the view adopted in this book.

A particular OHP ("Sam") is one and the same as a particular human animal. Sam comes into existence when the animal to whom Sam is identical—that animal that Sam *is*—does. Sam ceases to exist when that animal does.

A human animal comes into existence at some point in the time interval between the fertilization of its mother's egg by its father's sperm, and live birth—perhaps at the very beginning, perhaps at the very end, or in-between. To be sure, where that point lies is exceedingly controversial. This isn't a book on the morality of abortion, so I don't need to take a position on the question. OHPs come into existence no earlier than conception and no later than live birth.

Animalism rejects the position that an OHP comes into existence only when it possesses the cluster of psychological attributes sufficient to be a person. One-month-old infants fall far short of the full complement of psychological attributes of adult OHPs and indeed so far short as not to be persons. Still, one-month-old infants are fully alive and human.

A human being ceases to exist when it dies.[2] Animalism is, again, useful here. First, since a particular OHP is identical to a particular human being, the OHP ceases to exist when the animal does. Animalism precludes the view that an OHP ceases to exist when it loses the psychological characteristics required for personhood even if the human being continues.

Second, and relatedly, the "death" of a human being should be understood as the cessation of the processes that make it a living organism.[3] One proposed definition of human death, the "higher-brain" definition, is the "irreversible loss of the capacity for consciousness,"[4] which occurs when the cerebrum ceases to function. The higher-brain definition would imply that Latetia, who has a functioning brain stem and who breathes on her own and pumps blood without artificial aid—but is in a permanent vegetative state because of a profoundly impaired cerebrum—is dead. But Latetia is not dead. The animal that Latetia *is* dies

[2] Some animalists argue that an animal continues to exist as long as its body does, even if the body is dead. On this view, the "corpse" view, an animal ceases to exist only when its corpse disintegrates. The corpse view is problematic. See Luper (2009, pp. 46–48). Instead, this chapter adopts the common-sense position that an animal ceases to exist when it dies. That said, shifting to the corpse view would not (as far as I can tell) change any of the substantive conclusions of the chapter. In particular, the existence-ceases-with-death view, like the corpse view, allows for posthumous events to affect an animal's lifetime well-being. See Section 3.4.4.

[3] On the nature of death in general, see Belshaw (2009); Luper (2009). On the nature of death for human beings, see these sources and DeGrazia (2005, 2014).

[4] DeGrazia (2014, p. 87).

when it biologically dies—when it ceases to operate as a living organism. And that hasn't happened.

A plausible definition of the death of a human being is the "irreversible loss of functioning of the organism as a whole."[5] David DeGrazia offers a useful gloss on this definition.

> Proponents of this definition emphasize that death is a biological phenomenon common to all organisms. Organisms are those things that are literally alive . . . without being parts of larger biological entities (as cells and organs are parts of organisms). So an adequate definition must plausibly cover the deaths of non-human organisms—from paramecia to daisies to insects to coyotes—as well as human death. What is common to the deaths of all kinds of living creatures? In brief, the organism stops functioning as a more or less integrated unit. Where there was once a dynamic entity that extracted energy from the environment to maintain its own structure and functioning, there now is an inert piece (or pieces) of matter subject to disintegration and entropy. In the case of humans, no less than other organisms, death involves the irreversible loss of integrated bodily functioning.
>
> The qualifier "irreversible" is important here. . . . If the body of an organism stops functioning, even for a long time, but the condition is later reversed so that function resumes, it is presumably incorrect to say that the organism died before returning to life. . . . Suppose someone falls into a freezing lake and loses cardiopulmonary and brain function for an hour before being resuscitated. Even though this person might have appeared dead to observers prior to resuscitation, he did not actually die. . . . Rather than abandoning the traditional assumption that death is irreversible, we should abandon just the assumption that life and death are exhaustive. Between life and death, a state of *frozen, nonfatal inertness* is possible.[6]

This organism-as-a-whole definition of death might need to be revised to focus on the failure of the circulatory and respiratory systems. Death, on this approach, is understood as "the irreversible cessation of circulatory-respiratory function."[7] Indeed, traditionally, this was the medical definition. The case for focusing on the heart and lungs is that unlike "brain failure [or the failure of many other organs], loss of respiration and circulation leads relentlessly to the breakdown of cells, tissues, organs, bodily systems, and eventually the organism as a whole."[8]

[5] DeGrazia (2014, p. 82).
[6] DeGrazia (2014, pp. 82–83).
[7] DeGrazia (2014, p. 94).
[8] DeGrazia (2014, p. 94).

With both of these organismic (biological) accounts of death, questions arise regarding the extent to which life can be sustained via artificial means. Clearly, humans whose circulatory-and-respiratory systems, and thus whole bodies, can't function without *some* artificial aid may still be alive. Mechanical ventilators clearly illustrate this point: Patients who need a ventilator to breathe are *alive.* (If they weren't, the allocation of ventilators wouldn't be a matter of life and death—as of course it is.) But imagine a human being whose lungs, heart, and brain all fail; an emergency operation is performed, replacing the lungs and heart with machines, and the brain with a computer to direct the lungs, heart, and other organs. Does the human being die and thereby cease to exist when their biological lungs, heart, and brain fail, or do they continue to live and to exist after the operation?

This isn't a book about the criteria that healthcare workers should use to determine when a person is dead, and so I don't need to choose between the organism-as-a-whole and circulatory-respiratory definitions. The typical sources of human fatality risk that are abated by risk-regulation policies (pollutants, hazardous workplaces, dangerous vehicles, consumer products, etc.) cause both circulatory-respiratory and organism death in rapid succession. Nor is it a book about the ethics of heroic body rebuilds (e.g., brain, lung, and heart replacement) to extend life. Thus, identifying the maximal extent of artificial organs consistent with a human's remaining human is also not a topic I need to grapple with.

3.2 The Ethical Significance of Death (at the Level of Worlds)

How does lifetime welfarism conceptualize the ethical significance of death? Because this ethical account is consequentialist, it does so in two steps. First, it considers: what is the ethical significance of death *at the level of worlds*? How does an individual's death in a given world affect the ethical goodness of that world, i.e., the world's position in the world-ranking? Second, the account considers: what is the ethical significance of death *at the level of action*? How should individual decisionmakers, choosing among actions that cause or prevent death, or that increase or reduce the risk of death, evaluate those actions?

The second question is answered in Chapter 5. I show how the SWF framework, a decision-procedure for lifetime welfarism, gives guidance with respect to actions that cause or prevent death, or that increase or reduce the risk of death. The second question can't be answered until the first is. The SWF procedure is designed to give choice guidance in light of the world-ranking—by modeling worlds as "outcomes" (simplified representations of worlds) and actions as probability distributions across outcomes. This can't be done until we grasp the structure of the world-ranking and how death figures into that structure. We can't build our models, and incorporate death into those models, until it's clear what the ethical significance of death is *at the level of worlds.*

That's the question addressed here. In what follows, the "ethical significance of death" or cognate phrases include the elided qualifier "at the level of worlds."

Lifetime welfarism, of course, is a specific version of consequentialism. It sees the world-ranking as determined by the pattern of lifetime well-being (more precisely, as satisfying the axiom cluster Lifetime Pareto Indifference, Lifetime Anonymity, and Lifetime Strong Pareto). Thus, the ethical significance of death is reducible to its effect on lifetime well-being.

Here's first an informal statement of the view (for short, "LWB Reducibility," with "LWB" indicating "lifetime well-being").

LWB Reducibility: Death is ethically significant just insofar as it affects lifetime well-being (informal version)

Consider any two worlds which are such that some individual ("Sofia") dies earlier in the second world than the first, producing some change (Δ_{Sofia}) in her lifetime well-being and perhaps some changes (Δ_j, Δ_k, . . .) in the lifetime well-being of other persons (*j*, *k*, . . .).

The ethical impact of Sofia's death on the second world's position in the world-ranking is exactly the same as if she had not died earlier but her lifetime well-being had changed by Δ_{Sofia} and the other persons' lifetime well-being had changed by Δ_j, Δ_k, ...

And now a more precise rendition:

LWB Reducibility: Death is ethically significant just insofar as it affects lifetime well-being (more precise version)

Let d_{later}, $d_{earlier}$, d_{later}* be any three worlds that fit the following pattern: (1) There is one individual ("Sofia") who has the same birth date in d_{later} and $d_{earlier}$, but dies earlier in $d_{earlier}$ than she does in d_{later}; (2) her birth and death dates in d_{later}* are the same as in d_{later}; and (3) she is equally well off in d_{later}* and $d_{earlier}$, in terms of lifetime well-being. Moreover, for every other person in the population, it is the case that (4) that person's birth date is the same in all three worlds; their death date is the same in all three worlds; and they are at the same level of lifetime well-being in d_{later}* and $d_{earlier}$.

If so, d_{later}* is ethically equally good as $d_{earlier}$; and the ethical ranking of d_{later}* versus any world *d* (d_{later} or any other) is the same as the ranking of $d_{earlier}$ versus that world.[9]

[9] In a world set D that contains d_{later} and $d_{earlier}$ as described by LWB Reducibility, a d_{later}* as there described may not exist ("exist" meaning being a member of D: being one of the worlds each compared to the others by an ethical ranking $\succcurlyeq^E$ on D). But it will exist in some larger D^+ of which D

Note that Sofia might suffer a loss of well-being because of death, a gain of well-being, no change, or an incomparable change. LWB Reducibility covers all four cases.

Death may have a first-person effect on lifetime well-being: Sofia's level of lifetime well-being in an earlier-death world ($d_{earlier}$) may be higher, lower, or incomparable with her level of lifetime well-being in a later-death world (d_{later}). Death may also have third-person effects on lifetime well-being—effects on the lifetime well-being of persons other than the one who dies (Sofia). These other persons' levels of lifetime well-being in the world where Sofia dies earlier ($d_{earlier}$) may be higher, lower, or incomparable with their levels of lifetime well-being in a world where Sofia dies later (d_{later}).

LWB Reducibility covers both first-person effects and third-person effects.[10]

LWB Reducibility would be an empty principle if lives of different longevities could never attain the same level of lifetime well-being. If that were the case, there could never *be* two worlds d_{later}* and $d_{earlier}$ such that Sofia is equally well off despite having different longevities—and the principle would never apply. But in fact any plausible account of lifetime well-being *will* allow for the possibility that lives with different durations might be equally good (see Section 3.4.1 on this topic) and so the principle of LWB Reducibility is *not* empty.

Sofia, an OHP, is not immortal. What's of interest, then, is not the ethical significance of her death as compared to immortality but rather the ethical significance of her dying "prematurely," i.e., dying earlier in one world as compared to another. The answer that lifetime welfarism gives is quite straightforward. By virtue of Sofia's death, the earlier-death world is shifted in the world-ranking (relative to the later-death world and any other world) in exactly the same manner as would occur if Sofia and everyone else affected were to suffer/enjoy the loss/increase in lifetime well-being that results from Sofia's earlier death but without a reduction in Sofia's longevity. This is what LWB Reducibility says.

LWB Reducibility is an immediate consequence of Lifetime Pareto Indifference.[11] If LWB Reducibility were not true, this axiom would be violated.

is a subset; and, by World Set Well-Being and Ethical Consistency (see Chapter 1, notes 60–62), $d_{earlier}$ and other worlds in D must be ranked the same way by the D ranking as by the D$^+$ ranking. In effect, if no d_{later}* exists in D, $d_{earlier}$ is ranked vis-à-vis any *d′* that exists in D the same way as d_{later}* would be ranked vis-a-vis *d′*, were d_{later}* to exist (as it would in D$^+$).

[10] The world d_{later}* is constructed so as to mirror the change in *any* person's lifetime well-being that occurs with Sofia's earlier death, but without Sofia dying earlier. Note that each person in the population, both Sofia and everyone else, has the same lifetime well-being in d_{later}* that they do in $d_{earlier}$. Thus, the difference in any person's lifetime well-being between $d_{earlier}$ and d_{later}—whether that person is Sofia or someone else—equals the difference in their lifetime well-being between d_{later}* and d_{later}.

[11] Each person in the population has the same level of lifetime well-being in $d_{earlier}$ that they do in d_{later}*. Thus, by Lifetime Pareto Indifference, the two worlds are equally ethically good. Moreover, because $d_{earlier}$ and d_{later}* are equally good, it follows from the transitivity of the world-ranking that the two are ranked the same way vis-à-vis any third world.

LWB Reducibility should not be surprising. It just codifies, as applied to death, the *welfarist* cast of lifetime welfarism. *Everything* about someone's life matters just insofar as it affects well-being—and death is no different.

What is less obvious is how the lifetime-welfarist account of the ethical significance of death—as codified by LWB Reducibility—relates to the vast body of philosophical scholarship on the "badness" or "harmfulness" of death. Let's now turn to that topic.

3.3 The Badness/Harmfulness of Death

The Greek philosopher Epicurus argued that death is not bad for the individual who dies. His argument was crystallized in an oft-quoted letter to Menoeceus.

> Become accustomed to the belief that death is nothing to us. For all good and evil consists in sensation, but death is deprivation of sensation. So death, the most terrifying of ills, is nothing to us, since as long as we exist death is not with us; but when death comes, then we do not exist.[12]

Epicurus' denial of the badness of death has spurred much discussion over the centuries, continuing right up to the present. There is a quite substantial contemporary philosophical literature on whether death is bad.[13]

The main objection to the badness of death that this literature gleans from Epicurus' letter (following Jens Johansson, let's call it the Epicurean Argument) can be expressed as follows: "(1) Anything that is bad for a person is bad for her at a time. (2) There is no time at which death is bad for the person who dies. (3) Hence, death is not bad for the person who dies."[14] A second argument, the Experience Argument, is that well-being consists in good and bad experiences, but death is the absence of experiences.

Some contemporary philosophers agree (in light of the Epicurean Argument or Experience Argument) that death is not a bad; while others, in particular "deprivationists," affirm that death can be a bad. In what follows, I first discuss "deprivationism," illustrating its features by way of example: the version presented by Ben Bradley in his book *Well-Being and Death*.[15] I then contrast

[12] Quoted in Johansson (2013, p. 255).

[13] Overviews of this literature are provided by Bradley (2009, 2016); Luper (2009, 2021); and various of the chapters in volumes on the philosophy of death edited by Luper (2014) and Bradley, Feldman, and Johansson (2013). Timmerman (2019) cites (and critiques) the major contemporary Epicureans. A recent anthology on the badness of death, covering both theory and policy, is Gamlund and Solberg (2019).

[14] Johansson (2013, p. 255).

[15] Bradley (2009).

Bradley's view with my own: the lifetime-welfarist account of the ethical significance of death. Third, I discuss the Symmetry Argument against the badness of death, associated with Lucretius, and describe how my account responds to that argument. Finally, I discuss Jeff McMahan's influential notion of time-relative interests and how this relates to deprivationism and to the lifetime-welfarist account.

This section does *not* attempt to survey the literature on the badness of death or the deprivationist component of that literature. The reason is not merely lack of space. More fundamentally, the lifetime-welfarist account of the ethical significance of death—as codified by LWB Reducibility—doesn't use the concept of the badness of death. Whether death can be bad is the core concern of this literature but not a concern of my account. The account is not a contribution *to* the literature on the badness of death, and thus a survey of that literature would be otiose, here. Although the lifetime-welfarist account does have certain superficial similarities to deprivationism, it does not in fact attempt to explain why death can be bad. This will become evident (I hope) in what follows.

3.3.1 A Deprivationist Account of Why Death Is Bad: Ben Bradley's Account

Examining a specific deprivationist account of the badness of death will bring into focus the similarities and differences between deprivationism and my own view of the matter—the lifetime-welfarist view. Ben Bradley's book-length exposition of deprivationism, *Well-Being and Death*, is thorough, sophisticated, and fairly recent (hence Bradley is positioned to incorporate and build from the substantial body of deprivationist writing that preceded his book)[16]. And *Well-Being and Death* is exemplary of deprivationism in explaining death's badness with reference to a counterfactual: Death is bad in depriving the individual of the welfare goods they would have received had they not died.

Bradley's primary focus, like mine, is lifetime well-being. He generally does not use this term. He says instead that a theory of well-being will explain "what makes someone's life go well for her,"[17] what "counts as a good life for [a] person,"[18] or the "value of a life."[19] But I take all of these formulations, as used by Bradley, to be synonyms for "lifetime well-being."

[16] See, e.g., Broome (1999); Brueckner and Fischer (1986); Feldman (1991, 1992); Nagel (1979a); Quinn (1984).
[17] Bradley (2009, p. 1).
[18] Bradley (2009, p. 3).
[19] Bradley (2009, p. 8).

In my more precise formulation, the objects of a theory of lifetime well-being are not lives but "histories," each history being a pairing of an individual and a world. Bradley says something similar. In *his* more precise formulation, a theory of well-being is a theory of the value of worlds relativized to subjects.

> There may be many notions of lives—biographical, biological, psychological, etc.—and I have no interest in picking one out as being particularly important. So I propose to bypass this discussion altogether by taking *worlds*, rather than *lives*, as the items of prudential evaluation. We can say that a world is good or bad for a person without ever mentioning her life at all. The value of a world for someone is nothing mysterious; it is just how well things go for her at that world. . . . For ease of exposition, I will sometimes continue to refer to lives. But talk of the value of a life should be understood as talk about the subject-relative value of a world.[20]

Bradley's understanding of a "world," i.e., a "possible world," is exactly the same as mine: "Let us think of a possible world as a complete story about the universe: a maximal consistent set of propositions."[21] And lifetime well-being understood as the ranking of histories (Adler), or instead as the "subject-relative value of a world" (Bradley), are close if not identical.

Bradley endorses "pure hedonism": the lifetime well-being of a given life depends upon its pain and pleasure states. But he also explains that his account of the badness of death does not, in many respects, depend upon pure hedonism.[22]

That account, in a nutshell, is that a particular death is bad for the person who dies just insofar as the lifetime well-being of the life in which that death occurs is lower than the lifetime well-being of the life the person would have led, had the death not occurred.

> According to the deprivation account of the evil of death, death is bad because it deprives us of a good life. Like most people, I accept that death is bad, and I accept the deprivation account of its badness. But there are versions of the deprivation account that differ in philosophically interesting ways. . . . I argue for a *difference-making* account of deprivation, according to which the badness of a death is determined by a comparison between the life its victim actually lives and the life she would have lived had that death not occurred.[23]

20 Bradley (2009, pp. 7–8).
21 Bradley (2009, p. 49).
22 Bradley (2009, p. 45).
23 Bradley (2009, p. xiv).

To be more precise, Bradley's account explains how death in the *event* sense—the event, in some world, that brings someone's life to an end—can be a bad. Bradley's "Difference-Making Principle" is a general account of the badness of events. This principle uses the standard notion, in the possible-worlds literature, of a similarity relation between worlds. Worlds are similar and different in various respects. A similarity relation *R* will be such that, for any world *d*, other worlds will be ranked as more or less similar to *d*; and (if things go well) for any event *E* that occurs in *d*, there will be a single world in which *E* does not occur and which, of all such non-*E* worlds, is the one most similar to *d* as per the *R* similarity relation. What Bradley offers is an account of the badness of an event relativized to a similarity relation.

> [Difference-Making Principle]. The value of event E, for person S, at world *w*, relative to similarity relation R = the intrinsic value of *w* for S, minus the intrinsic value for S of the most R-similar world to *w* where E does not occur.[24]

The "intrinsic value of w for S" is, in my terminology, just the lifetime well-being of person S's life in that world.

Applied to the death-event of some person in a given world *d* (the event in that world whereby that person dies), Bradley's account says that this death-event in *d* is bad, relative to similarity relation *R*, just insofar as the person's lifetime well-being in *d* is lower than their lifetime well-being in the most *R*-similar world to *d* in which that event does not occur. Thus, a death-event can be bad for the person who dies, but not necessarily so. If the most *R*-similar world to *d* in which the death-event does not occur yields a *lower* level of lifetime well-being for the person than their level of lifetime well-being in *d*, the death-event in *d* is good for them.

By relativizing the value of events to similarity relations, Bradley's account reflects the truism that situations (including worlds: complete situations) are similar or different in various respects. Relativization also allows Bradley to accommodate conflicting verdicts about the badness of particular deaths. He considers the case of a 20-year-old pedestrian who accidentally steps into the path of a bus and is instantly and painlessly killed.[25] During the autopsy, it's discovered that the pedestrian had a cerebral aneurysm that would have burst within a week and killed him had he not been killed by the bus. Is the young pedestrian's death bad for him? Very bad, ignoring the aneurysm; not so bad, considering it. That is (as per Bradley), the death-event is very bad relative to one similarity relation, and not so bad relative to another. If *d* is the world under

[24] Bradley (2009, p. 50).
[25] See Bradley (2009, pp. 52–60). This case was introduced by McMahan (2002, p. 117).

discussion and *E* the event of the pedestrian's being killed by the bus, let R_1 be a similarity relation such that the closest world relative to *d* in which *E* doesn't occur is one in which the pedestrian dies in old age; and let R_2 be a similarity relation such that the closest world relative to *d* in which *E* doesn't occur is one in which the pedestrian dies as a result of the aneurysm. Then (on Bradley's analysis) the pedestrian's death-event in *d* is very bad for him relative to R_1, and not so bad relative to R_2.

While Bradley mainly trains his attention on the goodness or badness of death, he also discusses whether death is a *harm*.[26] (This is characteristic of the contemporary philosophical literature on death. Epicureans and anti-Epicureans often consider whether death is *bad*, but they also or instead consider related notions, e.g., whether death is a "harm" or a "misfortune.")[27] The difficulty with saying that an event (such as death) is a harm iff it is bad according to the Difference-Making Principle arises with cases in which someone is, intuitively, harmed by an event but overall benefited by it. Bradley considers, for example, a case in which a man is imprisoned in a concentration camp—surely a harm—but this experience so deepens his character that he ends up living a better life than had he not been imprisoned.

Bradley handles this sort of case by differentiating between prima facie and all-things-considered harms. The imprisonment is a prima facie harm for the prisoner (in virtue of the terrible suffering he experiences in the camp) but not an all-things-considered harm. Bradley proposes that an event (and, in particular, a death-event) is an all-things-considered-harm iff it is bad according to the Difference-Making Principle.

So Bradley is an Anti-Epicurean: death *can* be a bad (and *can* be a harm). How does he answer the Epicurean Argument? In a lengthy response to that Argument, Bradley pursues the following strategy.[28] Bradley accepts prong (1), that anything bad for someone must be bad for them at a time. (A different anti-Epicurean strategy, so-called atemporalism, is to deny (1) and assert that death is a timeless harm.) Thus Bradley needs to identify a time or stretch of time at which death is bad. The possibilities he considers are eternalism (death is bad for the victim at all times); priorism (before death); concurrentism (at the time of death); and subsequentism (after death).

Bradley argues for subsequentism, here drawing upon the notion of momentary well-being (my term, not Bradley's). He claims that a person, after death, has a zero well-being level. Thus, he proposes that an individual's death in some world *d* is bad for that person, at times after death, relative to similarity relation

[26] See Bradley (2009, pp. 65–69).
[27] On misfortune, see, e.g., McMahan (2019).
[28] See Bradley (2009, ch. 3).

R, iff the individual's momentary well-being level at those times in the closest world in which death doesn't occur is positive (above zero).

Finally, how does Bradley answer the Experience Argument: that well-being consists in good and bad experiences, but death is the absence of experiences? Bradley contends that even if pure hedonism (his preferred theory of well-being) is true, the argument can be answered. The answer is to distinguish between the *intrinsic* well-being value of death, and its "extrinsic" (non-intrinsic value).

> [W]hile it is at least arguable, and hedonists assert, that the only things that can be *intrinsically* good or bad for someone are sensations, sensations are not the only things that can be *extrinsically* good or bad for someone. In particular, the *causes* and *preventors* of our sensations, anything that *makes a difference* to our experiences, may be extrinsically good or bad for us. Deprivation theorists attribute extrinsic value, not intrinsic value, to death; death causes us not to have any sensations, which is worse for us than having good sensations.[29]

3.3.2 Comparing My Account to Bradley's

My account—the lifetime-welfarist account of the ethical significance of death—and Bradley's deprivationist analysis of death's badness have important similarities. Lifetime well-being and possible worlds are central to both analyses. Further, both accounts revolve around *comparisons* of lifetime well-being. My account: Whether a world in which someone dies at a particular point in time is better or worse than a world in which they live longer depends upon a comparison of the patterns of lifetime well-being in the two worlds. Bradley's: Whether a death-event in some world is good or bad for the individual who dies hinges on a comparison of their lifetime well-being in that world, with their lifetime well-being in the closest possible world (as per some similarity relation) in which that particular death-event doesn't occur.

But there is also a quite fundamental difference between our accounts, which is this: *I say nothing about how to characterize a death as good or bad.* (This is why I choose to label mine as an account concerning the "ethical significance of death"—avoiding the term "badness of death.") My account doesn't use the concept of a death being good or bad—and thus doesn't need to explain that concept.

According to lifetime welfarism, the objects of ethical assessment are whole worlds. What matters, for any given world, is not whether it is ethically good or bad (a non-comparative notion), but a comparative feature of the world—namely,

[29] Bradley (2009, p. 80).

where it sits in the overall ranking of worlds $\succcurlyeq^E$, which compares each world to every other and does so in a transitive fashion.

Further, per lifetime welfarism, the ethical comparison of any two worlds depends upon the histories in each and the patterns of lifetime well-being associated with those histories. The death-event of some person in a given world is ethically significant *only* as one determinant of the lifetime well-being level of the history in which that event occurs (the first-person effect of death, on the lifetime well-being of the person who dies), and perhaps as one determinant of the lifetime well-being levels of other persons' histories (the third-person effect of death, on the lifetime well-being of other persons). The proposition that death has ethical significance just insofar as it affects lifetime well-being levels is a basic feature of lifetime welfarism, and is given precise expression in the principle of LWB Reducibility.

Because a death-event is ethically significant *only* as one determinant of the lifetime well-being level of the history in which the death occurs and perhaps the levels of other histories, the question whether death itself is good or bad is *ethically inert*—for purposes of lifetime welfarism. Assume that individual i is born at the same time in worlds d and d^*, but dies later in d^*. World d is associated with the array of histories $((d; 1), \ldots, (d; N))$, and world d^* with the array $((d^*;1), \ldots, (d^*; N))$. Whether d is ethically better than, worse than, equally good as, or incomparable with d^* depends upon the patterns of lifetime well-being associated with the two arrays. The fact that individual i's death-event in history $(d; i)$ occurs at an earlier point in time than i's death-event in history $(d^*; i)$ is ethically relevant insofar as it helps to determine the lifetime well-being facts about these two histories (and perhaps the lifetime well-being facts about other histories). But this *exhausts* the ethical relevance of the death-event in d. For purposes of lifetime welfarism, there is no reason to ask whether a death-event, taken alone, is good or bad. Such an assessment is ethically inert; it plays no ethical role.

The fact that my account involves comparisons and that Bradley's account also involves comparisons shouldn't obscure the fundamental difference between the accounts that I'm now highlighting. Bradley employs a comparison of lifetime well-being in order to analyze a value concept—the badness of a death-event—which my account doesn't use and doesn't need to analyze.

To see why the goodness or badness of death is ethically inert, for purposes of lifetime welfarism, let's use Bradley's example of the young pedestrian (let's call him Adam). In world d, Adam steps in front of a bus at age 20 and dies instantly (event E). Consider any other world d^+. Whether Adam's death in d is good or bad as per Bradley's analysis is just irrelevant to the ethical comparison of d and d^+ as per lifetime welfarism. Let d^* be a world in which Adam isn't hit by the bus but instead dies in old age: the closest world to d in which E doesn't occur, according to similarity relation R_1. Let d^{**} be a world in which Adam isn't hit by the bus but instead dies of an aneurysm a week later: the closest world to *d* in which *E* doesn't occur, according to similarity relation R_2. And let d^{***} be a world in which Adam isn't hit by the bus but instead is later kidnapped and tortured: the closest world to *d* in which *E* doesn't occur, according to similarity relation R_3.

So Adam's death in *d* is very bad (relative to R_1), slightly bad (relative to R_2), and good (relative to R_3)—in virtue of a comparison of his lifetime well-being in *d* with his lifetime well-being in d^*, d^{**}, and d^{***}, respectively. But none of this has any relevance to the comparison of *d* and d^+. That just depends on Adam's lives in *those two worlds* (and the lives of everyone else).

For example, Adam in d^+ might live until middle age and then die of a freak accident. Then it is a comparison of the well-being of Adam's living to middle age and dying in a freak accident, versus Adam's being killed by a bus at age 20, that matters to the d^+/d comparison—not a comparison of Adam's living to old age versus being killed by a bus, or dying of an aneurysm versus being killed by a bus, or being kidnapped and tortured versus being killed by a bus.

While the concept of the badness of death plays no role in lifetime welfarism, it doesn't follow—of course—that this concept is ethically inert within the framework of other ethical theories. Analyzing this concept might well be important for various types of non-consequentialist ethical views. It may also be important as a matter of understanding ordinary discourse. My intention here is *not* to cast cold water on Bradley's work or the many other contributions to the literature on the badness of death, but just to say that the question confronted by this literature—Is death bad and, if so, how?—is not a problem that *this* book needs to engage.

Bradley focuses on the badness of death in the event sense. Alternatively, one might attempt to analyze the badness of the state-of-affairs of someone being dead. The badness of death in *either* sense is ethically inert, for purposes of lifetime welfarism. So, too, are related concepts regarding "harm" and "misfortune." Whether death (in the event or state-of-affairs sense) is a harm or a misfortune plays no role in lifetime welfarism, just as the badness of death doesn't.

My lifetime well-being account of the ethical significance of death might be described as a kind of *deflated deprivationism.* I affirm that a life cut short by premature death may well be worse, for lifetime well-being, than a life in which death occurs later. If so, the first life will be worse in virtue of a shortfall of well-being goods—worse because there are contributors to well-being that occur in the second life but not the first, or are realized more fully in the second life than in the first. These claims are in the spirit of deprivationism; but since the badness of death (the core concern of Bradley and other full-blown deprivationists) doesn't figure within my account, it is only a *deflated* deprivationism.

Still, the account might be challenged to answer a variant of Epicurus' argument. I claim this: An individual *i* who dies earlier in one world (*d*) as compared to a second (d^*) can be worse off in the first. But *when* does this difference in well-being occur? Well-being, of course, is goodness *for* a subject. The well-being level of *i* in *d* is lower than that of *i* in d^* iff *d* is worse *for i* than d^*. The subject, individual *i*, is the possessor of a relational property. That relational property is a three-part relation between them and the two worlds: world *d* worse for *i* than world d^*. But no property can be possessed by a nonexistent individual. So an Epicurean challenge can be raised: At what time is it true both that *i* exists and that they possess the relational property of being worse off in *d* than d^*?

Bradley, curiously, analyzes the badness of death in lifetime terms but then uses momentary well-being to answer the timing question.[30] *My* answer to the *variant* of the timing problem that my account needs to answer (the variant described in the preceding paragraph) sticks to lifetime well-being. Momentary well-being has no role in my account; why should I introduce it here? What we're trying to understand is how the *lifetime* well-being of *i* in *d* can be lower than the *lifetime* well-being of *i* in d^*. That is true iff *d* is worse for *i* than d^*. When does *i* have that relational property? The answer is straightforward. First, *i* has the relational property of being worse off in *d* than d^* in world *d*, at all times that they exist in *d*; and, second, *i* has that property in d^*, at all times that they exist in d^*.[31]

Finally, my account readily answers Epicurus' Experience Argument. Even if we assume that lifetime well-being reduces to good and bad sensations—or, more generally, to good and bad experiences—there is no difficulty in explaining how *i* can be worse off in *d* than d^*. The histories (*d*; *i*) and (d^*; *i*) don't contain the same experiences. At times in d^* after the time of *i*'s death in *d*, *i* has mental states that they don't have in *d*. So even if the theory of well-being is such as to satisfy the experientialist restriction,[32] that constraint doesn't require the histories (*d*; *i*) and (d^*; *i*) to be ranked equally good.

3.3.3 The Symmetry Argument

The Symmetry Argument against the badness of death is also associated with Epicurus. It trades upon a symmetry between prenatal and postmortem nonexistence, as expressed by Epicurus' follower Lucretius: "Look back at the

[30] That said, other deprivationists have also defended subsequentism. See sources cited in Timmerman (2022). Bradley (2016) amplifies his defense of subsequentism.

[31] It is important to distinguish between two timing questions. (1) When is it true that *i*'s lifetime well-being level in *d* is lower than their lifetime well-being in d^*? I.e., when is it true that history (*d*; *i*) is at a lower level of lifetime well-being than history (d^*; *i*)? The answer: this is true in any world (*d*, d^*, or any other world) at all times. (2) At what times does *i* have the relational property of being worse off in *d* than d^*? The answer: *i* has that property in any world (*d*, d^*, or any other world) at all and only those times when *i* exists in that world. (It can't be true that *i* has this relational property, or any other property, at a time when they don't exist.)

[32] See Section 1.2.1.

eternity that passed before we were born, and mark how utterly it counts to us as nothing. This is a mirror that Nature holds up to us, in which we may see the time that shall be after we are dead."[33]

The Symmetry Argument might be framed as follows. (1) It is not bad for us that we were born later than we might have been. (2) Our posthumous non-existence is like our pre-vital non-existence in all relevant respects. (3) If two things are alike in all relevant respects, and one of them is not bad for us, then the second is not bad for us either. (4) So it is not bad for us that we died earlier than we might have.[34]

In assessing the Symmetry Argument, we need to keep in mind the identity conditions for human beings.[35] On some such views, birth timing is itself an essential property. (On such views, Matt Adler, who was born in the actual world in 1962, couldn't have been born at a significantly earlier or later date. In every possible world where Matt Adler exists, he is born in 1962 or not too much later or earlier.) On other views, birth timing is not an essential property.

The Symmetry Argument does not seem to pose a challenge to the deprivationist account of the badness of death.[36] Whatever strategy deprivationists employ to explain the badness of death can also be used to explain why a particular birth of some individual is bad, as opposed to a differently timed birth of that individual (insofar as this timing change is consistent with the identity conditions for humans).

In any event, the Symmetry Argument does not undermine the lifetime-welfarist account of the ethical significance of death. The badness of birth is an ethically inert notion for lifetime welfarism, just as the badness of death is. Assume that some individual, Jason, is born at time t in world d and dies at time t'. Let d^+, d^{++}, d^{+++}, . . . be alternative worlds in which Jason is born at the same time as in d but dies at a different time. In ranking each of these alternative worlds against d, lifetime welfarism take account of Jason's lifetime well-being levels in the two, and the lifetime well-being levels of everyone else in the population. In making these comparisons, we never need to ask whether Jason's death in d is bad (or good). That characterization is just irrelevant to the lifetime-welfarist analysis.

Similarly, let d^*, d^{**}, d^{***}, . . . be alternative worlds in which Jason is born at a different time than in d (to the extent this is consistent with the identity conditions for humans). In ranking each of *these* alternative worlds against

[33] Quoted in Luper (2009, p. 61).

[34] This formulation is similar, but not identical, to that of Luper (2009, p. 61).

[35] See Luper (2009, pp. 60–67); Warren (2014).

[36] Bradley argues as much in Bradley (2009, pp. 62–65). Cf. Brueckner and Fischer (1986), Fischer (2006), arguing that a later birth can deprive someone of well-being but that it is rational not to care about such deprivation, because our rational attitudes are temporally asymmetric. For an overview of scholarship on the Symmetry Argument, see Warren (2014).

d, lifetime welfarism—once more—takes account of Jason's lifetime well-being levels in the two, and the lifetime well-being levels of everyone else in the population. In making *these* comparisons, we never need to ask whether Jason's *birth* in *d* is bad (or good). *That* question is just irrelevant to the lifetime-welfarist analysis.

3.3.4 Jeff McMahan's Time-Relative Interest Account

In his influential book, *The Ethics of Killing*, Jeff McMahan defends a "time-relative interest" account of the badness of death.[37] McMahan sees his account as a variant of deprivationism. In a recent restatement of the view, McMahan contrasts the time-relative approach with *standard* deprivationism, which McMahan terms the "Life Comparative Account"—according to which "[t]he badness of death . . . consists in the difference in value between the life a person has if he dies at a certain time and the life he would have had if he had not died at that time."[38] Ben Bradley's view, discussed in detail above, is an exemplar of the Life Comparative Account. McMahan criticizes standard deprivationism for its implications with respect to the deaths of fetuses and infants.

> [The Life Comparative Account] implies that the worst death that an individual can suffer is death immediately after the individual has begun to exist. Suppose that we begin to exist, as I believe, when the fetal brain develops the capacity for consciousness, sometime between 22 and 28 weeks after conception, probably closer to the later end of this period. It is hard to believe that a 28-week-old fetus suffers a greater misfortune in dying than a teenager does.[39]
>
> McMahan continues:
>
> I have sought to develop an account of the misfortune of death that explains and justifies the common intuition that the death of a fetus is a substantially lesser misfortune for that fetus than the death of a person normally is for that person. It is based . . . on Derek Parfit's argument that the fact that an individual at an earlier time and an individual at a later time are the same individual (that is, that they are *identical*) is *not* what makes it rational for the former to care in an egoistic way about what may happen to the latter. The basis of such rational egoistic concern is instead the *relations* that are constitutive of our identity over

37 McMahan (2002, pp. 165–88).
38 McMahan (2019, p. 116).
39 McMahan (2019, pp. 116–17).

> time. [These are] psychological relations grounded in physical, functional, and organizational continuities in the brain, such as continuities of memory, character, desire, belief, and intention. Whereas identity is all-or-nothing, the relevant relations are matters of degree. . . .
>
> According to the account I have defended, the extent to which death is a misfortune at time *t* is a function primarily of two variables: (1) the amount of good life lost (which is the sole factor recognized by the Life Comparative Account) and (2) the strength of the relevant relations that would have held between the individual at *t* and himself at those later times at which the good things in his life would have occurred. . . . Because there would be virtually no psychological relations between a barely conscious 28-week-old fetus and itself as a child or adult, the misfortune it suffers in dying at 28 weeks may be negligible even though the amount of good life it loses is great. . . . Even though the fetus would have a much better life if it were not to die, its interest at the time (or "time-relative interest") in avoiding death is very weak. . . . I have labeled this account of the misfortune of death the *Time-Relative Interest Account.*[40]

The case of infant or fetal deaths takes us beyond the Focal Case. I'll address this issue in Chapter 8. The resolution that I will propose involves the age of integration—the age prior to which events are not integrated into lifetime well-being. Assume that Sofia dies as an infant in world *d* and survives to adulthood in *d**. If the age of integration is zero, then the comparison of the two worlds depends upon Sofia's lifetime well-being in each world and everyone else's lifetime well-being in each. Alternatively, if the age of integration is non-zero (and Sofia in *d* is younger than the age of integration), the comparison of the two worlds depends upon Sofia's lifetime well-being in *d** (as a function of post-integration events); her pre-integration momentary well-being in *d**; and her pre-integration momentary well-being in *d*—as well as the lifetime well-being and pre-integration momentary well-being of everyone else in the population.

In either event—whether the age of integration is zero or non-zero—the badness of Sofia's death in *d* is ethically inert for purposes of the ethical framework developed in this book. The comparison of *d* to *d** depends on the pattern of lifetime well-being in both worlds, or on the pattern of lifetime well-being and pre-integration momentary well-being. Whether Sofia's death is bad—in a standard deprivationist sense (Bradley), or alternatively in McMahan's time-relative-interest sense—is not going to make a difference to this world-to-world comparison, or to the comparison of *d* to any third world.

In any ethical context where it *is* necessary to assess the badness of a death, the debate between McMahan and standard deprivationists is an important one.

[40] McMahan (2019, pp. 117–18).

This is true, at least, for non-welfarist ethical theories that take account of the badness of death; and it may well be true in other contexts too. But for purposes of the ethical framework elaborated in this book, lifetime welfarism, adjudicating the dispute between McMahan and standard deprivationists is not an important topic—because the issue of the badness of death (be it an adult's death or an infant's death) just doesn't arise.

3.4 Death and Lifetime Well-Being

How does death impact lifetime well-being? Consider any given history for an individual, and any alternative history of that individual in which they die later. How does the lifespan of the individual in each history, together with their attributes in that history while alive, determine their lifetime well-being levels?

A full answer to this question clearly depends on the specifics of the theory of well-being. This book is agnostic about the content of well-being and so will not propose a detailed explanation of how the longevity and non-longevity features of histories interact to yield lifetime well-being. Rather, in this section, I consider four general questions regarding the impact of death on lifetime well-being that are central to the book's project: developing a welfarist account of fatality risk regulation. First, does longevity have lexical priority over the non-longevity components of lives? Second, is life-extension always beneficial? Third, is the risk of death itself a welfare setback? Finally, can posthumous events change lifetime well-being?

3.4.1 Lexical Priority to Longevity?

A theory of lifetime well-being *could* assign lexical priority to longevity in ranking histories.

> <u>Lexical priority to longevity</u>: If the lifespan of one history is shorter than a second's, then the first history has a lower level of lifetime well-being than the second's.

Lexical priority to longevity means that longer lives are always better than shorter ones, regardless of what occurs during the longer and shorter lives. If two histories have the same birth date but different death dates, the history with the earlier death date is *necessarily* worse than the other. No feature of the individual's life during the earlier-death history could be good enough to compensate for the shorter lifespan and raise that history to a level of lifetime well-being equal to or greater than that of the later-death history; and no feature of the individual's life during the later-death history could be bad enough to counterbalance the longer lifespan and lower that history to a level equal to or lower than that of the earlier-death history.

Lexical priority to longevity is not inconsistent with lifetime welfarism. The formal constraints on the lifetime well-being comparison structure allow for lexical priority to longevity, as do the basic ethical axioms of lifetime welfarism: Lifetime Pareto Indifference, Lifetime Anonymity, and Lifetime Strong Pareto.

Still, lexical priority to longevity would be in serious tension with the project of this book. To begin, it would render LWB Reducibility an empty principle. If lexical priority to longevity is true, LWB Reducibility is trivially satisfied—no world-ranking violates it—because a loss Δ_i in individual *i*'s lifetime well-being that occurs by virtue of *i*'s loss of longevity can never be the same as a loss that occurs holding *i*'s longevity constant. Moreover, lexical priority to longevity would undermine the SWF framework. That framework uses attribute bundles to model histories and assumes that the well-being of bundles is measurable via a well-being measure $w(\cdot)$. But if lexical priority to longevity holds true of histories and, thus, of the bundles representing histories, well-being may not be measurable.[41]

Surely, however, lexical priority should be rejected.[42] Any plausible theory of well-being will allow for some degree of trade-off between lifespan and the non-longevity components of lives. Specifically, I'll posit the following principle, *Downward Trade-offs*.

> Downward Trade-offs: For any history h with a lifespan l, and any longer lifespan l^*, there is some history with lifespan l^* which is equally good as h.[43]

The Downward Trade-offs principle suffices to negate lexical priority to longevity and make LWB Reducibility a non-empty principle, and is independently plausible. To motivate Downward Trade-offs, consider a history $h^{neutral\text{-}l^*}$ in which the individual has lifespan l^*, but the individual's life is so devoid of non-longevity well-being components that $h^{neutral\text{-}l^*}$ is equally good for well-being as non-existence. If h is better than non-existence, then we can arrive at a history

[41] If well-being is determined by two or more lexically ordered dimensions, with an uncountable number of locations on at least one of the dimensions, and with this dimension lexically superior to a dimension with at least two locations, then well-being is not measurable—for reasons first identified by Debreu (1954). In particular, then, if attribute bundles are structured so that longevity is continuous rather than discrete, i.e., longevity can take any value in some uncountable interval of real numbers, lexical priority to longevity will preclude the existence of a $w(\cdot)$ that represents the well-being ranking of bundles. On the modeling of longevity, see Chapter 4, note 7.

[42] See Broome (2004, pp. 23–25).

[43] This statement should be qualified in a manner analogous to the qualification for LWB Reducibility stated in note 9. Although a history with lifespan l^* equally good as h may not exist

with longevity l^* equally good as h by improving the non-longevity well-being components of $h^{neutral\text{-}l^*}$. If h is equally good as non-existence, then h is equally good as $h^{neutral\text{-}l^*}$. Finally, if h is worse than non-existence, we start with $h^{neutral\text{-}l^*}$ and make its non-longevity well-being components even worse so as to arrive at a history equally good as h.

Two further principles regarding trade-offs will be needed to support the methodology advanced in Chapter 4 for constructing the SWF framework's well-being measure, $w(\cdot)$. That methodology will rely upon two trade-off principles: Archimedean I and Archimedean II. These principles are stated in terms of attribute bundles. But, if the well-being measure $w(\cdot)$ is to be a reasonable implementation of an underlying lifetime well-being comparison structure, then presumably counterparts to Archimedean I and Archimedean II should hold true at the level of histories. Let's denote these counterpart principles, respectively, as Archimedean I$^+$ and Archimedean II$^+$. More precisely:

> Archimedean I$^+$: Let $h_1, h_2, \ldots, h_n, \ldots$ be a finite or infinite sequence of histories such that the well-being difference between each history and the one before in the sequence is a constant, non-zero difference. If there are two histories h^* and h, h^* better than h, such that the well-being difference between h^* and h is larger than the well-being difference between h_n and h_1, for any n, and the well-being difference between h and h^* is less than the well-being difference between h_n and h_1, for any n, then the sequence is finite.[44]

What Archimedean I$^+$ means, in a nutshell, is that no well-being difference between two histories is so large as to be larger than any finite concatenation of a fixed difference.

> Archimedean II$^+$: Let L, L^*, L^{**} be three history lotteries such that the third is better than the second, in turn better than the first. Then there is some probability p, strictly less than 1, such that a (p, 1-p) mixture of L^{**} and L is better

in D, it will exist in some larger D$^+$ of which D is a subset; and World Set Well-Being Consistency will apply.

[44] The reader may find Archimedean I$^+$ easier to grasp after engaging with the formal discussion of history differences in Section 1.A.2. Leaving aside incomparability, well-being differences can be positive, negative, or zero. The zero difference is the difference between any history and itself. The difference between two histories is positive iff greater than the zero difference and negative iff less than the zero difference. (It's also true that the difference between two histories is positive iff the first history is at a higher well-being level than the second, and negative iff the first history is at a lower well-being level than the second.) The statement of Archimedean I$^+$ here is the verbal rendition of Archimedean I (stated in terms of well-being bundles) in Section 4.2.1, which in turn is taken from Krantz, Luce, Suppes, and Tversky (2007, ch. 4).

than L^*; and some probability q, strictly greater than 0, such that a $(q, 1\text{-}q)$ mixture of L^{**} and L is worse than L^*.[45]

Archimedean I$^+$ and I^{++} are quite general principles—principles that go well beyond trade-offs between the longevity and non-longevity components of lifetime well-being—but these principles do have implications for such trade-offs. Note that the Downward Trade-offs principle itself does not rule out the following: there is a history h with lifespan l and a shorter lifespan l' such that every history with lifespan l' is worse than h.[46] Archimedean I$^+$ and II^{++} will have implications here. Archimedean I$^+$ means that if we take a history with the shorter lifespan l' that is worse than h, and our well-being theory allows us to make constant, positive improvements to well-being at that lifespan, we will eventually end up with a history with lifespan l' that is no worse than h.[47] Archimedean II$^+$ means that, given any history even better than h, and any history with the shorter lifespan l' that is worse than h, there will be a lottery with a chance of the yet better history and some downside risk of the history with the shorter lifespan that will be better than h.

Downward Trade-offs, Archimedean I$^+$, and Archimedean II^{++} are the only principles regarding well-being trade-offs that are required for the project of this book. They are consistent with a wide range of views about how a life's longevity together with its non-longevity components give rise to lifetime well-being.

3.4.2 Is Life-Extension Always Beneficial?

Policy analysis of risk regulation, as it currently stands, generally assumes that reducing an individual's fatality risk and thereby increasing their expected lifespan is a benefit to that individual. The so-called "value of statistical life" (VSL), the linchpin of cost-benefit analysis (CBA), quantifies the value of reducing fatality risk in monetary terms. VSL is the individual's willingness to pay per unit of risk reduction.[48] The US government evaluates risk-reducing policies using a *positive*

[45] See Chapter 1, note 32, and Section 1.A.2 (positing that the lifetime well-being comparison structure includes a lottery ranking). See Chapter 4, note 19, explaining what it means to mix lotteries.

[46] Imagine that lifetime well-being is measurable by $w(\cdot)$ and that the set of possible w values for any longevity l is bounded above at a value w_l but unbounded below. Downward Trade-offs holds true. However, if $w(h) > w_{l'}$, every history with lifespan l' is worse than h.

[47] I don't say that this history is "better" than h because it might be incomparable with h. If the ranking of histories is complete, "no worse" can be replaced with "better."

[48] See Chapter 6.

VSL; and the proposition that VSL is positive is endorsed by the academic literature on VSL.[49] A positive VSL means that the individual is willing to pay some positive sum of money for an increase in their expected lifespan.

But is an increase in lifespan invariably a benefit?[50] Within a particular policy-assessment context, the assumption that it is could well be justified on pragmatic grounds. This is an issue I'll turn to in Chapter 5. The question I wish to address here is more fundamental: is such an assumption demanded by the very structure of lifetime well-being?

At the level of possible worlds and the lifetime well-being comparison structure, the proposition that life-extension (an increase in lifespan) is invariably beneficial can be stated as follows.

Life Extension Always a Benefit:

Let h and h^+ be two histories of the same individual i which are as follows: (1) i has the same birth date in both histories; (2) i dies at a later date in h^+ than in h; and (3) at all times that i is alive in h, their attributes at that time are the same as their attributes at the same time in h^+.

If so, h^+ is better for lifetime well-being than h.

A bit less formally: extending a life by pushing back the date of death from t to t^+, and holding constant what happens up until t, always increases lifetime well-being.

Is *Life Extension Always a Benefit* a plausible principle? Note, to begin, that the principle of Downward Trade-offs, which I endorsed earlier, doesn't entail rejecting Life Extension Always a Benefit. Downward Trade-offs says that if we take a history h with a lifespan l, then for any longer lifespan l^*, there is at least one history h^* with lifespan l^* that is equally good as h. Downward Trade-offs *doesn't* imply that there must be one such equally-good-but-longer history h^* which is identical to h up to the point that the individual dies. See note 51 for

[49] On US government values for VSL, see sources cited Chapter 6, note 6. Although empirical studies of VSL do, occasionally, find negative values (see, e.g., Aldy and Viscusi [2007, pp. 249-50], mentioning one example), the best estimates of VSL reported by articles reviewing the empirical literature are invariably positive (see sources cited Chapter 6, note 5). Economic theory does recognize the possibility of rational suicide (see Hamermesh and Soss [1974]); but the theory literature on VSL generally places to one side the possibility of rational suicide and assumes a positive VSL (see sources cited Chapter 6, note 4).

[50] To be sure, an individual might end up with a positive VSL even if some ways of increasing their lifespan are harmful rather than beneficial. That is, the conclusion that reducing an individual's fatality risk increases their expected lifetime well-being (and thus that the individual has a positive VSL for that reduction) need not reflect the premise that every increase in lifespan is beneficial. But it might. The question I am asking here is whether such a premise is warranted by the structure of lifetime well-being.

an example of a ranking of histories that satisfies Downward Trade-offs but also satisfies Life Extension Always a Benefit.[51]

Still, as a substantive matter, Life Extension Always a Benefit is hard to endorse.[52] Indeed, it seems that life extension can sometimes be a cost—extension may reduce lifetime well-being—rather than invariably being a benefit.[53] Given the histories h and h^+ as described by the antecedent condition to Life Extension Always a Benefit, let the "extension period" be the period of time during which the individual i is alive in h^+ but no longer alive in h. On any plausible theory of lifetime well-being, it seems that i's temporal attributes during the extension period could be sufficiently bad that the longer life, h^+, is worse for lifetime well-being than the shorter life, h. Imagine that, during the extension period, individual i's experiential life is terribly bad. They experience horrible physical pain, unremitting feelings of unhappiness, a profound and constant sense of suffering, etc. On any plausible experientialist theory of welfare, these negative mental states can be sufficiently bad to make the extension a net negative contributor to i's lifetime well-being: h^+ is worse than h.

Suppose now that individual i's intense pain and profound suffering during the extension period incapacitates them from realizing whatever objective goods are posited by a given objective-good theory. That will mean, presumably, that the extension period adds nothing to i's lifetime well-being. If so, Life Extension Always a Benefit is falsified. Moreover, an objective-good theory that has no hedonic component, and that therefore insists that pain and suffering however intense do not reduce lifetime well-being, is difficult to believe. Thus, on any plausible objective-good theory, h^+ is worse than h.

[51] Assume that time is divided into discrete periods (moments); lifetime well-being is measurable, with the lifetime well-being of a history equaling the sum total of the momentary well-being during the periods the individual is alive. Momentary well-being values are drawn from a set $(0, K)$ or $(0, K]$, $K > 0$, or $(0, \infty)$, i.e., they can be a range of positive values, bounded below by 0 but never equaling 0. Then Life Extension Always a Benefit holds true: if a life is extended, with past momentary well-being held fixed, lifetime well-being must increase, since momentary well-being in the new periods must be positive. However, Downward Trade-offs is also satisfied: Any history h with lifespan l will have some positive lifetime well-being value w; for any longer lifespan l^* (meaning, here, the number of moments) a history h^* with momentary well-being in each period equaling w/l^* will be equally good as h.

[52] See Kagan (2012a, ch. 12); Sharp and Millum (2018, p. 117). Broome's supposition of a "neutral level for continuing to live"—"living an extra period at the neutral level is equally good as dying, for the person herself" (Broome 2004, p. 234)—is also inconsistent with Life Extension Always a Benefit. Frances Kamm argues that death is bad not merely insofar as it deprives a person of goods but also because of the "insult factor" ("death happens to a person who has already existed and undoes him") and the "extinction factor" ("death means that the possibility of anything significant for the person in the future is over"). See Kamm (1993, p. 54). But Kamm does not contend that, in light of these additional factors, life extension is always a benefit.

[53] Note that rejecting Life Extension Always a Benefit doesn't entail that life extension is sometimes a cost (a reduction in lifetime well-being). A "trivial" theory of lifetime well-being on which all life-histories are equally good rejects Life Extension Always a Benefit but also rejects that life extension is sometimes a cost. Still, such a theory is very implausible! The plausible arguments for rejecting Life Extension Always a Benefit do so by showing that life extension sometimes is a cost.

Finally individual i, in light of the experiential horrors of the extension period and its disabling effect on their ability to pursue a range of goods, could well have a global preference for h over h^+—and this preference could surely survive plausible idealization conditions for a global preference (being well-informed, formally rational, etc.). In short, on any plausible global-preference theory, h^+ could well be worse than h.

Rejecting the principle Life Extension Always a Benefit, and affirming instead that life extension can sometimes reduce lifetime well-being, implies that the decision to commit suicide *may* be rational and self-interested. There are choice situations in which an agent's choice to end their own life is a rational choice in light of the agent's well-being (self-interest). If life extension can sometime reduce lifetime well-being, the agent can rationally believe as much. Thus, there can be choice situations in which the agent rationally believes that remaining alive has a lower *expected* lifetime well-being than dying. In such (dire) situations, suicide is rational and self-interested.[54]

It hardly follows from the proposition that suicide *may* be rational and self-interested that government should encourage suicide! Many suicides are impulsive responses to immediate distress rather than being carefully premeditated.[55] An impulsive decision to end one's own life hardly indicates that remaining alive has a lower expected benefit than dying. And, of course, even a premediated suicide (e.g., by someone suffering mental illness) may well not be rational.

Nor does it follow from denying Life Extension Always a Benefit that policy analysts should eschew *modeling* life extension as invariably beneficial. Within the SWF framework, histories are perspicuously modeled as lifetime bundles, each bundle describing an individual's longevity l (the number of periods the individual is alive, up to some maximum possible lifespan T); their "period bundle" (a bundle of attributes such as income, health, happiness, etc.) for each period from 1 to l; and the attribute of Dead for each period from $l + 1$ until T. A policy, in turn, is conceptualized as an array of lotteries over lifetime bundles—one such lottery for each cohort of similarly situated individuals in the population.[56]

Life extension is modeled as invariably beneficial by the SWF framework in a given policy-choice situation if: for each cohort, in every lottery over lifetime bundles faced by that cohort, every lifetime bundle assigned a non-zero probability is such that all of its period bundles other than Dead have a higher period well-being value than Dead. When and why the analysis might be appropriately structured in this manner is discussed in Chapter 5.

[54] See Kagan (2012a, ch. 15). More precisely, a rational choice at time t between dying and continuing to live, in light of the individual's expected lifetime well-being, should factor in the "option value" of continuing to live (Burri 2021).

[55] See Rimkeviciene, O'Gorman, and De Leo (2015).

[56] See Chapters 4–5.

3.4.3 Is the Risk of Death Itself a Welfare Setback?

Claire Finkelstein has argued that the risk of harm is itself a harm. She endorses the "Risk Harm Thesis."

> The Risk Harm Thesis suggests that exposing someone to a risk of harm itself harms him. That is, exposure to risk entails a reduction of [someone's] welfare, regardless of whether the risk eventuates in outcome harm. This is obviously not to say that outcome harm is irrelevant to addressing the harmfulness of risk. Without the possibility of outcome harm there is no risk. But it does suggest that the harm a person suffers by being exposed to risk does not evaporate the moment it is clear no outcome harm will result.[57]

Finkelstein motivates the Risk Harm Thesis with various examples, such as this one:

> Suppose that unbeknownst to you, an airline on which you regularly fly is negligent in maintaining its planes. On one particular trip, one of two engines on the plane on which you are flying quits in midflight, a fact you only learn after you have disembarked. It seems plausible to suppose that flying under these conditions has harmed you, as compared with similarly situated passengers on a flight without engine failure. You have been harmed because you are worse off, from the standpoint of your baseline welfare, than passengers who fly in nondefective planes.[58]

By contrast, Stephen Perry denies that the risk of harm is itself a harm: "[R]isk, at least as that notion is ordinarily understood in moral and legal contexts, cannot plausibly be regarded as harm in itself."[59] John Oberdiek concurs with Finkelstein that the risk of harm can be a harm, although he offers a different account from hers; he sees risk as harmful in virtue of infringing an individual's autonomy.[60]

Finkelstein, Perry, and Oberdiek all see a close connection between harm and well-being, although none go so far as to equate "harm" with "setback to well-being." In any event, the issue of concern for lifetime welfarism—brought to the fore by the debate between Finkelstein, Perry, Oberdiek, and others in the risk-harm literature[61]—is the nexus between risk and lifetime well-being.

[57] Finkelstein (2003, p. 967).
[58] Finkelstein (2003, p. 970–71).
[59] Perry (2007, p. 196).
[60] Oberdiek (2017, p. 9).
[61] The risk-harm literature includes Adler (2003); Bowen (2022); Finkelstein (2003); Maheshwari (2021); Oberdiek (2017); Perry (1995, 2001, 2003, 2007, 2014); Placani (2017); Rowe (2021). The

Is the risk of death itself a setback to lifetime well-being? We need to be careful in framing this question. No doubt, risks of death have ethical significance *at the level of action*. If two actions, P and P^*, available to some decisionmaker are identical in all ethically relevant respects except for the fact that some individual's risk of premature death is higher with P, then surely this will normally be grounds for counting P^* to be the ethically better choice. P^* provides the individual more favorable prospects for lifetime well-being. This book aims (in Chapter 5) to offer a detailed account of the ethical significance of risks of death at the level of action. A theory of risk regulation will do exactly that.

The interesting possibility, suggested by the risk-harm literature, is that the risk of death might have ethical significance *at the level of worlds*, not merely at the level of action. Individuals' lifetime well-being levels in worlds (and differences in lifetime well-being between worlds) might depend, in part, on their risks of death in those worlds. To put this in terms of histories: the fact that individual i in world d faces a heightened risk of death (in some sense) might be one of the determinants of the lifetime well-being of history $(d; i)$—on top of the individual's actual lifespan in the history and standard (non-risk) determinants of well-being.

Risk will have ethical significance at the level of action even if it has no ethical significance at the level of worlds—even if being at risk is not an ingredient of the lifetime well-being of histories. But risk could have the latter role as well as the former. Does it? In what follows, I use "risk as a setback to lifetime well-being" and similar phrases to mean as an ingredient of the lifetime well-being of histories.

Conceptualizing the risk of death as a feature of a history requires some care. OHPs are not immortal; *every* history ends with the individual's death. What's at issue is not the risk of death but the risk of *premature* death (in some sense). For purposes here, this notion can be specified as follows. Event E in world d imposes a risk of premature death on individual i if there is some non-zero probability in d that E will cause i's death; the *magnitude* of that risk is the magnitude of this probability. Individual i's overall risk of premature death in history $(d; i)$ is a function of the risk-magnitudes of all the events that occur in d which impose a risk of premature death on i.

Let's leave aside the details of this intra-history risk aggregation. However it is specified, we can say this: (1) If event E in world d imposes a risk of premature death on i, and E does not occur in world d^*, then—ceteris paribus—i's risk of premature death is higher in history $(d; i)$ than in history $(d^*; i)$. (2) If E occurs in both worlds and has a higher probability in d of causing individual i's death,

position advanced in this section is most similar to Perry's, in arguing that risk in the frequentist sense is not an objective welfare setback; and to Placani's, in arguing that risk in the third-party epistemic sense may be a dignitary harm.

then—ceteris paribus—individual *i*'s risk of premature death is higher in history (*d*; *i*) than in history (*d**; *i*).

In the literature on risk harm, it is rightly stressed that "probability" has two, quite different meanings. Probability in the relative-frequency ("frequentist") sense is the proportion of items in a reference class. Probability in the epistemic or Bayesian sense is someone's degree of belief in a proposition.[62] Consider the probability that Felix will suffer a heart attack. To determine this probability in the frequentist sense, we identify some class of items (here, persons) that includes Felix. The probability of Felix suffering a heart attack, relative to that reference class, is just the percentage of those persons who suffer a heart attack.

There are many different reference classes that include Felix. For the sake of illustration, assume that Felix is a married 60-year-old male of French ancestry who eats meat, exercises regularly, and smokes. Then each of these reference classes includes Felix: all persons, all males, all married persons, all persons of French ancestry, all 60-year-old males who eat meat, all persons of French ancestry who are smokers, etc. For each such class of persons, there is a proportion that will suffer a heart attack; and this proportion is Felix's frequentist probability of suffering a heart attack, relative to the class. Because the proportions, in general, are not the same—the proportion of heart attacks among 60-year-old male meat-eating smokers is much higher than among persons who exercise regularly—frequentist risk must be relativized to reference classes.

The epistemic probability of Felix suffering a heart attack is just someone's degree of belief that he will do so. Epistemic probability is relativized to cognizers (different persons can have different degrees of belief in a given proposition). A given person's belief in a proposition may be based upon information about relative frequencies; but probability in the epistemic and frequentist senses are still, conceptually, quite distinct.

So there are now two quite different ways to specify the probability that an event *E* causes individual *i*'s death. First, there's the frequentist risk of *E* causing *i*'s death. This is relativized to a class of events; it is the proportion of events in that class that cause someone's death. Second, there's the epistemic risk of *E* causing *i*'s death. This is relativized to a cognizer: it is someone's degree of belief that *E* causes *i*'s death.

Although a theory of well-being *could* allow for frequentist risk to be a welfare setback, it seems clear that two of the major types of well-being

[62] The philosophical literature on probability has advanced a number of objective (non-epistemic) conceptions of risk in addition to the frequentist conception, such as propensities or objective chances. See Hájek (2023). The risk-harm literature has focused on frequentism rather than alternative objective views. I will not address, in this section, whether non-frequentist objective risks might be welfare setbacks even if (as I will argue) frequentist risks are not. It may well be that the best account of non-frequentist objective risk ends up being fairly close to frequentism (Hoefer 2007) and that the argument carries over. In any event, this is an issue that must be left for another day.

theories—experientialist and objective-good theories—will not do so. As for the first: The fact that Kayla is subject to a frequentist risk (as opposed to Kayla's beliefs about that risk, her fears regarding it, etc.) is not itself a component of her experiences.

As for the second: Stephen Perry's line of argumentation shows why a classic objective-good theory, despite allowing for non-experiential well-being goods, will not count risk in the frequentist sense to be a setback to well-being.

> [T]he extent and indeed the very existence of the risk that one person can be said to have imposed on another is relative to the reference class with respect to which the relative frequency of harm is stated, and there is no unique or canonically correct way to specify the appropriate reference class. The only plausible candidate for such canonical status would be the narrowest causally relevant reference class that would in principle be specifiable in a world of perfect knowledge, and, at least in a deterministic universe, the relative frequency of harm within that class will always be 100 per cent or 0 per cent; either way, there is no basis for saying that risk is a form of harm in itself.[63]

Choosing a reference class for event *E* other than the maximally specified class (one that includes all the causally relevant features of *E*) seems arbitrary. Why would an objective-good theory do that? If causal laws are deterministic, the frequentist risk of *E* causing *i*'s death, relative to the maximally specified class, is non-zero only if this risk is 1; the putative setback to well-being from frequentist risk is nothing other than the setback from death itself. If causal laws are indeterministic, this risk might be between 0 and 1; but why a frequentist risk relative to the maximally specified class would itself be a reduction in objective goods is hard to see. Indeed, none of the exemplary objective-good theories presented earlier would hold that risk in this sense is a welfare setback.[64]

By contrast, on a preference theory, frequentist risk will be a welfare setback to the extent that individuals disprefer it and the preference is not screened out by idealizing conditions. Such preference, although *possible*, seems quite idiosyncratic. What's at issue is whether an individual disprefers the frequentist risk of death as such, apart from other differences between histories. Imagine that Abby's birth date, death date, and all non-risk features of her life are the same in two histories. In the first history, her frequentist risk of death (aggregating over all events, and with some specification of reference classes) is higher. Why would that difference, alone, motivate her to disprefer the first history?

[63] Perry (2007, pp. 196–97).
[64] See Section 1.2.1.

In short, only the combination of a preference theory and quite idiosyncratic preferences will make frequentist risk a welfare setback. This is a possibility that can safely be ignored at the level of the SWF framework, our decision-procedure. One relatively "low-cost" way to enhance the tractability of that framework is to ignore highly atypical sources of well-being.

What about the risk of death in the epistemic sense? Intuitively, there are at least two different plausible ways in which epistemic risk might figure into lifetime well-being.

(a) First-party epistemic risk and fear. Event *E* occurs in world *d*. Individual *i* in this world believes, to some degree, that *E* will cause their death. This belief is a component of a fear state: individual *i*'s beliefs produce unpleasant feelings. Plausibly, *i*'s probabilistic belief itself has welfare significance: that is, it is worse for them to have the experiential package of belief plus bad feeling, as opposed to bad feeling with no grounding belief.

(b) Third-party epistemic risk and dignity. Event *E* is an action of some third party, the "risk-imposer," which they undertake with a probabilistic belief that *E* will cause *i*'s death. If this belief is coupled with certain other beliefs, desires, or intentions on the part of the risk-imposer, then—intuitively—their action is a dignitary harm to individual *i*. (Consider the case in which the risk-imposer feels contempt for the victim and plays Russian Roulette with the victim behind the victim's back.)

First-party epistemic risk as part of an experiential package of this belief state plus fear or other bad feelings could be counted as a welfare setback by an experientialist theory; an objective-good theory; and a preference theory to the extent that individuals disprefer this experiential package. Third-party epistemic risk as a component of a dignitary harm could be counted as a welfare setback by an objective-good theory, or a preference theory to the extent that individuals disprefer *that*. Neither a preference not to be afraid nor a preference not to be disrespected seems idiosyncratic.

In short, risk is a plausible setback to lifetime well-being at the level of worlds in two ways, both involving epistemic risk: as part of a fear state and as part of a dignitary harm. Being afraid and suffering dignitary harms are features of a life that can make it go worse. Further, a nuanced application of the SWF framework could be structured to take account of these setbacks to lifetime well-being. It would do so by including the relevant beliefs (first-party or third-party) as one of the possible types of attributes in each person's bundle of attributes. There is nothing mysterious here: beliefs can be modeled as attributes for purposes of policy analysis, no less so than income, health, happiness, leisure, and other more conventional modeled attributes.

3.4.4 Posthumous Events

Consider two histories of one individual that have the same birth and death dates and that are identical during the time the individual is alive. However, the histories differ with respect to occurrences after the individual dies. Might the histories have different levels of lifetime well-being?

In academic disciplines other than philosophy that engage with the concept of well-being—such as economics, law, and psychology—a "yes" answer to this question would generally be seen as ludicrous. However, numerous philosophers have endorsed the possibility of posthumous harm.[65] Work in this area tends to be trained on posthumous harm rather than benefit, but there certainly are philosophers who have explicitly attended to posthumous benefit and argued that this, too, is possible. The specifics of "harm" and "benefit" are contested, but these concepts—however precisely construed—involve some significant link to well-being. So an argument for posthumous harm or benefit would tend to show that two histories identical except for posthumous occurrences *can* differ in lifetime well-being.

Joel Feinberg offers an example well constructed to elicit intuitions in favor of posthumous harm, involving a person whose achievement of life-goals is frustrated by posthumous events. He describes a "Case A" and "Case B," as follows:

> Case A: A woman devotes thirty years of her life to the furtherance of certain ideals and ambitions in the form of one vast undertaking. She founds an institution dedicated to these ends and works single-mindedly for its advancement. ... One month before she dies, the "empire of her hopes" collapses utterly as the establishment into which she has poured her life's energies crumbles into ruin, and she is personally disgraced. She never learns the unhappy truth, however, as her friends, eager to save her from disappointment, conceal or misrepresent the facts. She dies contented.
>
> Case B: The facts are the same as in Case A, except that the institution in which the woman had so great an interest remains healthy, growing and flourishing, until her death. But it begins to founder a month later, and within a year, it collapses utterly, while at the same time, the woman and her life's work are totally discredited.[66]

[65] The list of "works cited" in David Boonin's recent book on posthumous harm comprises a comprehensive list of references to the literature on posthumous harm. See Boonin (2019). See Keller (2014) for a review chapter.

[66] Feinberg (1993, pp. 181–82).

Feinberg then observes: "It would not be very controversial to say that the woman in Case A had suffered grievous harm to her interests although she never learned the bad news. Those very same interests are harmed in Case B to exactly the same extent."[67]

The examples are easily reframed in terms of lifetime well-being. In Case A, imagine two histories. In one history, the institution flourishes; in another, it collapses (unbeknownst to the founder) one month *before* her death. In Case B, we again have two histories, now identical during the founder's lifetime; in one, the institution flourishes, in the second it collapses one month *after* her death. Why allow that the two Case A histories differ for the founder's lifetime well-being but insist that the two Case B histories cannot?

To be sure, experientialists about well-being will deny that posthumous occurrences can affect lifetime well-being; whatever the occurrences might be, they aren't changes in the subject's experiences. The interesting question is why well-being theories that reject the experientialist restriction[68] and that therefore *can* allow that the two Case A histories differ for lifetime well-being should conclude that the two Case B histories don't.

Recall the timing problem raised by Epicurus: At what time does the event of death harm the deceased? Scholarship about posthumous harm engages a very similar question: At what time do posthumous events harm the deceased? However, I don't think that the timing puzzle jeopardizes the view that posthumous events can be an ingredient in lifetime well-being, any more than it jeopardizes the view that premature death can be. Let d and d^+ be two worlds that are identical except for occurrences after *i*'s death. If a non-experientialist well-being theory posits that d is better for *i*'s lifetime well-being, it can answer the timing question as follows. World d is better for individual i than world d^+—individual i has that relational property; they stand in that relation to the two worlds—at all times during their life in d, and at all times during their life in d^+.

Consider, then, the two main types of well-being theories that reject the experientialist restriction: objective-good theories and preferentialist theories. The goods posited by objective-good theorists are generally *not* such as to be affected by posthumous occurrences. The clear exception is the good of achievement. Feinberg's Case B shows clearly how posthumous events can undermine what an individual achieves with their life and can thereby affect their lifetime well-being (insofar as lifetime well-being depends in part on achievement). Simon Keller makes achievement (fulling goals) the centerpiece of his account of posthumous harm.[69]

[67] Feinberg (1993, p. 182).
[68] See Section 1.2.1.
[69] See Keller (2014).

Preferentialists can also allow for posthumous occurrences to affect lifetime well-being, insofar as individuals have preferences regarding such occurrences. A general problem for preferentialist views, which I've elsewhere discussed at some length, is that preferences are welfare-relevant only if appropriately restricted.[70] Derek Parfit's famous "stranger" example illustrates the need for a restriction.[71] Imagine that I meet a stranger on a train, learn that she has some disease, and develop a preference that the disease be cured. She is then cured, unbeknownst to me; thus, my preference is satisfied; but surely (without more) that event doesn't make me better off.

How a preferentialist theory should specify the restriction is a difficult and, I believe, still unresolved question in the philosophy of well-being. But it doesn't seem plausible that the best account will screen out all preferences concerning posthumous events. Indeed, this can be seen by tweaking Feinberg's examples. The founder, let's imagine, strongly prefers that her institution flourish (a) during her life and (b) after her death. This is a preference about what actually happens to the institution, not about her beliefs and feelings regarding the institution—but unless the best account requires restricted preferences to be about experiences (and *that* seems wrong[72]) the preference is welfare-relevant. So, in Case A, the history in which the institution collapses a month before the founder's death is worse in terms of her welfare-relevant preferences. Why insist, then, that in Case B the history in which the institution collapses a month after the founder's death is *not* worse in terms of her welfare-relevant preferences?

In sum, the relation between death and well-being may include an element generally ignored by non-philosophers, namely, posthumous occurrences. Theories of well-being, if they deny that well-being is solely a product of an individual's experiences—if they reject the experientialist restriction—*can* plausibly suppose that posthumous occurrences may be one ingredient of lifetime well-being. A full account of death and well-being should recognize this.

However, it should also now be noted that the nexus between posthumous events and lifetime well-being may well have little significance for the modeling of fatality-risk-regulation policies (the concern of this book). Leaving aside individuals' preferences for the flourishing of family members (as evidenced by the purchase of life insurance policies and the drafting of wills to bequeath assets to relatives), it seems fairly unusual for individuals to have welfare-relevant preferences with posthumous scope or to pursue goals the accomplishment of which depends substantially on posthumous events. Further, risk regulation policies are aimed at conditions in the world (toxins, dangerous workplaces,

[70] Adler (2012, ch. 3).
[71] Parfit (1987, p. 494).
[72] See Adler (2013, pp. 1570–80).

etc.) that reduce lifetime well-being by *shortening lives*, not by frustrating the posthumous realization of individuals' goals and preferences.

Thus, specifying the SWF framework for the case of risk-regulation policies by limiting an individual's welfare-relevant attributes to their attributes during their lifetime—such as their income, health, happiness, or leisure, all standard attributes in economic models—and ignoring the effect of posthumous occurrences on well-being is a reasonable choice.[73] The view outside philosophy that well-being can't be affected posthumously is a reasonable one at the level of the SWF decision-procedure (for purposes of evaluating risk-regulation policies), even if rejected (by those holding non-experientialist theories of well-being) at the level of worlds.

[73] The modeling setup in Chapter 4 ignores posthumous occurrences. An individual's lifetime well-being is determined by their period attributes during periods they are alive.

4
Measuring Lifetime Well-Being

This chapter discusses the measurement of lifetime well-being. Recall that the SWF framework includes a well-being measure $w(\cdot)$, which converts each outcome into a list ("vector") of lifetime well-being numbers, one for each person in the population. The SWF proper is a rule for ranking these vectors (for example, the utilitarian SWF or a prioritarian SWF); and the SWF framework also includes an uncertainty module for the SWF, which ranks policies understood as probability distributions across vectors. This chapter covers the construction of the well-being measure $w(\cdot)$.

Recall, too, that each outcome is a simplified model of a possible world. An outcome is characterized with respect to *some* of the features of a world that are relevant to individuals' well-being. In particular, in a given outcome x, each individual i is assigned a bundle of attributes, $b_i(x)$. The types of attributes in a bundle are *some* of the individual attributes (properties) that constitute or causally contribute to well-being. The attribute bundles are *lifetime* bundles; they describe the individual's attributes over their entire lifetime. For example, if income is included as an attribute, a bundle will specify individual i's income for each period that they are alive. If health is included as an attribute, the bundle will describe their health in each period.

Thus, a given outcome x corresponds to a list of lifetime bundles: one for each person in the population. The list of bundles associated with x is $(b_1(x), \ldots, b_i(x), \ldots, b_N(x))$. Our well-being measure $w(\cdot)$ maps bundles onto lifetime well-being numbers. Bundle b is assigned the number $w(b)$. Outcomes are converted into well-being vectors via the mapping from bundles to lifetime well-being numbers. An individual's lifetime well-being number in the vector associated with a given outcome is just the lifetime well-being number assigned to their bundle in that outcome by $w(\cdot)$. Formally: $\mathrm{w}_i(x) = w(b_i(x))$.

Death shows up in this modeling framework as a source of variation in individuals' lifespan. One of the attributes in a bundle is a lifespan (longevity) attribute. If Jim is born at the same time in two outcomes but dies earlier in one of the two, his bundle in that outcome will have a shorter lifespan attribute than his bundle in the other.

Section 4.1 discusses the content of attribute bundles. Section 4.2 provides a fully generic methodology for the construction of the well-being measure $w(\cdot)$. This methodology is agnostic as between different accounts of well-being; nor

Risk, Death, and Well-Being. Matthew D. Adler, Oxford University Press. © Oxford University Press 2025.
DOI: 10.1093/9780197505984.003.0004

does it make any assumption regarding temporal additivity. Section 4.3 discusses the specific form that well-being measurement takes in the case of a preference-based well-being measure. Here, there arises a link between $w(\cdot)$ and the *utility* functions representing individual preferences.

A common assumption in both economics and public health scholarship is that lifetime well-being is temporally additive. That is, $w(b) = \sum_{t=1}^{T} w^p(b^t)$, with b^t attributes in period t, and $w^p(.)$ a period well-being function; or this formula with a discount factor attached. Temporal additivity has important advantages in terms of tractability but also may have downsides. Section 4.4 addresses temporal additivity, both in general and in the case of a preference-based well-being measure.

The lifetime well-being measure $w(\cdot)$, as constructed in Sections 4.2 through 4.4, is an *interval-scale* measure of lifetime well-being. Well-being numbers as assigned by $w(\cdot)$ contain information about levels and differences of lifetime well-being, but its zero point is not meaningful. For some purposes, however, it is important to measure lifetime well-being on a ratio scale rather than an interval scale. The reason that this might matter is covered in Section 4.5, as is the well-being information that might be embodied in the zero point.

Sections 4.2 through 4.4 contain a substantial amount of mathematical formalism. This material is inherently fairly technical and is difficult to present informally. The sections present and analyze the axioms sufficient to derive an interval-scale measure $w(\cdot)$ of lifetime well-being: in general (4.2), in the specific case of a preference-based well-being account (4.3), and if that measure takes the additive form (4.4). Readers who wish to skip these sections can do so. They *are* an important intellectual component of the book—in demonstrating that an interval-scale $w(\cdot)$ exists and in describing how it is constructed—but the material in other chapters can be fully comprehended without a detailed engagement with these sections.

4.1 Attribute Bundles

4.1.1 Background

The enterprise of modeling and measuring an individual's well-being as a function of their attributes is hardly new, nor is it limited to scholarship in the SWF tradition. That enterprise is long-standing and widespread in economics and public health. Much work in economics sees an individual's *utility* (a measure of preference-satisfaction) as based upon some or all of the following attributes: the individual's material resources, meaning specifically their income, consumption (expenditure on goods or services), or their wealth; the individual's leisure; and/or the nature and level of certain public goods that the individual accesses, e.g., environmental quality in the location where they reside. Although economists often simplify matters by using one-period models, there is certainly plenty of scholarship that adopts a multiperiod framework. An individual's life is divided into multiple periods, e.g., years; this allows the analyst to consider both heterogeneity in individuals' longevity and intertemporal change in attributes within the life of any one individual.[1]

Health economists and other scholars of public health often employ the "QALY" (quality-adjusted life year) format for quantifying an individual's lifetime health-and-longevity attainment.[2] An individual's health for each year that they are alive is measured on a 0–1 scale, with 1 the number for perfect health (no impairments) and 0 for a health state equivalent to being dead. Their lifetime health-and-longevity number is the sum of these health quality numbers.

The QALY literature ignores an individual's material resources (income/consumption/wealth) in calculating lifetime numbers. However, some work in health economics takes account of longevity, health, *and* material resources. An individual's lifetime well-being is seen as a function of their longevity, their health state each period that they are alive, and their income/consumption/wealth each period that they are alive.[3]

A revisionary school within economics trains its attention on individual happiness or, more generally, "subjective well-being" (SWB).[4] SWB surveys are a mainstay of this literature; an SWB survey asks the respondent to quantify their happiness, life-satisfaction, hedonic states, or some other aspect of their experiential life. The implicit or explicit normative premise of this literature is experientialist: an individual's well-being is determined by their mental states. (See Section 1.2.1, defining experientialist theories of well-being in terms of an "experientialist restriction.")

An SWB scholar interested in modeling an individual's well-being might do so with traditional economic attributes (income/consumption/wealth, leisure, health, public goods) on the assumption that these correlate with experiential attributes such as happiness or life-satisfaction. However, a general empirical finding in the SWB literature is that the correlation between the traditional attributes and SWB may be weak; for example, work on the so-called Easterlin paradox shows that increased income above a poverty threshold may produce

[1] See Adler (2012, pp. 241–45), for citations to scholarship illustrating the various approaches to modeling utility described in this paragraph.
[2] See Pinto-Prades, Herrero, and Abellán (2016).
[3] See, e.g., Cookson et al. (2021); Cookson, Norheim, and Skarda (2022).
[4] See Graham (2016) for a review.

little increase in happiness.[5] An alternative approach, therefore, is to characterize individuals with respect to experiential states. A lifetime bundle might describe an individual's happiness, feelings of life-satisfaction, degree of pain or pleasure, etc., rather than their material resources, leisure, health, and/or access to public goods. A second alternative is to include both non-experiential and experiential attributes in a bundle. This latter modeling choice might appeal to well-being accounts that don't satisfy the experientialist restriction—the accounts are non-experientialist—but that include experiential states as one component of well-being.

Yet another corpus of scholarly work that attends to the modeling of well-being, as an input to policy assessment, is the literature on "capabilities." This literature grew out of writings by Amartya Sen from the 1980s and is now large and multifaceted, with theoretical, formal, and empirical components.[6] Capabilities theorists are skeptical of resource-based indicators of individual attainment. They emphasize that what matters for well-being are not resources but "functionings," that is, more specific states of the person—such as being nourished, having shelter, or having a certain quantum of skills or knowledge. Resources are converted into functionings at variable individual rates. (Capabilities, in turn, are opportunities to achieve functionings.) Capabilities theorists are also skeptical of the hedonic tradition in philosophizing about well-being and of SWB work. The empirical work in this literature tends to characterize individuals in terms of some list of functionings rather than resources or SWB.

4.1.2 Constructing Attribute Bundles for the SWF Framework

What follows draws upon and synthesizes the various modeling and measurement literatures that have just been mentioned and adapts them to the needs of the SWF framework.

I will use the symbol "b" to denote a lifetime bundle of attributes. The well-being metric $w(\cdot)$ operates upon b bundles. It maps each such bundle onto a number, quantifying the lifetime well-being of an individual with that bundle.

In the specific case of a preference-based theory of well-being, the modeler will distinguish between an individual's non-preference attributes and their preferences (preferences being a kind of attribute). See Section 4.3. For now, however, no such distinction need be made; b includes all of the attributes

[5] See Graham (2016, pp. 428–31); and see Killingsworth, Kahneman, and Mellers (2023) for an important recent contribution.

[6] See Robeyns (2017).

modeled as relevant to well-being. This will include, at least, various non-preference attributes; and in addition, in the case of a preference theory of well-being, it will include information about preferences.

It's standard in the measurement of lifetime well-being to divide an individual's life into *periods*, and I will do so as well.[7] A "period" might be a decade, a year, a month, a day, an hour, etc. How should we determine period length? This depends upon how intertemporal variation in attributes is modeled, which in turn depends upon tractability and data availability. The period length is the *longest interval of time during which all attributes are modeled as constant*. To be concrete, assume that we have good data regarding individuals' monthly incomes but not about their monthly health states—only about their health states on an annual basis. We are inclined to calculate lifetime well-being as a function of longevity, income, and health, and to take account of month-by-month income variation in undertaking this calculation. If so, the period length should be one month. A period length of one day is unnecessarily short; since each individual will be assigned an income amount for each month and a health state for each year, dividing each month into days adds complexity with no gain in accuracy. A period length of more than one month, e.g., one year, is too long. We wish to allow that, for example, Jada's income in January of a given year is different from her income in February. If the period length is a whole year, we can't register this variation.

Different modeled attributes may vary on different time scales. In the example now under discussion, income varies on a monthly scale while health varies on an annual scale. So a month is the longest interval over which the more variable attribute (income) remains constant. Health also remains constant over that interval and indeed over a yet longer interval, namely, a whole year. But the month-by-month periodization does no violence to the measurement of health. If we divide a year into twelve months, we can assign the individual a monthly income and still allow for the variation in health that the data permit us to recognize. An individual's health in each month of a given year is just their health in that year.

The temporal structure of bundles includes not merely a period length but also a maximum longevity T. This is the maximum number of periods that we consider to be possible. There will be some bundle b^* such that the individual

[7] The framework that I set out here is a discrete-time framework: there are a countable (indeed, finite) number of periods in each bundle. Economists also employ continuous-time models. Adapted to the bundle framework, that would mean a real-valued $l > 0$ and a quality of life variable, $q(t)$, for all times $0 \leq t \leq l$, with $q(t)$ a function of attributes at t and, perhaps, preferences. The well-being value of a bundle is the integral of $q(t)$ from 0 to l.

Extant scholarship on the SVRR concept (see Chapter 5, note 21)—scholarship that is part of the foundation for Chapter 5—employs a discrete-time setup. Moreover, many readers will likely find integrals more difficult to comprehend and manipulate than summations. For these reasons, this chapter and Chapter 5 work within discrete rather than continuous time. Translating this chapter and Chapter 5 into a continuous-time setup is a topic for future research.

lives for T periods and no bundle b such that the individual lives for more than T periods. If the period length is one year, then T might be, for example, 100 years.

Every b bundle is divided into T periods: $1, 2, \ldots, T$. Period 1 is the first period of the individual's life; the individual is modeled as being born at the beginning of that period.

For each period, the lifetime bundle specifies, first, whether the individual is alive or dead during the period; and second, if alive, what their bundle of attributes is during that period (their "period bundle"). I'll use the symbol b^t to denote this period bundle. Stretching the term "attributes" a bit, an individual's "attributes" in a period when dead is just the status Dead, and in a period when alive is some bundle of attributes that might be possessed by a living person. That is, if the individual is dead in period t, then b^t is just the status of Dead. If the individual is alive in period t, then b^t denotes their living-person attributes (some cluster of the types of attributes that might be held by a living person) during that period.

The "longevity" of an individual with a given bundle is just the number of periods during which they are alive rather than being Dead. For a given bundle b, let l denote the longevity of that bundle.

It bears emphasis that longevity l is a *variable* whose value depends upon the bundle. A given individual can live different lifespans; fatality risk regulation changes the probabilities of these possible lifespans. A core feature of the modeling apparatus now being described—the lifetime bundle concept—is that this apparatus can represent variation in an individual's lifespan. It does so via the "l" variable, which can take different values in different bundles. In what follows, the reader should be careful to keep in mind that "l" means longevity (the number of periods that the individual is alive) in the particular bundle b under discussion.

Summing up: A given lifetime bundle b consists of a series of period bundles of living-person attributes from period 1 through period l, the individual's longevity in that bundle, and the status of Dead for every period from $l + 1$ through T. That is, a given bundle b has the structure: $(b^1, b^2, \ldots, b^l, b^{l+1} = \text{Dead}, b^{l+2} = \text{Dead}, \ldots, b^T = \text{Dead})$.

Here's a concrete example that may make the abstract notation a bit easier to grasp. Assume that the period length is annual and that the maximum number of periods T is 100 years. Assume also that an individual's period attributes include their consumption and their health. In a particular bundle b, the individual lives for 50 years. That is, $l = 50$. So b^1 (their period attributes in year 1) tells us the individual's consumption and health during their first year of life, b^2 the individual's consumption and health during their second year of life, . . . , b^{49} their consumption and health during their 49th year of life, and $b^l = b^{50}$ their consumption and health during their last, 50th year of life. $b^{l+1} = b^{51} = \text{Dead}$, $b^{52} = \text{Dead}, \ldots, b^T = b^{100} = \text{Dead}$.

Recall that lifetime welfarism posits that the "age of integration" is zero.[8] Every event during the individual's life, from birth, is incorporated into their lifetime well-being. A non-zero age of integration has some plausibility, but this takes us beyond lifetime welfarism, since it requires modification of the fundamental axioms of Lifetime Pareto Indifference, Lifetime Anonymity, and Lifetime Strong Pareto.

This chapter assumes a zero age of integration. But, it should be noted, the modeling setup presented here for measuring lifetime well-being is readily modified for a non-zero such age. In that case, the individual's attribute bundle describes their life *after* the age of integration. The first period starts not with birth but with the age of integration. Lifetime well-being measures are constructed exactly the same way as presented below, but operate upon bundles that begin with the age of integration rather than birth.

What types of individual characteristics can be included in a period bundle? The format just proposed is very flexible in this regard. First, by "attribute" I mean any property of an individual, including both non-relational ("monadic") properties and relational properties. An individual's health, income, or happiness is a monadic property; this is a feature of them alone, not of them in relation to others. An individual's relative income—where their income sits in the population distribution of incomes—is relational. b^t might include monadic attributes, relational attributes, or both.[9]

Second, attributes might be constitutive of well-being (a component of well-being, according to the theory of well-being being implemented), or instrumental to well-being. Consider the income attribute, used pervasively in traditional economic modeling. An individual's income is not itself constitutive of well-being. Rather, income is useful in producing a range of welfare goods.

Actually, economics recognizes that income's welfare value is instrumental, not intrinsic. Standard economic theory regarding income and utility is that particular marketed goods and services ("commodities") are the intrinsic sources of preference satisfaction. Individuals are supposed to have a "direct" utility function with commodities as inputs and an "indirect" utility function depending on income and prices; income's "indirect" utility is a measure of its instrumental value in enabling an individual to purchase commodities.[10]

To be sure, the view of commodities as intrinsically preferred is itself problematic. Someone *may* intrinsically prefer a commodity (I've just got to have a 1957 Chevy) or instead might do so instrumentally (I want this car because it's

[8] See Section 2.5.
[9] Relational attributes are one way to capture the third-party impacts of an individual death. See Section 5.5.1.
[10] See Mas-Colell, Whinston, and Green (1995, ch. 3).

a safe and reliable source of transportation, which I care about because having *that* helps me to satisfy my intrinsic preferences). If indeed I want higher income because it enables me to purchase more commodities, which in turn I value only instrumentally, then income's role in my preference-satisfaction is doubly instrumental. In any event, economists' use of income as an argument in individual utility functions illustrates that some or all of the inputs to a well-being metric (in our setup, some or all of the period attributes in a period bundle b^t) may have instrumental rather than intrinsic value for well-being.

Third, as already mentioned, information about an individual's preferences *may* be included in their lifetime bundle *b*. If so, period bundles will tell us not only about (some of) their non-preference characteristics but also about their preferences.

To sum up: Period bundles may include monadic attributes, relational attributes, or both; attributes that are constitutive of well-being (on the theory of well-being at hand), attributes that are instrumentally useful in producing well-being, or both; and information about individual preferences in addition to non-preference attributes.

This is all to underscore the flexibility of the format—but it doesn't tell us *which* types of attributes to include in the period bundles. Existing modelling practices are a starting point. We could use traditional economic attributes (income/consumption/wealth, leisure, health, public goods), or the experiential attributes that figure importantly in the SWB literature (happiness, life-satisfaction, hedonic states), or specific functionings or capabilities—or some mixture of the above. But how to choose among these? And are there approaches worth entertaining that diverge from all of the above?

The choice of attributes depends both upon the well-being theory at hand and pragmatic factors (tractability and data availability). Ignore pragmatic factors for the moment. Then the selection of period attributes is, conceptually, straightforward. If the theory is experientialist, a period bundle describes all the types of mental states that the theory counts as intrinsically good for well-being. If we're working with an objective-good theory of well-being, then the period bundle describes every characteristic that partly or wholly instantiates one or more goods on the theory's list of such goods. If the theory is a preferentialist one, then the period bundle describes any type of attribute (monadic or relational) that anyone in the population intrinsically prefers, as well as the individual's preferences. For short, call this specification of attribute bundles as per the theory of well-being at hand, leaving aside pragmatic factors, the "theoretical benchmark."

With pragmatic factors in play, the bundle components may be different—perhaps *very* different—than as per the theoretical benchmark. A full account of how pragmatic factors influence attribute selection is well beyond the scope of this book. In bare outline, they do so as follows. Tractability pushes in three directions. (1) To reduce the number of types of attributes. If there are *M* types of attributes, then each period bundle is an *M*-dimensional bundle. An individual's level on each of the *M* dimensions needs to be specified. Describing a given lifetime bundle, and the set of possible bundles, becomes a more onerous task as *M* increases. (2) To represent attribute levels numerically. Consider the health attribute. An individual's health might be described qualitatively, as a particular health state (emphysema, angina, tinnitus, etc.), or by means of a number. Clearly the latter is more tractable, and indeed this is (in part) why the QALY literature represents an individual's health condition during a year as a health quality number on a zero-one scale. (3) To use a single instrumentally valuable attribute as a stand-in for a plurality of intrinsically valuable attributes. If attribute type *A* is instrumentally valuable as a means to *M* different types of intrinsically valuable attributes, then using *A* as a stand-in for all of the latter cuts down the number of dimensions needed to represent these attributes from *M* to 1.

Tractability needs to be balanced against accuracy. Departing from the theoretical benchmark means that the set of possible bundles isn't a fully accurate representation of the way in which individuals' histories might truly vary with respect to well-being (as per the theory on hand). This departure is "costly" to the extent that policy analysis with bundles that depart from the theoretical benchmark leads to recommendations that are different from those that would be given with fully accurate bundles. If two bundle descriptions both depart from the theoretical benchmark, with equal "costs" in accuracy, and one description is more tractable, then that description should be preferred to the other. As of yet, no formal methodology exists for balancing the accuracy "cost" of a departure from the theoretical benchmark against the tractability "benefit." (The SWF framework itself can't be used to perform that balancing; that framework can be set in motion only *after* the balancing has occurred and period attributes have been chosen.) The balancing is, unfortunately, somewhat qualitative and unstructured.

Pragmatic factors include not merely tractability but also data availability. The better our information about how a particular characteristic varies among individuals and how it is affected by policy interventions, the more accurate our mapping from policies onto probability-distributions-across-outcomes will be. For example, data about annual income is much more fully collected by government than data about specific functionings. This makes it easier not merely to estimate the status quo distribution of income (as opposed to the status quo distribution of bundles of functionings) but also to calibrate models that predict the causal impact of some type of policy on an individual's income (as compared to models that predict the causal impact of that type of policy on an individual's functionings).

4.2 Constructing a Measure of Lifetime Well-Being: A General Methodology

I here present a very general account of measuring lifetime well-being—one that is fully generic with respect to different views of well-being (experientialist, preferentialist, objective-good, etc.) and also makes no assumption about temporal additivity.[11] The account will rely upon two literatures within measurement theory: scholarship regarding the measurement of orderings of *differences*, as specifically set forth by David Krantz, R. Duncan Luce, Patrick Suppes, and Amos Tversky in their pathbreaking text, *Foundations of Measurement*;[12] and scholarship regarding the measurement of orderings of *lotteries*, as pioneered by John von Neumann and Oskar Morgenstern.[13] I'll refer to the difference-measurement theory that I rely upon as "KLST theory"; and the lottery-measurement theory as "vNM theory."

These measurement frameworks, especially vNM theory, are often applied to preferences, yielding *utility* functions representing the preferences; but the theories are much more general. For *any* ordering that meets the axioms set forth by the theory, there is a measure representing the ordering. In this section, we'll be using KLST theory to construct a measure of the well-being ordering of attribute bundles and bundle differences, as per any given account of well-being; we'll be using vNM theory to construct a measure of the well-being ordering of bundle lotteries, as per that account; and then we'll bring this all together, using the Bernoulli axiom, to specify our well-being measure $w(\cdot)$.[14]

4.2.1 KLST Theory and the Measurement of Well-Being Differences

Recall (Chapter 1) that I posited a formal structure for any account of lifetime well-being: a ranking of histories and history differences, denoted as "$\succcurlyeq^L$" and "$\succcurlyeq^D$". This lifetime well-being comparison structure, which operates at the level of *histories* (each history a pairing of a possible world and an individual) is modeled by the SWF framework via rankings at the level of *bundles*. A given bundle

[11] The account here builds upon Adler (2016b; 2019b, ch. 2 and appendix).

[12] Krantz, Luce, Suppes, and Tversky (2007, ch. 4). An important contribution to difference-measurement theory that advances upon Krantz, Luce, Suppes, and Tversky (2007) and synthesizes existing results is Köbberling (2006). References to other work in this literature can be found in Köbberling (2006) and in Adler (2016b, p. 509).

[13] von Neumann and Morgenstern (1944). For presentations of the theory of utility measurement that has developed from von Neumann and Morgenstern's insights ("vNM utility theory"), see, e.g., Kreps (1988; 2013, chs. 1–2, 5–6); Gilboa (2009); Mas-Colell, Whinston, and Green (1995, ch. 6).

[14] The account presented here is similar to that of Broome in *Weighing Lives* (2004, ch. 5), in using the Bernoulli axiom to measure lifetime well-being. But there is a major difference between our views. I provide two different routes to constructing the well-being measure $w(\cdot)$: one, the KLST route, which does not employ expected-utility theory or Bernoulli; and a second, the vNM route,

b is a simplified representation of a history; and the rankings $\succcurlyeq^L$ and $\succcurlyeq^D$ have counterpart rankings with respect to bundles. So as to avoid multiplying symbolism, I'll now use "$\succcurlyeq^L$" and "$\succcurlyeq^D$" to denote the bundle rankings. I'll show how KLST theory yields a measure $\theta(\cdot)$ representing $\succcurlyeq^L$ and $\succcurlyeq^D$.

Let **B** be the set of bundles, and **B**×**B** the set of pairs of bundles. $\succcurlyeq^L$ is a complete quasiordering of **B**, and $\succcurlyeq^D$ a complete quasiordering of **B**×**B**. Although the history-level rankings need not be complete, an incomplete ranking is not representable by a well-being measure.[15] I therefore impose completeness on $\succcurlyeq^L$ and $\succcurlyeq^D$ in the service of constructing such a measure, which is in turn critical to the SWF framework. Think of completeness as one of the simplifying premises that this framework adopts so as to operate as a tractable decision-procedure.

I'll denote how $\succcurlyeq^L$ ranks bundles and $\succcurlyeq^D$ bundle pairs as follows. "$b \succcurlyeq^L b^*$" indicates that $\succcurlyeq^L$ ranks b at least as good as b^*. According to the theory of well-being at hand, b is at least as good for lifetime well-being as b^*. "$(b^+, b^{++}) \succcurlyeq^D (b', b'')$" indicates that $\succcurlyeq^D$ ranks the first pair at least as large as the second pair.

which does. On my account, Bernoulli is a very useful but contingent feature of well-being measurement; even if Bernoulli is rejected, one can still construct $w(\cdot)$ via the KLST route. (The same approach is taken in Adler [2016b] and Adler [2019b, ch. 2 and appendix].) By contrast, for Broome, Bernoulli is essential. He writes, "I am using Bernoulli's hypothesis as a *definition* of quantities of well-being" (p. 90). KLST theory plays no role in Broome's analysis; expected-utility theory and Bernoulli are the only avenue he provides to well-being measurement.

This also means that we define Bernoulli somewhat differently. Broome defines "Bernoulli's hypothesis" as follows: "One prospect is better for a person than another if and only if it gives the person a greater expectation of wellbeing than the other" (p. 89). What this statement means depends on how "greater expectation of well-being" is spelled out. Because Broome uses *only* expected-utility theory to arrive at an interval-scale measure of well-being, "greater expectation of well-being" is precisified, by Broome, as: greater expectation of well-being, with well-being measured on an interval scale using expected-utility theory. Thus Bernoulli's hypothesis ends up being necessarily true. My approach, instead, is to define the Bernoulli axiom as the risk-neutrality of lotteries with respect to the KLST measure of well-being; it need not hold true.

Broome's position in *Weighing Lives* is somewhat different than in his earlier *Weighing Goods* (1991), as discussed in *Weighing Lives* (see 2004, p. 90). Whatever the differences between the two works, KLST theory also plays no role in *Weighing Goods.*

[15] A well-being measure, throughout the book, is understood as a real-valued function that maps histories (see Section 1.3, Section 1.A.4) or bundles (this chapter) onto real numbers. Those numbers *represent* well-being levels and differences as per $\succcurlyeq^L$ and $\succcurlyeq^D$. Representation: The well-being level of one history/bundle is at least as high as the well-being level of a second history/bundle iff the well-being number assigned to the first is at least as large as the well-being number assigned to the second; and the well-being difference between the members of one pair of histories/bundles is at least as large as the well-being difference between the members of a second pair of histories/bundles iff the difference in well-being numbers between the members of the first pair is at least as large as the difference in well-being numbers between the members of the second pair. (See Section 1.A.4, stating this representation formally with respect to histories; and this section, below, with respect to bundles.) But any real number is larger, smaller, or equal to a second. Thus, if Representation holds true, it must be the case that any history/bundle is at a higher, lower or equal well-being level as a second (not an incomparable level); and that the well-being difference between the members of any pair of histories/bundles is larger, smaller, or equal to the well-being difference between the members of any other pair of histories/bundles (and not that the well-being differences are incomparable).

According to the theory of well-being at hand, the well-being difference between b^+ and b^{++} is at least as large as the well-being difference between b' and b''.

I posit that $\succcurlyeq^L$ and $\succcurlyeq^D$ satisfy the following axioms. These axioms (for short, the "substantive axioms") capture the structural features of well-being levels and differences. They are intended to express uncontroversial truisms about how comparisons of well-being levels and differences work (uncontroversial for those who accept such comparisons). In these and subsequent axioms, $\sim^D$ and $\succ^D$ indicate, respectively, that the differences are of the same size or that the first is greater; these relations are derived from $\succcurlyeq^D$.[16]

Linkage: $b \succcurlyeq^L b^*$ iff $(b, b^*) \succcurlyeq^D (b^*, b^*)$.

Reversal: $(b, b^*) \succcurlyeq^D (b^+, b^{++})$ iff $(b^{++}, b^+) \succcurlyeq^D (b^*, b)$.

Separability: If $(b, b^+) \succcurlyeq^D (b^*, b^+)$, then $(b, b') \succcurlyeq^D (b^*, b')$; and if $(b^+, b) \succcurlyeq^D (b^+, b^*)$, then $(b', b) \succcurlyeq^D (b', b^*)$.

Neutrality: $(b, b) \sim^D (b^*, b^*)$.

Concatenation: If $(b, b^*) \succcurlyeq^D (b', b'')$ and $(b^*, b^{**}) \succcurlyeq^D (b'', b''')$, then $(b, b^{**}) \succcurlyeq^D (b', b''')$.

In addition to these axioms, I posit an Archimedean I axiom (with "I" attached to differentiate it from the Archimedean axiom of vNM theory). Archimedean I rules out a certain kind of lexical priority with respect to the sources of well-being. It says, roughly, that no difference between two bundles is so large as to be larger than any finite concatenation of a fixed difference. More precisely:

Archimedean I: Let $b_1, b_2, \ldots, b_n, \ldots$ be a finite or infinite sequence of bundles such that $(b_2, b_1) \sim^D (b_{n+1}, b_n)$ for all n, and it is not the case that $(b_2, b_1) \sim^D (b_1, b_1)$. If there exist b^*, b such that $(b^*, b) \succ^D (b_n, b_1) \succ^D (b, b^*)$ for all n, then the sequence is finite.

Finally, I posit a technical axiom, "Solvability." Essentially, this requires that there be no "holes" in the bundle set.

Solvability: If $(b, b^*) \succcurlyeq^D (b', b'') \succcurlyeq^D (b, b)$, then there exist b^+, b^{++} such that $(b, b^+) \sim^D (b', b'') \sim^D (b^{++}, b^*)$.

Assume that $\succcurlyeq^L$ and $\succcurlyeq^D$ are complete quasiorderings of **B** and **B** × **B**, respectively, that satisfy the substantive axioms, Archimedean I, and Solvability. Then KLST theory shows that these rankings are jointly representable by a well-being

[16] See Section 1.A.1.

measure $\theta(\cdot)$. There exists a $\theta(\cdot)$ such that (1) $b \succcurlyeq^L b^*$ iff $\theta(b) \geq \theta(b^*)$; and (2) $(b^+, b^{++}) \succcurlyeq^D (b', b'')$ iff $\theta(b^+) - \theta(b^{++}) \geq \theta(b') - \theta(b'')$. $\theta(\cdot)$ is such that it assigns real numbers to bundles so that the *numerical* relations between the numbers mirror the well-being relations between bundles and bundle pairs.

$\theta(\cdot)$ is not unique. KLST theory, however, shows that $\theta(\cdot)$ is unique up to a positive affine transformation. If another measure $\theta^*(\cdot)$ also represents $\succcurlyeq^L$ and $\succcurlyeq^D$ as per above, then there must exist a positive constant r and a constant s such that $\theta^*(\cdot) = r\theta(\cdot) + s$.[17]

In other words, KLST theory shows the following: If $\succcurlyeq^L$ and $\succcurlyeq^D$ are complete quasiorderings of **B** and **B** × **B**, respectively, that satisfy the substantive axioms, Archimedean I, and Solvability, then there exists a non-empty set of well-being measures $\boldsymbol{\theta}$ such that $\theta(\cdot)$ belongs to $\boldsymbol{\theta}$ if, and only if, $\theta(\cdot)$ represents well-being in the manner above. Moreover, if $\theta(\cdot)$ belongs to $\boldsymbol{\theta}$, then so does another $\theta^*(\cdot)$ if, and only if, $\theta^*(\cdot)$ is a positive affine transformation of $\theta(\cdot)$.

Let's call $\boldsymbol{\theta}$ the KLST set of well-being measures for our well-being theory. This yields an immediate route to constructing $w(\cdot)$—namely, $w(\cdot)$ is any member of the KLST set of well-being measures. But there's another possible route, more indirect. I'll build that route with the tools of vNM theory and, then, the Bernoulli axiom.

4.2.2 vNM Theory and the Measurement of Well-Being Lotteries

Recall that our theory of well-being was also posited to have a ranking of history lotteries, $\succcurlyeq^{Lott}$. This history-level ranking is modeled as a ranking of lotteries over attribute bundles.

Let **B**, again, be the set of bundles; and let **L** be the set of all lotteries over **B**. A lottery L is such as to assign probabilities to bundles; $p_L(b)$ indicates the probability assigned to b by lottery L. $0 \leq p_L(b) \leq 1$, $p_L(b) > 0$ for a finite number of bundles, and $\sum_b p_L(b) = 1$. Note that each bundle is itself a kind of lottery: a lottery that assigns probability 1 to that bundle, and 0 to every other bundle.

$\succcurlyeq^{Lott}$ is a complete quasiordering of **L**. "$L \succcurlyeq^{Lott} L^*$" indicates that lottery L is at least as good for well-being as L^*.

Let's say that a measure $\zeta(\cdot)$ on the set of bundles "expectationally represents" the lottery ranking $\succcurlyeq^{Lott}$ if the ranking of lotteries as per $\succcurlyeq^{Lott}$ is mirrored by the *expected value* of the numbers assigned to bundles as per $\zeta(\cdot)$. That is, $L \succcurlyeq^{Lott} L^*$ iff $\sum_{b \in \mathbf{B}} p_L(b)\zeta(b) \geq \sum_{b \in \mathbf{B}} p_{L^*}(b)\zeta(b)$.

[17] That is: for every b, $\theta^*(b) = r\theta(b) + s$.

vNM theory shows that there exists a $\zeta(\cdot)$ that expectationally represents $\succcurlyeq^{Lott}$ if the following two axioms are satisfied.[18]

> Lottery Independence: Let $[p, L; (1-p), L']$ denote a p, $(1-p)$ mixture of lotteries L and L'.[19] Lottery Independence requires: $L \succcurlyeq^{Lott} L^*$ iff $[p, L; (1-p), L'] \succcurlyeq^{Lott} [p, L^*; (1-p), L']$.
>
> Archimedean II: If $L \succ^{Lott} L^* \succ^{Lott} L^{**}$, then there exists p less than 1 such that $[p, L; (1-p), L^{**}] \succ^{Lott} L^*$, and there exists p' greater than 0 such that $L^* \succ^{Lott} [p', L; (1-p'), L^{**}]$.

Lottery Independence is, plausibly, a requirement of rationality. Archimedean II, like Archimedean I, rules out a kind of lexical priority with respect to well-being sources. No bundle is so much worse than a second that no risk of the first is worth incurring for the chance of an improvement to the second.

vNM theory demonstrates not merely that there exists a measure $\zeta(\cdot)$ expectationally representing $\succcurlyeq^{Lott}$, but that $\zeta(\cdot)$ is unique up to a positive affine transformation. That is, vNM theory shows: If $\succcurlyeq^{Lott}$ is a complete quasiordering of the lottery set **L** that satisfies Lottery Independence and Archimedean II, then there is a non-empty set $\boldsymbol{\zeta}$ of measures that expectationally represent $\succcurlyeq^{Lott}$. Moreover, if $\zeta(\cdot)$ belongs to $\boldsymbol{\zeta}$, then so does another $\zeta^*(\cdot)$ if, and only if, $\zeta^*(\cdot)$ is a positive affine transformation of $\zeta(\cdot)$. Let's call $\boldsymbol{\zeta}$ the vNM set of well-being measures for our well-being theory. While the KLST set $\boldsymbol{\theta}$ consists of well-being measures that represent one component of our theory ($\succcurlyeq^L$ and $\succcurlyeq^D$), the vNM set $\boldsymbol{\zeta}$ consists of well-being measures that represent a different component of our theory ($\succcurlyeq^{Lott}$).

4.2.3 The Bernoulli Axiom: Linking the KLST and vNM Measures

Suppose that our ranking of histories and differences satisfies the KLST axioms, hence is represented by a KLST set $\boldsymbol{\theta}$ of well-being measures; and that our ranking of lotteries satisfies the vNM axioms, hence is represented by a vNM set $\boldsymbol{\zeta}$ of lottery measures.

The Bernoulli axiom now stipulates that the ranking of lotteries is *risk neutral* in well-being, as measured by any KLST measure $\theta(\cdot)$. To see the idea here, imagine that we have a bundle b, with well-being level $\theta(b)$. The symbol Δ denotes some increment in well-being; $\Delta > 0$. A lottery L gives a 50% probability of a bundle with

[18] See Gilboa (2009, ch. 8).

[19] A p, $(1-p)$ mixture of two lotteries L and L' is a new lottery that assigns bundle b the probability $pp_L(b) + (1-p)p_{L'}(b)$.

well-being level $\theta(b) + \Delta$, and a 50% probability of a bundle with well-being level $\theta(b) - \Delta$. Bernoulli requires that L and b be ranked equally good.

More generally:

Bernoulli: For any lottery over bundles L and bundle b^*, $L \sim^{Lott} b^*$ iff $\sum_{b \in \mathbf{B}} p_L(b)\theta(b) = \theta(b^*)$.[20]

Our theory of well-being is always indifferent between a lottery L the expected $\theta(\cdot)$ value of which is a particular value θ^*, and a bundle b^* such that $\theta(b^*) = \theta^*$.

Bernoulli, it should be stressed, does *not* preclude risk aversion in the components of well-being.[21] For example, it's often supposed that individual preferences are such as to be risk averse in *income*. A well-being theory is risk averse in income if it favors receiving a certain amount of income y for certain, as opposed to a lottery whose expected income is y. Bernoulli does not preclude risk aversion in income or any other attribute. Rather it stipulates that, once we've measured well-being *itself* with a measure of well-being levels and differences—the measure $\theta(\cdot)$—our ranking of lotteries will be risk neutral in terms of *that* (not necessarily income or any input to well-being).

Bernoulli seems like a reasonable default assumption for a well-being theory. What considerations would justify risk aversion in well-being and (if so) a particular degree of risk aversion, or risk proneness in well-being and (if so) a particular degree of risk proneness? Moreover, Bernoulli has major benefits in terms of tractability, now to be explained.

Let $\theta(\cdot)$ be some member of the KLST set of well-being measures, and let $\zeta(\cdot)$ be some member of the vNM set of well-being measures. Bernoulli implies that, for any such $\theta(\cdot)$ and $\zeta(\cdot)$, $\zeta(\cdot)$ is a positive affine transformation of $\theta(\cdot)$.[22] But, if $\zeta(\cdot)$ is a positive affine transformation of $\theta(\cdot)$, it follows by KLST theory that $\zeta(\cdot)$ itself represents well-being levels and differences, hence is a member of the KLST set $\boldsymbol{\theta}$. The same is true for every other vNM measure. In short, $\boldsymbol{\zeta}$ is a subset of $\boldsymbol{\theta}$. But, further, if $\zeta(\cdot)$ is a positive affine transformation of $\theta(\cdot)$, it follows by vNM theory that $\theta(\cdot)$ itself expectationally represents the ranking of lotteries, hence is a member of the vNM set $\boldsymbol{\zeta}$. The same is true for every other KLST measure. In short, $\boldsymbol{\theta}$ is a subset of $\boldsymbol{\zeta}$.

[20] b^* is equivalent to a "degenerate" lottery that assigns probability 1 to bundle b^* and 0 to all others. The statement "$L \sim^{Lott} b^*$" indicates that the lottery ranking is indifferent between L and this degenerate lottery.

[21] See Adler (2019b, p. 57), for an example.

[22] See Adler (2019b, pp. 269–70).

But θ and ζ can only be subsets of each other if they are identical. In short, Bernoulli has a dramatic implication: *It means that the KLST set is the same as the vNM set.* There is a single set of well-being measures $\theta = \zeta$. Each well-being measure $w(\cdot)$ in this set is both a KLST measure that represents $\succcurlyeq^L$ and $\succcurlyeq^D$ and a vNM measure that expectationally represents $\succcurlyeq^{Lott}$.

If Bernoulli is not satisfied, then θ and ζ are *not* the same set. Indeed, if Bernoulli is not satisfied, θ and ζ are disjoint.

If Bernoulli is not satisfied, we *still* have the direct route to constructing $w(\cdot)$. Namely, use our well-being theory to construct the KLST set of measures and pick $w(\cdot)$ as any member of that set. But Bernoulli yields a second, indirect route to constructing $w(\cdot)$—namely, use our well-being theory to construct the vNM set of measures and pick $w(\cdot)$ as any member of *that* set.

4.2.4 Constructing the $w(\cdot)$ Measure: A Summary

To recapitulate, the account of well-being measurement adopted here relies upon the KLST axioms (the cluster of axioms set forth by KLST theory), the vNM axioms (the cluster of axioms set forth by vNM theory), and the Bernoulli axiom.

The KLST axioms imply the existence of the KLST set of measures, θ. Any measure $\theta(\cdot)$ in θ represents the well-being levels of bundles and the well-being differences between bundles: $b \succcurlyeq^L b^*$ iff $\theta(b) \geq \theta(b^*)$; and $(b^+, b^{++}) \succcurlyeq^D (b', b'')$ iff $\theta(b^+) - \theta(b^{++}) \geq \theta(b') - \theta(b'')$.

The vNM axioms imply the existence of the vNM set of measures, ζ. Any measure $\zeta(\cdot)$ in ζ expectationally represents the well-being ranking of lotteries: $L \succcurlyeq^{Lott} L^*$ iff $\sum_{b \in \mathbf{B}} p_L(b)\zeta(b) \geq \sum_{b \in \mathbf{B}} p_{L^*}(b)\zeta(b)$.

The Bernoulli axiom implies that θ and ζ are the very same set. Any measure $\theta(\cdot)$ that represents well-being levels and differences is *also* such as to expectationally represent the well-being ranking of lotteries. Conversely, any measure $\zeta(\cdot)$ that expectationally represents the well-being ranking of lotteries is *also* such as to represent well-being levels and differences.

This account affords two routes to constructing the well-being measure, $w(\cdot)$, one direct and the second indirect. The direct route is to construct the KLST set, θ, by deliberating about how our favored theory of well-being (whatever it may be) ranks bundles and bundle differences. Any member of the KLST set can then be selected as our $w(\cdot)$. The indirect route is to construct the vNM set, ζ, by deliberating about how our favored theory of well-being ranks bundle lotteries. Any member of the vNM set can then be selected as our $w(\cdot)$.

The indirect route is available for *any* account of well-being. For example, the proponent of an objective-good account *might* find it reasonably straightforward to construct the KLST set, θ—by reflecting about how the various objective goods posited by their account translate into a ranking of bundles and bundle differences. Alternatively, they might feel that doing so is difficult and might find it easier to construct the vNM set, ζ—by reflecting about how those goods translate into a ranking of bundle lotteries.

As we'll now see, the indirect route is especially useful for a preference-based account of well-being, because there is an analytical connection between the vNM set ζ and the *utility* functions representing individuals' preferences. In the case of a preference-based theory, the indirect route means constructing ζ with reference to those utility functions, and then setting $w(\cdot)$ as any member of ζ. See Section 4.3, immediately below.

Some readers may be skeptical about the Bernoulli axiom. If Bernoulli is dropped, the indirect route for constructing $w(\cdot)$ is no longer available. Without Bernoulli, the KLST and vNM sets are disjoint. A vNM measure, $\zeta(\cdot)$, will no longer be such as to represent well-being levels and differences. The only path to $w(\cdot)$, therefore, is the direct route of assembling the KLST set.

In the subsequent sections of this chapter, I assume Bernoulli.[23]

4.3 Preference-Based Well-Being Measurement

I'll operationalize the measurement of lifetime well-being for a preference-based theory as follows.[24] Each lifetime bundle b is now a "hybrid bundle" (a, R). The symbol a here denotes a lifetime bundle of non-preference attributes. R is a global preference structure. Specifically, it is a ranking of a bundles and lotteries over a bundles. A lifetime hybrid bundle b is some combination of a lifetime bundle of non-preference attributes and a global preference structure. This is what is indicated by the symbolism $b = (a, R)$.

The temporal structure of bundles remains the same as in the generic case. An individual can live a maximum of T possible periods. Their longevity l is the

[23] Using Bernoulli, I show how a preference-based well-being measure can be derived from individuals' vNM utility functions, representing individuals' preferences with respect to bundle lotteries. See Section 4.3, Section 4.4.2. If Bernoulli were dropped, a preference-based well-being measure could instead be derived from "difference utility" functions representing individuals' preferences with respect to bundle differences. See Adler (2016b, pp. 491, 497), citing scholarship regarding difference utility. Because difference utility is a much less familiar concept in economics and policy analysis than vNM utility, I focus on the vNM-utility approach.

[24] This section, like Section 4.2, is based upon Adler (2016b; 2019b, ch. 2 and appendix). What follows derives a preference-based well-being measure from vNM utility functions. A different type of preference-based measure, the so-called "equivalence" approach, employs ordinal utility functions. See Fleurbaey and Blanchet (2013); Fleurbaey (2016). See also Adler and Decancq (2022), contrasting the two approaches. Space constraints preclude a discussion of the equivalence approach here.

number of periods they are alive; a^t denotes a period bundle of non-preference attributes—either a bundle of living-person non-preference attributes (the sorts of non-preference attributes that a living person might possess) or the status Dead. A lifetime bundle a of non-preference attributes is a sequence of a^t bundles, one for each of the T periods, with a^t = Dead for periods when the individual is dead.

Thus, the individual's lifetime bundle b is a series of period bundles—as in the generic case. $b = ((a^1, R), (a^2, R), \ldots, (a^l, R), b^{l+1} = \text{Dead}, b^{l+2} = \text{Dead}, \ldots, b^T = \text{Dead})$.[25]

The set of lifetime bundles, **B**—now specifically a set of hybrid bundles—is constructed as follows. There is a set **A** of a bundles; and a set **R** of preferences, i.e., rankings of **A** and of lotteries over **A**. Included in **B** is every pairing of an element of **A** and an element of **R**, or a subset of such pairings.

Preferentialist theories may "idealize" (launder) preferences in various ways. The preferences that figure into well-being might be required to be well-informed, to meet some standard of rational deliberation, and so on.[26] If so, the global preference structure R will be required to meet these idealization criteria. (a, R) represents a life in which the individual's non-preference attributes are a and their idealized preferences (according to whichever criteria of idealization are posited by the theory) are R. If the theory has no standards of idealization and looks instead to an individual's actual preferences, then (a, R) represents a life in which the individual's non-preference attributes are a and their actual preferences are R.

A large body of scholarship documents that individuals' actual preferences fall short of the vNM axioms.[27] Still, it is often—although certainly not universally—supposed by decision theorists that the vNM axioms are one component of what it takes for preferences to be rational.[28]

Let's suppose, then, that the preference theory being implemented *does* include the axioms of vNM theory as idealization criteria. In short, **B** is a set of hybrid bundles, (a, R) bundles; and every global preference structure R included in these hybrid bundles is a ranking of a bundles and lotteries over a bundles that satisfies vNM theory.

[25] I posit that if a^t is Dead then b^t = Dead. Alternatively, one might posit that b^t = (Dead, R)—but this is odd, since it suggests that the individual has preferences while dead.

[26] See Adler (2012, ch. 3); Goodin (1995, ch. 9); Harsanyi (1982, pp. 54-56).

[27] See, e.g., Friedman, Isaac, James, and Sunder (2014).

[28] For a review of the normative defenses of expected utility theory, see Briggs (2023); Thoma (2019b). Buchak (2013), a book much discussed in the recent philosophical literature on decision theory, offers a critique of expected utility theory—proposing instead what she terms "risk-weighted expected utility." This account, in turn, has attracted criticism. See, e.g., Thoma (2019a); Thoma and Weisberg (2017).

Because each R satisfies vNM theory, each R can be represented by a vNM *utility* function $u^R(\cdot)$. The symbol "u" indicates "utility": a numerical function that represents *preferences*. The superscript R indicates that $u^R(\cdot)$ is a vNM utility function that expectationally represents preference R.

It's important to understand that vNM theory is now coming into play at *two* different places in our account of well-being measurement. First, as above in the generic case, we continue to assume that $\succcurlyeq^{Lott}$ is represented by a set of vNM well-being measures $\boldsymbol{\zeta}$. Every vNM well-being measure $\zeta(\cdot)$ is such that the following is true: For any two lotteries L and L^* over b bundles, $L \succcurlyeq^{Lott} L^*$ iff $\sum_{b \in \mathbf{B}} p_L(b)\zeta(b) \geq \sum_{b \in \mathbf{B}} p_{L^*}(b)\zeta(b)$. This applies, as before—the only difference here being that each b bundle is a hybrid bundle (a, R).

Second, each preference structure R is expectationally represented by a vNM utility function $u^R(\cdot)$. More precisely, let l be a lottery over a bundles, with $\pi_l(a)$ the probability of bundle a with that lottery. Then, for any two lotteries over a bundles, l and l^*, preference R weakly prefers l to l^* iff $\sum_{a \in \mathbf{A}} \pi_l(a)u^R(a) \geq \sum_{a \in \mathbf{A}} \pi_{l^*}(a)u^R(a)$.

The strategy, now, is to use this latter equation as a way to construct a vNM well-being measure; and from there, via Bernoulli, to construct a well-being measure $w(\cdot)$.

What allows us to do this is an axiom of Sovereignty. Sovereignty is meant to express the *deference to preferences* that makes a theory preference-based.

> Sovereignty: If L and L^*, two lotteries over b bundles (hybrid bundles), are such that all of the bundles assigned a non-zero probability by L and all of the bundles assigned a non-zero probability by L^* contain the very same preference structure R, then the ranking of the lotteries tracks R's ranking of the corresponding lotteries over a bundles.

To see why the Sovereignty axiom indeed expresses the deference to preferences that is the hallmark of a preference view of well-being, consider the following. (1) Let Hussein's preferences be denoted R^{Hussein}. Assume that Hussein prefers bundle a to bundle a^*. If so, a preference-based well-being theory will count Hussein as better off with a than with a^*. More abstractly, it assigns a higher level of well-being to (a, R^{Hussein}) than to $(a^*, R^{\text{Hussein}})$. The first hybrid bundle is Hussein's life if his non-preference attributes are a; the second hybrid bundle is Hussein's life if his non-preference attributes are a^*. And this is just what is required by Sovereignty: that (a, R^{Hussein}) be assigned a higher well-being level than $(a^*, R^{\text{Hussein}})$. (2) Let l and l^* be two lotteries over a bundles. Assume, now, that Hussein prefers lottery l to lottery l^*. (Hussein's preference structure is not just a ranking of a bundles but also a ranking of lotteries over a bundles; and all this information is encoded in R^{Hussein}.) If so, a preference-based well-being theory will count Hussein as better off with lottery l than with lottery l^*. More abstractly, a preference-based well-being theory will assign a higher level of well-being to a lottery L over *hybrid* bundles with probabilities corresponding to l, as compared to a lottery L^* over *hybrid* bundles with probabilities corresponding to l^*, if the preference structure in all of these hybrid bundles is R^{Hussein}. Again, this is just what is required by Sovereignty: that L be ranked above L^*.

If Sovereignty is adopted, every vNM measure of well-being $\zeta(\cdot)$ within the vNM set $\boldsymbol{\zeta}$ must be closely connected to individuals' vNM utility functions. Sovereignty implies the following.

<u>The Implications of Sovereignty for the vNM Measure of Well-Being</u>

Let $u^R(\cdot)$ be a vNM utility function representing preference structure R. Then $\zeta(a,R) = c(u^R)u^R(a) + d(u^R)$, with $c(u^R) > 0$.

The formula $\zeta(a,R) = c(u^R)u^R(a) + d(u^R)$ requires some clarification. $c(u^R)$ and $d(u^R)$ are two scaling factors. They are written in this form, rather than simply as "*c*" and "*d*", because these two scaling factors are specific to each vNM utility function. To illustrate, assume that the set **R** of preferences includes R^*, R^{**}, and R^{***}. Some hybrid bundles include R^*, others R^{**}, others R^{***}. Then we select vNM utility functions $u^{R^*}(\cdot)$, $u^{R^{**}}(\cdot)$, and $u^{R^{***}}(\cdot)$. For each of these utility functions we select two scaling factors. And the vNM measure of the well-being of a given hybrid bundle (a, R)—with $R = R^*$, R^{**}, or R^{***}—is then calculated using the formula $\zeta(a,R) = c(u^R)u^R(a) + d(u^R)$.

In order to operationalize the formula $\zeta(a,R) = c(u^R)u^R(a) + d(u^R)$, we will need to pick the scaling factors $c(u^R)$ and $d(u^R)$ for each vNM utility function. The scaling factors are irrelevant to well-being comparisons among hybrid bundles all of which have the same preference R as their preference component; they function, rather, to determine the comparisons among bundles that incorporate different preferences.[29]

Let $\zeta(\cdot)$ be a vNM measure of well-being constructed using the formula $\zeta(a,R) = c(u^R)u^R(a) + d(u^R)$. The set $\boldsymbol{\zeta}$, then, is all positive affine transformations of $\zeta(\cdot)$. If we now add Bernoulli, we have (as above) that the KLST set of well-being measures $\boldsymbol{\theta}$ is identical to the vNM set of well-being measures $\boldsymbol{\zeta}$, and $w(\cdot)$ is any member of this set.

In summary, the methodology here for constructing a preference-based lifetime well-being measure uses the general methodology set forth above in Section

[29] On the role and selection of scaling factors, see Adler (2016b, pp. 499–503; 2019b, pp. 55–64, 190-92); Fleurbaey and Zuber (2021).

4.2 and adds several additional assumptions. First, each lifetime bundle b takes the specific form (a, R), with a a lifetime bundle of non-preference attributes and R a preference (ranking of a bundles and lotteries over a bundles). Second, we adopt an axiom of deference to preferences—Sovereignty—which implies that the vNM measure $\zeta(\cdot)$ can be defined in terms of the vNM utility functions representing individual preferences. Adding Bernoulli, we can define our $w(\cdot)$ measure directly in terms of vNM utility functions: $w(a,R)=c(u^R)u^R(a)+d(u^R)$ or any positive affine transformation thereof.

What is striking, and powerful, about the formula $w(a,R)=c(u^R)u^R(a)+d(u^R)$ is that $w(\cdot)$ represents well-being levels and differences and yet is derived from vNM utility functions rather than via deliberation about well-being levels and differences. Starting from the collection of vNM utility functions for the various preferences being modeled, the analyst needs only to choose scaling factors $c(u^R)$, $d(u^R)$ for each such utility function. Doing so fully defines the well-being measure $w(\cdot)$.

4.4 Temporal Additivity

The temporally additive form is widespread in economics and public health. For example, economists studying individuals' investment and consumption decisions usually assume that a person's preferences over lifetime consumption streams can be represented by lifetime utility numbers equaling the (discounted) sum of period utility, as calculated with a period utility function taking each period's consumption as its input.[30] The QALY framework for quantifying lifetime health does so by summing up health quality in each period.[31]

Extrapolating such formulas to the context at hand, we have that $w(b)=\sum_{t=1}^{T} w^p(b^t)$, with $w^p(\cdot)$ a period well-being measure. In this section, I discuss the temporally additive formula in the general case, then in the specific case of a preference-based well-being measure. Finally, I discuss the possibility of this formula with a discount factor attached: $w(b)=\sum_{t=1}^{T}\lambda(t)w^p(b^t)$, $\lambda(t)$ a discount factor.

[30] On the common assumption of temporal additivity in economics, see, e.g., Gollier (2001, pp. 217–18); Mas-Colell, Whinston, and Green (1995, pp. 733–36).

[31] Pinto-Prades, Herrero, and Abellán (2016).

4.4.1 Temporal Additivity: The General Case

Temporal additivity, as I'll conceptualize it, starts with the generic account of well-being measurement set forth in Section 4.2. Namely, there is a KLST set of well-being measures $\boldsymbol{\theta}$; a vNM set of well-being measures $\boldsymbol{\zeta}$; and a Bernoulli axiom with the upshot that these two sets are identical. We then adopt axioms (for short, "temporal additivity axioms") sufficient to ensure that each KLST measure $\theta(\cdot)$ in $\boldsymbol{\theta}$ is temporally additive, and that each vNM measure $\zeta(\cdot)$ in $\boldsymbol{\zeta}$ is temporally additive.[32] By virtue of these axioms, each $\theta(\cdot)$ can be expressed in terms of a corresponding *period* KLST measure $\theta^p(\cdot)$. $\theta(b) = \sum_{t=1}^{T} \theta^p(b^t)$. And each vNM measure can be expressed in terms of a corresponding *period* vNM measure. $\zeta(b) = \sum_{t=1}^{T} \zeta^p(b^t)$.

In other words, the temporal additivity axioms imply that there is a set $\boldsymbol{\theta}^{\mathbf{p}}$ of period KLST measures, each corresponding to one KLST measure in the set $\boldsymbol{\theta}$. And they imply that there is a set $\boldsymbol{\zeta}^{\mathbf{p}}$ of period vNM measures, each corresponding to one vNM measure in the set $\boldsymbol{\zeta}$.

As in the generic case, we can construct our well-being measure $w(\cdot)$ via the direct route (construct $\boldsymbol{\theta}$ and set $w(\cdot)$ equal to some member of that set), or via the indirect route (construct $\boldsymbol{\zeta}$ and set $w(\cdot)$ equal to some member of that set). But each of these routes becomes easier, since the sets of KLST and vNM measures ($\boldsymbol{\theta}$ and $\boldsymbol{\zeta}$) can be specified by identifying, respectively, the sets of *period* KLST and *period* vNM measures ($\boldsymbol{\theta}^{\mathbf{p}}$ and $\boldsymbol{\zeta}^{\mathbf{p}}$).

Consider, first, the direct route. A period KLST measure $\theta^p(.)$ is such as to represent the well-being levels of period bundles and the well-being differences between period bundles. Let b_1^t, b_2^t, b_3^t, and b_4^t be any four period bundles. Then $\theta^p(.)$ will be such that (1) Period bundle b_1^t is at least as good for well-being as period bundle b_2^t iff $\theta^p(b_1^t) \geq \theta^p(b_2^t)$; and (2) the difference in well-being between b_1^t and b_2^t is at least as large as the difference in well-being between b_3^t and b_4^t iff $\theta^p(b_1^t) - \theta^p(b_2^t) \geq \theta^p(b_3^t) - \theta^p(b_4^t)$. By reflecting on how our theory of well-being ranks period bundles and period-bundle differences, we arrive at $\boldsymbol{\theta}^{\mathbf{p}}$. And we then set our period well-being measure, $w^p(.)$, equal to any period KLST measure in $\boldsymbol{\theta}^{\mathbf{p}}$.

[32] On axioms sufficient to ensure additivity of a KLST measure across multiple dimensions (such as multiple time periods), see Dyer and Sarin (1979); Smith and Dyer (2021). On axioms sufficient to ensure additivity of a vNM measure across multiple dimensions (such as multiple time periods), see Bleichrodt and Quiggin (1999); Fishburn (1982, ch. 6); Keeney and Raiffa (1993, chs. 5–6). Dyer (2005) and von Winterfeldt and Edwards (1986, ch. 9) provide a useful overview of both topics. Note that if Bernoulli holds true, the temporal additivity of the KLST measures in $\boldsymbol{\theta}$ imply the temporal additivity of the vNM measures in $\boldsymbol{\zeta}$, and vice versa.

Consider, next, the indirect route. A period vNM measure $\zeta^p(\cdot)$ is such as to expectationally represent the well-being ranking of lotteries over period bundles. By reflecting on how our theory of well-being ranks such lotteries, we arrive at $\boldsymbol{\zeta}^{\mathbf{p}}$. And we then set our period well-being measure, $w^p(\cdot)$, equal to any period vNM measure in $\boldsymbol{\zeta}^{\mathbf{p}}$.

A concrete example may be useful in explicating these quite abstract formulations. Let's assume (to make the example simple) that lifetime well-being is modeled as depending upon an individual's income and their longevity. For each period, an individual's period bundle specifies their income during that period if they are alive then, or their status as Dead if not. Assume a non-preference-based theory of well-being: the period well-being measure $w^p(\cdot)$ is to be identified without reference to individuals' preferences. The set $\mathbf{B^p}$ of possible period bundles includes possible income amounts, plus the status Dead. That is, $\mathbf{B^p} = \{y, y^*, y^{**}, \ldots, \text{Dead}\}$, with y a possible period income, y^* a different possible period income, and so forth.

If we follow the direct route, we identify a KLST period measure by determining how amounts of period income translate into levels of period well-being (here, it is standard to adopt a monotonicity assumption, namely, that period well-being increases with period income); and by determining how differences between amounts of period income translate into differences in period well-being. For example, is the difference in period well-being between a period income of \$60,000 and a period income of \$40,000 larger, smaller, or equal to the difference in period well-being between a period income of \$90,000 and a period income of \$60,000? Finally, we need to bring death into the picture (Dead is a possible period bundle), and we can do so by identifying a threshold income amount y^{Thresh} such that extending someone's life by one period with y^{Thresh} is equally good as not-extending their life.[33]

Why is this last step necessary? Assume that $\theta^p(.)$ and $\theta^{p*}(.)$ are identical in terms of the well-being numbers they assign to period income amounts but assign different numbers to the status Dead. For example, the first KLST measure is such that $\theta^p(\text{Dead}) = \theta^p(\$1000)$, while the second KLST measure is such that $\theta^{p*}(\text{Dead}) = \theta^{p*}(\$500)$. If so, the two measures imply *different* rankings of the period bundles in the set $\mathbf{B^p}$, and *different* rankings of differences between period bundles. $\theta^p(.)$ is such that a period income of \$1000 is equally good as Dead (and, given monotonicity, that a period income of \$500 is worse than Dead), while $\theta^{p*}(.)$ is such that a period income of \$500 is equally good as Dead. And

[33] If there is no such y^{Thresh}, we specify $\theta^p(\text{Dead})$ directly—by setting $\theta^p(\text{Dead})$ so that (1) it is lower than/greater than $\theta^p(y)$ iff Dead is worse than/better than income y for period well-being, and (2) differences between $\theta^p(\text{Dead})$ and $\theta^p(y)$ for various period income amounts track our judgments about differences in period well-being between Dead and those income amounts.

specifying our lifetime well-being measure $w(\cdot)$ by setting $w^p(\cdot) = \theta^p(\cdot)$ yields a different lifetime well-being measure than if we set $w^p(\cdot) = \theta^{p*}(\cdot)$.

If we follow the indirect route, we identify a vNM measure for the case at hand by determining how our well-being theory ranks lotteries over the set $\mathbf{B}^p = \{y, y^*, y^{**}, \ldots, \text{Dead}\}$. Specifically, we compare lotteries over possible period income amounts. For example, is a lottery with a 50% probability of \$50,000 and a 50% probability of \$100,000 better, worse, or equally good for well-being as getting \$70,000 for sure? And (as with the direct route) we identify a threshold income amount y^{Thresh} such that extending someone's life by one period with y^{Thresh} is equally good as not-extending their life.[34]

It's important to clarify that the well-being number assigned to the state Dead need not be zero. This is true whether we adopt the direct or indirect route to identifying $w^p(\cdot)$. Consider the direct route. The set $\mathbf{\theta}^\mathbf{p}$ of period KLST measures is unique up to a positive affine transformation.[35] Each member of this set contains the very same information regarding the levels and differences of period bundles. There will be a KLST measure in this set, $\theta^p(\cdot)$, which is such that $\theta^p(\text{Dead}) = 0$; but there will also be another KLST measure $\theta^{p+}(\cdot)$, a positive affine transformation of the first, which is such that $\theta^{p+}(\text{Dead}) \neq 0$. We might set $w^p(\cdot) = \theta^p(\cdot)$, but we might equally well set $w^p(\cdot) = \theta^{p+}(\cdot)$. In the first case $w^p(\text{Dead}) = 0$, while in the second case $w^p(\text{Dead}) \neq 0$. A parallel analysis applies to the indirect route.

We are free to set $w^p(\text{Dead}) = 0$ or $w^p(\text{Dead}) \neq 0$ because we are using this period well-being measure to define a lifetime measure, $w(\cdot)$, which assigns numbers on an *interval* scale of lifetime well-being. $w(\cdot)$ tells us about the levels of lifetime well-being associated with lifetime bundles, and about differences in

[34] If there is no such y^{Thresh}, we specify $\theta^p(\text{Dead})$ directly—here, by considering lotteries that include both period income amounts and Dead.

[35] $\mathbf{\theta}^\mathbf{p}$ is unique up to a positive affine transformation because $\mathbf{B}^p$ includes the status Dead as one of the possible period bundles—which in turn is why each $\theta^p(\cdot)$ assigns a value to Dead as well as the other elements of $\mathbf{B}^p$. If $\theta^{p*}(\cdot)$ is a positive affine transformation of $\theta^p(\cdot)$—namely, $\theta^{p*}(\cdot) = r\theta^p(\cdot) + s$, $r > 0$—the two period measures imply the same comparisons of the members of $\mathbf{B}^p$ with respect to period well-being levels and differences. And the lifetime well-being measure corresponding to $\theta^p(\cdot)$ and $\theta^{p*}(\cdot)$, respectively—$\theta(b) = \sum_{t=1}^{T} \theta^p(b^t)$ and $\theta^*(b) = \sum_{t=1}^{T} \theta^{p*}(b^t)$—imply the same comparisons of lifetime bundles with respect to lifetime well-being levels and differences.

If, instead, $\mathbf{B}^p$ were defined to *exclude* Dead and include only living-person period bundles, with $\theta(b) = \sum_{t=1}^{T} \theta^p(b^t)$ summing over period bundles *excluding* Dead, then (implicitly) Dead is necessarily assigned a period well-being of 0, and $\theta^p(\cdot)$ is unique up to a positive ratio (not affine) transformation. But this is *not* the approach taken here. Again, Dead is treated as one possible period bundle among others.

An exactly parallel analysis shows that the set ζ^p of period vNM measures is unique up to a positive affine transformation.

lifetime well-being. If we wished to specify a *ratio* scale of lifetime well-being, then we might be required to set w^p(Dead) = 0. See Section 4.5.[36]

We've been exploring the workings of temporal additivity but haven't yet addressed the question of justification. Namely, why adopt an assumption of temporal additivity? And what are its downsides?

The advantage of temporal additivity is tractability. Formulating a period measure of well-being $w^p(\cdot)$, and then arriving at the lifetime well-being measure via the summative formula $w(b) = \sum_{t=1}^{T} w^p(b^t)$, is *easier* than constructing $w(\cdot)$ by thinking in terms of whole lifetime bundles. If we follow the direct route (constructing $w(\cdot)$ by constructing a KLST measure), then temporal additivity allows us to derive $w(\cdot)$ by thinking about the well-being levels of period bundles and the well-being differences between period bundles, as opposed to thinking about the well-being levels of whole lifetime bundles and the well-being differences between whole lifetime bundles. If we follow the indirect route (constructing $w(\cdot)$ by constructing a vNM measure), then temporal additivity allows us to derive $w(\cdot)$ by thinking about lotteries over period bundles, as opposed to lotteries over lifetime bundles.

The temporal-additivity assumption makes it easier to construct $w(\cdot)$—whether by the direct or indirect route—because the set of period bundles $\mathbf{B}^p$ is smaller than the set of lifetime bundles **B**. If the maximum number of periods is *T*, then the latter set includes every possible *T*-period combination of elements from the former set. Thinking about well-being comparisons with respect to a smaller set of items is easier than doing so with respect to a larger set.

There is a downside. Temporal additivity precludes sequencing effects. Some philosophers argue that the sequencing of period well-being matters to lifetime well-being. A life that starts at a low level of well-being, and improves, is better than a second life with the same sum total of period well-being that starts high and deteriorates—or so it has been argued. Temporal additivity rules this out; all lifetime bundles with the same sum total of period well-being are assigned the same level of lifetime well-being, regardless of the sequence of period well-being within the lifetime bundles.

A different type of sequencing concerns the sequencing of period *bundles* (rather than period well-being). Let $b_1^t, b_2^t, \ldots, b_T^t$ be *T* different period bundles.

[36] As discussed in Section 4.5, a ratio-scale measure of lifetime well-being is defined by identifying a zero lifetime bundle, b^{zero}. Assume that b^{zero} is such that its lifetime well-being value is the same as a life with period bundle b^* in every period, for any longevity *l*. That is, $w(b^{zero}) = w(b^*, \ldots, b^*, \text{Dead}, \ldots, \text{Dead})$, for any lifetime bundle with longevity $l = 1$ to *T* and b^* the period bundle for periods 1 to *l*. We now define a ratio-scale measure of lifetime well-being $w'(\cdot)$ as follows: $w'(b) = w(b) - w(b^{zero})$. Assume, further, that $w(\cdot)$ and thus $w'(\cdot)$ are temporally additive, with $w^p(\cdot)$ and $w^{p\prime}(\cdot)$ the corresponding period well-being measures. It follows that $w^{p\prime}(b^*) = w^{p\prime}(\text{Dead}) = 0$.

Consider now the various lifetime bundles that are composed from the T period bundles—each lifetime bundle arranging the period bundles in some order. Temporal additivity implies that all of these lifetime bundles receive the very same level of lifetime well-being. But this result might well be criticized.[37]

It is possible to modify the temporally additive formula so as to allow for sequencing effects while retaining some of the tractability benefits of the formula. A bundle is divided into T periods, with $T = K \times D$. Periods are "clumped" together into groups of D periods, and there are K of these clumps in total. (For example, if each period is a month, clumped into years, and the maximum lifespan is 100 years = 1200 months, then $T = 1200$, $K = 100$, and $D = 12$.) Lifetime well-being is the sum of the well-being of each clump. Such an approach would allow for within-clump sequencing effects: the well-being of a given clump could depend upon the order of period well-being or period bundles within that clump.

4.4.2 Temporal Additivity with a Preference-Based Well-Being Measure

Recall the general setup from Section 4.3. In the case of a preference-based well-being measure, a lifetime bundle b is modeled as the combination (a, R), with a a lifetime bundle of non-preference attributes. $a = (a^1, a^2, \ldots, a^T)$; a^t is a period bundle of living-person non-preference attributes, if the individual is alive in period t, or otherwise Dead. **A** is the set of a bundles. There is also a set **R** of preferences, i.e., rankings of **A** and of lotteries over **A**. Included in **B**, the set of lifetime bundles, is every pairing of an element of **A** and an element of **R**, or a subset of such pairings.

In the general case, recall, we derived a lifetime well-being measure via the indirect route. By adding an axiom of Sovereignty to the KLST axioms, vNM axioms, and Bernoulli, we ended up with the formula: $w(a,R) = c(u^R)u^R(a) + d(u^R)$. $u^R(\cdot)$ is a lifetime utility function representing preference R; $c(u^R)$ and $d(u^R)$ are scaling factors.

Temporal additivity, in this setup, means assuming that each preference R (in the set **R** that we are using to model well-being) is temporally additive. That is, the lifetime utility function $u^R(\cdot)$ takes the form of summing period utility.

[37] Sequencing effects are one of the issues engaged in the philosophical literature on the structure of lifetime well-being. See sources cited Chapter 2, note 1.

The inconsistency of temporal additivity and sequencing effects, as described in the text, does not apply to temporal additivity with a discount factor. But a discount factor is criticizable on other grounds, and in any event discounting yields only a quite specific kind of sequencing, namely, better bundles earlier. See Section 4.4.3.

$u^R(a) = \sum_{t=1}^{T} u^{R:p}(a^t)$. A given lifetime utility function $u^R(.)$ can be expressed in terms of a period utility function $u^{R:p}(\cdot)$. We assign a lifetime utility number to a given *a* bundle by adding up by the numbers assigned to each period bundle a^t as per the period utility function $u^{R:p}(\cdot)$.

Putting together this formula with that in the paragraph preceding it, we end up with the following formula for a preference-based, temporally additive measure of lifetime well-being:

$$w(a,R) = \sum_{t=1}^{T} [c(u^{R:p})u^{R:p}(a^t) + d(u^{R:p})]$$

Lifetime well-being for a given combination of a lifetime *a* bundle and a preference structure *R* is the sum of scaled period utility.

Much scholarship in economics indeed assumes that lifetime utility is temporally additive: it assumes the formula $u^R(a) = \sum_{t=1}^{T} u^{R:p}(a^t)$, or that formula with a discount factor attached. The reason for doing do is, again, tractability. If we adopt an assumption of temporal additivity, we can specify a given preference *R* and its utility function by specifying its ranking of period bundles. Let $\mathbf{A^p}$ be the set of a^t bundles—period bundles of non-preference attributes. **A** is the set of lifetime sequences of period bundles, comprised from $\mathbf{A^p}$—each element of **A** being a temporal sequence of the elements of $\mathbf{A^p}$. Temporal additivity means that we can "nail down" the content of a given preference by identifying how it ranks $\mathbf{A^p}$ and lotteries over $\mathbf{A^p}$. Without temporal additivity, we'll instead need to consider a much more complicated question: how the preference ranks lifetime sequences of period bundles (the elements of **A**), and lotteries over such sequences.[38]

4.4.3 A Discount Factor?

We've been using the following general formula for temporally additive lifetime well-being: $w(b) = \sum_{t=1}^{T} w^p(b^t)$. However, economists often posit a lifetime well-being function that is not merely temporally additive but also incorporates a discount factor (specifically, a utility-discount factor, since economists adopt a preference view of welfare and thus measure well-being with utility numbers).[39]

[38] Parallel to the philosophical literature on sequencing effects and lifetime well-being, there is an empirical literature in economics that examines whether individuals' preferences exhibit sequencing effects. See sources cited in Adler (2012, pp. 419–20).

[39] See Frederick, Loewenstein, and O'Donoghue (2002), discussing the pervasiveness of the discounted-utility model in economics.

If the preceding formula were revised to incorporate a discount factor, it would read as follows: $w(b) = \sum_{t=1}^{T} \lambda(t) w^p(b^t)$, with $\lambda(t) > 0$—the discount factor—decreasing with time. Is such an approach justified?

Consider first a well-being theory that is not preference-based. The formula $w(b) = \sum_{t=1}^{T} \lambda(t) w^p(b^t)$ is certainly *possible* within the context of such a theory. We identify our period well-being measure $w^p(\cdot)$, as per the methodologies discussed in Section 4.4.1, and then specify the discount factor $\lambda(t)$. But the inclusion of this term within the temporally additive formula seems hard to defend. Let b_1^t and b_2^t be two period bundles such that the first is assigned a higher level of period well-being by our theory than the second. And let b and b^* be two lifetime bundles which are identical, except that the two period bundles swap temporal locations: In b, the better period bundle occurs earlier in time and the worse bundle later; in b^* the better period bundle occurs later in time and the worse one earlier. Then the discounted temporally additive formula *necessarily* ranks b better than b^*. Why would that be warranted?[40]

Well-being theorists do sometimes posit that a life goes better if it is "upward sloping."[41] The discounted temporally additive formula, however, favors a downward- over an upward-sloping life—and not only favors a life that is consistently downward-sloping over one that is upward-sloping, but indeed (as in the previous paragraph) counts any shift of better period bundles to a position earlier in life as an improvement in lifetime well-being. Such a view is downright weird, and I'm not aware of any non-preference theorist of well-being who adopts it.

If our theory is instead a preference-based theory, then the period well-being measure $w^p(\cdot)$ is derived from individuals' period utility functions, with $u^{R;p}(\cdot)$ the period utility function of someone with preference R. Whether our formula for temporally additive lifetime well-being should include the discount factor, or not, now depends upon whether the formula for lifetime *utility* includes such a factor. $u^R(\cdot)$ is the lifetime utility function of someone with preferences R. It represents how someone with those preferences ranks lifetime bundles and lotteries over such bundles. If temporally additive, $u^R(\cdot)$ could take the form $u^R(a) = \sum_{t=1}^{T} u^{R;p}(a^t)$, omitting a discount factor; or it could take the form $u^R(a) = \sum_{t=1}^{T} \lambda^R(t) u^{R;p}(a^t)$, with $\lambda^R(\cdot)$ the discount factor. Which formula is more appropriate?

The simple answer is that it depends on the preference. It might be that Fred is a discounter while Ginger is not. Fred's lifetime utility is the

[40] See Sullivan (2018), generally arguing against the rationality of "time biases" such as discounting.

[41] See sources cited Chapter 2, note 1.

discounted sum of period utility; Ginger's, the undiscounted sum of period utility.

Such an answer is too quick, in two ways. First, our preference theory might idealize preferences. If the idealization component includes a rational-deliberation screen, discounting may be screened out. Suppose that Fred has a brute preference for preferred period bundles (those with a higher period utility) to occur earlier in his life. Were he to deliberate about this preference, Fred might realize that it lacks any substantive basis (the fact that a period bundle occurs earlier rather than later in life doesn't, as such, increase its impact on lifetime well-being) and thereby come to reject it.

Second, we should distinguish between present-bias and utility discounting. Present-bias means that individuals, at a given point in time, care more about what occurs now rather than later. A temporally discounted lifetime utility function is *one* source of present-bias, but not the only possibility. Imagine that Hilda prefers period bundle b_1^t over period bundle b_2^t. Faced with the choice between having b_1^t now and b_2^t later, or having b_2^t now and b_1^t later, Hilda prefers the first option. This preference might be explained by the fact that Hilda's preference over lifetime bundles, like Fred's, is such as to prefer better period bundles to occur earlier. But another possibility is that Hilda, like Ginger, has an undiscounted lifetime utility function—and yet tends to give extra decisional weight to what occurs in the present. Present-bias, in this case, means that she *departs* from the maximization of lifetime utility and, instead, upweights what is occurring now. It would be a mistake to infer from Hilda's behavior that her lifetime utility function is like Fred's rather than Ginger's.

In short, calculating lifetime well-being as the sum of discounted period well-being seems quite problematic for a non-preference theory of well-being and may well be unwarranted even for a preference theory. That said, it would be dogmatic to insist that temporally additive lifetime well-being must take the form $w(b) = \sum_{t=1}^{T} w^p(b^t)$. We should also allow for the possibility that $w(b) = \sum_{t=1}^{T} \lambda(t) w^p(b^t)$. The methods for constructing the period well-being measure discussed earlier are compatible with both formulas, indeed agnostic as between them.

4.5 Moving from an Interval Scale to a Ratio Scale of Lifetime Well-Being

Our lifetime well-being measure, $w(\cdot)$, is an *interval-scale* measure of lifetime well-being. That is, $w(\cdot)$ is unique up to a positive affine transformation.[42]

[42] It may to useful to recall the definition of "positive affine transformation." $w^*(\cdot)$ is a positive affine transformation of $w(\cdot)$ if there exists a $r > 0$, s, such that $w^*(\cdot) = rw(\cdot) + s$. That is, for every bundle b, $w^*(b) = rw(b) + s$.

All the specific methodologies presented in sections 4.2 through 4.4 operate to define an interval-scale measure of lifetime well-being. This is true whether $w(\cdot)$ is constructed directly, via the KLST set of well-being measures, or indirectly, via the vNM set; whether or not $w(\cdot)$ is preference-based; and whether or not $w(\cdot)$ is temporally additive. In each case, we arrive at a lifetime well-being measure unique up to a positive affine transformation. Note that $w(\cdot)$ has been constructed to embody our judgments of lifetime well-being and differences in lifetime well-being; any positive affine transformation of $w(\cdot)$ does so equally well.[43]

In some contexts, however, it may be useful to define a *ratio-scale* measure of lifetime well-being. $w(\cdot)$ is a *ratio-scale* measure of lifetime well-being if it is unique up to a positive *ratio* transformation.[44] In general, an interval scale can be converted into a ratio scale by specifying a meaningful zero point. What this means, with respect to our interval scale of lifetime well-being, is that we convert $w(\cdot)$ into a ratio-scale measure by identifying a zero bundle b^{zero}, and then rescaling $w(\cdot)$ so that it assigns 0 to the zero bundle. That is, from $w(\cdot)$, we define a new measure $w^+(\cdot)$ as follows: $w^+(b) = w(b) - w(b^{zero})$.[45]

Although defining a ratio scale of lifetime well-being *can* be useful, care is needed in doing so. The bundle b^{zero} should be *meaningful*—it should embody ethically relevant information about well-being—but there are a number of different candidates for such information, depending on which version of welfarism is being used. Even with a specific theory of well-being in hand, and the interval scale of lifetime well-being it defines, there is no *unique* way to move to a ratio scale. There will be a variety of ways to identify b^{zero}.

Consider, to start, the utilitarian SWF—which just adds up well-being numbers. In the fixed-population context, with the utilitarian SWF, there is no advantage to defining a ratio scale of well-being. The outcome ranking is the same whether we use our interval-scale well-being measure, $w(\cdot)$, or instead convert that into a ratio-scale measure $w^+(\cdot)$.

Things change when we move to the variable-population context.[46] The population is now a set of individuals, finite or infinite, each of whom exists in some

[43] $w(\cdot)$ is such that $w(b) \geq w(b')$ iff bundle b is at least as good for lifetime well-being as bundle b'; and $w(b) - w(b') \geq w(b'') - w(b''')$ iff the difference in lifetime well-being between bundle b and bundle b' is at least as large as the difference in lifetime well-being between bundle b'' and bundle b'''. If $w^*(\cdot)$ is a positive affine transformation of $w(\cdot)$, it will imply the very same comparisons of bundle lifetime well-being levels and differences as $w(\cdot)$.

[44] $w^*(\cdot)$ is a positive ratio transformation of $w(\cdot)$ if there exists a $r > 0$ such that $w^*(\cdot) = rw(\cdot)$.

[45] Why does identifying a zero bundle define a ratio scale? Note that if $w'(\cdot)$ is a positive affine transformation of $w^+(\cdot)$ *and* is such that $w'(b^{zero}) = 0$, it follows that $w'(\cdot) = rw^+(\cdot)$, $r > 0$.

[46] See Blackorby, Bossert, and Donaldson (2005); Greaves (2017).

(not necessarily all) of the outcomes. Each outcome corresponds to a well-being vector with a slot for each person in the population, but with a Ω rather than a well-being number in the slot if the person doesn't exist in that outcome. Assume that, naively, we try to define the utilitarian rule for this context by stipulating that the score assigned to a vector is just the sum total of well-being numbers for existing people. This rule is not well-defined with an interval scale of well-being, as shown in the accompanying note.[47]

One utilitarian rule for the variable-population context that *is* well-defined with an interval-scale well-being measure, and that some scholars support, is to assign a score to a well-being vector by summing over existing people, each time subtracting the well-being level of a life equally good as nonexistence. This is the so-called total utilitarian rule. Let b^{NE} be a bundle that our well-being theory judges to be equally good as non-existence. The total-utilitarian rule works as follows: For a given outcome x, it assigns the vector corresponding to x the following score (summing over the individuals who exist in x, and ignoring the Ωs): $\Sigma[w(b_i(x)) - w(b^{NE})]$. Outcomes are ranked according to the scores of their corresponding vectors.

Again, this rule *is* well-defined with an interval-scale measure of lifetime well-being. But we might find it useful to simplify the statement and application of the total-utilitarian rule by defining a ratio scale of well-being, as follows. Let $b^{zero} = b^{NE}$, the bundle equally good for well-being as non-existence. And let our ratio-scale measure $w^+(\cdot)$ be defined as follows: $w^+(b) = w(b) - w(b^{NE})$. The total-utilitarian rule can now be expressed, more compactly, as follows: Rank outcomes according to the score $\Sigma[w^+(b_i(x))]$.

A different proposed utilitarian rule for the variable-population context is so-called critical-level utilitarianism. Note that the total-utilitarian rule prefers to add people to the population even if their lives are barely better than non-existence. This leads to the so-called repugnant conclusion, and to avoid that some have proposed a "critical-level" rule—which sums over existing people, now subtracting the well-being of a "critical-level" life. This is a "good" life, better than non-existence. Let b^{crit} be the critical-level life, with $w(b^{crit}) > w(b^{NE})$. The critical-level rule assigns the vector corresponding to outcome x the following score (summing over the individuals in x, and ignoring the Ωs): $\Sigma[w(b_i(x)) - w(b^{crit})]$.

[47] For example, assume that only individual i exists in x, while only j and k exist in y. $w(\cdot)$ is such that $w(b_i(x)) = 10$, $w(b_j(y)) = 3$, $w(b_k(y)) = 3$. $w^*(\cdot) = w(\cdot) + 15$, hence a positive affine transformation. Then the naïve rule using $w(\cdot)$ assigns x and y scores of 10 and 6, respectively (hence yields the verdict that x is the better outcome): but using $w^*(\cdot)$ assigns x and y scores of 25 and 36, respectively (hence the opposite verdict).

The rule thus stated can be more crisply stated by defining a ratio-scale measure of well-being, $w^{++}(b) = w(b) - w(b^{crit})$. But note that this is a *different* ratio scale of well-being from the one above, since $w(b^{crit}) \neq w(b^{NE})$. The critical-level rule can be stated using this new ratio scale, not the earlier one: Rank outcomes according to the score $\Sigma[w^{++}(b_i(x))]$.

Yet a different kind of ratio scale arises with a prioritarian SWF. Even in the fixed-population context, the prioritarian rule is not well-defined with an interval scale of well-being. Let $g(\cdot)$ be the prioritarian transformation function: any strictly increasing, strictly concave, and continuous function. Outcome x will be mapped onto the vector $(w(b_1(x)), \ldots, w(b_N(x)))$, and y onto the vector $(w(b_1(y)), \ldots, w(b_N(y)))$. We assign the first vector the score $\Sigma g(w(b_i(x)))$ and the second the score $\Sigma g(w(b_i(y)))$, and rank the two outcomes according to these scores. If instead we map outcomes onto vectors using a positive affine transformation of our initial well-being measure, the ranking of the outcomes may change.

We can circumvent this problem by using a specific prioritarian SWF, the Atkinson SWF.[48] The Atkinson $g(\cdot)$ function is as follows: $g(v) = \frac{1}{1-\gamma}(v)^{1-\gamma}$, $\gamma > 0$, or log (v) in the special case of $\gamma = 1$. The degree of priority for the worse off is captured by γ, the "priority parameter," and increases as γ does. If we assign each outcome x the following score using the Atkinson $g(\cdot)$ function, and rank outcomes in the order of the scores, the ranking *is* well-defined with an interval scale of well-being: $\Sigma g(w(b_i(x)) - w(b^{Atk}))$.[49] b^{Atk} is a special "zero bundle" selected for use with the Atkinson SWF. Suffice it to say that $w(b^{Atk})$ need not be equal to $w(b^{NE})$, nor need it be equal to $w(b^{crit})$.[50]

We can more crisply state the Atkinson-prioritarian rule by defining a ratio scale of well-being as follows: $w^{+++}(b) = w(b) - w(b^{Atk})$. If so, the Atkinson-prioritarian rule for ranking outcomes can be stated as follows: $\Sigma g(w^{+++}(b_i(x)))$. But note that this ratio scale is a different scale from either of the ones discussed above.

To recapitulate: $w(\cdot)$ as constructed in previous sections is an interval-scale measure of lifetime well-being. It can be converted into a ratio scale, by

[48] See Adler (2012, ch. 5; 2019b, ch. 4; 2022b).

[49] The reader may well be puzzled as to why ranking outcomes according to the score $\Sigma g(w(b_i(x)))$ is *not* invariant to positive affine transformations of the well-being measure for any prioritarian transformation function $g(\cdot)$, and yet ranking outcomes according to the score $\Sigma g(w(b_i(x)) - w(b^{Atk}))$ *is* invariant to positive affine transformations of the well-being measure with an Atkinson $g(\cdot)$. The answer is that, in the first case, we are using a "profile-independent" $g(\cdot)$ function—one that is applied to vectors of well-being numbers regardless of the well-being measure—while in the second case we are using a "profile-dependent" $g(\cdot)$ function, one that changes as the well-being measure changes. The distinction between profile-independent and profile-dependent prioritarianism is discussed at length in Adler (2022b).

[50] See Adler and Treich (2015).

identifying a b^{zero}. But there are a variety of possible candidates for this bundle, depending on the ethical view being implemented. b^{zero} could be b^{NE}, b^{crit}, b^{Atk}, or perhaps some other bundle. There is no "natural" zero point; if $w(\cdot)$ is converted into a ratio-scale measure of lifetime well-being, this should be done with a clear stipulation about how the zero point has been picked.

5

Evaluating Risk-Regulation Policies

Simple Utilitarianism and Ex Post Prioritarianism

What follows is the most important chapter in this book. It shows, in detail, how utilitarianism and prioritarianism can be brought to bear to evaluate risk-regulation policies.

The analysis here rests upon the various arguments, concepts, and tools developed in the four previous chapters. Without the intellectual work of those previous chapters, this chapter would be a non-starter: it *presupposes* those arguments, concepts, and tools. Still, the present chapter is more significant in light of the book's aims than the preceding ones. We are finally in a position to do what the book promises: to demonstrate how welfarism gives systematic and specific guidance in making the difficult trade-offs involved in selecting policies to reduce fatality risk. The chapter focuses on utilitarianism (the historically dominant version of welfarism) and prioritarianism (the most plausible alternative to utilitarianism, or so I believe).

How does welfarism provide policy guidance? Via the SWF framework (or so I have argued).[1] Recall that a given SWF has multiple uncertainty modules.[2] I believe that the most attractive utilitarian module is *simple utilitarianism* and that the most attractive prioritarian module is *ex post prioritarianism*. The chapter, thus, focuses on these modules. In short, the chapter demonstrates how utilitarianism and prioritarianism can be brought to bear to evaluate risk-regulation policies by way of simple utilitarianism and ex post prioritarianism, respectively.

Chapter 7 argues in favor of these approaches, as against competing utilitarian and prioritarian modules—by considering an array of uncertainty axioms that one might wish a module to satisfy. The reader eager to see the argument *for* simple utilitarianism and ex post prioritarianism can jump to Chapter 7 and then return to this chapter.

The first section of the current chapter, Section 5.1, is a preliminary section that discusses the tractability properties of simple utilitarianism and ex post

[1] See Section 1.4; Adler (2012, 2019b, 2022b).
[2] See Table 1.1.

Risk, Death, and Well-Being. Matthew D. Adler, Oxford University Press. © Oxford University Press 2025.
DOI: 10.1093/9780197505984.003.0005

prioritarianism and also addresses the general question of how the components of the SWF modeling framework correspond to real-world entities.

Section 5.2 sets forth a conceptual apparatus for applying simple utilitarianism and ex post prioritarianism to risk-regulation policies. (This is done, specifically, in Section 5.2.1.) A given policy *P* assigns each individual a lottery over lifetime bundles. Simple utilitarianism and ex post prioritarianism calculate the ethical value of *P* as a function of the array of individual lotteries. In turn, each individual's policy-specific lottery over lifetime bundles can be seen as arising from their age; their policy-specific risk profile; and their policy-specific attribute profile. This conceptualization is closely linked to the *life table*, a standard tool of demographers.

Section 5.2 will also introduce the concept of the social value of risk reduction (SVRR). The SVRR is the social value of a small change in individual fatality risk: social/ethical value as per a given SWF-plus-uncertainty module (here, simple utilitarianism or ex post prioritarianism). The SVRR allows us to see how simple utilitarianism and ex post prioritarianism assign relative ethical values of fatality risk reduction to individuals differentiated by age, income, health, preferences, etc.

Section 5.3 illustrates the conceptual apparatus set forth in Section 5.2.1 with an empirical simulation. Underlying the empirical results are various general properties of the simple utilitarian and ex post prioritarian SVRRs. Section 5.4 reviews these properties.

Section 5.5 discusses a modification to the apparatus set forth in Section 5.2.1 (namely, to allow for individual attribute profiles that are stochastic rather than non-stochastic) and discusses how this modification is useful in handling the problem of interdependent fates and in accounting for the possibility that life extension may not be beneficial.

A terminological note: In what follows, "well-being" always means "lifetime well-being" unless I specify otherwise (e.g., "period well-being"). I will often explicitly say "lifetime well-being," but it is stylistically awkward to do so at every juncture, and so "lifetime" is sometimes dropped.

The focus of this chapter (as indeed the entire book until Chapter 8) is what I have termed the Focal Case: a fixed and finite population of ordinary human persons (OHPs).[3] The chapter demonstrates how simple utilitarianism and ex post prioritarianism can be brought to bear to evaluate risk-regulation policies in the Focal Case. One extension beyond the Focal Case, discussed in Chapter 8, concerns a "variable population": policies may change who comes into existence. Such effects are ignored in this chapter. In the apparatus set forth in Section 5.2.1,

[3] See Chapter 1.

everyone affected by the policies being modeled has already been born; policies change their fatality risks, not their chances of existence.

Two other topics are also beyond the scope of this chapter. One is the application of utilitarianism and prioritarianism to fatality risk-regulation policies under conditions of "ambiguity": the absence of well-defined probabilities.[4] While accounting for ambiguity is an important part of predictive decision theory, it is less clear whether ambiguity should also be a component of normative decision theory. Arguably, *rational* decisionmaking—in particular, rational policymaking via the SWF framework—should eschew ambiguity and instead strive to assign precise probabilities to outcomes.[5] In any event, extending the analysis of this chapter to account for ambiguity is a topic that must be left for future research.

Second, I assume (as throughout the book) that policies are finite probability distributions over outcomes.[6] Complications for policy modeling that arise with infinite lotteries (an infinite number of outcomes with a non-zero probability given some policy)[7] are ignored here and are a topic for future research.

5.1 Simple Utilitarianism and Ex Post Prioritarianism: Preliminaries

Recall that the SWF framework gives guidance in ranking any set of policies **P**. It does so via a number of key components, which are brought together to yield choice guidance with respect to **P**. These components are a model population $\mathbf{I}^{\text{Mod}}$; the outcome set **O**; a lifetime well-being measure $w(\cdot)$; the SWF; and an uncertainty module for the SWF.[8]

Outcomes are simplified representations of possible worlds. Outcomes are characterized with respect to *some* of the features of a world that are relevant to individuals' well-being. In particular, in a given outcome x, each individual i in $\mathbf{I}^{\text{Mod}}$ is assigned a bundle of attributes $b_i(x)$. The types of attributes in a bundle are *some* of the individual attributes (properties) that constitute or causally contribute to well-being. The attribute bundles are *lifetime bundles*: they describe the individuals' attributes over their entire lifetimes. In short, a given outcome x corresponds to a list of lifetime bundles $(b_1(x), \ldots, b_N(x))$, one for each of the N individuals in the model population.

4 See Berger (2022) for a recent review.
5 See Al-Najjar and Weinstein (2009); Fleurbaey (2018).
6 See Section 1.A.6.
7 See Goodsell (2021).
8 See Section 1.4.

With the well-being measure $w(\cdot)$ in hand, each outcome is mapped onto a well-being vector. Bundle $b_i(x)$, the lifetime bundle of individual i in outcome x, is assigned the well-being number $w(b_i(x))$; and x itself is mapped onto a vector (list) of N well-being numbers, namely, the vector $(w(b_1(x)), \ldots, w(b_N(x)))$. I also use a more compact notation for the well-being vector corresponding to x, namely, $\mathbf{w}(x)$.

An SWF—such as the utilitarian SWF; a prioritarian SWF; the leximin SWF; a sufficientist SWF; or an egalitarian SWF—is a rule for ranking well-being vectors.

The SWF framework captures the decisionmaker's uncertainty about policy outcomes by conceptualizing a given policy P as a probability distribution across outcomes. For each outcome x in the outcome set **O**, there is a probability $\pi_P(x)$: the probability of outcome x, given the choice of policy P. Because each outcome, in turn, is mapped onto a well-being vector, each policy corresponds to a probability distribution across well-being vectors.

An uncertainty module for a given SWF, denoted $\succcurlyeq^{E\text{-}P}$, ranks policies as a function of their associated probability distributions across well-being vectors. Each SWF has multiple such modules. The simple-utilitarian module (a module for the utilitarian SWF) and ex-post-prioritarian module (a module for a prioritarian SWF) employ, respectively, the following formulas.

Simple Utilitarian Module: $P \succcurlyeq^{E\text{-}P} P^*$ iff $\sum_x \pi_P(x) \sum_{i=1}^{N} \mathbf{w}_i(x) \geq \sum_x \pi_{P^*}(x) \sum_{i=1}^{N} \mathbf{w}_i(x)$

Ex-Post-Prioritarian Module: $P \succcurlyeq^{E\text{-}P} P^*$ iff $\sum_x \pi_P(x) \sum_{i=1}^{N} g(\mathbf{w}_i(x)) \geq \sum_x \pi_{P^*}(x) \sum_{i=1}^{N} g(\mathbf{w}_i(x))$, with $g(\cdot)$ strictly increasing, strictly concave, and continuous.

In other words, simple utilitarianism assigns each policy a score equaling the expected sum of individual well-being and ranks policies according to these scores; while ex post prioritarianism assigns each policy a score equaling the expected sum of individual *transformed* well-being (transformed by the $g(\cdot)$ function) and ranks policies according to *these* scores.

Simple utilitarianism and ex post prioritarianism are especially *tractable* uncertainty modules. To be precise, they satisfy two tractability axioms: Decomposability and Policy Separability. These axioms are discussed in Section 5.1.1 immediately below. Section 5.1.2 discusses how these axioms help to address a general question for policy analysts employing the SWF framework—namely, how the *notional* individuals and *notional* probabilities that operate within the framework correspond to real-world humans and actual probabilities.

5.1.1 Tractability Axioms: Decomposability and Policy Separability

Tractability axioms reduce the analytic burden in evaluating policies.[9] One such axiom is "Decomposability." To grasp this axiom, note that each policy is associated with a lottery over attribute bundles for each individual in the population $\mathbf{I}^{\mathbf{Mod}}$—and thus (given the well-being measure $w(\cdot)$) a lottery over well-being levels, one for each person in the population. Decomposability stipulates that two policies mapping onto the same array of individual well-being lotteries are equally good.

> Decomposability: Let P and P^* be such that, for each individual i, i's lottery over well-being levels is the same with P as with P^*. Then the uncertainty module should rank P equally good as P^*.

Decomposability means that the decisionmaker (or the policy analyst advising the decisionmaker) does not need to explicitly characterize a policy as a probability distribution over whole outcomes. Instead, it is sufficient to characterize a policy as an array of individual bundle lotteries. This individual-level information is a "sufficient statistic" for evaluating policies. Two policies, P and P^*, might correspond to quite different outcome lotteries, but as long as they generate the same list of individual bundle lotteries, the analyst can treat them as equivalent—if Decomposability holds. See Table 5.1 for an illustration.

A second tractability axiom, Policy Separability, states that if some individuals face the same well-being lotteries with two policies, P and P^*, the P/P^* ranking is invariant to what those lotteries are.

> Policy Separability: Let P, P^*, P^+, and P^{++} be as follows. There is a subset $\mathbf{M}$ of the population $\mathbf{I}^{\mathbf{Mod}}$ such that for each individual in $\mathbf{M}$, their well-being lottery with P is the same as their well-being lottery with P^*, and their well-being lottery with P^+ is the same as their well-being lottery with P^{++}. Policies P^+ and P^{++} are the same as P and P^*, respectively, as regards the well-being lotteries faced by individuals who do not belong to $\mathbf{M}$. If so, the uncertainty module's ranking of P^+ as compared to P^{++} should be the same as its ranking of P as compared to P^*.

[9] The Decomposability axiom discussed in this section is discussed in Adler (2019b, pp. 287–88), where it is referred to as "correlation-insensitivity." (Decomposability is referred to by McCarthy [2017] and McCarthy, Mikkola, and Thomas [2020] as "Anteriority.") Policy Separability as discussed in this section is a logically stronger version of an axiom by the same name in Adler (2019b, pp. 285–87) and Adler (2022b).

See chapter appendix, Section 5.A.1.1, for formal statements of Decomposability and Policy Separability.

Table 5.1 Decomposability

	Policy P		Policy P*	
	Outcome *x*	Outcome *y*	Outcome *z*	Outcome *zz*
	$\pi_P(x) = .5$	$\pi_P(y) = .5$	$\pi_{P^*}(z) = .5$	$\pi_{P^*}(zz) = .5$
Ariella	50	10	10	50
Brianna	50	40	40	50
Caleb	50	70	50	70
Dev	50	100	50	100

Explanation: The table shows individuals' lifetime well-being levels with the different possible outcomes of each policy. Policy *P* will lead to outcome *x* or *y*, each with probability 0.5. Policy *P** will lead to outcome *z* or *zz*, each with probability 0.5. Note that the two policies lead to different possible vectors of lifetime well-being numbers, but each individual faces the same lottery over lifetime well-being levels with *P* as with *P**. Decomposability therefore requires that the policies be ranked as equally good.

See Table 5.2 for an illustration.

Policy Separability is logically stronger than Decomposability. If an uncertainty module satisfies Policy Separability, it necessarily satisfies Decomposability—but not vice versa.[10]

As a shorthand, I'll say that an individual is "unaffected" if the individual faces the same lottery over bundles regardless of which policy in **P** (the set of policies) is chosen. Assume that some individuals are, indeed, unaffected. (This would be true, at least, of individuals who existed in the past and are now dead. Depending on the specific types of policies in **P**, it might also include current or future individuals.) Decomposability, alone, means that the ranking of policies in **P** depends upon the array of individual well-being lotteries associated with each policy—lotteries for both affected and unaffected individuals. Adding Policy Separability further reduces the decisional burden. Decomposability *plus* Policy Separability means that the ranking of policies depends upon the array of individual well-being lotteries *for affected individuals* associated with each policy. Unaffected individuals can be ignored.

If an uncertainty module satisfies both Decomposability and Policy Separability, the analyst has a very useful decisional shortcut for characterizing the policies in **P**. Policies need not be explicitly characterized as probability distributions over whole outcomes, or even as probability distributions over whole outcomes dropping the bundles of the unaffected. Instead, each policy can

[10] See chapter appendix, Section 5.A.1.1, for an example of an uncertainty module that satisfies Decomposability but not Policy Separability.

Table 5.2 Policy Separability

	Policy P		Policy P*	
	Outcome x	Outcome y	Outcome z	Outcome zz
	$\pi_P(x) = .5$	$\pi_P(y) = .5$	$\pi_{P*}(z) = .5$	$\pi_{P*}(zz) = .5$
Ariella	7	20	11	11
Brianna	21	5	13	12
Caleb	30	40	30	40
Dev	8	1	8	1
	Policy P$^+$		Policy P^{++}	
	Outcome x^+	Outcome y^+	Outcome z^+	Outcome zz^+
	$\pi_{P+}(x^+) = .5$	$\pi_{P+}(y^+) = .5$	$\pi_{P++}(z^+) = .5$	$\pi_{P++}(zz^+) = .5$
Ariella	20	7	11	11
Brianna	21	5	12	13
Caleb	6	3	6	3
Dev	50	100	100	50

Explanation: Caleb faces the same well-being lottery with P as P^*, and with P^+ as P^{++}. The same is true of Dev. Caleb and Dev are the members of subset M. The other members of the population, Ariella and Brianna, are each situated the same way with respect to the P^+/P^{++} choice as with respect to the P/P^* choice—namely, each faces the same lottery with P^+ as she does with P, and the same lottery with P^{++} as she does with P^*. Policy Separability requires that the P^+/P^{++} ranking be the same as the P/P^* ranking.

be characterized as an array of bundle lotteries, one for each *affected* individual. Knowing how each policy assigns bundle lotteries to the affected subset of the population is a "sufficient statistic" for ranking the policies in P.

5.1.2 Individuals and Cohorts

As explained in Chapter 1, the "individuals" that figure into the SWF framework—the members of the model population I^{Mod}—are not flesh-and-blood human beings (OHPs). The numerical designator "i" that refers to a particular member of I^{Mod}, individual i, is not meant as a proper name that actually designates a particular, existing, OHP. Rather, I^{Mod} is a theoretical construct that functions as a model of a population of actual OHPs, and individual 1, individual 2, . . . , individual i are members of this made-up population. They are *notional*, not actual, humans.

As also stated in Chapter 1, each outcome is a simplified model of a possible world. The designator "x" for a particular outcome is not meant to refer to a world or to a set of worlds. In effect, each outcome is a *notional* world, not a genuinely possible world or set of worlds.

Because outcome x is neither a world nor a set of worlds, the policy-specific probabilities assigned to outcomes by the SWF framework—$\pi_P(x)$ the probability of outcome x given policy P—are not the actual epistemic probabilities (degrees of belief) of a governmental decisionmaker or policy analyst. Rather, these probabilities are *notional* degrees of belief. Outcome x specifies a bundle for each individual in $\mathbf{I}^{\mathbf{Mod}}$. Thus, $\pi_P(x)$ is the probability that the individuals receive the array of bundles specified by x: the probability that individual 1 receives bundle $b_1(x)$ and individual 2 receives bundle $b_2(x)$ . . . and individual N receives bundle $b_N(x)$. But since each individual i in $\mathbf{I}^{\mathbf{Mod}}$ is a representation of an OHP, not an actual OHP, the decisionmaker or policy analyst can't believe *to any degree* that i exists and has bundle $b_i(x)$.

Why should the SWF framework (as I interpret it) construe outcomes as models of worlds (not genuine worlds or sets of worlds), the individuals in $\mathbf{I}^{\mathbf{Mod}}$ as representations of actual OHPs (not actual OHPs), and decisionmaker probabilities as notional (not actual) degrees of belief? Doing so dramatically increases the framework's capacity to employ tractable, simplified models in evaluating policies.

For example, much SWF scholarship uses one-period models[11]—which tend to be considerably simpler to work with than multiperiod models. Individuals have attributes during a single period, and policies affect these attributes. But there is no differentiation of individuals by lifespan. (Such differentiation is only possible in a multiperiod model, which allows for variation in the number of periods that each individual exists.) Consider, then, the outcome set **O** for an SWF application employing the single-period setup. In each outcome x in **O**, everyone in $\mathbf{I}^{\mathbf{Mod}}$ lives for a single period: Everyone has the same lifespan. Although it is *possible* that everyone in the actual human population has the same lifespan, a decisionmaker's actual degree of belief that this is the case should be *zero* or close to zero. Consider a US governmental decisionmaker, Kylie, concerned about the effect of her choices on US citizens who have already been born and are still alive. Actual demographic processes in the United States are such that individuals do not all die at the same age. If Kylie is reasonably informed about these processes, she should believe to a very high degree that individuals in the

[11] This is true, notably, of the canonical model in optimal-tax scholarship. Individuals are differentiated by consumption and leisure but not lifespan; each individual ends up with a single amount of consumption and a single amount of leisure, rather than (as in a multiperiod model) different such amounts in different periods. See, e.g., Kaplow (2008, ch. 4).

actual population of humans that she is concerned about will not all die at the same age. Her *actual* degree of belief in a world *d* in which all currently living US citizens die at the same age should be zero or close to zero. But if Kylie is using the single-period outcome set O to evaluate her choices, *every* outcome *x* to which Kylie assigns a non-zero probability, given any policy *P*, is such that everyone in $\mathbf{I}^{\mathbf{Mod}}$ dies at the same age. Thus $\pi_p(x)$ can't be Kylie's *actual* degree of belief that, were she to choose *P*, outcome *x* would occur. Rather, $\pi_p(x)$ must be a notional degree of belief: a model-based representation of Kylie's epistemic probabilities.

To be sure, the application of the SWF methodology to risk regulation employed in this book employs a multiperiod rather than single-period setup. Individuals can live varying lifespans, from 1 to *T* periods; governmental policies affect individuals' lifespan probabilities. Still, within this setup, there is plenty of scope for simplifications that don't correspond to genuine possibilities. For example, individuals might be modeled as having a constant level of some attribute, one that remains the same in each period when the individual is alive. Imagine that a given individual's lifetime bundle is specified to include their lifespan and, for each period alive, their health and income. Health and/or income are allowed to vary between individuals but are stipulated to be constant within each individual's life. Doing so avoids the additional computational burden that would arise with health and income varying both interpersonally and intertemporally. But it is exceedingly unlikely that each individual's health or income will in fact remain constant over their lifespan. If O is such that individual health and/or income are intertemporally constant in every outcome *x*, $\pi_p(x)$ can't be Kylie's *actual* degree of belief that were she to choose *P*, outcome *x* would occur. Kylie must surely know that income and health are intertemporally variable, not constant.

The use of simplified models that don't map onto real possibilities is characteristic not just of SWF-based modeling but also of other policy-analytic methodologies and of economic scholarship generally.[12]

But we now face a tricky question. If the designator "*i*" for a given member of $\mathbf{I}^{\mathbf{Mod}}$ is not mean to designate an actual OHP, and $\pi_p(x)$ is not understood as the decisionmaker's or policy analyst's actual epistemic probability (degree of belief), what *is* the correspondence between these constructs and real OHPs and probabilities, respectively? There must be *some* nexus between the components of the SWF framework and the real entities that the components are meant to represent. Otherwise, the framework can hardly provide useful guidance to a decisionmaker in making *real* choices.

I'll now explain how this nexus should be understood in the case of an uncertainty module (such as simple utilitarianism or ex post prioritarianism) that

[12] On modeling in economics, decision theory, and ethics, see, e.g., Gilboa, Postlewaite, Samuelson, and Schmeidler (2014); Sugden (2013); Roussos (2022); Weymark (2022).

satisfies the Decomposability axiom. Given Decomposability, each policy P can be conceptualized as a list of bundle lotteries, one for each member of the model population $\mathbf{I}^{\mathbf{Mod}}$. The actual population of OHPs should be divided into *cohorts*. A cohort of the actual population is a group of individuals that the SWF analyst *treats as similarly situated*, in the sense that cohort members are modeled as facing the same bundle lotteries as each other, for every policy in **P**. Each cohort C of actual OHPs corresponds to a cohort C^{Mod} of notional individuals (a subset of $\mathbf{I}^{\mathbf{Mod}}$). Let $\rho_{P,i}(b)$ denote the probability that notional individual i receives bundle b with policy P. A cohort C^{Mod} of $\mathbf{I}^{\mathbf{Mod}}$ is such that if i and j are two members of the cohort, then $\rho_{P,i}(b) = \rho_{P,j}(b)$ for every bundle b and every policy P in **P**. These *notional* cohort bundle probabilities will be based upon the *real* probabilities that the actual humans in cohort C will receive the types of attributes included in the b bundles.

For example, the apparatus for modeling risk policies presented below, in Section 5.2.1, supposes that (a) each lifetime bundle consist of a lifespan l plus a period bundle for each period alive, and (b) individuals in $\mathbf{I}^{\mathbf{Mod}}$ of different ages generally face different lifespan probabilities. (Older individuals tend to have a greater chance of living a longer lifespan.) Thus, cohorts of $\mathbf{I}^{\mathbf{Mod}}$ are differentiated, at least, by age. A cohort of $\mathbf{I}^{\mathbf{Mod}}$ is a group of notional individuals with the same age, or a subset of each such age group. Each such cohort C^{Mod} will correspond to a real-world cohort C consisting of everyone of the same age, or a subgroup of an age group. For example, suppose that period bundles are specified as including the notional individual's health and income. Then a real-world cohort C will consist either of everyone of the same age; or an age group subdivided in a way that is useful in predicting the effect of policies on longevity, health, and income. Educational attainment, work history, gender, race, place of residence, marital status, prior income, and prior health are among the types of individual characteristics that serve to predict the life expectancy of an individual of a given age and their current and future income and health. Thus, each age group will constitute a real-world cohort C; or age groups will be partitioned by some combination of educational attainment, work history, gender, race, residence, marital status, prior income, and prior health (or other demographic characteristics), and a real-world cohort C will be a subset of an age group arising from this partition. For each C there is a corresponding C^{Mod} of notional individuals. If i is a member of C^{Mod}, i's lottery over lifetime bundles for a given policy (that is, $\rho_{P,i}(b)$ for each bundle b and policy P) is based upon the lifespan probabilities and health and income experience of the actual humans in C.[13]

[13] What about the outcome probabilities, namely, $\pi_P(x)$ for a given policy P and outcome x? How are *these* derived from real-world data? If the uncertainty module satisfies Decomposability, the $\rho_{P,i}(b)$ values are sufficient to rank policies. $\pi_P(x)$ values can be specified implicitly. Real-world data grounds the $\rho_{P,i}(b)$ values; and once those are specified, the array of $\pi_P(x)$ values (the probability of each outcome x for each policy P) is *any* such array that is consistent with the $\rho_{P,i}(b)$ values.

5.2 Simple Utilitarianism and Ex Post Prioritarianism Applied to Risk-Regulation Policies

The apparatus for applying simple utilitarianism and ex post prioritarianism to risk-regulation policies is presented in Section 5.2.1. (As we'll see, this apparatus is grounded in the tractability axioms.) Section 5.2.2 introduces the concept of the social value of risk reduction (SVRR), which illuminates how the simple-utilitarian and ex-post-prioritarian values of policies depend upon the policies' distributions of risk reduction among the affected population.[14]

Lest there be any confusion, in this section and for the remainder of this chapter, "individual" means a member of I^{Mod}, i.e., a notional individual belonging to the model population that is a key component of the SWF framework.

5.2.1 Conceptualizing Risk-Regulation Policies

Recall that lifetime bundles are divided into T periods: 1, 2, . . . , T, with T the maximum possible length of life. Each lifetime bundle consists of a longevity l, the number of periods that the individual lives; a series of *period bundles* (bundles of period attributes) for periods 1 through l; and the status of Dead for each period from $l + 1$ through T.[15]

The decisionmaker is selecting among a group of policies **P** at some point in calendar time: "the present" or "the current time." I'll assume that each individual has an "age," namely, the number of periods that the individual has survived as of the current time. For example, if Luis has survived 50 periods (he was born 50 periods ago), his age is 50; the current period of his life is period 51.

Simple utilitarianism and ex post prioritarianism satisfy the Decomposability axiom. Each policy can, therefore, be characterized as an array of lotteries over lifetime bundles—one lottery over lifetime bundles for each person in the population. Such characterization is sufficient to determine the ethical value of each policy (as per simple utilitarianism and ex post prioritarianism).[16]

[14] See chapter appendix, Section 5.A.2, for a more precise statement of some of the material presented in this section.

[15] See Chapter 4.

[16] This Section—conceptualizing a risk policy as an array of lotteries over lifetime bundles, one lottery for each member of the population—grows out of my earlier work, in particular Adler (2017; 2019b, ch. 5; 2020a; 2020b) and Adler, Ferranna, Hammitt, and Treich (2021).

In turn, an individual's lottery over lifetime bundles, with a given policy *P*, is fully determined by three pieces of information. The first is the individual's current age. Let's denote this as A_i. Thus, the current period of individual *i*'s life is period number $A_i + 1$.[17]

The second is the individual's *risk profile*. Let p_i^t denote individual *i*'s "survival probability" for period *t*, meaning the probability that they survive to the end of period *t*, conditional on being alive at the beginning of period *t*. (The individual's probability of dying before the end of period *t*, conditional on being alive at the beginning of period *t*, is just 1 minus their survival probability.) A given policy *P* endows the individual with a *risk profile*, namely, a list of survival probabilities, one for each period beginning with the current period: $(p_i^{A_i+1}, p_i^{A_i+2}, \ldots, p_i^T)$.

In particular, what is distinctive about a fatality-risk-regulation policy is that it *improves* individuals' risk profiles, relative to baseline. Let *B* denote the baseline policy, i.e., the policy of inaction: government leaves in place the status quo. *B* is one of the policies in **P**, the policy set; inaction is one of the choices available to government. Other policies in **P**, if they are risk-regulation policies, will endow (some) individuals with risk profiles that are an improvement on their baseline profiles, in the sense that those individuals have survival probabilities in the current period and/or future periods that are *larger* than baseline survival probabilities.[18]

Finally, a given policy *P* endows the individual with an *attribute profile*. An attribute profile takes the form $(b_i^1, \ldots, b_i^T)$. Each b_i^t in this attribute profile is a *conditional period bundle*: it denotes the bundle that individual *i* will receive in period *t*, if they survive to the end of that period. For example, assume that Mira's current age is 30. It is possible that Mira does not survive through the end of period 50, i.e., that her status in period 50 is Dead. However, if Mira *does* survive through the end of period 50, she will have some period bundle in that period: b_{Mira}^{50} is that period bundle.

A risk-regulation policy will not merely change individuals' risk profiles, relative to the baseline policy. It may well also change their attribute profiles. In

[17] I assume that $1 \le A_i \le T - 1$. Individuals are already in existence ($1 \le A_i$; the individual has been born and survived at least a single period; note that if $A_i = 0$ and $p_i^{A_i+1} < 1$, there is a non-zero probability that that individual does not come into existence). As already mentioned, the issue of variable-population policy impacts is postponed to Chapter 8. Further, no individual has lived the maximum lifespan ($A_i \le T - 1$). Such individuals are dead at present and hence unaffected; thus they can be dropped from the analysis given Policy Separability.

[18] That said, the apparatus here does not *require* that a policy improve individuals' risk profiles, relative to baseline. Although that is a typical feature of risk-regulation policies, the apparatus is more general. An individual's age, risk profile with a given policy *P*, and attribute profile with that policy suffice to determine their policy *P* lottery over lifetime bundles—and thus to enable the analyst to assign a simple-utilitarian or ex-post-prioritarian value to policy *P*, once the analyst has this information for all individuals—regardless of whether individuals' risk profiles are improvements or worsenings relative to baseline.

particular, improving survival probabilities is rarely costless. Doing so typically requires some resource expenditure, which is ultimately incurred by individuals in the form of reduced income. So, if period bundles describe individual incomes, the attribute profiles that individuals receive with a risk-regulation policy *P* will differ from the baseline attribute profiles as regards individuals' incomes.

To sum up, each individual *i* has an age A_i; and each policy *P* in **P** endows each individual *i* with a policy-specific risk profile $(p_i^{A_i+1}, p_i^{A_i+2}, \ldots, p_i^T)$ and with a policy-specific attribute profile $(b_i^1, \ldots, b_i^T)$, namely, a list of period bundles received in each period conditional on surviving to the end of the period rather than being Dead then. The probabilities in *i*'s risk profile will be based upon the *real-world* survival probabilities of the real-world cohort of individuals that the cohort of notional individuals including *i* corresponds to; and *i*'s attribute profile will be derived from information about this actual group's attributes and how these attributes change as a result of policy interventions.[19]

These three pieces of information for individual *i*—age, risk profile, and attribute profile—are sufficient to calculate individual *i*'s lottery over lifetime bundles as a result of policy *P*. Why is it sufficient information? From the policy *P* risk profile, we can calculate a policy *P* lottery over longevities (lifespans) for individual *i*. That is, we can calculate the probability that *i* lives exactly A_i periods, the probability that they live exactly $A_i + 1$ periods, the probability that they live exactly $A_i + 2$ periods, . . . , the probability that they live exactly *T* periods. Then, for each possible longevity *l*, the policy *P* attribute profile determines which *l*-period series of period bundles the individual receives if they live exactly *l* periods.

Imagine now that some individuals are unaffected. More precisely, these individuals (1) have the same risk profile for every policy in **P**, and (2) have the same attribute profile for every policy in **P**. Because simple utilitarianism and ex post prioritarianism satisfy the axiom of Policy Separability, the unaffected can be dropped from the analysis.

How does simple utilitarianism *evaluate* policies understood as lotteries over lifetime bundles for affected individuals? It does so by taking the expected sum of individual well-being or, equivalently, by summing individuals' expected well-being. Let $E^{SU}(P)$ be the sum of affected individuals' expected well-being for a given policy *P*, taking account of the lottery over lifetime bundles that *P* confers upon each affected person. Formally, let $\rho_{P,i}(b)$ denote the probability for individual *i* of bundle *b*, given policy *P*. And let $E^{SU}(P) = \sum_i \sum_b \rho_{P,i}(b) w(b)$, with the

[19] Given the modeling apparatus set forth here, a cohort of $\mathbf{I}^{\text{Mod}}$ consists of individuals who are the same age and who have the same risk profile and attribute profile for every policy in **P**. This notional cohort corresponds to an actual cohort of OHPs. See Section 5.1.2.

summation taken over all affected individuals, and with $w(\cdot)$ our lifetime well-being measure. Then it's not difficult to show that the simple-utilitarian rule as stated at the beginning of this chapter (the expected sum of individual well-being) can be restated as ranking policies according to this rule: P is at least as good as P^* iff $E^{SU}(P) \geq E^{SU}(P^*)$.

In parallel fashion, ex post prioritarianism evaluates policies by taking the expected sum of individual *transformed* well-being or, equivalently, by summing individuals' expected *transformed* well-being. Let $E^{EPP}(P)$ be the sum of affected individuals' expected transformed well-being for a given policy P, taking account of the lottery over lifetime bundles that P confers upon each affected person. Again, let $\rho_{P,i}(b)$ denote the probability for individual i of bundle b, given policy P. And let $E^{EPP}(P) = \sum_i \sum_b \rho_{P,i}(b) g(w(b))$, with the summation taken over all affected individuals, and with $w(\cdot)$ our lifetime well-being measure and $g(\cdot)$ the prioritarian transformation function. Then it's not difficult to show that the ex-post-prioritarian rule as stated at the beginning of this chapter (the expected sum of transformed well-being) can be restated as ranking policies according to this rule: P is at least as good as P^* iff $E^{EPP}(P) \geq E^{EPP}(P^*)$.

To recapitulate: Simple utilitarianism assigns each policy an ethical value $E^{SU}(P)$ which is the sum across affected individuals of individual expected well-being—as determined by the individual's age, risk profile for the given policy, and attribute profile for the given policy, together with the well-being measure $w(\cdot)$. Ex post prioritarianism assigns each policy an ethical value $E^{EPP}(P)$ which is the sum across affected individuals of individual expected transformed well-being—as determined by the individual's age, risk profile for the given policy, and attribute profile for the given policy, together with the well-being measure $w(\cdot)$ and prioritarian transformation function $g(\cdot)$.

It's worth noting that the conceptual apparatus proposed here is closely related to the standard tools of demography. One standard task of demographers is to estimate a so-called cohort life table, for cohorts of individuals defined by birth year (equivalently, current age) and, perhaps, other characteristics.[20] And one quantity in a cohort life table, typically, is the probability of surviving each year of life, conditional on being alive at the beginning of that year. This probability is (to use the terminology above) an annual survival probability. In short, a cohort life table tells us the baseline *risk profile* for the cohort. The framework here combines this type of standard demographic information with non-risk information (attribute profiles) to determine the simple-utilitarian and ex-post-prioritarian value of policies.

[20] See, e.g., Preston, Heuveline, and Guillot (2001, ch. 3).

5.2.2 The Social Value of Risk Reduction (SVRR)

The social value of risk reduction (SVRR) is a useful concept in understanding how changes to survival probabilities contribute to the value of policies, as per simple utilitarianism or ex post prioritarianism.[21] A given policy *P* endows each individual with a risk profile and attribute profile. Equivalently, a given policy *P* endows each individual with a profile of risk and attribute *deltas*—that is, a list of changes in the individual's risk profile and attribute profile, for each period starting with the current period, relative to their baseline risk and attribute profiles. Starting with the individual's baseline risk and attribute profiles, and altering these by the deltas for a given policy *P*, we end up with the individual's policy *P* risk and attribute profiles.

$\text{SVRR}_i^{\text{SU}}$ denotes the simple-utilitarian SVRR for individual *i*. This is defined as the partial derivative of E^{SU} with respect to *i*'s current survival probability, with this partial derivative evaluated at *i*'s baseline risk and attribute profile.[22] Intuitively, $\text{SVRR}_i^{\text{SU}}$ is the change in simple-utilitarian value per unit of current risk reduction for individual *i*, as evaluated for a marginal such reduction. Further, simple-utilitarian value is just the sum of individuals' expected lifetime well-being. So we can also say that $\text{SVRR}_i^{\text{SU}}$ is the change in an individual's expected lifetime well-being and, thus, in the sum total of expected lifetime well-being (simple-utilitarian value), per unit of current risk reduction for individual *i*—as evaluated for a marginal such reduction.

Why *is* $\text{SVRR}_i^{\text{SU}}$ a useful concept? Assume that a policy changes individuals' current survival probabilities by Δp_i for each individual *i*, as well as (perhaps) changing individuals' future survival probabilities and their attribute profiles. Then the total change in E^{SU} relative to baseline is approximately equal to the sum across individuals of $\text{SVRR}_i^{\text{SU}} \times \Delta p_i$, plus sums of corresponding terms for the deltas to individuals' future survival probabilities and to individuals' attribute profiles. In other words, $\text{SVRR}_i^{\text{SU}}$ captures that *portion* of a policy's impact on simple-utilitarian value that results from the delta to individual *i*'s current survival probability.

Moreover, by comparing $\text{SVRR}_i^{\text{SU}}$ to $\text{SVRR}_j^{\text{SU}}$ for two individuals *i* and *j*, we can determine the relative simple-utilitarian value of risk reductions for the two. Consider a change Δp to someone's current survival probability. That risk change, if accruing to individual *i*, results in a change of simple-utilitarian value

[21] See Adler, Ferranna, Hammitt, and Treich (2021); Adler, Hammitt, and Treich (2014); Ferranna, Hammitt, and Adler (2023); Ferranna, Sevilla, and Bloom (2022); Hammitt and Treich (2022).

[22] See chapter appendix, Section 5.A.2, for a formal presentation of the SVRR concept. In some contexts, it may be useful to generalize SVRR as discussed in the text so as to define SVRR_i for an unaffected individual *i*. On this topic, see Section 5.A.2.5.

by approximately $SVRR_i^{SU} \times \Delta p$. The very same risk change, accruing instead to individual *j*, results in a change of simple-utilitarian value by approximately $SVRR_j^{SU} \times \Delta p$. Thus (for a small Δp) the first change in ethical value is larger than/smaller than/equal to the second iff $SVRR_i^{SU}$ is larger than/smaller than/equal to $SVRR_j^{SU}$.

An ex-post-prioritarian SVRR is defined analogously. $SVRR_i^{EPP}$, the ex-post-prioritarian SVRR, is the partial derivative of E^{EPP} with respect to *i*'s current survival probability, with this partial derivative evaluated at *i*'s baseline risk and attribute profile. $SVRR_i^{EPP}$ is the change in *ex-post-prioritarian* value per unit of current risk reduction for individual *i*, as evaluated for a marginal such reduction. Ex-post-prioritarian value is just the sum of individuals' expected transformed lifetime well-being. So we can also say that $SVRR_i^{EPP}$ is the change in an individual's expected transformed lifetime well-being and, thus, in the sum total of expected transformed lifetime well-being (ex-post-prioritarian value), per unit of current risk reduction for individual *i*—as evaluated for a marginal such reduction.

Simple-utilitarian and ex-post-prioritarian SVRRs are individual-specific. This is indicated via the "*i*" subscript, with $SVRR_i$ denoting the SVRR of individual *i*. To avoid clutter, however, I sometimes drop the subscript and refer just to "SVRR." This is *not* meant to suggest that SVRRs are the same across individuals.

5.3 An Empirical Illustration

This section uses a simulation model, based on the US income distribution and survival curve, to illustrate the theory of policy evaluation presented in the previous section. I assume an affected population of 25 age-income cohorts. I calculate SVRRs and evaluate exemplary risk-regulation policies, using a simple-utilitarian module and an ex-post-prioritarian module—the latter with an Atkinson-prioritarian SWF with two different degrees of priority for the worse off (moderate and higher).

Section 5.3.1 explains the building blocks of the simulation. Section 5.3.2 presents and discusses the SVRRs. Section 5.3.3 evaluates exemplary policies. Section 5.3.4 varies the simulation by allowing for preference heterogeneity.

5.3.1 The Simulation Model: Building Blocks

So that the simulation results are easy to present, I use a simple, one-dimensional period bundle: each period bundle is just an income amount. The period length is one year. Thus, each lifetime bundle consists of a longevity and an income for each year alive. $b = (y^1, y^2, \ldots, y^l, \text{Dead}, \text{Dead}, \ldots, \text{Dead})$, with y^t the income in year t. The maximum longevity, T, is 100 years.

The well-being measure is a temporally additive measure,[23] $w(b) = \sum_{t=1}^{T} w^p(y^t)$, with $w^p(y^t) = (\log y^t - \log(\$1000))$,[24] and $w^p(\text{Dead}) = 0$. This period well-being measure is based on the logarithmic utility function, widely employed in economics. Note that the threshold income is $1,000: the period well-being of $1,000 equals the period well-being of Dead, i.e., extending a life of any duration by adding one year at an income of $1,000 leaves lifetime well-being unchanged. $1,000 is roughly equal to the World Bank extreme poverty level of $2.15/day.[25]

Lifetime bundles do not describe individual preferences. The bundle structure and well-being measure, thus, can be understood either as (1) implementing a non-preference-based theory of well-being, or as (2) implementing a preference-based theory with the simplifying assumption that individuals have an identical preference structure R and thus identical lifetime utility functions, specifically temporally additive utility functions with period utility $u^{R;p}(y^t) = (\log y^t - \log(\$1000))$, and $u^{R;p}(\text{Dead}) = 0$. (Below, in Section 5.3.4, I refine the simulation model by allowing for preference heterogeneity.)

The affected population is divided into 25 equal-size cohorts: five age groups (ages 20, 30, 40, 50, and 60), each divided into five income quintiles ("Low," "Moderate," "Middle," "High," and "Top"). Income by quintiles is based on US data.[26] I estimated post-tax-and-transfer individual income for the five quintiles to be as follows (2016 dollars), Low to Top: $21,961; $30,118; $41,349; $57,538; and $134,840. Data about the age distribution of income was then used to estimate a time profile of income. I estimated time factors for each year of life, and multiplied the quintile incomes here by the time factors to arrive at the income in that quintile in that year of life.[27] This yields the baseline *attribute profile* for each cohort. (I'll also refer to this attribute profile as an "income profile," since the only described attribute is income.)

[23] As discussed in Chapter 4, temporal additivity means that lifetime well-being is the sum of period well-being. See Section 4.4.

[24] Here, "log" denotes the natural logarithm (ln). Using logarithms to a different base (e.g., base 10) would not change the results of the simulation; switching the base has the effect of multiplying everyone's lifetime well-being number by a common positive constant, which does not change policy recommendations by the utilitarian SWF or an Atkinson-prioritarian SWF.

[25] See World Bank (2022, p. 3).

[26] The data sources for this simulation were the same as for the simulation in Adler (2020b) and are described in Adler (2020b, appendix A).

[27] The time factors were as follows (rounding to 0 decimal places). Ages 0 to 24: 38%. Ages 25 to 29: 84%. Ages 30 to 34: 101%. Ages 35 to 39: 121%. Ages 40 to 44: 129%. Ages 45 to 49: 130%. Ages 50 to 54: 131%. Ages 55 to 59: 124%. Ages 60 to 64: 114%. Ages 65 to 69: 97%. Ages 70 to 74: 90%. Ages 75 and over: 67%.

A baseline *risk profile* for each of the 25 cohorts was taken from a life table for the entire US population. For the Middle income quintile, the survival probability in each year of life was set equal to the survival probability for that year in the life table. Survival probabilities for the other quintiles were adjusted so as to roughly match the estimates of life expectancy by income group in Chetty et al. (2016).[28]

For purposes of the ex-post-prioritarian analysis, the transformation function used was an Atkinson transformation function. The Atkinson $g(\cdot)$ function, recall, is as follows: $g(v) = \frac{1}{1-\gamma}(v)^{1-\gamma}$, $\gamma > 0$, or log (v) in the special case of $\gamma = 1$. The degree of priority for the worse off is captured by γ, the "priority parameter," and increases as γ does. I consider two different levels of γ: 1 and 2. $\gamma = 1$ has the special property of neutralizing permanent differences in period well-being on the ex-post-prioritarian SVRR.[29] $\gamma = 2$ is chosen to illustrate the effect of yet more priority for the worse off.

In order to use the Atkinson $g(\cdot)$ function, we need to choose a zero point of lifetime well-being, b^{Atk}.[30] The well-being measure plugged into the ex-post-prioritarian formula using the Atkinson $g(\cdot)$ function—$E^{EPP}(P) = \sum_i \sum_b \rho_{P,i}(b) g(w(b))$—should be such that $w(b^{Atk}) = 0$. Here I select b^{Atk} to be a life of any duration with the threshold income, \$1,000, in each period alive. Note that the well-being measure set out five paragraphs above indeed satisfies the condition $w(b^{Atk}) = 0$.

Ex-post-prioritarian SVRRs with $\gamma = 1$ and $\gamma = 2$ will be displayed momentarily. Table 5.3 provides a different perspective on the impact of γ. The well-being measure employed here displays *diminishing marginal well-being impact*: ceteris paribus, a dollar increment for a higher-income person has a smaller effect on well-being than the same increment for a lower-income person. Thus, the utilitarian SWF will approve some "leaky transfers" in income. If the richer person's income is reduced by some amount, and the poorer person's income is increased by some fraction *f* of the amount, the utilitarian SWF will approve this transfer as long as *f* is not too small. Prioritarianism tolerates a greater degree

[28] The mortality risk at each age is 1 minus the survival probability. Mortality risks were taken from the 2017 US life table and then adjusted by a multiplicative factor in each year. The adjusted survival probabilities are 1 minus the adjusted mortality risks. The multiplicative factors for the Low, Moderate, Middle, High, and Top quintiles were, respectively, 1.5, 1.2, 1, 0.9, 0.75. These multiplicative factors were chosen so that the ratio between life expectancy at age 40 for individuals in that quintile, and life expectancy at age 40 for 50th percentile individuals, was approximately equal to the ratio as estimated by Chetty et al. (2016).

[29] See Section 5.4.3.

[30] On the Atkinson $g(\cdot)$ and the need to specify a zero bundle when using it, see Adler (2012, ch. 5; 2019b, ch. 4; 2022b); Section 4.5.

of leakage: as γ increases, the minimum acceptable fraction becomes smaller. Table 5.3 illustrates how moving from the utilitarian SWF to an Atkinson SWF with increasing values of γ affects the minimum acceptable fraction for a leaky transfer between the Top and Middle income groups, and between the Middle and Low groups.

Policies are changes (deltas) to cohorts' baseline risk profiles and attribute (income) profiles. A given such policy *P* endows each cohort with a new risk profile and attribute (income) profile. From that information, using the well-being measure $w(\cdot)$, we determine each cohort's expected well-being score with *P*; adding up these scores across the cohorts, we end up with $E^{SU}(P)$, the simple-utilitarian value of the policy. From the same information, using the well-being measure $w(\cdot)$ and now also our Atkinson transformation function ($\gamma = 1$ or $\gamma = 2$), we determine each cohort's expected *transformed* well-being score with *P*; adding up *these* scores across the cohorts, we arrive at $E^{EPP}(S)$, the ex-post-prioritarian value of the policy.

In general, a policy can change a cohort member's risk profile by changing current and/or future survival probabilities; and it can change their income profile by changing current and/or future income. Because the simulation is meant to be illustrative, I will focus on policies that reduce current risks (increase current survival probabilities) at the expense of some reduction in current incomes. Focusing on policies of this sort will bring to light the core features of ex post prioritarianism and simple utilitarianism as methodologies for assessing risk regulation, without the extra complexity of intertemporal risk/risk, risk/income, or income/income trade-offs.

Table 5.3 The Atkinson SWF Priority Parameter (γ) and Leaky Income Transfers

	Utilitarian	$\gamma = .5$	$\gamma = 1$	$\gamma = 1.5$	$\gamma = 2$	$\gamma = 5$	$\gamma = 20$
Top to Middle	31%	27%	23%	20%	18%	8%	0.1%
Middle to Low	53%	48%	44%	40%	37%	21%	1.3%

Explanation: This table assumes that each of the two individuals has a constant income, equaling that of the Top, Middle, or Low quintile; that the two individuals have the same lifespan; that the richer individual's income is reduced by a small Δy during one year; and that the poorer individual's income is increased by $f\Delta y$, $0 < f < 1$, in one year. It calculates the minimum value of *f* such that the transfer is an improvement, for a utilitarian SWF and for an Atkinson prioritarian SWF with various values of γ. The lifetime well-being measure is the same as in the simulation. See Adler (2019b, p. 294 n. 56) for the formula used in this calculation. Because income is constant, the results using the formula are independent of the individuals' common lifespan.

5.3.2 SVRRs in the Simulation Model

Table 5.4 displays the simple-utilitarian SVRRs ($SVRR^{SU}$) for the various cohorts, while Tables 5.5 and 5.6 display the ex-post-prioritarian SVRRs ($SVRR^{EPP}$) $\gamma = 1$ and $\gamma = 2$. These results are normalized so that 1 indicates the SVRR of a member of the 60-year-old, Low income cohort. (In other words, the tables show the ratio between the SVRR of a given cohort, and the SVRR of the 60-year-old, Low income cohort.)[31]

Recall that $SVRR^{SU}$ for the member of a given cohort is the change in that individual's expected lifetime well-being (and thus the change in the sum total of expected lifetime well-being across cohorts: the change in simple-utilitarian

Table 5.4 Simple-Utilitarian SVRRs

	Income: Low	Moderate	Middle	High	Top
Age 20	2.8	3.3	3.7	4.1	5.2
30	2.5	2.8	3.2	3.6	4.5
40	2.0	2.3	2.6	2.9	3.7
50	1.5	1.7	2.0	2.2	2.8
60	1.0	1.2	1.4	1.6	2.1

Explanation: This table shows $SVRR^{SU}$ values for the various cohorts, normalized so that 1 indicates $SVRR^{SU}$ for a member of the 60-year-old, Low income cohort.

Table 5.5 Ex-Post-Prioritarian (γ =1) SVRRs

	Income: Low	Moderate	Middle	High	Top
Age 20	5.3	5.3	5.3	5.3	5.3
30	3.8	3.8	3.9	3.8	3.8
40	2.5	2.6	2.7	2.7	2.7
50	1.6	1.7	1.8	1.8	1.8
60	1.0	1.1	1.1	1.2	1.2

Explanation: This table shows $SVRR^{EPP}$ ($\gamma = 1$) values for the various cohorts, normalized so that 1 indicates $SVRR^{EPP}$ ($\gamma = 1$) for a member of the 60-year-old, Low income cohort.

[31] The entries are rounded to one decimal place.

Table 5.6 Ex-Post-Prioritarian ($\gamma = 2$) SVRRs

	Income: Low	Moderate	Middle	High	Top
Age 20	12.2	10.7	9.5	8.5	6.6
30	6.5	5.8	5.2	4.6	3.6
40	3.5	3.1	2.9	2.6	2.1
50	1.9	1.7	1.6	1.5	1.2
60	1.0	1.0	.9	.8	.7

Explanation: This table shows $SVRR^{EPP}$ ($\gamma = 2$) values for the various cohorts, normalized so that 1 indicates $SVRR^{EPP}$ ($\gamma = 2$) for a member of the 60-year-old, Low income cohort.

value) per unit of current risk reduction to the individual, for a marginal such reduction. With this definition squarely in view, let's be clear about the meaning of the numbers in Table 5.4. Note that the entry in Table 5.4 for a 40-year-old, High income individual is 2.9. This means that a given increment Δp to the current-year survival probability of that individual produces an increase in their expected lifetime well-being that is 2.9 times the increase in expected lifetime well-being produced by the very same increment Δp to the current-year survival probability of a 60-year-old, Low income person. Inverting, simple utilitarianism sees equal value in a Δp increase in the survival probability of a 60-year-old, Low income person, and a *smaller* increase ($\Delta p/2.9$) in the survival probability of a 40-year-old, High income individual.

Similarly, $SVRR^{EPP}$ for the member of a given cohort is the change in that individual's expected transformed lifetime well-being (and thus the change in the sum total of expected transformed lifetime well-being across cohorts: the change in ex-post-prioritarian value) per unit of current risk reduction to the individual, for a marginal such reduction. Note that the entry in Table 5.5 for a 30-year-old, Moderate income individual is 3.8. This means that a given increment Δp to the current-year survival probability of that individual produces an increase in their expected *transformed* lifetime well-being ($\gamma = 1$) that is 3.8 times the increase in expected *transformed* lifetime well-being ($\gamma = 1$) produced by the very same increment Δp to the current-year survival probability of a 60-year-old, Low income person. Inverting, ex post prioritarianism sees equal value in a Δp increase in the survival probability of a 60-year-old, Low income person, and a *smaller* increase ($\Delta p/3.8$) in the survival probability of a 30-year-old, Moderate income person.

How the SVRRs in these tables vary by age and income is noteworthy. Let's start with $SVRR^{SU}$. First, within each income quintile, $SVRR^{SU}$ becomes smaller with age (moving down each column). For example, $SVRR^{SU}$ for Top income individuals of the five ages is, respectively, 5.2 (age 20), 4.5 (age 30), 3.7 (age 40), 2.8 (age 50), and 2.1 (age 60). A similar pattern holds for the other quintiles. Second, within each age group, $SVRR^{SU}$ increases with income (moving rightward in each row). For example, $SVRR^{SU}$ for 30-year-olds in the five income quintiles is, respectively, 2.5 (Low income), 2.8 (Moderate), 3.2 (Middle), 3.6 (High), and 4.5 (Top). A similar pattern holds for the other ages.

What explains these patterns? It can be shown that $SVRR_i^{SU}$ equals *the difference between individual i's expected lifetime well-being, conditional on surviving the current period, and their realized lifetime well-being if they die now.*[32] Consider the limiting case in which an individual would die for certain in the current period absent a life-saving policy intervention, and the policy ensures their survival to the end of the period. The simple-utilitarian value of such intervention is, clearly, equal to the quantity just stated. More generally, consider a policy that increases someone's current survival probability by Δp. The change in simple-utilitarian value from such a policy is Δp times the quantity just stated. Thus $SVRR_i^{SU}$, the change in simple-utilitarian value per unit of risk reduction to individual *i*, is equal to that quantity.

We can now grasp why $SVRR^{SU}$ (1) decreases with age and (2) increases with income in Table 5.4. (1) *The age pattern.* Let's say that the current "life expectancy remaining" of a given individual is the difference between the individual's expected longevity, if they survive the current period, and their longevity if they die now. A typical risk profile, at least in more affluent countries, is such that life expectancy remaining decreases with age. Indeed, this is true of the risk profiles for each of the five income quintiles in the simulation model. Consider now a group of individuals of different ages with a common risk profile and *constant* period income. Among these individuals, if life expectancy remaining decreases with age, then $SVRR^{SU}$ (the difference between the individual's expected lifetime well-being, conditional on surviving the current period, and their realized lifetime well-being if they die now) also decreases with age. In the simulation model, income is not constant but rises and then falls with age. Still, this variation is not strong enough to overturn the basic pattern of $SVRR^{SU}$ falling with age because life expectancy remaining does. (2) *The income pattern.* Consider two individuals of the same age and with the same risk profile, Rachel and Pete. Rachel is richer than Pete: her income in every period is greater than Pete's. Rachel's life expectancy remaining is the same as Pete's, but her $SVRR^{SU}$ is greater than Pete's. For each year of life subsequent to Rachel's and Pete's current age, the difference between the period well-being of that year and the period well-being of the state Dead (not being alive during the year) is *greater* with Rachel's

[32] See Section 5.4 and chapter appendix, Section 5.A.2.

income than with Pete's. This is an immediate consequence of the fact that period well-being increases with period income, as per our logarithmic well-being measure $w^P(\cdot)$. Choosing a period well-being measure with this property in turn reflects the truism that income is good for well-being rather than being bad or neutral. But if period well-being increases with period income, we have the (unwelcome) upshot that a given extension to life expectancy leads to a larger increase in expected lifetime well-being if conferred upon someone with greater period income.

The formula for $SVRR^{EPP}$ is parallel to that for $SVRR^{SU}$. Just as $SVRR_i^{SU}$ equals the difference between individual *i*'s expected lifetime well-being, conditional on surviving the current period, and their realized lifetime well-being if they die now, so $SVRR_i^{EPP}$ equals the difference between the individual *i*'s expected *transformed* lifetime well-being, conditional on surviving the current period, and their *transformed* lifetime well-being if they die now.[33]

As for age preference, within each column (quintile) $SVRR^{EPP}$ ($\gamma = 1$) decreases more sharply with age than $SVRR^{SU}$, and $SVRR^{EPP}$ ($\gamma = 2$) even more so. For example, within the Low income column, $SVRR^{SU}$ decreases from 2.8 (age 20) to 1 (age 60), while $SVRR^{EPP}$ ($\gamma = 1$) decreases from 5.3 (age 20) to 1 (age 60), and $SVRR^{EPP}$ ($\gamma = 2$) from 12.2 (age 20) to 1 (age 60). A similar pattern obtains in the other columns. In short, shifting from simple utilitarianism to ex post prioritarianism *intensifies the simple-utilitarian preference for the young.*

To gain some insight into why this occurs, consider a simpler case than the simulation model. There are two individuals, Young and Old, with the same income profile, but Young is at a lower current age than Old. Each individual would die in the current period absent governmental intervention. The lifetime well-being of Young if Young dies now is w_Y, while the lifetime well-being of Old if Old dies now is w_O—with $w_O > w_Y$.

If government were to intervene and ensure that either Young or Old survives the period, that individual would live a determinate lifespan of *M* years (longer than their current age). Let w_M be the lifetime well-being of Young or Old if government intervenes to save their life, with $w_M > w_O > w_Y$. The utilitarian benefit of saving Young is $\Delta w_Y = w_M - w_Y$, while the utilitarian benefit of saving Old is $\Delta w_O = w_M - w_O$. There is greater utilitarian benefit to saving Young: $\Delta w_Y / \Delta w_O > 1$.

Turning now to prioritarianism, we have that the prioritarian benefit from saving Young is $\Delta g_Y = g(w_M) - g(w_Y)$, while the prioritarian benefit from saving Old is $\Delta g_O = g(w_M) - g(w_O)$. It's not difficult to show that $\Delta g_Y / \Delta g_O > \Delta w_Y / \Delta w_O$. The prioritarian benefit of lifesaving decreases more quickly with age than the utilitarian benefit. The utilitarian sees a greater value in saving Young's life than Old's because the increment to lifetime well-being is greater. The prioritarian sees a

[33] See Section 5.4 and chapter appendix, Section 5.A.2.

greater value in saving Young's life than Old's for this reason, *and* for the additional reason that the increment to lifetime well-being is benefiting someone at a lower *level* of lifetime well-being ($w_Y < w_O$), hence is upweighted.

Generalizing from the simple case, it can be shown that among individuals with the same income profiles and risk profiles, $SVRR^{EPP}$ decreases with age more quickly than $SVRR^{SU}$.[34] And this is what we're observing in tables 5.5 and 5.6.

The second difference between $SVRR^{EPP}$ and $SVRR^{SU}$ concerns the income pattern. While $SVRR^{SU}$ increases with income (holding fixed age), $SVRR^{EPP}$ is close to constant[35] or decreases with income, given the values of γ considered here. For example, while $SVRR^{SU}$ for 30-year-olds is, respectively, 2.5 (Low income), 2.8 (Moderate), 3.2 (Middle), 3.6 (High), and 4.5 (Top), $SVRR^{EPP}$ ($\gamma = 1$) for 30-year-olds in these same income quintiles is 3.8, 3.8. 3.9, 3.8, and 3.8; and $SVRR^{EPP}$ ($\gamma = 2$) values decline from 6.5 to 5.8, 5.2, 4.6, and 3.6. In short, shifting from simple utilitarianism to ex post prioritarianism *neutralizes and then reverses the simple-utilitarian preference for the rich as the degree of priority for the worse off (γ) increases.*

To see why ex post prioritarianism has this effect, consider again our pair of individuals, Rachel and Pete, with the same current age and the same risk profile, but Rachel richer than Pete (greater income in each period). To make the case easier to grasp, assume that each will live to a determinate age of *M* years, greater than their current age, if they survive the period. Let w^C_R be the lifetime well-being of Rachel if she does not survive the current period, and w^M_R if she survives and lives to the age of *M* years. Similarly, let w^C_P be the lifetime well-being of Pete if he does not survive the current period, and w^M_P his lifetime well-being if he does and lives *M* years. $SVRR^{SU}$ for each individual is just the difference in their lifetime well-being between living *M* years and dying now: $SVRR^{SU}$ for Rachel is $w^M_R - w^C_R$, while $SVRR^{SU}$ for Pete is $w^M_P - w^C_P$.

We established earlier that $SVRR^{SU}$ for Rachel is larger than for Pete. $SVRR^{EPP}$ for each individual is the difference in their transformed lifetime well-being between living *M* years and dying now; $SVRR^{EPP}$ for Rachel is $g(w^M_R) - g(w^C_R)$, while $SVRR^{EPP}$ for Pete is $g(w^M_P) - g(w^C_P)$. How the two $SVRR^{EPP}$ values compare depends on the concavity of $g(\cdot)$. In extending Rachel's life from her current age to *M* years, we are producing a bigger increase in lifetime well-being ($w^M_R - w^C_R$) than if we extend Pete's life ($w^M_P - w^C_P$), but the first increase would benefit

[34] See Section 5.4.1.

[35] $SVRR^{EPP}$ ($\gamma = 1$) is not perfectly flat by income in Table 5.5. For example, it increases from 1.6 to 1.8 in the 50-year-old row. Small changes would be seen in all rows if the entries in Table 5.5 were not rounded to one decimal point. As discussed in Section 5.4.3, $SVRR^{EPP}$($\gamma = 1$) *is* perfectly flat by income as between individuals of the same age and risk profile and with a permanent proportional difference of period well-being by some factor *k*. In the simulation here, that condition would be satisfied if risk profiles did not vary by income and income profiles were constant (the same income in each period).

someone at a higher level of lifetime well-being ($w^C{}_R > w^C{}_P$). If $g(\cdot)$ is close to linear, Rachel's SVRR^{EPP} is greater than Pete's. As the concavity of $g(\cdot)$ increases, the SVRR^{EPP} values become equal and then Pete's becomes larger.

5.3.3 Illustrative Policies

In this section, I use the simulation model to illustrate the application of simple utilitarianism and ex post prioritarianism to exemplary policy choices. In all the choice situations, policies reduce individuals' current fatality risks (relative to baseline) by 1 in 100,000 on average. But the choice situations vary on two dimensions. (1) The risk reduction may be uniform, i.e., each individual in every one of the 25 cohorts receives a 1-in-100,000 risk reduction ("Uniform Risk Reduction"), or instead may be concentrated on a subset of the population. "Risk Reduction for the Youngest" means that policies confer a 5-in-100,000 risk reduction upon each 20-year-old; "Risk Reduction for the Oldest" means that policies confer a 5-in-100,000 risk reduction upon each 60-year-old. "Risk Reduction for the Poorest" means that policies confer a 5-in-100,000 risk reduction upon each individual in the Low income quintile; "Risk Reduction for the Richest" means that policies confer a 5-in-100,000 risk reduction upon each individual in the Top income quintile. (Note that in these latter four cases, individuals in 5 cohorts out of 25 receive a risk reduction of 5-in-100,000—hence the average individual risk reduction across all 25 cohorts is 1-in-100,000). (2) For a given type of risk reduction (whether uniform or concentrated on the youngest, oldest, poorest, or richest), the costs of that reduction in terms of lost income may be spread uniformly across the 25 cohorts or spread proportionally to income. In the first case, everyone in all 25 cohorts incurs the very same reduction Δy in current income. In the second case, individuals in cohort C^{Mod} incur a reduction $\Delta y_{C^{Mod}}$ in current income, which is the same fraction of baseline income for all 25 cohorts.

Crossing these two dimensions (the incidence of the risk reduction and the incidence of the income costs of risk reduction), we end up with 10 types of policy choice situations. For each such situation, I calculate the *breakeven* cost as per simple utilitarianism and ex post prioritarianism. If a policy's average individual cost in lost income, across the 25 cohorts, is *below* the breakeven, then the module (simple utilitarianism or ex post prioritarianism) evaluates the policy as better than the baseline; if the policy's average individual income cost is *above* the breakeven, then the module evaluates the policy as worse than the baseline; and if the policy's average individual cost is *equal* to the breakeven, then

Table 5.7 Policy Breakevens: Simple Utilitarianism and Ex Post Prioritarianism

	Simple Utilitarian	Ex-Post-Prioritarian ($\gamma = 1$)	Ex-Post-Prioritarian ($\gamma = 2$)
Uniform Risk Reduction			
Uniform Cost Incidence	\$50	\$65	\$94
Proportional Cost Incidence	\$73	\$105	\$165
Risk Reduction for Youngest			
Uniform Cost Incidence	\$72	\$118	\$223
Proportional Cost Incidence	\$105	\$191	\$392
Risk Reduction for Oldest			
Uniform Cost Incidence	\$27	\$24	\$20
Proportional Cost Incidence	\$39	\$40	\$37
Risk Reduction for Poorest			
Uniform Cost Incidence	\$36	\$63	\$118
Proportional Cost Incidence	\$53	\$102	\$208
Risk Reduction for Richest			
Uniform Cost Incidence	\$68	\$66	\$67
Proportional Cost Incidence	\$99	\$107	\$118

the module evaluates the policy as equally good as the baseline. These policy breakevens are displayed in Table 5.7.

Table 5.7 underscores that the SWF framework is an implementable policy-assessment framework. Here, that framework is being employed to address a standard policy problem in risk regulation: calculating breakeven costs. Table 5.7 also shows that the choice between simple utilitarianism and ex post prioritarianism and—if the latter—the selection of the priority parameter (here,

$\gamma = 1$ versus $\gamma = 2$) can have substantial consequences for policy evaluation. In most of the ten rows, the breakevens vary significantly as between the three methodologies.

What explains the pattern of breakevens in Table 5.7? Let's begin with the first type of policy choice situation, displayed in the first row of this table: Uniform Risk Reduction and Uniform Cost Incidence. If individuals in all 25 cohorts each receive a 1-in-100,000 risk reduction and incur the very same reduction in income, simple utilitarianism prefers the policy over baseline up to a breakeven cost of $50; ex post prioritarianism ($\gamma = 1$) does so up to a breakeven cost of $65; and ex post prioritarianism ($\gamma = 2$) does so up to a breakeven cost of $94.

The breakevens increase in the case at hand because ex post prioritarianism is willing to expend more of a given individual's current income to reduce that individual's current fatality risk, as compared to simple utilitarianism—and all the more so as the degree of priority for the worse off increases. The well-being *benefit* of a current risk reduction is an increased chance of the lottery over lifetime well-being levels that the individual will face if they survive the period—a benefit relative to the lifetime well-being level that the individual will attain if they die now. The well-being *cost* of a reduction in current income is a decrease in the individual's current period well-being—a cost that will be borne at all lifespans if they survive the current period. In short, the risk-reduction benefit adds to the lifetime well-being level that the individual attains if they die now, and the income cost reduces each of the possible lifetime well-being levels that they might obtain if they survive the period. Because ex post prioritarianism gives priority to lower levels of lifetime well-being, it upweights the risk reduction benefit relative to the income cost. This is illustrated by Table 5.8, which

Table 5.8 The Ratio between SVRR and Its Income Analogue

	Income: Low	Moderate	Middle	High	Top
Age 20	13.8/24.7/46.5	21.8/39.6/77.2	33.9/62.2/124.2	52.4/96.4/194.6	153.7/283.8/580.8
30	31.6/48.8/78.0	50.0/78.2/127.3	77.8/122.6/202.4	120.2/189.8/315.1	352.1/557.3/931.3
40	32.5/43.7/59.5	51.8/70.6/97.6	81.1/111.5/156.0	125.8/173.5/244.1	370.8/514.1/729.2
50	24.4/29.5/35.5	39.5/48.2/59.0	62.4/76.9/95.2	97.4/120.6/150.0	290.4/362.3/454.8
60	14.7/16.4/18.3	24.2/27.2/30.7	38.7/44.1/50.1	61.0/69.7/79.6	184.5/212.6/245.0

Explanation. This table shows the ratio between the SVRR and the analogous quantity on the income side (the partial derivative of E^{SU} or E^{EPP} with respect to income, i.e., the change in simple-utilitarian or ex-post-prioritarian ethical value per unit of increase in current income, calculated for a marginal such improvement). The first entry is the ratio for simple utilitarianism; the second for ex post prioritarianism $\gamma = 1$; the third for ex post prioritarianism $\gamma = 2$. These ratios are divided by 100,000 so as to be readable.

shows the ratio between the SVRR for each cohort and the parallel quantity on the income side. Note that in each of the 25 cohorts, this ratio increases as we move from simple utilitarianism to ex post prioritarianism (γ = 1) to ex post prioritarianism (γ = 2).

We have thus far gained some insight into the first row of the breakeven table, Table 5.7 (the row for Uniform Risk Reduction and Uniform Cost Incidence). The pattern of breakevens in the other rows can be explained in terms of how they differ from the first row, on either the risk-reduction side (who benefits from the risk reduction), the cost side (uniform versus proportional incidence), or both.

Consider, first, policy-choice situations that differ from Uniform Risk Reduction and Uniform Cost Incidence on the risk-reduction side. Cost incidence remains uniform, but the beneficiaries of risk-regulation policies are a subset of the population (youngest, oldest, poorest, richest) rather than the entire population. Table 5.9 shows the breakevens for these policy types, as a multiple of the breakeven for Uniform Risk Reduction and Uniform Cost Incidence.

Table 5.9 Policy Breakevens and the Beneficiaries of Risk Regulation

	Simple Utilitarian	Ex-Post-Prioritarian (γ = 1)	Ex-Post-Prioritarian (γ = 2)
Uniform Risk Reduction			
Uniform Cost Incidence	1	1	1
Risk Reduction for Youngest			
Uniform Cost Incidence	1.44	1.82	2.37
Risk Reduction for Oldest			
Uniform Cost Incidence	.54	.37	.21
Risk Reduction for Poorest			
Uniform Cost Incidence	.72	.97	1.26
Risk Reduction for Richest			
Uniform Cost Incidence	1.36	1.02	.71

Explanation: This table shows the ratio of the breakeven, relative to that for Uniform Risk Reduction and Uniform Cost Incidence, as the beneficiaries of the policy are varied (from Uniform Risk Reduction to Risk Reduction for the Youngest, Oldest, Poorest, or Richest)

Shifting risk reduction to the youngest increases the simple-utilitarian breakeven by a factor of 1.44, and the ex-post-prioritarian breakevens even more so (1.82 for $\gamma = 1$, 2.37 for $\gamma = 2$). Conversely, shifting risk reduction to the oldest decreases the simple-utilitarian breakeven by a factor of .54, and the ex-post-prioritarian breakevens even more so (.37 or .21). These patterns reflect the fact that $SVRR^{SU}$ decreases with age in this simulation model, and $SVRR^{EPP}$ even more so. Risk reduction for the young is more valuable than for the old, and so—holding constant the pattern of cost incidence—both simple utilitarianism and ex post prioritarianism are willing to expend more/less total costs for the same overall risk reduction if the risk reduction is concentrated on the young/old rather than being spread uniformly.

Shifting risk reduction to the poorest decreases the utilitarian breakeven (by a factor of .72); leaves the ex-post-prioritarian ($\gamma = 1$) breakeven virtually unchanged (.97); and increases the ex-post-prioritarian ($\gamma = 2$) breakeven (1.26). Conversely, shifting risk reduction to the richest increases the utilitarian breakeven (by a factor of 1.36); again leaves the ex-post-prioritarian ($\gamma = 1$) breakeven virtually unchanged (1.02); and decreases the ex-post-prioritarian breakeven (by a factor of .71). These patterns reflect that $SVRR^{SU}$ increases with income (holding constant age, the simple-utilitarian module prefers to allocate a risk reduction to a richer person, since doing so yields a greater increase in expected lifetime well-being); and that this simple-utilitarian skew toward the rich will be neutralized or reversed by shifting to ex post prioritarianism as γ becomes sufficiently large.

Consider, next, how a change in cost incidence affects policy breakevens. Holding constant the pattern of risk reduction (whether it be uniform or concentrated on the youngest, oldest, poorest, or richest), how does the breakeven change if cost incidence shifts from uniform to proportional? Table 5.10 displays this information. For each of the five patterns of risk reduction, Table 5.10 shows the breakeven for *proportional cost incidence* as a multiple of the breakeven for uniform cost incidence.

Moving from uniform to proportional cost incidence increases the simple-utilitarian breakeven by a factor of roughly 1.5. This reflects the diminishing marginal well-being impact of income. Consider once more our two individuals, Rachel and Pete, who are the same age and have the same risk profile but differ in income: Rachel is richer than Pete. A given reduction Δy in Rachel's current income produces a *smaller* reduction in her expected lifetime well-being than the same reduction Δy in Pete's current income. Thus, a given overall dollar cost (that is, a given average individual cost across the 25 cohorts) represents a smaller loss in the sum of expected lifetime well-being if that cost is shifted from poorer to richer individuals. Moving from uniform to proportional cost incidence effectuates such a shift.

Table 5.10 Policy Breakevens and Cost Incidence

	Simple Utilitarian	Ex-Post-Prioritarian ($\gamma = 1$)	Ex-Post-Prioritarian ($\gamma = 2$)
Uniform Risk Reduction	1.46	1.62	1.76
Risk Reduction for Youngest	1.46	1.62	1.76
Risk Reduction for Oldest	1.44	1.67	1.85
Risk Reduction for Poorest	1.47	1.62	1.76
Risk Reduction for Richest	1.46	1.62	1.76

Explanation: This table shows the ratio of the breakeven for Proportional Cost Incidence relative to that for Uniform Cost Incidence for each of the patterns of risk reduction.

Ex-post-prioritarian breakevens increase even more as we move from uniform to proportional cost incidence: by a factor of roughly 1.6 for $\gamma = 1$ and 1.8 for $\gamma = 2$. A given reduction Δy in Rachel's current income produces a *smaller* reduction in expected transformed lifetime well-being than the same reduction Δy in Pete's current income, for two reasons: because of the diminishing marginal well-being impact of money, *and* because Rachel can expect to be at a higher level of lifetime well-being than Pete.

5.3.4 Preference Heterogeneity

Chapter 4 discussed how to construct a preference-based measure of lifetime well-being, using vNM utility functions. The well-being measure $w(\cdot)$ takes as its input lifetime bundles, which are now understood as "hybrid bundles." A hybrid bundle takes the form (a, R), with a a lifetime bundle of non-preference attributes and R a global preference. The formula for preference-based lifetime well-being, derived in Chapter 4, was as follows: $w(a, R) = c(u^R)u^R(a) + d(u^R)$, with $u^R(\cdot)$ a vNM utility function representing preference R. $c(u^R)$ and $d(u^R)$ are scaling factors applied to this vNM utility function.

Less formally: The lifetime well-being value of a hybrid bundle (a, R) is the *utility* value of the component bundle a of non-preference attributes, as measured by a vNM utility function that represents preference R, with this function adjusted by scaling factors. If lifetime vNM utility is temporally additive (the sum of period utility), then lifetime well-being is temporally additive too, with period well-being equal to the utility value of the period bundle as per a period vNM utility function representing R, adjusted by scaling factors.[36]

I now illustrate how the Chapter 4 account of preference-based well-being measurement can be integrated with the apparatus for simple-utilitarian and ex-post-prioritarian evaluation of risk policies set forth in this chapter, specifically in Section 5.2.1.

Recall the structure of the Section 5.2.1 apparatus. Each individual i has an age A_i. A given policy P endows individual i with a risk profile $(p_i^{A_i+1}, p_i^{A_i+2}, \ldots, p_i^T)$, i.e., a list of survival probabilities, one for each period beginning with the current period; and an attribute profile $(b_i^1, \ldots, b_i^T)$, listing the attribute bundle that the individual will receive in each period if they survive to its end. Putting together these three pieces of information, we can derive the individual's lottery over lifetime bundles with policy P.

In the case of preference-based well-being measurement, each period bundle b_i^t in the attribute profile is a *hybrid* period bundle. It takes the form (a_i^t, R_i), with a_i^t a period bundle of non-preference attributes and R_i a global preference. The attribute profile for a given policy P becomes: $((a_i^1, R_i), \ldots, (a_i^T, R_i))$. What this mean is, if individual i lives l periods as a result of policy P, the lifetime hybrid bundle that individual i receives will be: $(a_i^1, R_i), \ldots, (a_i^l, R_i)$, b^{l+1} = Dead, ..., b^T = Dead. Equivalently, if individual i lives l periods as a result of policy P, they will receive the lifetime bundle of non-preference attributes $(a_i^1, \ldots, a_i^l$, Dead, Dead, ..., Dead), together with preference structure R_i.[37] Individual i's lifetime well-being, in this case, will be the *utility* value of the lifetime bundle of non-preference attributes $(a_i^1, \ldots, a_i^l$, Dead, Dead, ..., Dead), as per a vNM utility function that represents preference R_i, this function adjusted by scaling factors.

I implement this approach in the simulation model by dividing each of the 25 age-income cohorts into 2 subcohorts: one with the logarithmic period utility function employed above, and a second with a more risk-averse period utility function. The so-called coefficient of relative risk aversion captures the degree of risk aversion (curvature) of a utility function with respect to income and will be denoted here as "λ."[38] The coefficient of relative risk aversion for the logarithmic period utility

36 $w(a,R) = \sum_{t=1}^{T}[c(u^{R:p})u^{R:p}(a^t) + d(u^{R:p})]$. See Section 4.4.2.

37 R_i need not be fixed; different policies may endow a given individual i with different global preferences. (R_i *is* fixed over time; in any hybrid lifetime bundle, the global preference structure is the same in all periods.) In the simulation below, however, I assume that each of the two subcohorts ($\lambda = 1$ and $\lambda = 2$) has the same preferences with all policies.

38 Let utility $u(y)$ be a function of income y. Then the coefficient of relative risk aversion at income y is: $\frac{-u''(y)y}{u'(y)}$.

function is 1; the more risk-averse period utility function will have a risk-aversion coefficient equaling 2. I'll refer to these, respectively, as the "$\lambda = 1$" and "$\lambda = 2$" period utility functions.[39] Lifetime utility is assumed to be temporally additive.

Each of the 25 age-income cohorts has an age, baseline income profile, and baseline risk profile (as above); a given policy P endows each cohort with a different income and/or risk profile. The two subcohorts for a given cohort have the same age and the same baseline and policy P income and risk profiles; but the two subcohorts differ in their preferences. One subcohort has a preference structure represented by a $\lambda = 1$ period utility function; the second, a preference structure represented by a $\lambda = 2$ period utility function. In the baseline and with a given policy P, the two subcohorts face the *same* lottery over longevity/income bundles, but a lifetime well-being number is assigned to a given longevity/income bundle using two *different* utility functions: a $\lambda = 1$ period utility function for the first subcohort, and a $\lambda = 2$ period utility function for the second subcohort, each adjusted by scaling factors.[40] The scaling factors are chosen via "high-low" scaling, here by identifying two period income amounts ($1,000 the low amount and $1 million the high amount) and choosing scaling factors so that the scaled utility functions are equal at these amounts.[41]

[39] I'll denote the $\lambda = 1$ and $\lambda = 2$ period utility functions as $u^{1:p}(\cdot)$ and $u^{2:p}(\cdot)$, respectively. With y^t period income, they are as follows. $u^{1:p}(y^t) = \log y^t$; $u^{2:p}(y^t) = -(1/y^t)$. "log" here is the natural logarithm; see note 24. The coefficient of relative risk aversion is constant for each utility function and, respectively, 1 and 2.

[40] In the context at hand, a lifetime bundle a of non-preference attributes is a longevity/income bundle, namely, a longevity l and an income amount y^t for each period 1 to l. A given risk and income profile for some age-income cohort defines a lottery over longevity/income bundles. Let R^1 and R^2 be the global preference structure of the $\lambda = 1$ and $\lambda = 2$ subcohorts, respectively. Then the *hybrid* lifetime bundle corresponding to a given longevity/income bundle a is (a, R^1) for the $\lambda = 1$ subcohort and (a, R^2) for the $\lambda = 2$ subcohort.

In short, a given risk and income profile for some age-income cohort yields a common lottery over longevity/income bundles, but two *different* lotteries over hybrid bundles: a lottery over (a, R^1) bundles for the $\lambda = 1$ subcohort and a lottery over (a, R^2) bundles for the $\lambda = 2$ subcohort.

The lifetime well-being value of an (a, R^1) bundle is the sum of scaled period utility as calculated using $u^{1:p}(\cdot)$, and the lifetime well-being value of an (a, R^2) bundle is the sum of scaled period utility as calculated using $u^{2:p}(\cdot)$—as per the formula in note 36. That is, with a specifying a longevity l and an income amount y^t for each period 1 to l, $w(a, R^1) = \sum_{t=1}^{l} \left[c(u^{1:p}) u^{1:p}(y^t) + d(u^{1:p}) \right]$ and $w(a, R^2) = \sum_{t=1}^{l} \left[c(u^{2:p}) u^{2:p}(y^t) + d(u^{2:p}) \right]$. I assume here that the scaling factors are such that the period well-being of Dead (the period bundle in periods $l + 1$ through T) is 0, hence the "Dead" terms can be dropped from the summation. See note 41.

[41] Note that $1,000 is the threshold income: the period income taken in the main simulation to have the same period well-being as Dead. Moreover, in the main simulation, the period well-being of Dead is 0, which I preserve here. I therefore chose scaling factors so that $c(u^{1:p})u^{1:p}(1000) + d(u^{1:p}) = c(u^{2:p})u^{2:p}(1000) + d(u^{2:p}) = 0$; and $c(u^{1:p})u^{1:p}(1000000) + d(u^{1:p}) = c(u^{2:p})u^{2:p}(1000000) + d(u^{2:p})$. This is accomplished as follows: $c(u^{1:p}) = 1$; $d(u^{1:p}) = -\log(1000)$; $c(u^{2:p}) = (1000000/999)(\log(1000000) - \log(1000))$; $d(u^{2:p}) = (1000/999)(\log(1000000) - \log(1000))$.

Table 5.11 Simple-Utilitarian SVRRs with Preference Heterogeneity

	Income: Low	Moderate	Middle	High	Top
Age 20	2.8/**6.1**	3.3/**6.5**	3.7/**6.8**	4.1/**7.0**	5.2/**7.3**
30	2.5/**5.1**	2.8/**5.5**	3.2/**5.8**	3.6/**5.9**	4.5/**6.2**
40	2.0/**4.1**	2.3/**4.4**	2.6/**4.7**	2.9/**4.8**	3.7/**5.1**
50	1.5/**3.1**	1.7/**3.4**	2.0/**3.6**	2.2/**3.8**	2.8/**4.0**
60	1.0/**2.2**	1.2/**2.5**	1.4/**2.7**	1.6/**2.8**	2.1/**3.0**

Explanation: This table shows $SVRR^{SU}$ values for the subcohorts ($\lambda = 1$ and $\lambda = 2$) of the various cohorts, with the $\lambda = 1$ $SVRR^{SU}$ to the left of the slash and the $\lambda = 2$ $SVRR^{SU}$ to the right of the slash (in bold). These values are normalized, so that 1 indicates $SVRR^{SU}$ for the $\lambda = 1$ subcohort of the 60-year-old, Low income cohort.

Tables 5.11 and 5.12 display the effect of preference heterogeneity on the simple-utilitarian SVRR ($SVRR^{SU}$) and ex-post-prioritarian SVRR ($SVRR^{EPP}$), respectively.[42]

Each of the 25 cells in Table 5.11 (one cell for each age-income cohort) has two entries, separated by a slash. The number to the left of the slash is the $SVRR^{SU}$ for the $\lambda = 1$ subcohort. (These numbers are the same as in Table 5.4.) The number to the right of the slash, set in bold so as to increase readability, is the $SVRR^{SU}$ for the $\lambda = 2$ subcohort. The numbers are normalized, with 1 indicating $SVRR^{SU}$ for the $\lambda = 1$ subcohort of the 60-year-old, Low income cohort. (That is, the normalized $SVRR^{SU}$ for a given age-income-preference subcohort is its $SVRR^{SU}$ divided by $SVRR^{SU}$ for the 60-year-old, Low income, $\lambda = 1$ subcohort.)

Recall that $SVRR^{SU}$ is the change in expected lifetime well-being per unit of current risk reduction, for a marginal such reduction. Since expected lifetime well-being for the two subcohorts of a given age-income cohort are calculated in two different ways—using, respectively, a $\lambda = 1$ and $\lambda = 2$ period utility

[42] In general, $SVRR^{SU}$ for an individual i is the partial derivative of E^{SU} with respect to i's current survival probability, evaluated at i's baseline risk and attribute profiles; and $SVRR^{EPP}$ is the partial derivative of E^{EPP} with respect to i's current survival probability, evaluated at i's baseline risk and attribute profiles. See chapter appendix, Section 5.A.2. In the case at hand, the attribute profile for the $\lambda = 1$ subcohort of a given age-income cohort is the income profile of that cohort, together with the global preference structure (R^1) of that subcohort; and the attribute profile for the $\lambda = 2$ subcohort of a given age-income cohort is the same income profile, together with the global preference structure (R^2) of that subcohort.

More concretely, $SVRR^{SU}$ and $SVRR^{EPP}$ for the $\lambda = 1$ or $\lambda = 2$ subcohort of a given age-income cohort is the partial derivative of the subcohort's expected lifetime well-being ($SVRR^{SU}$) or expected transformed lifetime well-being ($SVRR^{EPP}$), with respect to current survival probability, evaluated at the baseline risk and income profiles of the cohort—and with the lifetime well-being measure for each subcohort the sum of scaled period utility as per note 40.

Table 5.12 Ex-Post-Prioritarian SVRRs ($\gamma = 1$) with Preference Heterogeneity

	Income: Low	Moderate	Middle	High	Top
Age 20	5.3/**4.6**	5.3/**4.6**	5.3/**4.7**	5.3/**4.7**	5.3/**4.8**
30	3.8/**3.2**	3.8/**3.3**	3.9/**3.3**	3.8/**3.4**	3.8/**3.4**
40	2.5/**2.2**	2.6/**2.3**	2.7/**2.4**	2.7/**2.4**	2.7/**2.5**
50	1.6/**1.5**	1.7/**1.6**	1.8/**1.6**	1.8/**1.7**	1.8/**1.7**
60	1.0/**1.0**	1.1/**1.0**	1.1/**1.1**	1.2/**1.1**	1.2/**1.2**

Explanation: This table shows $SVRR^{EPP}$ ($\gamma = 1$) values for the subcohorts ($\lambda = 1$ and $\lambda = 2$) of the various cohorts, with the $\lambda = 1$ $SVRR^{EPP}$ to the left of the slash and the $\lambda = 2$ $SVRR^{EPP}$ to the right of the slash (in bold). These values are normalized, so that 1 indicates $SVRR^{EPP}$ for the $\lambda = 1$ subcohort of the 60-year-old, Low income cohort.

function—the $SVRR^{SU}$ values will be *different*. And this is what we observe in Table 5.11: the number to the left of the slash in each of the 25 cells in Table 5.11 is different from the number to the right.

How $\lambda = 1$ $SVRR^{SU}$ compares to $\lambda = 2$ $SVRR^{SU}$ depends on the choice of scaling factors. The reader will observe that in each of the 25 cells of Table 5.11, $\lambda = 2$ $SVRR^{SU}$ is always greater than $\lambda = 1$ $SVRR^{SU}$. Why this occurs is explained in the notes.[43]

The pattern of $\lambda = 2$ $SVRR^{SU}$ values is the same as the pattern of $\lambda = 1$ $SVRR^{SU}$ (the latter pattern already discussed in connection with Table 5.4). Whether $\lambda = 1$ or 2, $SVRR^{SU}$ decreases with age and increases with income.[44]

Table 5.12 uses the same format as Table 5.11, but now displaying $SVRR^{EPP}$ ($\gamma = 1$) for the two subcohorts. The number to the left of the slash is the $SVRR^{EPP}$ ($\gamma = 1$) for the $\lambda = 1$ subcohort (these numbers are the same as in Table 5.5), while the number to the right of the slash, set in bold, is the $SVRR^{EPP}$ ($\gamma = 1$) for the

[43] With high-low scaling, the scaling factors are such that scaled period utility with the more risk-averse utility function (here, $\lambda = 2$) exceeds scaled period utility with the less risk-averse utility function ($\lambda = 1$) at all period income levels in between the low and high levels. In effect, at these income levels, more risk-averse individuals are better off: they have a higher level of period well-being. See Adler (2019b, pp. 190–92); Fleurbaey and Zuber (2021).

Because $SVRR^{SU}$ increases with period well-being (as discussed in Section 5.4.2), and because all age-income cohorts here have period income levels in between low ($1,000) and high ($1,000,000), $\lambda = 2$ $SVRR^{SU}$ exceeds $\lambda = 1$ $SVRR^{SU}$.

[44] It will be noted that $\lambda = 2$ $SVRR^{SU}$ does not increase as steeply with income as $\lambda = 1$ $SVRR^{SU}$. This occurs because of the choice of scaling factors. With high-low scaling, the scaled period utility function for $\lambda = 2$ will first increase more steeply with income than the scaled period utility function for $\lambda = 1$, and then less steeply. See Adler (2019b, pp. 190–92). In the simulation, period income for all of the cohorts is in the region where $\lambda = 2$ rescaled period utility increases less steeply. Thus, period well-being increases less steeply with income for this subcohort than for $\lambda = 1$.

$\lambda = 2$ subcohort. The numbers are normalized, with 1 indicating SVRR^{EPP} ($\gamma = 1$) for the $\lambda = 1$ subcohort of the 60-year-old, Low income cohort.[45]

The SVRR^{EPP} values depend upon whether $\lambda = 1$ or $\lambda = 2$, just as SVRR^{SU} values do. (As with SVRR^{SU}, how $\lambda = 1$ SVRR^{EPP} compares to $\lambda = 2$ SVRR^{EPP} depends on the choice of scaling factors.) The pattern of $\lambda = 2$ SVRR^{EPP} values is the same as the pattern of $\lambda = 1$ SVRR^{EPP} (the latter pattern already discussed in connection with Table 5.5). Whether $\lambda = 1$ or 2, SVRR^{EPP} is roughly flat with income (unlike the corresponding SVRR^{SU} values)[46] and decreases with age (more steeply than the corresponding SVRR^{SU} values).

5.4 SVRR: Some General Results

This section reports some theoretical results regarding the SVRR.[47] These results deepen our understanding of simple utilitarianism and ex post prioritarianism as methodologies for evaluating fatality risk policies.

The setup is the same as in Section 5.2.1. Lifetime bundles are divided into T periods, with T the maximum length. Each individual i has a current age A_i. A given policy endows each individual with a risk profile: a list of survival probabilities, one for each period beginning with the current period. The risk profile takes the form $(p_i^{A_i+1}, \ldots, p_i^T)$. A given policy also endows each individual with an attribute profile, which takes the form $(b_i^1, \ldots, b_i^T)$. b_i^t is the bundle of attributes that individual i receives in period t, conditional on surviving to the end of period t.

The SVRR concept concerns how a change in an individual's current baseline survival probability changes simple-utilitarian or ex-post-prioritarian value. Thus, in what follows, I use $(p_i^{A_i+1}, \ldots, p_i^T)$ and $(b_i^1, \ldots, b_i^T)$ to denote individual i's *baseline* risk profile and attribute profile.

Let μ_i^t denote individual i's baseline probability of living exactly t periods. This value can be derived from the individual's risk profile. And let W_i^t denote individual i's lifetime well-being if they live exactly t periods with their baseline attribute profile. I assume that well-being is temporally additive. Thus $W_i^t = \sum_{s=1}^{t} w^p(b_i^s) + \sum_{s=t+1}^{T} w^p(\text{Dead})$. I assume (this was also true in the Section 5.3 simulation) that every bundle that an individual might receive, if alive, has

[45] While $\lambda = 2$ SVRR^{SU} always exceeds $\lambda = 1$ SVRR^{SU} in Table 5.11, because high-low scaling has the effect of making the first group better off for income levels in between low and high (see note 43), the pattern is reversed in Table 5.12: $\lambda = 2$ SVRR^{EPP} is always smaller than $\lambda = 1$ SVRR^{EPP} (not visible in the age-60 row because of rounding). This is because prioritarianism upweights well-being gains to the worse off (in this case, the $\lambda = 1$ subcohorts).

[46] SVRR^{EPP} ($\gamma = 1$) would be perfectly flat with income, for $\lambda = 1$, $\lambda = 2$, and any other period utility function, if risk profiles did not vary by income and income profiles were constant. See note 35.

[47] See chapter appendix, Section 5.A.2, regarding the derivation of these results.

a higher level of period well-being than Dead.[48] However, the results here regarding SVRR^{EPP} hold true for any prioritarian transformation function, whether or not of the Atkinson form used in the simulation.[49]

The simple-utilitarian value of the baseline, $E^{SU}(B)$, equals the sum of affected individuals' baseline expected lifetime well-being levels. That is, $E^{SU}(B) = \sum_i \sum_{t=A_i}^{T} \mu_i^t W_i^t$, summing over affected individuals. The ex-post-prioritarian value of the baseline, $E^{EPP}(B)$, equals the sum of affected individuals' baseline expected *transformed* lifetime well-being levels. That is, $E^{EPP}(B) = \sum_i \sum_{t=A_i}^{T} \mu_i^t g(W_i^t)$, summing over affected individuals.

Recall that $SVRR_i^{SU}$ is the partial derivative of E^{SU} with respect to *i*'s current survival probability, and $SVRR_i^{EPP}$ is the partial derivative of E^{EPP} with respect to *i*'s current survival probability—calculated at *i*'s baseline risk profile and attribute profile. These SVRRs can be shown to be equal to the following.

$$SVRR_i^{SU} = -W_i^{A_i} + \sum_{t=A_i+1}^{T} \frac{\mu_i^t}{p_i^{A_i+1}} W_i^t$$

$$SVRR_i^{EPP} = -g(W_i^{A_i}) + \sum_{t=A_i+1}^{T} \frac{\mu_i^t}{p_i^{A_i+1}} g(W_i^t)$$

That is, $SVRR_i^{SU}$ is the difference between *i*'s expected lifetime well-being, conditional on surviving the period, and their lifetime well-being if they die now. $SVRR_i^{EPP}$ is the difference between *i*'s expected *transformed* lifetime well-being, conditional on surviving the period, and their *transformed* lifetime well-being if they die now.[50]

5.4.1 The Effect of Age on the SVRR

In the empirical simulation, SVRR^{SU} decreased with age within each income quintile. However, this is not theoretically required. Consider two individuals, *i* and *j*, with the same risk and attribute profile, but *i* older than *j*: $A_i > A_j$.[51] It is *possible* that the older individual has a *larger* SVRR^{SU} ($SVRR_i^{SU} > SVRR_j^{SU}$).

[48] That is, the attribute profile of each individual *i* is such that, for all *t*, $w^P(b_i^t) > w^P(\text{Dead})$. See Section 5.5.2 for a discussion of how to account for the possibility that life extension may not be beneficial.

[49] The results also do not require that $w^P(\text{Dead}) = 0$.

[50] Although this section (Section 5.4) generally assumes temporal additivity, the formulas for $SVRR_i^{SU}$ and $SVRR_i^{EPP}$ in this paragraph can be derived without that assumption.

[51] If $A_i > A_j$, to say that the two individuals have the same risk profile means that in each period starting with $A_i + 1$, the two profiles have the same survival probability. (Note that *i*'s profile begins with period $A_i + 1$.)

To see intuitively how this might happen, imagine that the attribute profile (common to both individuals) is such that attribute bundles starting in period $A_i + 1$ have a much higher level of period well-being than bundles in previous periods. $\text{SVRR}_i^{\text{SU}}$ is the difference between *i*'s expected lifetime well-being conditional on surviving the current period (i.e., surviving to age $A_i + 1$) and their realized lifetime well-being if they die at age A_i. $\text{SVRR}_j^{\text{SU}}$ is the difference between *j*'s expected lifetime well-being conditional on surviving the current period (i.e., surviving to age $A_j + 1$) and their realized lifetime well-being if they die at age A_j. If the jump in period well-being starting at period $A_i + 1$ is large enough, the first difference will exceed the second.

A different way that SVRR^{SU} might actually increase with age involves the risk profile. Assume that period well-being is constant. The common risk profile is such that survival probability in period $A_j + 2$ is very low, while survival probabilities beginning in period $A_i + 2$ are quite high. As a result, if the younger individual does survive the current period, they are quite likely to die in the next period (period $A_j + 2$ of their life). If the older individual does survive the current period, they are likely to live much longer. Thus, the older individual's life expectancy remaining exceeds the younger individual's. Because period well-being is constant, it follows that $\text{SVRR}_i^{\text{SU}} > \text{SVRR}_j^{\text{SU}}$.

Under what conditions can we be sure that $\text{SVRR}_i^{\text{SU}} < \text{SVRR}_j^{\text{SU}}$? The following can be demonstrated: If the common attribute and risk profiles are such that period well-being does not increase over time and survival probabilities do not increase over time, $\text{SVRR}_i^{\text{SU}} < \text{SVRR}_j^{\text{SU}}$.[52]

Regardless of the time path of SVRR^{SU}, SVRR^{EPP} places more weight on risk reduction for the young than SVRR^{SU} does. Given two otherwise similarly situated individuals, one older than the other, the ethical value of a given Δp reduction in fatality risk if conferred upon the younger individual *relative* to the ethical value of that same reduction if conferred upon the older one is *greater* according to ex post prioritarianism than according to simple utilitarianism. Let's term this feature of ex post prioritarianism "Extra Priority for the Young."[53]

> Extra Priority for the Young: Let *i* and *j* be two individuals with the same risk profile and attribute profile, *i* older than *j*. Then $\text{SVRR}_j^{\text{EPP}}/\text{SVRR}_i^{\text{EPP}} > \text{SVRR}_j^{\text{SU}}/\text{SVRR}_i^{\text{SU}}$.

[52] The proof is provided in the on-line appendix to Adler, Ferranna, Hamrmitt, and Treich (2021).

[53] Ex ante prioritarianism also has this feature. See Section 7.3.1. Thus prioritarianism, in both its ex post and ex ante variants, validates the "fair innings" idea: that individuals who are younger have a stronger claim to a given life-extension than individuals who are older. See Bognar (2015); and see Adler, Ferranna, Hammitt and Treich (2021, p. 2), citing scholars who endorse this or related ideas.

Consider the implications of Extra Priority for the Young. (1) If the simple-utilitarian SVRR decreases with age, then the ex-post-prioritarian SVRR decreases more quickly with age. (This is what we observed in the simulation model.) (2) Even if the simple-utilitarian SVRR does not decrease with age, the ratio of the ex-post-prioritarian SVRRs, younger to older, will be greater than the ratio of the simple-utilitarian SVRRs, younger to older. For example, if the common risk and attribute profiles are such that simple utilitarianism sees equal value in conferring a Δp risk reduction upon the younger and older individuals, ex post prioritarianism prefers to confer the risk reduction upon the younger individual. (If $SVRR_j^{SU}/SVRR_i^{SU} = 1$, $SVRR_j^{EPP}/SVRR_i^{EPP} > 1$.) And if simple utilitarianism actually prefers the older individual ($SVRR_j^{SU}/SVRR_i^{SU} < 1$), ex post prioritarianism may be indifferent or may prefer the younger—or if it also prefers the older individual, will do so with less relative weight to the older than simple utilitarianism.

It makes intuitive sense that ex post prioritarianism has the Extra Priority for the Young feature. If Young and Old have the same risk and attribute profile, a given increment Δw in lifetime well-being for Young will be accorded more weight by ex post prioritarianism than the same increment Δw for Old—since Young can expect to end up with a lower level of lifetime well-being than Old. Such is the intuition supporting Extra Priority for the Young. That said, actually proving that Extra Priority for the Young holds true is not a trivial task.

5.4.2 The Effect of Quality of Life and Background Risk

How do differences in period well-being affect the simple-utilitarian and ex-post-prioritarian SVRRs? To analyze this question, let's consider two individuals of the same age and with the same risk profiles ("Ariela" and "Biff"), but with attribute profiles such that they have different levels of period well-being in a single period. The following can be demonstrated. (1) If Ariela is better off than Biff in the *current* period, then $SVRR^{SU}$ is greater for Ariela than Biff. Surprisingly, perhaps, the same is true for $SVRR^{EPP}$. (2) If Ariela is better off than Biff in a single *future* period, then $SVRR^{SU}$ is greater for Ariela than Biff. Again (and, once more, perhaps surprisingly), the same is true for $SVRR^{EPP}$. (3) If Ariela is better off than Biff in a single *past* period, then $SVRR^{SU}$ is the same for the two individuals. In this case, by contrast, $SVRR^{EPP}$ is greater for Biff than for Ariela.

Finally, how do differences in survival probabilities affect the simple-utilitarian and ex-post-prioritarian SVRRs (that is, how does the *level* of fatality risk affect the ethical value of a *change* in fatality risk, as captured by the SVRR)? To analyze *this* question, consider two individuals of the same age and with the same attribute profiles ("Camila" and "Daniel,"), but with risk profiles differing

Table 5.13 Simple-Utilitarian and Ex-Post-Prioritarian SVRRs: Comparative Statics

	Period Well-Being: Single-Period Difference	Survival Probability: Single-Period Difference
$SVRR^{SU}$	Past period: *Unchanged* Current period: *Increasing* Future period: *Increasing*	 Current period: *Unchanged* Future period: *Increasing*
$SVRR^{EPP}$	Past period: *Decreasing* Current period: *Increasing* Future period: *Increasing*	 Current period: *Unchanged* Future period: *Increasing*

Explanation: This table shows the comparative statics of $SVRR^{SU}$ and $SVRR^{EPP}$ with respect to a single-period change in period well-being or survival probability.

in survival probability in a single period. The following can be demonstrated. (1) If Camila's survival probability is greater than Daniel's in the *current* period, then $SVRR^{SU}$ is the same for Camila and Daniel. The same is true for $SVRR^{EPP}$. (2) If Camila's survival probability is greater than Daniel's in a single *future* period, then $SVRR^{SU}$ is greater for Camila than for Daniel. The same is true for $SVRR^{EPP}$.

Table 5.13 summarizes these results.

5.4.3 Equal Value of Risk Reduction?

It is sometimes asserted that the ethical value of lifesaving is the same for all individuals.[54] Simple utilitarianism and ex post prioritarianism differ in significant respects, but they concur in *rejecting* this proposition.[55] First, the analysis above of SVRR and age shows that neither $SVRR^{SU}$ nor $SVRR^{EPP}$ is constant with age. Even if the younger and older individuals have the same attribute and risk profiles, $SVRR^{SU}$ for the two will not generally be the same. $SVRR^{SU}$ is *guaranteed* to decrease with age if survival probabilities and period well-being do not increase with age. And whenever $SVRR^{SU}$ is greater for the younger individual, $SVRR^{EPP}$ must also be greater (by virtue of Extra Priority for the Young).

Second, even among individuals of the same age, $SVRR^{SU}$ and $SVRR^{EPP}$ can vary as a result of differences in period well-being and/or background risk. See Table 5.13.

[54] See Hasman and Østerdal (2004, pp. 20–22) and Fleurbaey and Ponthiere (2022, pp. 356–57), citing examples.

[55] Fleurbaey and Ponthiere (2022), Hasman and Østerdal (2004), and Moreno-Ternero and Østerdal (2023) all explore the possibility of equal value of lifesaving and reach negative conclusions.

Differences in the ethical value of risk reduction that flow from differences in period well-being (e.g., differences in income or health) may be intuitively troubling. In particular, many will rebel at the thought that someone who is *better off* (e.g., has a higher income or is in better health) should take priority with respect to fatality risk reduction.[56]

$SVRR^{SU}$ is intuitively troubling in this respect; it is skewed toward those with a higher level of period well-being. Assume that Ellie and Frank are of the same age and have the same risk profile. Then (an upshot of Table 5.13) if Ellie is better off than Frank in one or more current-or-future periods, and no worse off in any current-or-future period, $SVRR^{SU}$ for Ellie is greater than for Frank.

Surprisingly, shifting from simple utilitarianism to ex post prioritarianism cannot wholly eliminate the skew toward better-off individuals. If Ellie is better off than Frank in one or more current-or-future periods; no worse off in any current-or-future period; and equally well off in all past periods, then both $SVRR^{EPP}$ and $SVRR^{SU}$ will be greater for Ellie (also an upshot of Table 5.13). This is true regardless of the degree of concavity of the prioritarian transformation function.[57]

That said, ex post prioritarianism *can* neutralize the simple-utilitarian skew toward better-off individuals in one important class of cases. These are cases of a *permanent* difference in period well-being. Imagine, now, that Ellie and Frank are of the same age and have the same risk profile, but Ellie is better off than Frank in *all* periods. In such cases, $SVRR^{SU}$ for Ellie will exceed that for Frank, but $SVRR^{EPP}$ need not. The fact that Ellie is better off than Frank in the current period and future periods will tend to increase her $SVRR^{EPP}$ relative to Frank's;

[56] "Consensus exists that an individual person's wealth should not determine who lives or dies." Emanuel et al. (2020, p. 2051).

[57] It might be wondered whether this intuitively troubling feature of ex post prioritarianism (which it shares with simple utilitarianism) can be avoided by shifting to a different prioritarian uncertainty module, or from prioritarianism to a different type of non-utilitarian SWF. The answer is, essentially, "no." Consider a non-stochastic version of the case at hand. Ellie and Frank are the same age A. In the baseline, absent governmental intervention, each is sure to die. Government is choosing between intervening so as to ensure Ellie's survival to age $M > A$ (after which point Ellie would die) or intervening so as to ensure Frank's survival to age M (after which point Frank would die).

Assume that Ellie and Frank have had the same period well-being up until now (in periods 1 through A), but that—for each period from the current period $(A + 1)$ through M—Ellie would have greater period well-being (were she to survive that period) than Frank (were he to do so). W^A_{Ellie} and W^A_{Frank} are the individuals' lifetime well-being values were they to die now, and W^M_{Ellie} and W^M_{Frank} the values were each to live M periods. $W^A_{Ellie} = W^A_{Frank}$ and $W^M_{Ellie} > W^M_{Frank}$.

Given that $W^A_{Ellie} = W^A_{Frank}$ and $W^M_{Ellie} > W^M_{Frank}$, *any* SWF that satisfies Lifetime Strong Pareto and Lifetime Anonymity will prefer to save Ellie over saving Frank. To see this, assume (without loss of generality) that there are N individuals in the model population, with Ellie denoted as individual $(N - 1)$ and Frank as individual N. Individuals 1 through $(N - 2)$ are unaffected by government's intervening to save Ellie or, instead, Frank; in either event, they will have, respectively, lifetime well-being values of $W_1, \ldots, W_{(N-2)}$. Then the vector of lifetime well-being values that results from saving Ellie is $(W_1, \ldots, W_{(N-2)}, W^M_{Ellie}, W^A_{Frank})$, while the vector that results from saving Frank is $(W_1, \ldots, W_{(N-2)}, W^A_{Ellie}, W^M_{Frank})$. By Anonymity and Strong Pareto, the first vector is better than the second.

but the fact that she is also better off in *past* periods will tend to *decrease* her $SVRR^{EPP}$ relative to Frank's. Depending on how these two, conflicting effects of the permanent well-being difference balance out, it might be the case that $SVRR^{EPP}$ for Ellie is equal to or less than Frank's.

The following can be demonstrated.[58]

$SVRR^{SU}$ and $SVRR^{EPP}$ with permanent, proportional differences in well-being.

Consider two individuals, Ellie and Frank, of the same age and with the same risk profile, such that Ellie in each period is $k > 1$ times the well-being of Frank. In such a case, $SVRR^{SU}$ for Ellie is greater than for Frank.

Let $g(\cdot)$ be the Atkinson transformation function. (1) If the priority parameter γ is less than 1, $SVRR^{EPP}$ for Ellie is greater than for Frank. (2) If the priority parameter γ equals 1, $SVRR^{EPP}$ for Ellie and Frank are equal. (3) If the priority parameter γ exceeds 1, $SVRR^{EPP}$ for Ellie is less than for Frank

5.5 Stochastic Attribute Profiles

The conceptual apparatus that was set forth in Section 5.2.1, and that was the basis for the SVRR concept introduced in Section 5.2.2, the empirical illustration in Section 5.3, and the general results in Section 5.4, employs *nonstochastic* attribute profiles. For each period *t*—not only past periods, but the current period (period $A_i + 1$) and future periods too—individual *i*'s attribute profile specifies a single bundle b_i^t. This is the bundle that—the apparatus stipulates—individual *i* will receive *for certain* if *i* survives to the end of period *t* rather than dying earlier.

To employ a nonstochastic attribute profile is to constrain the types of uncertainty that are reflected in each individual's lottery over lifetime bundles with a given policy. The *only* uncertainty thus reflected is our uncertainty about the individual's longevity (as captured in the risk profile). Policy *P* confers a *lottery* over lifetime bundles on individual *i*—not a single lifetime bundle—because we are uncertain when *i* will die. A second type of uncertainty that might be seen as funneling into *i*'s lottery—uncertainty about what *i*'s attributes will be—is ignored by the Section 5.2.1 apparatus.

The apparatus is readily modified to incorporate this second type of uncertainty—by shifting to a *stochastic attribute profile*. For each period *t*, the stochastic attribute profile endows *i* with a conditional lottery over attribute bundles in that period: the lottery over period bundles that *i* will face, if *i* survives

[58] See chapter appendix, Section 5.A.2.4.

to the end of t.[59] Individual i's lottery over lifetime bundles with a given policy P is now determined as a function of i's current age, risk profile with P, and stochastic attribute profile with P.

It bears emphasis that the tractability axioms (Decomposability and Policy Separability) are fully applicable to simple utilitarianism and ex post prioritarianism, whether the analyst employs the Section 5.2.1 apparatus or instead shifts to stochastic attribute profiles.[60] Moreover, the simple-utilitarian and ex-post-prioritarian SVRRs remain well-defined.[61]

There are, of course, policy-analytic costs as well as benefits to using stochastic attribute profiles. The assessment of risk-regulation policies becomes more nuanced—by attending to *two* types of uncertainty that bear on individuals' lifetime well-being—but at the cost of increased complexity. Rather than try to craft a general recommendation about when to use stochastic profiles and when to stick with the Section 5.2.1 apparatus, I'll briefly discuss two contexts in which the analytic nuance afforded by stochastic attribute profiles is particularly useful: *interdependent fates* and the possibility that *life extension may not be beneficial.*

5.5.1 Interdependent Fates

I'll use the term "interdependent fates" to denote a scenario in which one individual's well-being depends on the longevity of another person or persons. At first blush, it seems that the Section 5.2.1 apparatus even modified for stochastic attributes cannot reflect interdependent fates. Actually, it *can*—or so I'll argue. But explaining this will require a bit of work.

59 Formally, there is a set $\mathbf{B}^{\mathbf{P}}$ of all possible period bundles. For each period t, individual i's policy-specific attribute profile specifies a probability value $\pi_i^t(b^*)$ for each period bundle b^* in $\mathbf{B}^{\mathbf{P}}$, namely, the probability that i receives b^* in period t if i survives to the end of t.

The period t lottery might be a "degenerate" lottery, i.e., $\pi_i^t(b^*) = 1$ for some period bundle b^*. This will be the case for past periods ($t \leq A_i$).

60 If two policies P and P^* are such that each person's lottery over lifetime well-being with P is the same as with P^*, P and P^* will be ranked equally good by simple utilitarianism and ex post prioritarianism (Decomposability); and unaffected individuals (those with the very same well-being lottery regardless of which policy is chosen) can be dropped from the analysis (Policy Separability). Using individual risk profiles together with nonstochastic attribute profiles or, instead, *stochastic* attribute profiles are simply different methodologies for specifying each individual's lottery over lifetime bundles with a given policy.

61 Simple utilitarianism and ex post prioritarianism each assign a given policy some score E as a function of the array of individual risk profiles and attribute profiles; $SVRR_i$ is the partial derivative of E with respect to i's current survival probability, calculated at the baseline array of risk and attribute profiles. The attribute profiles might be nonstochastic (the Section 5.2.1 setup; see chapter appendix, Section 5.A.2.3, displaying $SVRR_i$ formulas in this case) or stochastic.

Throughout the discussion, in illustrating the problem of interdependent fates, I'll use "Darsh" as the name of an individual whose well-being depends upon the longevity of one or more other persons and "Mario" as the name of another person whose longevity affects Darsh's well-being. This shorthand will enable a less wordy presentation of the problem, as opposed to repeatedly writing "the person whose well-being depends upon the longevity of another," etc.

It will be useful to distinguish between two different versions of an interdependent fates scenario. First, someone's well-being might be *causally* affected by the longevity of others. Call this the "causal" variant of interdependent fates. It can arise in many different ways.

For example, imagine that Mario's longevity affects Darsh's health (and that Darsh's well-being, in turn, is a function of Darsh's health). Mario is Darsh's spouse, relative, or friend; and Darsh's physical or mental health during some period *t* of Darsh's life would be better were Mario to be alive during *t* than if Mario were to be dead.

The Section 5.2.1 apparatus is insufficient to model the dependence of Darsh's health on Mario's survival. Assume that Darsh and Mario are currently both alive; Darsh's age at present is A_{Darsh}. Individuals' period bundles, if alive, include a health attribute: b_i^t, the bundle of individual *i* in period *t* if *i* is alive during *t*, has a health component h_i^t. We now posit that h_{Darsh}^t (the health of Darsh in period *t* of his life, if Darsh is alive during that period) will be better if Mario is alive rather than dead during period *t*.

A terminological note: In the *T*-period model of lifetime well-being set forth in Chapter 4 and used throughout this chapter, to say that an individual "survives to the end of period *t*" is synonymous with saying that they are "alive during period *t*." Either an individual is Dead during *t* (thus not alive, and thus does not survive until its end), or is alive and survives until the end of *t*.

Let *t* be either the current period of Darsh's life or a future period (that is, $t > A_{\text{Darsh}}$). It is currently uncertain if Mario will be alive during *t*. Assigning Darsh a nonstochastic attribute profile $(b_{\text{Darsh}}^1, \ldots, b_{\text{Darsh}}^T)$ does not reflect the impact of Mario's survival on Darsh's health. Assume that, if Mario is alive during period *t*, h_{Darsh}^t takes the value h^{**}; and that, if Mario dies before period *t*, h_{Darsh}^t takes the value h^*, with h^{**} a better health state than h^*. If Darsh's attribute profile is nonstochastic, then his bundle b_{Darsh}^t will have a determinate health component (be it h^{**}, h^*, or something else). But Darsh's health in period *t* is *uncertain*—or so we are supposing. It can be either h^{**} or h^*, depending on Mario's longevity.

At first blush, modifying the Section 5.2.1 apparatus to allow for stochastic attribute profiles still doesn't permit us to reflect the dependence of Darsh's health on Mario's longevity. Suppose that we try to construct a stochastic attribute profile for Darsh. For any period *t* in Darsh's life with $t > A_{\text{Darsh}}$, this profile endows Darsh with a conditional lottery over period bundles (the lottery over period bundles that Darsh will face, conditional on being alive during *t*). There is a probability π that h_{Darsh}^{t} takes the value h^{**} (this reflects the possibility that Mario might be alive during *t*, given that Darsh is) and a probability (1 – π) that h_{Darsh}^{t} takes the value h^{*} (this reflects the possibility that Mario might be dead during *t*, given that Darsh is alive).

The difficulty lies in *specifying* the probability π. That probability is just the probability that Mario is alive during period *t* of Darsh's life, conditional on Darsh being alive. If we try to assign Darsh a risk profile and a stochastic attribute profile, we (seem to) find ourselves at a loss. Darsh's lottery over period bundles for any period $t > A_{\text{Darsh}}$ can't be specified independently of *Mario*'s survival probabilities for that period.

I'll now show how the Section 5.2.1 apparatus modified to allow for a stochastic attribute profile *can* in fact reflect the causal dependence of one person's attributes on another's survival. Assume, for simplicity, that Darsh's health depends causally only on Mario's longevity (no one else's); and that Mario's attributes may or may not depend causally on Darsh's longevity, but in any event do not depend on anyone else's. A Darsh/Mario "suboutcome" is a joint specification of a possible lifespan l_{Darsh} for Darsh and a possible lifespan l_{Mario} for Mario, plus a possible lifetime bundle for Darsh (specifying Darsh's period bundles for each period from 1 to l_{Darsh} and "Dead" thereafter) and a possible lifetime bundle for Mario (specifying Mario's period bundles for each period from 1 to l_{Mario} and "Dead" thereafter). A given policy *P* induces a probability distribution over Darsh/Mario suboutcomes.

Note, critically, that these policy *P* probabilities of the various Darsh/Mario suboutcomes will *reflect* any causal dependence of Darsh's attributes on Mario's longevity (or vice versa). If, for example, Mario's being alive improves Darsh's health, then a suboutcome in which both are alive during a given period of Darsh's life and Darsh's health is good will be more probable—as compared to the probability of that suboutcome if Mario's survival has no impact on Darsh's health. (See Table 5.14, illustrating how assigning probabilities to Darsh/Mario suboutcomes allows us to capture the causal interaction between Mario's survival and Darsh's attributes.) Having assigned probabilities to Darsh/Mario suboutcomes for a given policy *P*, we can then *derive* a policy *P* risk profile and stochastic attribute profile for Darsh and for Mario. The probabilities in these risk profiles and stochastic attribute profiles are derived *from* the probability distribution over Darsh/Mario suboutcomes. (Again, see Table 5.14.)

Generalizing from this example, the causal variant of interdependent fates can be handled as follows. Partition the population into *M* "internally interdependent" groups, denoted by number as 1, . . . , *m*, . . . , *M*. Each group is such that (a) if the group has multiple members, the well-being of some members of that group causally depends upon the longevity of others in the group, and (b) no

Table 5.14 Accounting for Interdependent Fates via Suboutcomes

	Mario alive during period t of Darsh's life	Mario dead during period t of Darsh's life
Darsh alive during period t of Darsh's life	Probability: τ_1 Darsh's health during t: h^{**}	Probability: τ_2 Darsh's health during t: h^*
Darsh dead during period t of Darsh's life	Probability: τ_3	Probability: $\tau_4 = 1 - (\tau_1 + \tau_2 + \tau_3)$

Explanation: Period t is either the current period of Darsh's life ($A_{\text{Darsh}} + 1$) or a later period. The top left cell of the matrix represents one subset of the set of all Darsh/Mario suboutcomes, namely, those in which Darsh and Mario are both alive during period t; the top right cell, the subset in which Darsh is alive and Mario is dead; the bottom left cell, the subset in which Darsh is dead and Mario is alive; the bottom right cell, the subset in which both are dead. The probabilities of these subsets are, respectively, τ_1, τ_2, τ_3, and τ_4. Note that Darsh's health during t if alive during t depends on whether Mario is alive or dead then: it is h^{**} in the first case and h^* in the second (with h^{**} a better health state than h^*).

From this information we can derive Darsh's probability of being alive during t (that probability is $\tau_1 + \tau_2$)† and Darsh's lottery over health attributes, conditional on being alive during t: If Darsh is alive during t, there is a probability $\pi = \tau_1/(\tau_1 + \tau_2)$ of having health h^{**} and probability $(1 - \pi) = \tau_2/(\tau_1 + \tau_2)$ of having health h^*.

To see how these probabilities capture the causal interaction between Mario's survival and Darsh's health, consider a comparator case in which there is no interaction: Darsh has a 50% chance of health h^{**} and a 50% chance of h^* if alive during t regardless of whether Mario is alive then. In the case at hand, Darsh's probability of the better health state h^{**} if both he and Mario are alive during t is *higher* than in the comparator case (1 as opposed to 50%), and Darsh's probability of the worse health state h^* in this event is *lower* than in the comparator case (0 as opposed to 50%).

† Note that $\tau_1 + \tau_2$ is the unconditional probability of Darsh surviving to the end of period t. The relevant entry in his risk profile, p_{Darsh}^{t}, is the conditional probability of Darsh surviving to the end of period t, conditional on surviving to the end of period $(t - 1)$. That conditional probability can in turn be derived once we also know Darsh's unconditional probability of surviving to the end of period $(t - 1)$ (this information not displayed in table).

group member's well-being causally depends upon the longevity of anyone outside the group.[62] There is a set of possible suboutcomes for a given group m, each such suboutcome specifying a lifespan for each of the members of m and a lifetime bundle with that lifespan. A given policy P produces a probability distribution over the group suboutcomes for each group m. We model the effect of P by (1) determining the policy P probability distributions over group suboutcomes for each group m. From this information for a given group m we can (2) derive P-specific risk profiles and stochastic attribute profiles for the members of m. Doing this for each group, we arrive at (3) P-specific risk profiles and stochastic attribute profiles for the entire population. As in the case without interdependent fates, a P-specific risk profile and stochastic attribute profile for a given

[62] Further, this is the finest partition, in the sense that a new partition derived by replacing any group m with two subsets of m, m_1 and m_2—which are disjoint and whose union is m—no longer satisfies conditions (a) and (b).

person yields a *P*-specific lottery over lifetime bundles for that person. Thus, from (3) we arrive at (4) a *P*-specific lottery over lifetime bundles for everyone in the population, which (together with our well-being measure and prioritarian transformation function) yields a simple-utilitarian and ex-post-prioritarian value for policy *P*—as in the case without interdependent fates.

In short, the Section 5.2.1 setup modified for stochastic attribute profiles *can* handle the case of interdependent fates. In this case, however, the probabilities in individuals' stochastic attribute profiles are derived *from* probabilities of group suboutcomes rather than being specifiable for each individual independently of what occurs to anyone else.

I have been discussing the *causal* variant of interdependent fates. A second variant occurs when someone's well-being is *constitutively dependent* on someone else's longevity. In this case, the well-being theory is such that one person's attributes (including the attribute of being dead or alive during a given period) are seen as a direct determinant of someone else's well-being. Other-regarding preferences provide an illustrative example. Suppose that we have adopted a preference-based theory of well-being, which counts certain other-regarding preferences—preferences regarding the condition of other people—as relevant to the well-being of the preference-holder. Imagine, now, that Darsh has an other-regarding preference vis-à-vis Mario. Darsh prefers that Mario be alive and, if alive, that Mario be in good health, happy, with a high income, and otherwise flourishing. This can be captured, formally, by having Darsh's attribute bundle b_{Darsh}^{t} during a given period t of Darsh's life include not only Darsh's own (non-relational) attributes but also the attributes of Mario at that time that Darsh cares about (a kind of relational attribute of Darsh's).[63] The critical point, now, is that if $t > A_{\text{Darsh}}$, b_{Darsh}^{t} is stochastic—it depends on whether Mario is alive or not during t.

The difference between the causal and constitutive variants of the interdependent fates case is that, in the latter case, Mario's status as alive or dead is not merely a causal factor influencing Darsh's bundle but a component of that bundle. That being recognized, the modeling solution to the constitutive variant is the same as in the causal case: namely, partition the population into "internally interdependent" groups; for each group, predict probabilities over group suboutcomes for each given policy *P*; and from these probabilities derive risk profiles and stochastic attribute profiles for group members.

[63] I commented in Chapter 4 that the attributes in bundles might be monadic (non-relational) or relational. See Section 4.1.2. Mario's health, happiness, etc., are relational attributes of Darsh in the sense that they are not properties of Darsh alone (they are not properties Darsh could have in a world in which only he existed).

5.5.2 The Benefit of Life Extension

Chapter 3 rejected the proposition that life extension is invariably beneficial. Increasing a history's lifespan might reduce rather than increasing lifetime well-being. In particular, this will very plausibly be the case if the subject experiences great suffering during the added lifespan, is unable to realize objective goods, and prefers not to keep living.[64]

The Section 5.2.1 apparatus is not particularly well suited to reflect the possibility that life extension might be harmful rather than beneficial. To illustrate, and for simplicity, assume that the well-being measure is temporally additive. Consider, now, an individual i with age A_i; risk profile $(p_i^{A_i+1}, p_i^{A_i+2}, \ldots, p_i^T)$; and nonstochastic attribute profile $(b_i^1, \ldots, b_i^T)$. Life extension is being modeled as invariably beneficial for individual i if each of the period bundles that i stands to realize, if their lifespan is extended by one or more periods past their current age, is better than the status Dead. That is, each of the bundles $b_i^{A_i+1}, b_i^{A_i+2}, \ldots, b_i^T$ is better for period well-being than Dead.

Conversely, life extension is being modeled as *possibly* harmful for individual i if there is some possible number of periods e such that, if i were to live exactly e periods past their current age, lifetime well-being would be lower than dying now. That is, $w^p(b_i^{A_i+1}) + \cdots + w^p(b_i^{A_i+e}) < e \times w^p(\text{Dead})$. This in turn entails (of course) that at least one of the period bundles $b_i^{A_i+1}, b_i^{A_i+2}, \ldots, b_i^T$ is worse for period well-being than Dead.

But that, in turn, seems like a fairly crude way to translate Chapter 3's insight—that life extension is not invariably beneficial—into the policy-analysis context. To illustrate, consider an individual (Zia) diagnosed with a terminal disease. One policy P currently being considered by government is to enact a blanket ban on "assisted suicide": that is, to prohibit third parties (doctors, nurses, etc.) from helping anyone—Zia and others like her, as well as individuals not diagnosed with a terminal illness—in ending their lives.

Will Zia be better off if she lives past her current age, rather than dying now? Perhaps not. The future course of Zia's illness *might* be so bad that she would better off dying now.

Is there, then, some future time such that—were Zia to be alive at that time with the terminal disease—Zia's condition will be worse than being Dead? Again, perhaps not. The future course of Zia's illness might not be that bad. It's *possible* that, at all times before she dies from the disease, Zia is better off alive than Dead.

The Section 5.2.1 setup can't capture our uncertainty about the benefits of life extension for Zia. If we specify a nonstochastic attribute profile for Zia such that

[64] See Section 3.4.2.

each possible bundle in a period $t > A_{Zia}$ is better than Dead, then the possibility that life extension might be harmful for her is erased. Conversely, having some (or all) of the bundles in this profile be worse than Dead downplays our uncertainty about the course of her illness. We are uncertain not merely about how long Zia will live (as reflected in her risk profile) but also about how bad things will be if she does live beyond her current age.

A stochastic attribute profile provides the needed nuance. In the current period and each future period, Zia faces a lottery over bundles conditional on being alive. In some (or all) of these periods, some bundles assigned a non-zero probability are worse than Dead, while others assigned a non-zero probability are better than (or just as good as) Dead.

Consider a counterpart individual to Zia: Zane, who is the same age as Zia and has the same risk profile, but has a stochastic attribute profile more favorable than Zia's. In each period, Zane faces the same lottery over bundles as Zia, except that the cumulative probability (for Zia) of realizing bundles worse than or equally good as Dead is shifted (for Zane) to bundles better than Dead. (Thus, in no period does Zane have a chance of a period bundle worse than or equally good as Dead.)

The simple-utilitarian SVRR for Zia will be less than the simple-utilitarian SVRR for Zane; the ex-post-prioritarian SVRR for Zia will be less than the ex-post-prioritarian SVRR for Zane. It is less valuable to reduce Zia's risk of dying than to reduce Zane's; in both cases, the risk reduction increases the individual's chance of living longer, but in Zia's case (not Zane's) it is possible that the longer life she would lead would be worse than dying earlier. If Zia's prospects are sufficiently bad, her SVRRs will be negative; Zane's will always be positive.

In what policy contexts should stochastic attribute profiles be used so as to reflect the possibility that extending some persons' lives might be harmful rather than beneficial to them? Here's a rough, qualitative recommendation: Do so if a significant fraction of the individuals likely to be affected by the policies under consideration face a significant chance that life extensions for them would be harmful, not beneficial. That will be true, very plausibly, for policies regarding assisted suicide. That may well *not* be true for suicide-prevention policies in general (for example, funding "hotlines" or outreach to offer counseling to those considering suicide), let alone more typical risk-regulation policies (laws regulating pollution, food safety, automobile design, consumer product safety, occupational hazards, etc.).

A final word of caution. There is a huge gap between the fact that some individual articulates a desire to end their life or tries to commit suicide, and the conclusion that life extension for that individual would be harmful. First, the individual's desires may be conflicted or ephemeral; they may not have a robust, ongoing preference to cease living. Second, even individuals who *do* have such a preference may be mistaken about the probabilities of various possible life-courses; for example, they may significantly underestimate the chance of good treatment for a health condition that currently feels hopeless. Third, on many plausible theories of well-being, the fact that someone considers a possible future life-course (a specification of what might happen in their life in the future) to be worse than dying now doesn't imply that the life-course *is* worse for well-being than dying now. It needn't imply that even on a preference theory of well-being (since preference theories may well look to "laundered" preferences;[65] if so, what matters is whether the individual *would* consider the life-course to be worse than dying now, were they to have good information and deliberate calmly, not whether the individual does in fact consider it to be worse), let alone experientialist or objective theories.

These cautionary points should be kept firmly in view by policy analysts who wish to incorporate the possibility of non-beneficial life extensions into their assessments.

Chapter 5: Appendix

5.A.1 Tractability Axioms

5.A.1.1 Statement of the Axioms

Let $L_{P,i}$ denote the lottery over well-being levels for individual i that results from policy P. With v a real number, $L_{P,i}(v) = \sum_{x:w_i(x)=v} \pi_P(x)$, i.e., $L_{P,i}(v)$ is the probability to individual i of well-being level v with policy P.[66] $L_{P,i} = L_{P^*,i}$ indicates that i faces the same well-being lottery with policies P and P^*, that is, for every real number v, $L_{P,i}(v) = L_{P^*,i}(v)$.

Decomposability: If $L_{P,i} = L_{P^*,i}$ for all i, then $P \sim^{E\text{-}P} P^*$.

Policy Separability: Let $\mathbf{M}$ be a subset of $\mathbf{I}^{\mathbf{Mod}}$, and let $\mathbf{M}^+ = \mathbf{I}^{\mathbf{Mod}} \setminus \mathbf{M}$ (all individuals not in $\mathbf{M}$). Assume P, P^*, P^+, P^{++} are as follows. For all $i \in \mathbf{M}$, $L_{P,i} = L_{P^*,i}$ and $L_{P+,i} = L_{P++,i}$. For all $j \in \mathbf{M}^+$, $L_{P,j} = L_{P+,j}$ and $L_{P^*,j} = L_{P++,j}$. Then $P \succsim^{E\text{-}P} P^*$ iff $P^+ \succsim^{E\text{-}P} P^{++}$.

Policy Separability is logically stronger than Decomposability—it implies Decomposability (but not vice versa). To see that Policy Separability implies Decomposability, let P^+ and P^{++} be "degenerate" policies each of

[65] See Chapter 4, note 26.

[66] See Section 1.A.6 regarding summations over infinite sets.

which yields the same well-being level v_i' for sure for each individual i: $L_{P+,i}(v_i') = L_{P++,i}(v_i') = 1$. Assume that policies P and P^* meet the antecedent condition for Decomposability, namely, $L_{P,i} = L_{P^*,i}$ for all i. By Policy Separability, $P \succcurlyeq^{E\text{-P}} P^*$ iff $P^+ \succcurlyeq^{E\text{-P}} P^{++}$. By Pareto Indifference and Module Consistency, $P^+ \sim^{E\text{-P}} P^{++}$. Thus $P \sim^{E\text{-P}} P^*$.[67]

For an example of an uncertainty module that satisfies Decomposability but not Policy Separability, consider the module for a rank-weighted SWF that assigns a score to each policy equaling the rank-weighted sum of individuals' expected well-being ("ex ante rank weightism").[68]

5.A.1.2 The Relation between Separability and Policy Separability

Section 1.3 introduced the *Separability* axiom at the level of the world-ranking (see Section 1.A.5 for a formal statement) and offered a pragmatic defense of this axiom, namely, that satisfying this axiom is a necessary condition for the Policy Separability axiom under discussion in the current chapter. More precisely, a world-ranking $\succcurlyeq^{E\text{-D}}$ is appropriately implemented by an SWF $\succcurlyeq^{E}$ and a companion uncertainty module that satisfies Policy Separability *only if* $\succcurlyeq^{E\text{-D}}$ satisfies Separability.

Why is this so? Note first that Separability has a corresponding outcome-level axiom (call it Outcome Separability): The ranking of any two outcomes is invariant to the well-being levels of individuals whose levels are the same in the two outcomes.

> Outcome Separability: Let **M** be a subset of $\mathbf{I}^{\text{Mod}}$, and let $\mathbf{M}^+ = \mathbf{I}^{\text{Mod}} \setminus \mathbf{M}$ (all individuals not in **M**). Assume x, x^*, x^+, x^{++} are as follows. For all $i \in \mathbf{M}$, $\mathbf{w}_i(x) = \mathbf{w}_i(x^*)$ and $\mathbf{w}_i(x^+) = \mathbf{w}_i(x^{++})$. For all $j \in \mathbf{M}^+$, $\mathbf{w}_j(x) = \mathbf{w}_j(x^+)$ and $\mathbf{w}_j(x^*) = \mathbf{w}_j(x^{++})$. Then $\mathbf{w}(x) \succcurlyeq^{E} \mathbf{w}(x^*)$ iff $\mathbf{w}(x^+) \succcurlyeq^{E} \mathbf{w}(x^{++})$.

A world-ranking $\succcurlyeq^{E\text{-D}}$ is appropriately implemented by an SWF $\succcurlyeq^{E}$ that satisfies Outcome Separability iff the world-ranking satisfies Separability—or so I would argue. For the welfarist, $\succcurlyeq^{E\text{-D}}$ ranks worlds in light of the patterns of individual well-being. $\succcurlyeq^{E}$ does the same at the outcome level (with outcomes being simplified models of worlds). For $\succcurlyeq^{E}$ to satisfy (or violate) Outcome Separability

[67] On Module Consistency, see Section 1.A.6. The Pareto Indifference axiom being invoked here is Pareto Indifference at the level of well-being vectors, see Section 7.1. Strictly, Policy Separability implies Decomposability only if we suppose that **P** is "rich" enough to include at least one degenerate policy—or if we suppose that any **P** is a subset of a larger **P*** that includes at least one degenerate policy, and that the ranking of policies in **P** should be consistent with the ranking in **P*** (which seems very plausible). (Two distinct degenerate policies are not required, since P^+ and P^{++} might be the same policy.)

[68] See Section 7.A.2.

while $\succcurlyeq^{E\text{-D}}$ violates (or satisfies) Separability would be to misrepresent how well-being determines moral betterness.

Assume, then, that the world-ranking $\succcurlyeq^{E\text{-D}}$ violates Separability and hence its implementing SWF $\succcurlyeq^{E}$ violates Outcome Separability. It follows immediately that any uncertainty module for that SWF will violate Policy Separability. This follows from Module Consistency (see Section 1.A.6), namely, that the ranking of degenerate policies by any uncertainty module for a given SWF must track that SWF's outcome ranking: If P leads to outcome x for certain, and P^* to outcome x^* for certain, then $P \succcurlyeq^{E\text{-P}} P^*$ iff $\mathbf{w}(x) \succcurlyeq^{E} \mathbf{w}(x^*)$.

To see why Module Consistency means that $\succcurlyeq^{E}$ satisfying Outcome Separability is a necessary condition for its uncertainty module satisfying Policy Separability, assume that $\succcurlyeq^{E}$ violates Outcome Separability. Thus, there are four outcomes x, x^*, x^+, x^{++} that meet the antecedent conditions for Outcome Separability but it is *not* the case that $\mathbf{w}(x) \succcurlyeq^{E} \mathbf{w}(x^*)$ iff $\mathbf{w}(x^+) \succcurlyeq^{E} \mathbf{w}(x^{++})$. Consider then four policies P, P^*, P^+, P^{++} that lead with certainty to x, x^*, x^+, and x^{++}, respectively. These policies meet the antecedent conditions for Policy Separability. By Module Consistency, $P \succcurlyeq^{E\text{-P}} P^*$ iff $\mathbf{w}(x) \succcurlyeq^{E} \mathbf{w}(x^*)$ and $P^+ \succcurlyeq^{E\text{-P}} P^{++}$ iff $\mathbf{w}(x^+) \succcurlyeq^{E} \mathbf{w}(x^{++})$. Thus, it *cannot* be the case that $P \succcurlyeq^{E\text{-P}} P^*$ iff $P^+ \succcurlyeq^{E\text{-P}} P^{++}$, as required by Policy Separability.

5.A.2 Risk Policies and the SVRR: Theory

5.A.2.1 Equivalent Formulas for Simple Utilitarianism and Ex Post Prioritarianism

The simple-utilitarian uncertainty module assigns each policy P a score equaling $\sum_x \pi_P(x) \sum_{i=1}^{N} w_i(x)$, and ranks policies in the order of these scores. That is, $P \succcurlyeq^{E\text{-P}} P^*$ iff $\sum_x \pi_P(x) \sum_{i=1}^{N} w_i(x) \geq \sum_x \pi_{P^*}(x) \sum_{i=1}^{N} w_i(x)$.

Note now that the simple-utilitarian score as just stated (the expected sum of individual well-being) is equal to the sum of individuals' expected well-being. $\sum_x \pi_P(x) \sum_{i=1}^{N} w_i(x) = \sum_{i=1}^{N} \sum_x \pi_P(x) w_i(x)$.[69] In turn, as above, let $L_{P,i}(v)$

[69] Recall (see Section 1.A.6) that policies are *finite* probability distributions over outcomes. If so, it is straightforward that $\sum_x \pi_P(x) \sum_{i=1}^{N} w_i(x) = \sum_{i=1}^{N} \sum_x \pi_P(x) w_i(x)$.

be the probability to individual i of well-being level v with policy P. Then $\sum_{i=1}^{N}\sum_{x}\pi_P(x)\mathbf{w}_i(x)=\sum_{i=1}^{N}\sum_{v}L_{P,i}(v)v$. This reformulation makes it evident why simple utilitarianism satisfies Policy Separability.

Recall that $\mathbf{w}_i(x) = w(b_i(x))$, $b_i(x)$ the bundle of individual i in outcome x. Let $\rho_{P,i}(b)$ denote the probability that individual i receives bundle b with policy P. $\rho_{P,i}(b)=\sum_{x:b_i(x)=b}\pi_P(x)$. Then the simple-utilitarian score assigned to each policy can be reformulated, once more, as follows: $\sum_{i=1}^{N}\sum_{b}\rho_{P,i}(b)w(b)$.

Finally, let $\mathbf{A(P)}$ denote the subset of *affected* individuals for a given policy set $\mathbf{P}$. An individual is "unaffected" relative to $\mathbf{P}$ if they face the same lottery over bundles for every policy in $\mathbf{P}$; and they are "affected" if this is not the case. And let $E^{SU}(P)$ denote the sum of individuals' expected well-being, summing over affected individuals. That is, $E^{SU}(P)=\sum_{i\in\mathbf{A(P)}}\sum_{b}\rho_{P,i}(b)w(b)$.

Note now that $\sum_{i=1}^{N}\sum_{b}\rho_{P,i}(b)w(b)\geq\sum_{i=1}^{N}\sum_{b}\rho_{P^*,i}(b)w(b)$ iff $E^{SU}(P)\geq E^{SU}(P^*)$.[70] We established above that $P\succcurlyeq^{\text{E-P}}P$ iff $\sum_{i=1}^{N}\sum_{b}\rho_{P,i}(b)w(b)\geq\sum_{i=1}^{N}\sum_{b}\rho_{P^*,i}(b)w(b)$. It therefore follows that the simple-utilitarian uncertainty module can be restated as ranking policies according to $E^{SU}(\cdot)$ scores: $P\succcurlyeq^{\text{E-P}}P^*$ iff $E^{SU}(P)\geq E^{SU}(P^*)$.

A parallel analysis can be undertaken for ex post prioritarianism. The ex-post-prioritarian module assigns each policy a score equaling the expected sum of individual transformed well-being and ranks policies in the order of these scores. $P\succcurlyeq^{\text{E-P}}P^*$ iff $\sum_{x}\pi_P(x)\sum_{i=1}^{N}g(\mathbf{w}_i(x))\geq\sum_{x}\pi_{P^*}(x)\sum_{i=1}^{N}g(\mathbf{w}_i(x))$. But note that the expected sum of individuals' transformed well-being is equal to the sum of individuals' expected transformed well-being: $\sum_{x}\pi_P(x)\sum_{i=1}^{N}g(\mathbf{w}_i(x))=\sum_{i=1}^{N}\sum_{x}\pi_P(x)g(\mathbf{w}_i(x))$. In turn, with $L_{P,i}(v)$ the probability to individual i of well-being level v with policy P, we have that $\sum_{i=1}^{N}\sum_{x}\pi_P(x)g(\mathbf{w}_i(x))=\sum_{i=1}^{N}\sum_{v}L_{P,i}(v)g(v)$. This reformulation makes it evident why ex post prioritarianism satisfies Policy Separability.

[70] This is because $\sum_{b}\rho_{P,i}(b)w(b)=\sum_{b}\rho_{P^*,i}(b)w(b)$ if $i\notin\mathbf{A(P)}$

Note now that $\sum_{i=1}^{N}\sum_{x}\pi_P(x)g(\mathbf{w}_i(x))=\sum_{i=1}^{N}\sum_{b}\rho_{P,i}(b)g(w(b))$. Finally, let $E^{EPP}(P)$ equal the sum of individuals' expected transformed well-being for policy P, summing over affected individuals. $E^{EPP}(P)=\sum_{i\in\mathbf{A(P)}}\sum_{b}\rho_{P,i}(b)g(w(b))$. Then the ex post prioritarian uncertainty module can be restated as ranking policies according to $E^{EPP}(\cdot)$ scores: $P \succsim^{E\text{-}P} P^*$ iff $E^{EPP}(P) \geq E^{EPP}(P^*)$.

5.A.2.2 Conceptualizing Risk Policies

Individual i has a current age A_i; that is, the number of the current period in i's life is $A_i + 1$. T is the maximum possible length of life (number of periods). $1 \leq A_i \leq T-1$. A policy P endows individual i with a risk profile $(p_{P,i}^{A_i+1},\ldots,p_{P,i}^{T})$, with $p_{P,i}^{t}$ the probability with policy P that i survives to the end of period t, conditional on being alive at the beginning of that period. P also endows i with an attribute profile $(b_{P,i}^{1},\ldots,b_{P,i}^{T})$, with $b_{P,i}^{t}$ the bundle of attributes that i receives in period t, conditional on surviving to the end of period t.

The individual's policy-specific risk and attribute profiles, in turn, determine their lottery over lifetime bundles. Let $\mu_{P,i}^{l}$ denote the probability that individual i lives exactly l periods. If $l < A_i$, $\mu_{P,i}^{l} = 0$. If $l = A_i$, $\mu_{P,i}^{l} = 1 - p_{P,i}^{A_i+1}$. Finally, if $l > A_i$, $\mu_{P,i}^{l}=\left(\prod_{t=A_i+1}^{l} p_{P,i}^{t}\right)(1-p_{P,i}^{l+1})$. For a given longevity l, individual i's policy-P sequence of period bundles is just $b_{P,i}^{1},\ldots,b_{P,i}^{l}$ and then Dead for periods $l+1$ to T.

The individual's risk and attribute profiles also determine their expected lifetime well-being and expected transformed lifetime well-being. Let $W_{P,i}^{l}$ denote individual i's lifetime well-being if they live exactly l periods with their policy-P attribute profile. Individual i's expected lifetime well-being with P is $\sum_{t=A_i}^{T}\mu_{P,i}^{t}W_{P,i}^{t}$, while the individual's expected transformed lifetime well-being with P is $\sum_{t=A_i}^{T}\mu_{P,i}^{t}g(W_{P,i}^{t})$. Thus $E^{SU}(P)=\sum_{i\in\mathbf{A(P)}}\sum_{t=A_i}^{T}\mu_{P,i}^{t}W_{P,i}^{t}$ and $E^{EPP}(P)=\sum_{i\in\mathbf{A(P)}}\sum_{t=A_i}^{T}\mu_{P,i}^{t}g(W_{P,i}^{t})$.

5.A.2.3 The SVRR

Let B denote some baseline policy. Let **B** denote the baseline risk and attribute profiles of affected individuals. Assume that the uncertainty module for an SWF satisfies Policy Separability and ranks policies according to a score $E(P)$, with $E(P)$ determined by the risk profiles and attribute profiles of affected individuals. Then SVRR_i is defined as the partial derivative of $E(\cdot)$ with respect to individual i's current survival probability, this partial derivative evaluated at

B. That is: $SVRR_i = \frac{\partial E}{\partial p_i^{A_i+1}}(\mathbf{B})$. (This definition, of course, assumes that $E(\cdot)$ is differentiable with respect to individuals' survival probabilities.) With $SVRR_i^{SU}$ and $SVRR_i^{EPP}$ denoting, respectively, the simple-utilitarian and ex-post-prioritarian SVRRs, we have that $SVRR_i^{SU} = \frac{\partial E^{SU}}{\partial p_i^{A_i+1}}(\mathbf{B})$ and $SVRR_i^{EPP} = \frac{\partial E^{EPP}}{\partial p_i^{A_i+1}}(\mathbf{B})$. Because both $E^{SU}(\cdot)$ and $E^{EPP}(\cdot)$ are additive across individuals, $SVRR_i^{SU}$ and $SVRR_i^{EPP}$ are determined just by individual *i*'s baseline risk profile and attribute profile. So we can write that $SVRR_i^{SU} = \frac{\partial E^{SU}}{\partial p_i^{A_i+1}}\left((p_{B,i}^{A_i+1}, \ldots, p_{B,i}^{T}),(b_{B,i}^{1}, \ldots, b_{B,i}^{T})\right)$ and that $SVRR_i^{EPP} = \frac{\partial E^{EPP}}{\partial p_i^{A_i+1}}\left((p_{B,i}^{A_i+1}, \ldots, p_{B,i}^{T}),(b_{B,i}^{1}, \ldots, b_{B,i}^{T})\right)$.

It's straightforward to show that $SVRR_i^{SU} = -W_{B,i}^{A_i} + \sum_{t=A_i+1}^{T} \frac{\mu_{B,i}^t}{p_{B,i}^{A_i+1}} W_{B,i}^t$, that is, the difference between *i*'s expected lifetime well-being, conditional on surviving the current period, and their lifetime well-being if they die now. To see this, note that $\frac{\partial \mu_i^t}{\partial p_i^{A_i+1}}\left((p_{B,i}^{A_i+1}, \ldots, p_{B,i}^{T}),(b_{B,i}^{1}, \ldots, b_{B,i}^{T})\right) = -1$ for $t = A_i$ and $\frac{\mu_{B,i}^t}{p_{B,i}^{A_i+1}}$ for $t > A_i$.

Similarly, $SVRR_i^{EPP} = -g(W_{B,i}^{A_i}) + \sum_{t=A_i+1}^{T} \frac{\mu_{B,i}^t}{p_{B,i}^{A_i+1}} g(W_{B,i}^t)$, that is, the difference between *i*'s expected transformed lifetime well-being, conditional on surviving the current period, and their transformed lifetime well-being if they die now.

Note that these formulas for $SVRR_i^{SU}$ and $SVRR_i^{EPP}$ do *not* assume that lifetime well-being is temporally additive.

5.A.2.4 Some General Results

The results reported in the main text regarding the effect of age (section 5.4.1) and quality of life and background risk (section 5.4.2) presume that lifetime well-being is temporally additive. With $w^p(\cdot)$ the period well-being measure, $W_{P,i}^l = \sum_{t=1}^{l} w^p(b_{P,i}^t) + \sum_{t=l+1}^{T} w^p(\text{Dead})$. The extent to which these results can be generalized beyond temporal additivity is a matter for future research.

The results are essentially those reported in Adler, Ferranna, Hammitt, and Treich (2021)—who use a more specific setup, with period well-being determined by period income rather than, as here, a period bundle that may include non-income attributes. The results here can be derived following the derivations set forth in the text of Adler, Ferranna, Hammitt, and Treich (2021) or in the online appendix accompanying that article.

The results in section 5.4.3 regarding SVRR^{SU} and SVRR^{EPP} with permanent, proportional differences in well-being, which also assume temporal additivity, can be derived as follows.

Let A denote the common age of Ellie and Frank; $(p_B^{A+1}, \ldots, p_B^T)$ their common baseline risk profile; and μ_B^l the common probability (derived from the risk profile) that either individual lives exactly l periods. Ellie's baseline attribute profile is $(b_{B,E}^1, \ldots, b_{B,E}^T)$ and Frank's baseline attribute profile is $(b_{B,F}^1, \ldots, b_{B,F}^T)$, with "$E$" and "$F$" in the subscripts denoting Ellie and Frank, respectively. Ellie is $k > 1$ times better off in every period than Frank, i.e., $w^p(b_{B,E}^t) = kw^p(b_{B,F}^t)$ for all t. Assume also that $w^p(\text{Dead}) = 0$ and that $w^p(b) > 0$ for every bundle b in Ellie's or Frank's attribute profiles.[71]

With $w^p(\text{Dead}) = 0$, $W_{B,i}^l = \sum_{t=1}^{l} w^p(b_{B,i}^t)$ for any lifespan l, with i = Ellie or Frank. Since $w^p(b_{B,E}^t) = kw^p(b_{B,F}^t)$ for all t, we have that $W_{B,E}^l = \sum_{t=1}^{l} w^p(b_{B,E}^t) = \sum_{t=1}^{l} kw^p(b_{B,F}^t) = kW_{B,F}^l$.

$SVRR_i^{SU} = -W_{B,i}^A + \sum_{t=A+1}^{T} \frac{\mu_B^t}{p_B^{A+1}} W_{B,i}^t$. Since $W_{B,E}^l = kW_{B,F}^l$ for any lifespan l, we have that $SVRR_E^{SU} = kSVRR_F^{SU}$.

With the Atkinson $g(\cdot)$ function, $SVRR_i^{EPP} = (\frac{1}{1-\gamma})\left[-(W_{B,i}^A)^{1-\gamma} + \sum_{t=A+1}^{T} \frac{\mu_B^t}{p_B^{A+1}} (W_{B,i}^t)^{1-\gamma}\right]$ with $\gamma > 0$, $\gamma \neq 1$; and $SVRR_i^{EPP} = -\log(W_{B,i}^A) + \sum_{t=A+1}^{T} \frac{\mu_B^t}{p_B^{A+1}} \log(W_{B,i}^t)$ with $\gamma = 1$.

Since $W_{B,E}^l = kW_{B,F}^l$ for any lifespan l, we have that:

(1) With $\gamma > 0, \gamma \neq 1$: $\frac{SVRR_E^{EPP}}{SVRR_F^{EPP}} = k^{1-\gamma}$, which is greater than 1 if $\gamma < 1$ and less than 1 if $\gamma > 1$.

(2) With $\gamma = 1$: $SVRR_E^{EPP} = -\log(kW_{B,F}^A) + \sum_{t=A+1}^{T} \frac{\mu_B^t}{p_B^{A+1}} \log(kW_{B,F}^t) = -(\log k + \log W_{B,F}^A) + \left(\log k + \sum_{t=A+1}^{T} \frac{\mu_B^t}{p_B^{A+1}} \log(W_{B,F}^t)\right) = SVRR_F^{EPP}$. (Note that $\sum_{t=A+1}^{T} \frac{\mu_B^t}{p_B^{A+1}} = 1$.)

[71] The supposition that $w^p(\text{Dead}) = 0$ is required to ensure that Ellie's lifetime well-being at any duration is k times the lifetime well-being of Frank at that duration—which in turn is critical for the comparative statics results regarding SVRR^{EPP} for the two individuals as a function of γ.

5.A.2.5 Defining SVRR for Unaffected Individuals?

$SVRR_i$ as defined in this section and discussed in the main text captures the social value of risk reduction for *affected* individuals. (Note that it is defined as the partial derivative with respect to individual *i*'s current survival probability of E^{SU} or E^{EPP}, which sum expected well-being or expected transformed well-being over affected individuals.) In some contexts, it might be useful to consider the social value of risk reduction for all individuals, affected or not. If so, the definition of $SVRR_i$ naturally generalizes. Let $E^{*SU}(P) = \sum_i \sum_{t=A_i}^{T} \mu_{P,i}^t W_{P,i}^t$ and $E^{*EPP}(P) = \sum_i \sum_{t=A_i}^{T} \mu_{P,i}^t g(W_{P,i}^t)$. Then the generalized definition of $SVRR_i^{SU}$ and $SVRR_i^{EPP}$ is as the partial derivative of E^{*SU} and E^{*EPP}, with respect to *i*'s current survival probability: $SVRR_i^{SU} = \frac{\partial E^{*SU}}{\partial p_i^{A_i+1}}\left((p_{B,i}^{A_i+1}, \dots, p_{B,i}^T), (b_{B,i}^1, \dots, b_{B,i}^T)\right)$ and $SVRR_i^{EPP} = \frac{\partial E^{*EPP}}{\partial p_i^{A_i+1}}\left((p_{B,i}^{A_i+1}, \dots, p_{B,i}^T), (b_{B,i}^1, \dots, b_{B,i}^T)\right)$. For an affected individual, the value of $SVRR_i$ thus generalized is exactly the same as the original $SVRR_i$ value. What changes is that we can now define $SVRR_i$ for the unaffected.

6

Evaluating Risk-Regulation Policies

Cost-Benefit Analysis

Cost-benefit analysis (CBA) is the dominant economic methodology for evaluating governmental policies and, specifically, risk-regulation policies.[1] Although the SWF framework favored in this book has been elaborated by a substantial body of writing in theoretical economics, CBA is much more common in applied economics. Moreover, the SWF methodology has not yet gained a foothold within governments.[2] By contrast, CBA has been the linchpin of systematic policy analysis in the US government for more than four decades and plays a major role in other governments.[3]

The key concept in applying CBA to risk regulation is the so-called value of statistical life (VSL). CBA, in general, translates well-being effects on individuals into monetary equivalents. VSL, specifically, is a conversion factor that translates risk reductions into monetary equivalents. If the fatality risk of individual i is reduced by Δp, the monetary equivalent is $\Delta p \times \text{VSL}_i$.

VSL is a much-discussed topic in the economics literature. A great deal of scholarly effort has been expended in developing the theory of VSL[4] and in estimating VSL values.[5] In the US government, specifically, VSL is a central parameter for policy analysts at risk-regulatory agencies. VSL is the tool that these analysts use to quantify the benefits of fatality risk reduction.[6]

[1] On CBA, see Adler (2012, ch. 2; 2019b); Adler and Posner (2006); Boadway (2016); Boadway and Bruce (1984); Boardman, Greenberg, Vining, and Weimer (2018); Freeman, Herriges, and Kling (2014); Just, Hueth, and Schmitz (2004).

[2] Although distributionally weighted CBA, an approximation to the SWF framework, has entered governmental practice (see Section 6.1.3), the direct application of SWFs has not (as far as this author is aware, and as of the drafting of this book).

[3] The use of CBA within government is discussed by Renda (2011); Wiener (2013); and Wiener and Alemanno (2017).

[4] See, e.g., Eeckhoudt and Hammitt (2001); Evans and Smith (2010); Hammitt (2000, 2007); Hammitt, Morfeld, Tuomisto, and Erren (2020); Johansson (2002); Jones-Lee, Chilton, Metcalf, and Nielsen (2015); Viscusi (2018).

[5] For overviews of the empirical literature on VSL, see Aldy and Viscusi (2007); Cropper, Hammitt, and Robinson (2011); Kniesner and Viscusi (2019); Krupnick (2007); OECD (2012); Viscusi and Aldy (2003); Viscusi (2018).

[6] See Robinson, Hammitt, and O'Keeffe (2019, sec. 3), tabulating VSL values used by US regulatory agencies; Viscusi (2018, ch. 2), describing evolution of US government VSL practice.

Risk, Death, and Well-Being. Matthew D. Adler, Oxford University Press. © Oxford University Press 2025.
DOI: 10.1093/9780197505984.003.0006

This chapter compares the SWF framework and CBA with respect to risk regulation. This comparison serves to illustrate what is distinctive about the methodology proposed in this book—via juxtaposition with the currently dominant economic approach. Despite their common disciplinary roots, the two frameworks differ quite significantly. What's undertaken, specifically, is to contrast the two specific SWF uncertainty modules explored at length in Chapter 5—simple utilitarianism and ex post prioritarianism—with CBA.

As we'll see in this chapter, VSL is the CBA analogue to the SVRR. $SVRR_i^{SU}$ quantifies how fatality risk reduction for a given individual *i* contributes to simple-utilitarian ethical value; and $SVRR_i^{EPP}$ quantifies how it contributes to ex-post-prioritarian ethical value. Similarly, VSL_i quantifies how fatality risk reduction for a given individual *i* contributes to *CBA* value: ethical value as measured using CBA's scale, the sum of monetary equivalents. But the properties of VSL are quite different from those of $SVRR^{SU}$, let alone $SVRR^{EPP}$.

Section 6.1 provides an overview of CBA as applied to risk regulation. It discusses both textbook CBA (the sum of monetary equivalents) and two variations: CBA using population-average rather than heterogeneous VSL, and CBA using the "value of statistical life year" (VSLY) to value risk reduction.[7]

Section 6.2 contrasts textbook CBA with simple utilitarianism and ex post prioritarianism. This section analyzes the differences between VSL, on the one hand, and $SVRR^{SU}$ and $SVRR^{EPP}$, on the other. It deploys the simulation model presented in Chapter 5 to illustrate these differences. And, again using that model, it shows how the policy recommendations of textbook CBA diverge from those of the two SWF modules.

Section 6.3 turns to population-average and VSLY-based CBA—showing how these, too, diverge from the SWF approach.

The main aim of the chapter is to illustrate the substantial differences between the SWF framework and CBA. Section 6.4 addresses the question of justification. Why believe that shifting away from the leading methodology (CBA), to this newcomer (SWF), would be an ethical improvement?

6.1 CBA and Risk Regulation

This section reviews textbook CBA (the sum of monetary equivalents), population-average CBA, and VSLY-based CBA. A fourth version of CBA, CBA with distributional weights, is also discussed.

[7] CBA with distributional weights, a third variation, is also covered in Section 6.1, for completeness, but it isn't discussed in the remainder of the chapter. As will be explained in Section 6.1, CBA with distributional weights is an approximation to the SWF framework rather than a genuinely distinct approach.

6.1.1 Textbook CBA

"Textbook CBA" is the version thereof presented in standard academic treatments. In what follows, I'll omit "textbook"—using "CBA" simpliciter as synonymous with "textbook CBA." And I'll often do the same in later sections.

So as to facilitate comparison with the SWF framework, I'll present CBA using some of the apparatus of that framework, namely, a set of policies **P**; a model population $\mathbf{I}^{\mathbf{Mod}}$; and an outcome set **O**. Each outcome x in **O** assigns a bundle of attributes to each individual, so that x corresponds to the list of bundles $(b_1(x), \ldots, b_N(x))$.

CBA employs a preference-based account of welfare. It assumes (as is standard in economics) that an individual's preferences can be represented by a utility function $u(\cdot)$. Let $u_i(\cdot)$ denote the utility function of individual i. $u_i(\cdot)$ represents i's preferences in the sense that if i is indifferent between bundles b and b^*, $u_i(b) = u_i(b^*)$; and if i prefers bundle b to b^*, $u_i(b) > u_i(b^*)$. (Throughout the chapter, I will assume that $u_i(\cdot)$ is, specifically, a vNM utility function; it represents i's risk preferences as well as i's preferences with respect to sure bundles and, in so doing, satisfies the vNM axioms.)[8]

CBA translates well-being effects on individuals into *monetary equivalents*. I use "money" as an umbrella term, meaning some indicator of an individual's material resources. More specifically, depending on how individual preferences are modeled, "money" might mean an individual's income, their material consumption, or their wealth.

So as to permit the translation of well-being effects into money, CBA requires that bundles include, at least, a description of the individual's money holdings. For CBA purposes, then, a bundle $b = (m, c)$, with m denoting money (income, consumption, or wealth) and c other attributes.

The literature on CBA suggests various rules whereby outcomes might be compared using monetary equivalents. The specific such rule which is most attractive as a formal matter is as follows.[9] Let B denote some baseline outcome.[10] Individual i's bundle of attributes in the baseline is $(m_i(B), c_i(B))$; and their bundle of attributes in a given outcome x is $(m_i(x), c_i(x))$. Then individual i's monetary equivalent for x, $\mathrm{ME}_i(x)$, is the change to their baseline money holdings that makes them indifferent between the baseline and the outcome.

[8] On vNM utility theory, see sources cited Chapter 4, note 13; Sections 4.2–4.3.

[9] This rule defines an individual's monetary equivalent for a given outcome x as the baseline change in money holdings (the so-called equivalent variation) rather than the change in x (the so-called compensating variation). The advantages of this approach are discussed in Adler (2012, pp. 92–98); Adler (2016a, on-line supplementary materials). That said, the message of this chapter—that CBA as applied to risk regulation diverges significantly from the SWF approach—holds equally true with respect to CBA defined in terms of compensating variations.

[10] I use "B" capitalized so as not to risk confusion with "b" for bundle.

That is, $ME_i(x) = \Delta m$ such that $u_i(m_i(B) + \Delta m, c_i(B)) = u_i(m_i(x), c_i(x))$. CBA's rule for ranking outcomes is as follows: x is at least as good as y iff $\Sigma ME_i(x) \geq \Sigma ME_i(y)$. In other words, outcomes are ranked according to the sum of monetary equivalents.

A notational aside. The formula $\Sigma ME_i(x)$, the sum of individuals' monetary equivalents for x, or related formulas, will be used repeatedly in this chapter. Strictly, the formula should be $\sum_{i=1}^{N} ME_i(x)$, which makes explicit that the individuals whose monetary equivalents are summed are the members of the population I^{Mod}: individual 1, individual 2, . . . , individual N. However, I will reduce clutter and use the simpler formula $\Sigma ME_i(x)$.

Although CBA differs from the SWF framework (as will be explored in detail in Section 6.2), some broad similarities between the methodologies should be noted. First, all SWFs satisfy the axiom of Pareto Indifference in ranking outcomes; and the major SWFs satisfy the axiom of Strong Pareto.[11] If we assume that individuals' preferences are "monotonic" in money (more is always better), then CBA's ranking of outcomes also satisfies Pareto Indifference and Strong Pareto.

Second, although CBA does not employ an interpersonally comparable measure of well-being $w(\cdot)$, there *may* be a close connection between $w(\cdot)$ and the individual utility functions that CBA *does* use. If $w(\cdot)$ is constructed so as to respect individual preferences (as per the analysis in Section 4.3 and the empirical illustration in Section 5.3.4), then the number assigned by $w(\cdot)$ to bundle (m, c) in the hands of individual i will be equal to a rescaling of the utility value $u_i(m, c)$.

In short, *both* CBA *and* the SWF framework together with a preference-based well-being measure employ utility functions. The critical difference is that CBA translates each outcome into a list of monetary equivalents, while the SWF framework translates each into a list of interpersonally comparable well-being numbers derived from the utility functions.

Policies (as in the SWF framework) are probability distributions across outcomes. Let B now denote a baseline policy, e.g., leaving in place status quo legislation and other governmental programs rather than adopting new measures. The set of policies $\mathbf{P}$ includes the baseline policy B as well as others: $\mathbf{P} = \{B,$

[11] Pareto Indifference and Strong Pareto at the level of worlds were set forth in Section 1.3.1 (under the more precise labels "Lifetime Pareto Indifference" and "Lifetime Strong Pareto," since the well-being at issue is lifetime well-being). These axioms, at the level of outcomes, are as follows. *Pareto Indifference*: If each individual is equally well off in outcome x as they are in outcome y, the outcomes are equally good. *Strong Pareto*: If each individual is at least as well off in outcome x as they are in outcome y, and some individuals are strictly better off in x, then x is better than y.

P^*, P^{**}, P^{***}, . . .}. We can define the monetary equivalent of individual i for a given policy P as follow: This monetary equivalent, $ME_i(P)$, is the change to the individual's baseline monetary holdings that suffices to render them indifferent between B and P. Stated in terms of utility, $ME_i(P)$ is such as to equalize individual i's expected utility with B and with P.[12]

CBA then assigns each policy a number equaling the sum total of monetary equivalents and ranks policies in the order of these numbers. Let $E^{CBA}(P) = \Sigma ME_i(P)$. Then CBA's policy ranking rule is the following: P is at least as good as P^* iff $\Sigma ME_i(P) \geq \Sigma ME_i(P^*)$.

This formalism brings into view the similarities and differences between CBA, on the one hand, and simple utilitarianism and ex post prioritarianism, on the other. The simple-utilitarian value assigned to a policy, $E^{SU}(P)$, is the sum of individuals' expected well-being. The ex-post-prioritarian value assigned to a policy, $E^{EPP}(P)$, is the sum of individuals' expected transformed well-being. All three approaches assign a numerical *score* to each policy—be it $E^{CBA}(P)$, $E^{SU}(P)$, or $E^{EPP}(P)$—and rank policies in the order of these scores.[13]

Further, all three approaches satisfy axioms of Decomposability and Policy Separability;[14] thus policies need not be explicitly described as probability distributions over whole outcomes. Instead, each policy can be described (more economically) as an array of bundle lotteries for the affected subset of the population. This renders CBA, like simple utilitarianism and ex post prioritarianism, an especially tractable policy-assessment tool.[15]

The difference—of course—is in the "currency" of ethical value. CBA computes its score by summing up a *monetary* measure of a policy's impact on each individual, the monetary equivalent, rather than expected well-being or expected transformed well-being.

Let's turn now, specifically, to CBA's assessment of risk regulation and therewith the VSL concept.[16] I'll explain how CBA works, here, via the same general

[12] Let $\rho_{P,i}(m, c)$ denote the probability that individual i receives bundle (m, c) given the choice of policy P. $\rho_{B,i}(m, c)$ is, specifically, the probability that i receives (m, c) in the baseline. Then $ME_i(P) = \Delta m$ such that $\sum_{(m,c)} \rho_{B,i}(m,c)u_i(m+\Delta m,c) = \sum_{(m,c)} \rho_{P,i}(m,c)u_i(m,c)$.

[13] The attentive reader will notice an inaccuracy in the paragraph to which this note is appended. E^{SU} and E^{EPP}, as I defined them in Section 5.2.1, sum individuals' expected well-being or expected transformed well-being over affected individuals. E^{CBA}, to be strictly parallel to these values, should also be defined as summing just over affected individuals. However, since CBA is not typically defined this way, I will define $E^{CBA}(P)$ as $\Sigma ME_i(P)$, summing over all individuals. The choice of definition doesn't change how CBA ranks policies, since CBA satisfies Decomposability and Policy Separability.

[14] These axioms are discussed in Section 5.1.1 and stated formally in Section 5.A.1.1.

[15] Moreover, CBA, like simple utilitarianism (although not ex post prioritarianism), satisfies the ex ante Pareto axioms. See Chapter 7.

[16] Scholarship presenting the VSL concept and comparing it to SVRR includes Adler (2017; 2019b, ch. 5; 2020b); Adler, Ferranna, Hammitt, and Treich (2021); Adler, Hammitt, and Treich (2014); Hammitt and Treich (2022).

setup used earlier for conceptualizing risk policies (in Section 5.2.1). Each individual has an age A_i. A given policy P endows each individual i with a risk profile (a list of survival probabilities, one for each period beginning with the current period). Each policy P also endows each individual i with an attribute profile: a list of period bundles, specifying for each period t the bundle b_i^t that the individual receives if they survive to the end of this period. Period bundles, for CBA purposes, are conceptualized as combinations of money and other attributes; $b^t = (m^t, c^t)$. Thus, the attribute profile of individual i with a given policy P is $((m_i^1, c_i^1), \ldots, (m_i^T, c_i^T))$.

Monetary equivalents could be defined in terms of money holdings in any of the T periods. Typically, however, CBA specifies these values in terms of *current* money holdings—and I'll do so here. Thus, individual *i*'s monetary equivalent for policy P, $\mathrm{ME}_i(P)$, is the change Δm to their baseline money holdings in the current period that equalizes their expected utility as between the baseline B and policy P.

VSL is standardly defined as the baseline marginal rate of substitution between money holdings and survival probability. In the setup here (with monetary equivalents defined in terms of current money holdings), this means specifically: *VSL_i is the marginal rate of substitution, for individual i, between current money holdings and current survival probability.*

This definition will be opaque to readers unfamiliar with the concept of a "marginal rate of substitution." Equivalent definitions of VSL are as follows:

— Assume that individual *i*'s current survival probability changes by Δp. Let Δm be *i*'s monetary equivalent for this change. Then VSL_i is the limit of $(\Delta m/\Delta p)$ as Δp goes to zero.

— VSL_i is a *conversion factor* that translates risk changes into monetary equivalents. Assume individual *i*'s current survival probability changes by Δp. Individual *i*'s monetary equivalent for this change is approximately $\mathrm{VSL}_i \times \Delta p$, with this approximation becoming increasingly accurate as Δp approaches zero.

— VSL_i is the partial derivative of E^{CBA} with respect to *i*'s current survival probability, evaluated at *i*'s baseline risk and attribute profile. That is, VSL_i is the change in CBA value (the sum of monetary equivalents) per unit of current risk reduction for individual i, as evaluated for a marginal such reduction.

This final definition of VSL_i highlights the parallelism with the SVRR concept. Just as SVRR_i^{SU} and SVRR_i^{EPP} are, respectively, the change in simple-utilitarian and ex-post-prioritarian value per unit of risk reduction to individual i (as evaluated for a marginal such reduction), so VSL_i is the corresponding such change in CBA value (the sum of monetary equivalents).

It bears emphasis that VSL_i varies among individuals (as do $SVRR_i^{SU}$ and $SVRR_i^{EPP}$). VSL_i depends upon individual *i*'s age, baseline risk profile, and baseline attribute profile. VSL_i is an individual risk-to-money conversion factor, not a universal constant. As with SVRR, I will sometimes omit the "*i*" subscript from "VSL" to avoid clutter; but the reader should keep in mind that VSL as per textbook CBA is an individual-level quantity.

VSL is useful for CBA purposes in just the way that SVRR is useful for SWF purposes. Assume that a policy changes individuals' current survival probabilities by Δp_i for each individual *i*, as well as (perhaps) changing individuals' future survival probabilities and their attribute profiles. Then the total change in E^{CBA} relative to baseline is approximately equal to the sum across individuals of $VSL_i \times \Delta p_i$ plus sums of corresponding terms for the deltas to individuals' future survival probabilities and to individuals' attribute profiles. VSL_i captures the *portion* of a policy's impact on CBA value (the sum of monetary equivalents) that results from the delta to individual *i*'s survival probability.

6.1.2 Population-Average CBA and VSLY-Based CBA

CBA, as practiced in the US government with respect to risk policies, is not textbook CBA. Instead, a single, population-average value (currently on the order of $10 million) is used to monetize risk reductions.[17] That is, if a policy changes individual *i*'s current survival probability by Δp, *i*'s monetary equivalent for that portion of the policy is estimated to be $\Delta p_i \times VSL^{average}$—$VSL^{average}$ being the average VSL across the US population. Thus, if one policy delivers a risk reduction of Δp to individual *i* and a second policy delivers a risk reduction of Δp to individual *j*, the two individuals are estimated to have the *same* monetary equivalent for the risk-reduction portion of the respective policies. By contrast, according to textbook CBA, individual *i*'s monetary equivalent for the risk-reduction portion of the policy that benefits them is $VSL_i \times \Delta p$, while individual *j*'s monetary equivalent for the risk-reduction portion of the policy that benefits them is $VSL_j \times \Delta p$. Since VSL_j need not equal VSL_i, these two monetary equivalents need not be equal.

Population-average CBA yields a simple formula for valuing risk reductions. Assume that a policy produces one or another pattern of risk reduction in the current period among the population, such that the expected number of deaths in the current period declines by ΔD. Then the aggregate monetary equivalent for that reduction is $\Delta D \times VSL^{average}$. This or similar formulas are pervasive in CBA documents undertaken by US regulatory agencies. We simply apply

17 See Adler (2020b), citing sources.

$VSL^{average}$ to total lifesaving, rather than summing up individuals' risk reductions multiplied by individual-specific VSLs.

What explains this departure from textbook CBA? Part of the explanation, surely, is an ethical aversion to differentiating monetary equivalents by income. Those with higher incomes will tend to have higher VSLs. Thus, textbook CBA will prefer to allocate a reduction Δp to richer rather than poorer individuals, ceteris paribus. Many will find this problematic, even repugnant.[18] Surveys of citizen views show no support for preferring the rich in allocating lifesaving effort or risk reduction.[19]

Population-average CBA goes further—eschewing *any* differentiation with respect to VSL. In particular, there is no differentiation with respect to age. A given Δp reduction is assigned the same value regardless of whether the beneficiary is a 20-year-old, a 50-year-old, or an 80-year-old. Neutrality with respect to *age* in risk reduction or lifesaving finds less support in citizen surveys than neutrality with respect to income.[20] The political clout of older individuals (who have tended, in US politics, to be better organized and more engaged than the young) may help to explain the use of population-average values. To be sure, the story need not only be a political one; some surely do have the intuition that the value of lifesaving is equal, regardless of individual income, or age, or any other characteristics.

VSLY (the "value of statistical life year") is a construct proposed by some scholars that circumvents the counterintuitive features of both textbook and population-average CBA.[21] $VSLY_i$ for a given individual i is their VSL_i divided by their life expectancy remaining. Formally, let LE_i denote the difference between an individual's expected lifespan conditional on surviving the current period, and their current age (their lifespan if they die now). An increment Δp to i's current survival probability produces an increase in expected lifespan of $LE_i \times \Delta p$. $VSLY_i$ is the limit, as Δp becomes small, of $\Delta m/(\Delta p \times LE_i)$. It is the individual's monetary equivalent per unit of expected-lifespan gain.

VSLY-based CBA computes a population-average VSLY ($VSLY^{average}$) and then values the monetary equivalent for a risk reduction Δp to a given individual i as $VSLY^{average} \times (\Delta p \times LE_i)$. Note that VSLY-based CBA differentiates among individuals in valuing risk reduction *only* insofar as they differ in life expectancy remaining. Differences in income or the other sources of quality of life do not, as such, produce heterogeneous valuations.

18 See, e.g., Emanuel et al. (2020); Hemel (2022).
19 See Dolan, Shaw, Tsuchiya, and Williams (2005).
20 See Dolan, Shaw, Tsuchiya, and Williams (2005); Huseynov, Palma, and Nayga (2020).
21 On VSLY, see Adler (2020b); Aldy and Viscusi (2007); Hammitt (2007, 2023); Hammitt, Morfeld, Tuomisto, and Erren (2020); Jones-Lee, Chilton, Metcalf, and Nielsen (2015); Kniesner and Viscusi (2019); Viscusi (2018, ch. 5).

6.1.3 Distributionally Weighted CBA

Some academic work on CBA discusses the possibility of adjusting individuals' monetary equivalents with so-called distributional weights.[22] While textbook CBA assigns policy P the score $\Sigma ME_i(P)$, distributionally weighted CBA assigns it a score equaling $\Sigma\alpha_i \times ME_i(P)$, with α_i the distributional weight for individual i – this weight depending on i's baseline characteristics. Distributional weights are sometimes used in governmental CBA practice.[23]

In the scholarly literature that examines it, distributional weighting is understood as a technique for modifying CBA so as to approximate the SWF methodology. In particular, if the weights are chosen appropriately, distributionally weighted CBA can approximate simple utilitarianism. (For reasons I have discussed elsewhere, there are not weights that will approximate ex post prioritarianism.)[24]

Distributionally weighted CBA with simple-utilitarian weights is not precisely equal to simple utilitarianism. They will tend to converge in ranking a set P of risk-regulation policies only if all policies are "close" to baseline (policy deltas in individuals' attribute and risk profiles are small). That said, the methodology is not a qualitative departure from the SWF framework; rather, and again, it is designed to approximate that framework. Since the aim of this chapter is to describe and criticize versions of CBA that *are* substantially distinct from SWF-based assessment, distributional weighting won't be further addressed here.

6.2 Textbook CBA versus Simple Utilitarianism and Ex Post Prioritarianism

6.2.1 SVRR versus VSL: A Theoretical Analysis

In this subsection, I extend the apparatus that was employed in Chapter 5 to illustrate the features of $SVRR^{SU}$ and $SVRR^{EPP}$—now using this apparatus to illuminate the differences between these constructs and VSL.

Each individual i, age A_i, has a baseline risk profile $(p_i^{A_i+1}, p_i^{A_i+2}, \ldots, p_i^T)$ and attribute profile $(b_i^1, \ldots, b_i^T)$. Each period bundle b^t is a combination of an income amount y^t and other attributes c^t. Thus an attribute profile for individual i takes the form $((y_i^1, c_i^1), \ldots, (y_i^T, c_i^T))$.

[22] See, e.g., Adler (2016a); Boadway (2016); Fleurbaey and Abi-Rafeh (2016); Nurmi and Ahtiainen (2018).

[23] See HM Treasury (2022). The Biden administration issued a guidance document that endorsed the use of distributional weights. See US Office of Management and Budget (2023). After the final draft of this book was completed, and while the book was being readied for publication, the Trump administration rescinded this guidance document. See White House (2025).

[24] See Adler (2016a, on-line supplementary materials).

CBA defines monetary equivalents in terms of individual preferences. The SWF framework revolves around a well-being measure $w(\cdot)$ which *may* be based upon individual preferences, but need not be. It is hardly remarkable that $SVRR^{SU}$ and $SVRR^{EPP}$, defined using a non-preference-based well-being measure, can depart from VSL. What is noteworthy, and worth examining in detail, is that such divergence can occur even with a preference-based $w(\cdot)$.

In Section 4.3, I showed that a preference-based well-being measure $w(\cdot)$ can be constructed by taking individuals' utility functions and then applying *scaling factors*.[25] Let $u_i(\cdot)$ be the rescaled utility function of individual *i*. Then, as per the theory developed in Section 4.3, the $w(\cdot)$ number of individual *i* with a given lifetime attribute bundle is just equal to the bundle's utility number as per $u_i(\cdot)$.

These (rescaled) individual utility functions can now be used to calculate *both* VSL_i *and* the SVRRs.

Assume that utility is temporally additive, with $u_i^p(.)$ the period utility function of individual *i*. Let U_i^t denote individual *i*'s lifetime utility if they live exactly *t* periods with their baseline attribute profile. Then $U_i^t = \sum_{s=1}^{t} u_i^p(y_i^s, c_i^s) + \sum_{s=t+1}^{T} u_i^p(\text{Dead})$. That is, U_i^t is the sum of period utility during the *t* periods alive as a function of baseline income and other attributes, plus the utility of Dead during the remaining periods.

In the earlier analysis, $SVRR_i^{SU}$ was the difference between *i*'s expected lifetime well-being conditional on surviving the current period, and *i*'s lifetime well-being if they die now. $SVRR_i^{EPP}$ was the same, but in terms of transformed lifetime well-being.[26] These analyses carry over here, but specifically in terms of *utility*—since $w(\cdot)$ is now, specifically, utility-based. That is, $SVRR_i^{SU}$ is the difference between *i*'s expected lifetime utility conditional on surviving the current period and *i*'s lifetime utility if they die now. $SVRR_i^{EPP}$ is the difference between *i*'s expected transformed lifetime utility conditional on surviving the current period and their transformed lifetime utility if they die now. That is,

$$SVRR_i^{SU} = -U_i^{A_i} + \sum_{t=A_i+1}^{T} \frac{\mu_i^t}{p_i^{A_i+1}} U_i^t$$

$$SVRR_i^{EPP} = -g(U_i^{A_i}) + \sum_{t=A_i+1}^{T} \frac{\mu_i^t}{p_i^{A_i+1}} g(U_i^t)$$

(Recall that μ_i^t denotes individual *i*'s baseline probability of living exactly *t* periods. This value can be derived from *i*'s risk profile.)

[25] This was illustrated empirically in Section 5.3.4.

[26] See Sections 5.4, 5.A.2.

Let MU_i denote the expected marginal utility of current income for individual i. Then VSL_i can be shown to be equal to $SVRR_i^{SU}$ divided by MU_i.[27]

$$VSL_i = \left(-U_i^{A_i} + \sum_{t=A_i+1}^{T} \frac{\mu_i^t}{p_i^{A_i+1}} U_i^t \right) / MU_i = SVRR_i^{SU} / MU_i$$

The intuition behind this formula for VSL_i is as follows. If individual i's current survival probability is increased by Δp, the change in their expected lifetime utility is $\Delta p \times SVRR_i^{SU}$. Individual i's monetary equivalent for the increase in current survival probability by Δp is the change in i's current income Δy that produces the very same change in expected lifetime utility. The change in expected lifetime utility from a Δy change to i's current income is approximately $\Delta y \times MU_i$. So Δy should be approximately such that $\Delta y \times MU_i = \Delta p \times SVRR_i^{SU}$, i.e., $\Delta y \approx (SVRR_i^{SU}/MU_i)\, \Delta p$. But VSL_i is just $\Delta y/\Delta p$ (at the limit, as Δp approaches zero), hence equal to $(SVRR_i^{SU}/MU_i)$.

How VSL_i varies among individuals is different from both $SVRR^{SU}$ and $SVRR^{EPP}$.[28] Let's first analyze how these indicators vary by age. Consider two individuals i and j, who differ in age (i older than j) but are otherwise similarly situated—meaning, in this setup, that they have the same risk profile and attribute profile and the same preferences (the same utility function). $SVRR^{EPP}$ has the property of "Extra Priority for the Young": $SVRR_j^{EPP}/SVRR_i^{EPP} > SVRR_j^{SU}/SVRR_i^{SU}$. VSL_i does not have this property. Nor does it track the simple-utilitarian age preferences. The young-to-old VSL ratio is not the simple-utilitarian ratio but the latter ratio adjusted by a relative-marginal-utility term. That is, $(VSL_j/VSL_i) = (SVRR_j^{SU}/MU_j)/(SVRR_i^{SU}/MU_i) = (SVRR_j^{SU}/SVRR_i^{SU}) \times (MU_i/MU_j)$. This relative-marginal-utility term, MU_i/MU_j, is the old-to-young ratio of expected marginal income utilities.

The young-to-old ratios of VSL and $SVRR^{SU}$ will be equal only if the relative-marginal-utility term equals 1. If the attribute and risk profiles are such that income and/or survival probability vary over time, this will generally not be the case. For example, if the older individual (i) has more current income than the younger individual (j) and a survival probability that is less than or equal to

[27] This follows directly from the definition of VSL_i that I'm using—namely, the marginal rate of substitution, for individual i, between current money holdings (specifically, income) and current survival probability. See the derivation in Adler, Ferranna, Hammitt, and Treich (2021).

[28] The results discussed in the following four paragraphs and summarized in Table 6.1 are taken from Adler, Ferranna, Hammitt, and Treich (2021). That article assumes that individuals have a common utility function, while I am allowing here for heterogeneous preferences and utility functions. However, the results here are comparative statics results comparing $SVRR^{SU}$, $SVRR^{EPP}$, and VSL between two individuals who differ on some dimension but have the same preferences. Thus the derivations in Adler, Ferranna, Hammitt, and Treich (2021) carry over directly. Adler, Ferranna, Hammitt, and Treich (2021) assume positive and diminishing marginal utility of income ($u' > 0, u'' < 0$).

that of the younger individual, the older individual will have a lower expected marginal income utility. (This assumes that income has diminishing marginal utility—a standard feature of utility functions.) Thus MU_i/MU_j is less than 1. In this case, textbook CBA gives *less* priority to the younger individual than simple utilitarianism. Conversely, if the older individual has less current income than the younger individual and a survival probability that is not too much lower, MU_i/MU_j will exceed one; if so, textbook CBA gives *more* priority to the young.

Consider, next, how VSL's pattern of variation among individuals of the same age compares to that of $SVRR^{EPP}$ and $SVRR^{SU}$. To make this comparison tractable, let's focus on how differences in income or background risk affect $SVRR^{SU}$, $SVRR^{EPP}$, and VSL. Imagine that two individuals have the same preferences, are the same age, and are similarly situated with respect to non-income attributes but either (1) have different amounts of income in some single period (past, present or future) or (2) have different survival probabilities in some single period (present or future). Table 6.1 summarizes the comparative statics of $SVRR^{SU}$, $SVRR^{EPP}$, and VSL with respect to these single-period differences in income or survival probability.

As Table 6.1 shows, the comparative statics of VSL are different from those of $SVRR^{EPP}$ with respect to both income and survival probability. The comparative statics of VSL are the same as those of $SVRR^{SU}$ with respect to income but not survival probability. If Eddie and Fran are similarly situated except that Eddie's current survival probability is lower than Fran's, the simple-utilitarian SVRRs are the same but the VSLs are not. Eddie will have a greater VSL than

Table 6.1 SVRRs and VSL: Comparative Statics

	Period Income: Single-Period Difference	**Survival Probability: Single-Period Difference**
$SVRR^{SU}$	Past period: *Unchanged* Current period: *Increasing* Future period: *Increasing*	Current period: *Unchanged* Future period: *Increasing*
$SVRR^{EPP}$	Past period: *Decreasing* Current period: *Increasing* Future period: *Increasing*	Current period: *Unchanged* Future period: *Increasing*
VSL	Past period: *Unchanged* Current period: *Increasing* Future period: *Increasing*	Current period: *Decreasing* Future period: *Increasing*

Explanation: This table shows the comparative statics of $SVRR^{SU}$, $SVRR^{EPP}$, and VSL with respect to a single-period change in income or survival probability.

Fran.[29] Ceteris paribus, CBA prefers to allocate a risk reduction to someone whose current survival probability is lower, while simple-utilitarianism is indifferent.

A further difference between VSL and $SVRR^{SU}$ is not apparent from Table 6.1. Although both VSL and $SVRR^{SU}$ increase with current income, VSL increases more quickly. Here, as elsewhere, the divergence in the patterns of $SVRR^{SU}$ and VSL occurs because of the expected-marginal-income-utility term in the denominator of VSL: again, $VSL_i = SVRR_i^{SU}/MU_i$. Consider two individuals, Rich and Poor, of the same age and otherwise identical, except that Rich's current income is greater than Poor's. Then simple utilitarianism prefers to allocate a risk reduction to Rich: $SVRR_{Rich}^{SU}/SVRR_{Poor}^{SU} > 1$. VSL also prefers to allocate a risk reduction to Rich. Moreover, the Rich-to-Poor VSL ratio exceeds the simple-utilitarian ratio—again, assuming diminishing marginal utility. $VSL_{Rich}/VSL_{Poor} = (SVRR_{Rich}^{SU}/SVRR_{Poor}^{SU}) \times (MU_{Poor}/MU_{Rich})$. If income has diminishing marginal utility, $MU_{Poor}/MU_{Rich} > 1$, and so $VSL_{Rich}/VSL_{Poor} > SVRR_{Rich}^{SU}/SVRR_{Poor}^{SU} > 1$. The simple-utilitarian value of risk reduction is skewed toward the rich, but the CBA value is even more skewed.

6.2.2 SVRR versus VSL: An Empirical Illustration

Here, I illustrate the differences between the SVRRs and VSL using the simulation model of Chapter 5.[30] Table 6.2 shows the ratio between the VSL of each

[29] This is because Eddie has a lower expected marginal utility of current income than Fran (marginal utility multiplied by the probability of surviving the period), hence a larger VSL given the formula $VSL_i = SVRR_i^{SU}/MU_i$.

[30] See Section 5.3. All of the building blocks of the Chapter 5 simulation, regarding incomes of the 25 cohorts, risk profiles, etc. (see Section 5.3.1), are carried over here. The Chapter 5 simulation employed the following well-being measure: $w(b) = \sum_{t=1}^{T} w^P(y^t)$, with $w^P(y^t) = (\log y^t - \log(\$1{,}000))$, and $w^P(\text{Dead}) = 0$. I here use the same well-being measure, here specifically interpreted as individuals' common utility function. That is, $u^P(\cdot)$ is the common period utility function; $u^P(y^t) = (\log y^t - \log(\$1{,}000))$, and $u^P(\text{Dead}) = 0$.

U_i^t, i's lifetime utility if they live exactly t periods, with bundle $(y_i^1, \ldots, y_i^t, \text{Dead}, \text{Dead}, \ldots, \text{Dead})$, equals $\sum_{s=1}^{t} u^P(y_i^s) + \sum_{s=t+1}^{T} u^P(\text{Dead})$. VSL values were calculated using the formula $VSL_i = SVRR_i^{SU}/MU_i$.

In order to calculate monetary equivalents for purposes of calculating CBA breakevens in Section 6.2.3, I used the following approximation: the monetary equivalent of a given individual i (the member of one or another cohort) for a policy that increases i's current survival probability by Δp and reduces current income by Δy is approximately $\Delta p \times VSL_i - \Delta y$. This approximation is quite accurate for the small changes in individuals' risk and income at issue in Section 6.2.3. See Adler (2017, pp. 72–74).

Table 6.2 VSLs

	Income: Low	Moderate	Middle	High	Top
Age 20	0.9	1.5	2.3	3.6	10.5
30	2.2	3.4	5.3	8.2	24.0
40	2.2	3.5	5.5	8.6	25.3
50	1.7	2.7	4.3	6.6	19.8
60	1.0	1.6	2.6	4.2	12.6

Explanation: This table shows VSLs for the various cohorts, normalized so that 1 indicates VSL for a member of the 60-year-old, Low income cohort.

Table 5.4 Simple-Utilitarian SVRRs

	Income: Low	Moderate	Middle	High	Top
Age 20	2.8	3.3	3.7	4.1	5.2
30	2.5	2.8	3.2	3.6	4.5
40	2.0	2.3	2.6	2.9	3.7
50	1.5	1.7	2.0	2.2	2.8
60	1.0	1.2	1.4	1.6	2.1

Explanation: This table shows $SVRR^{SU}$ values for the various cohorts, normalized so that 1 indicates $SVRR^{SU}$ for a member of the 60-year-old, Low income cohort.

cohort and that of the 60-year-old, Low income cohort. Tables 5.4, 5.5, and 5.6 from Chapter 5, reproduced here for the reader's convenience, show $SVRR^{SU}$, $SVRR^{EPP}$ ($\gamma = 1$), and $SVRR^{EPP}$ ($\gamma = 2$) in the same format: the ratio between the SVRRs and that of the SVRR for a 60-year-old, Low income individual.

Two of the differences discussed in the theoretical analysis above are strikingly apparent from these tables. The first is the effect of income. Within each age band (each row of the tables), $SVRR^{EPP}$ is approximately neutral with income ($\gamma = 1$) or decreases ($\gamma = 2$). $SVRR^{SU}$ increases with income. VSL also does, but much more dramatically. Moving from the lowest income quintile to the highest, $SVRR^{SU}$ increases by roughly a factor of 2. By contrast, VSL increases by roughly a factor of 11! Inverting, simple utilitarianism sees as equally valuable a Δp risk reduction for the poorest individual and a smaller ($\Delta p/2$) reduction for the richest, while CBA sees as equally valuable a Δp risk reduction for the poorest individual and a *much* smaller ($\Delta p/11$) reduction for the richest. The decreasing marginal utility of income strongly skews upward CBA's preference for risk reduction among the rich, as compared to that of simple utilitarianism.

Table 5.5 Ex-Post-Prioritarian (γ =1) SVRRs

	Income: Low	Moderate	Middle	High	Top
Age 20	5.3	5.3	5.3	5.3	5.3
30	3.8	3.8	3.9	3.8	3.8
40	2.5	2.6	2.7	2.7	2.7
50	1.6	1.7	1.8	1.8	1.8
60	1.0	1.1	1.1	1.2	1.2

Explanation: This table shows $SVRR^{EPP}$ (γ = 1) values for the various cohorts, normalized so that 1 indicates $SVRR^{EPP}$ (γ = 1) for a member of the 60-year-old, Low income cohort.

Table 5.6 Ex-Post-Prioritarian (γ = 2) SVRRs

	Income: Low	Moderate	Middle	High	Top
Age 20	12.2	10.7	9.5	8.5	6.6
30	6.5	5.8	5.2	4.6	3.6
40	3.5	3.1	2.9	2.6	2.1
50	1.9	1.7	1.6	1.5	1.2
60	1.0	1.0	.9	.8	.7

Explanation: This table shows $SVRR^{EPP}$ (γ = 2) values for the various cohorts, normalized so that 1 indicates $SVRR^{EPP}$ (γ = 2) for a member of the 60-year-old, Low income cohort.

The second, stark divergence in these tables between VSL and SVRR concerns the effect of age. $SVRR^{SU}$ decreases with age in each income quintile, and $SVRR^{EPP}$ does so even more quickly (as per Extra Priority for the Young). By contrast, VSL has a "hump" pattern, first increasing with age (from age 20 to age 40 in each income quintile) and then decreasing. Within each income quintile, VSL for 20-year-olds is *less* than VSL for 60-year-olds, while $SVRR^{SU}$ for 20-year-olds is at least 2.5 times that of $SVRR^{SU}$ for 60-year-olds.

As explained above, the age pattern of VSL can diverge from that of SVRR because of change in the expected marginal utility of income over time. In the simulation model, this mainly occurs by virtue of the time path of income. In line with empirical data regarding earnings over time, current-year incomes of the 25 cohorts are as follows (Table 6.3). Because current-year income increases with age in this model (up to age 50), the expected marginal utility of current income decreases with age (up to age 50). Returning to the formula $VSL_i = (SVRR_i^{SU}/MU_i)$, we see that the numerator ($SVRR_i^{SU}$) decreases with

Table 6.3 Current-Year Incomes

	Income: Low	Moderate	Middle	High	Top
Age 20	$8,331	$11,425	$15,686	$21,827	$51,152
30	$22,098	$30,306	$41,607	$57,896	$135,680
40	$28,426	$38,984	$53,522	$74,476	$174,536
50	$28,681	$39,334	$54,003	$75,145	$176,103
60	$24,930	$34,189	$46,939	$65,316	$153,069

age, but the denominator also decreases with age (up to age 50). The interaction of these factors yields a "hump" shape for VSL with age that diverges significantly from the smooth decline of $SVRR^{SU}$, let alone the even steeper decline of $SVRR^{EPP}$.

6.2.3 Illustrative Policies

Recall that Chapter 5 considered illustrative types of policies, all conferring an average 1-in-100,000 risk reduction across the 25 cohorts but differing (1) in who receives the reduction (all cohorts uniformly, or a reduction concentrated on the youngest, oldest, poorest, or richest cohorts); and (2) in how the cost burdens of the policy are spread (either uniformly or in proportion to income). Breakeven costs were calculated for the various policy types, as per simple utilitarianism and ex post prioritarianism ($\gamma = 1$ and $\gamma = 2$). The same is now done for textbook CBA. Table 6.4 presents the breakevens for all four policy-analytic approaches.

All the policies confer a reduction in current fatality risk on the various cohorts, at the cost of a reduction in current income. How CBA evaluates these policies, and specifically the breakevens it calculates, can therefore differ from simple utilitarianism and ex post prioritarianism for two reasons: (1) because of a divergence in how risk reduction is valued or (2) because of a divergence in how income costs are valued. The first divergence (between VSL, on the one hand, and $SVRR^{SU}$ and $SVRR^{EPP}$, on the other) has been reviewed at length. Let's now, more briefly, discuss the second.

CBA is (approximately) neutral to the distribution of income costs. The intuition, here, is that CBA measures policy impact by summing up monetary equivalents—and thus a transfer of money from one individual to another that holds constant this sum, merely changing the distribution of monetary impacts, is a matter of indifference to CBA.

Table 6.4 Policy Breakevens: Textbook CBA, Simple Utilitarianism, and Ex Post Prioritarianism

	Textbook CBA	Simple Utilitarian	Ex-Post-Prioritarian ($\gamma = 1$)	Ex-Post-Prioritarian ($\gamma = 2$)
Uniform Risk Reduction				
Uniform Cost Incidence	\$96	\$50	\$65	\$94
Proportional Cost Incidence	\$96	\$73	\$105	\$165
Risk Reduction for Youngest				
Uniform Cost Incidence	\$55	\$72	\$118	\$223
Proportional Cost Incidence	\$55	\$105	\$191	\$393
Risk Reduction for Oldest				
Uniform Cost Incidence	\$64	\$27	\$24	\$20
Proportional Cost Incidence	\$64	\$39	\$40	\$37
Risk Reduction for Poorest				
Uniform Cost Incidence	\$23	\$36	\$63	\$118
Proportional Cost Incidence	\$23	\$53	\$102	\$208
Risk Reduction for Richest				
Uniform Cost Incidence	\$270	\$68	\$66	\$67
Proportional Cost Incidence	\$270	\$99	\$107	\$118

To make this intuition a bit more precise in the present setup, consider first a purely redistributive policy P that deviates from baseline by increasing individual i's current income by Δy, while reducing j's by Δy. Individual i's monetary equivalent for P ($ME_i(P)$) is Δy, while individual j's is $-\Delta y$. The sum total of monetary equivalents is 0; CBA is indifferent between baseline and this purely redistributive policy.

Consider next a policy P that increases individual i's and individual j's survival probabilities, relative to baseline, by Δp_i and Δp_j, respectively, while reducing their incomes by Δy_i and Δy_j. Individual i's monetary equivalent for this policy is (approximately) $\Delta p_i \times \text{VSL}_i - \Delta y_i$, while individual j's is (approximately) $\Delta p_j \times \text{VSL}_j - \Delta y_j$. Consider a different policy P^* that provides the same risk reductions as P but changes the incidence of income costs as between the two individuals. Individual i's cost burden decreases by Δy, while individual j's increases by Δy. Thus, individual i's monetary equivalent for P^* is (approximately) Δy greater than their monetary equivalent for P, while individual j's monetary equivalent is (approximately) Δy less. Once more, then, the sum total of monetary equivalents doesn't change: CBA is (approximately) neutral as between P and P^*.[31]

By contrast, simple utilitarianism is *not* indifferent to the distribution of policy costs. As a result of the declining marginal utility of income, it prefers that a given quantum Δy in costs be borne by a richer rather than a poorer person, ceteris paribus. Ex post prioritarianism prefers to shift policy costs from poor to rich for this reason and for the additional reason that the poor are at a lower level of well-being (hence their well-being losses from income costs are upweighted).

To get a handle on the variation in breakevens in Table 6.4, let's start with Uniform Risk Reduction and Uniform Cost Incidence (top row) and then examine how the breakeven changes as the pattern of risk reduction shifts (holding constant uniform cost incidence). With Uniform Risk Reduction and Uniform Cost Incidence, CBA's breakeven (\$96) is greater than the SWF-based breakevens and almost twice that of simple utilitarianism (\$50). With risk reduction shifted to the youngest individuals, CBA's breakeven *decreases* (to \$55), while the SWF-based breakevens *increase* (so that all now exceed the CBA breakeven; the simple-utilitarian breakeven is now \$72, and the ex-post-prioritarian breakevens are considerably larger). This differential effect of a concentration of risk reduction on the young reflects the fact that CBA gives significantly less relative weight to the youngest, in this simulation, than the SWFs do. Conversely, with risk reduction shifted to the oldest individuals, the CBA breakeven does decrease, but it does so less substantially than the simple-utilitarian breakeven and much less substantially than the ex-post-prioritarian breakevens.

With risk reduction shifted to the poorest individuals, CBA's breakeven drops precipitously (from \$96 to \$23); the simple-utilitarian breakeven falls, but much less steeply (\$50 to \$36). Conversely, with risk reduction shifted to the richest

[31] CBA may not be precisely neutral between P and P^* because each individual's marginal utility of income may be different with P than with P^*. This means that the difference between individual i's monetary equivalent for P^* and for P may not be precisely Δy, and that the difference between individual j's monetary equivalent for P^* and for P may be not be precisely $-\Delta y$. If Δp_i, Δp_j, Δy_i, and Δy_j are small, any such change-in-marginal-utility effect will be small.

individuals, CBA's breakeven rockets skyward (from $96 to $270); the simple-utilitarian breakeven increases, but again less steeply ($50 to $68). Because VSL is much more biased to the rich than $SVRR^{SU}$, moving from a uniform risk reduction to one concentrated on the poor or the rich has a much larger effect on the CBA breakeven than on the simple-utilitarian one. Ex-post-prioritarian breakevens are essentially unchanged when risk reduction is concentrated on the poor or rich ($\gamma = 1$) or move in the opposite direction than CBA and simple utilitarianism ($\gamma = 2$).

On the cost side, the difference between CBA and the SWFs is straightforward. For every pattern of risk incidence, CBA's breakeven remains the same whether income costs are borne uniformly by the population or in proportion to income. This reflects the fact that CBA is neutral to the distribution of policy costs.[32] By contrast, simple-utilitarian breakevens increase with a shift from uniform to proportional incidence—and ex-post-prioritarian breakevens even more so.

6.3 Population-Average CBA and VSLY-Based CBA

I'll use the simulation model to illustrate, first, how population-average CBA and VSLY-based CBA value risk reduction across the various cohorts and, second, how they evaluate the illustrative policies—as compared to textbook CBA and the SWFs.

6.3.1 The Value of Risk Reduction

Population-average CBA, recall, employs a single, population-average VSL to value anyone's risk reduction. In the simulation model, the population-average VSL is $9,626,462. (This value is consistent with the population-average VSL figures that are used in US governmental practice—typically on the order

[32] Let Δy be the cost that each cohort bears under uniform cost incidence, and let Δy_{CMod} be the cost that a given cohort C^{Mod} bears under proportional cost incidence, holding fixed total costs. Because total costs are fixed, $\Sigma(\Delta y - \Delta y_{CMod}) = 0$. If monetary equivalents were calculated precisely, a cohort member's monetary equivalent for the shift from uniform to proportional cost incidence would be approximately $\Delta y - \Delta y_{CMod}$. (For why precise monetary equivalents are approximately rather than necessarily exactly equal to this quantity, see note 31.) Thus, the sum of monetary equivalents for the shift would be approximately 0.

In fact, monetary equivalents in this simulation were estimated using the formula provided in note 30. Each cohort member's thus-estimated monetary equivalent for the shift is exactly $\Delta y - \Delta y_{CMod}$, and the sum of monetary equivalents is exactly 0.

Table 6.5 The Value of Risk Reduction: Population-Average CBA

	Income: Low	Moderate	Middle	High	Top
Age 20	1.0	1.0	1.0	1.0	1.0
30	1.0	1.0	1.0	1.0	1.0
40	1.0	1.0	1.0	1.0	1.0
50	1.0	1.0	1.0	1.0	1.0
60	1.0	1.0	1.0	1.0	1.0

Explanation: This table shows the value of risk reduction across the various cohorts as per population-average CBA, normalized so that 1 indicates the value of reducing the risk of a 60-year-old, Low income individual.

Table 6.6 Life Expectancy Remaining (LE_i)

	Income: Low	Moderate	Middle	High	Top
Age 20	54.3	56.8	58.9	60.1	62.1
30	45.1	47.5	49.5	50.6	52.5
40	36.1	38.4	40.2	41.3	43.1
50	27.4	29.5	31.2	32.2	33.9
60	19.6	21.4	23.0	23.8	25.3

of \$10 million.)[33] A population-average VSL of \$9,626,462 means that risk-reduction to *any* cohort of Δp is valued at $\$9,626,462 \times \Delta p$.

Table 6.5 shows the relative value of risk reduction across the 25 cohorts as per population-average CBA, normalized so that 1 indicates the value of risk reduction to a 60-year-old, Low income individual. Table 6.5 is the counterpart to tables 6.2, 5.4, 5.5, and 5.6, showing VSL, $SVRR^{SU}$, and $SVRR^{EPP}$. There is a "1" in each cell in Table 6.5 because the valuation of risk reduction is constant. Clearly, this table looks *very* different from the simple-utilitarian and ex-post-prioritarian tables, as well as that for textbook CBA.

Turning to VSLY-based CBA: Table 6.6 shows the life expectancy remaining (LE_i) for the 25 cohorts. VSLY for each cohort is its VSL divided by life expectancy remaining. The average VSLY, across the 25 cohorts, is \$248,372.

According to VSLY-based CBA, the relative value of risk reduction, across the 25 cohorts, tracks the life expectancy remaining. Table 6.7 shows these values,

33 See Viscusi (2018, p. 28).

Table 6.7 The Value of Risk Reduction: VSLY-Based CBA

	Income: Low	Moderate	Middle	High	Top
Age 20	2.8	2.9	3.0	3.1	3.2
30	2.3	2.4	2.5	2.6	2.7
40	1.8	2.0	2.0	2.1	2.2
50	1.4	1.5	1.6	1.6	1.7
60	1.0	1.1	1.2	1.2	1.3

Explanation: This table shows the value of risk reduction across the various cohorts as per VSLY-based CBA, normalized so that 1 indicates the value of reducing the risk of a 60-year-old, Low income individual.

with the now-familiar normalization of 1 for a risk-reduction to the 60-year-old, Low income cohort.

The pattern of valuation, here, has some similarity to that of $SVRR^{EPP}$ ($\gamma = 1$) in Table 5.5. In both cases, the effect of income on the relative value of risk reduction is small; moving rightward in each row, the numbers increase only slightly. The slight increase in VSLY-based values reflects the fact that richer individuals have a more favorable survival curve (risk profiles).[34]

However, VSLY-based values differ significantly from those of $SVRR^{EPP}$ ($\gamma = 1$) with respect to the influence of age. $SVRR^{EPP}$ ($\gamma = 1$) decreases more steeply with age than VSLY-based values. The latter decrease with age because (in this simulation model) life expectancy remaining decreases with age; the former, for that reason *and* because of the extra weight that ex post prioritarianism accords to those at lower levels of lifetime well-being (including those who die at a younger age).

6.3.2 Illustrative Policies

Table 6.8 shows policy breakevens for all the approaches: the three variations on CBA (textbook, population average, VSLY-based), simple utilitarianism, and ex post prioritarianism.

[34] If the risk profiles were the same for all five quintiles, the VSLY-based values would be identical in each row. If the risk profiles were the same for all five quintiles *and* each quintile's period well-being in every period were some constant multiple of the Low income quintile's period well-being in that period (as would occur, e.g., with a constant income profile for all quintiles), the $SVRR^{EPP}$ ($\gamma = 1$) values would be identical in each row. See Chapter 5, note 35, and Section 5.4.3.

Table 6.8 Policy Breakevens: CBA (Textbook, Population-Average, and VSLY-Based), Simple Utilitarianism, and Ex Post Prioritarianism

	Textbook CBA	Population-Average CBA	VSLY-Based CBA	Simple Utilitarian	Ex-Post- Prioritarian ($\gamma = 1$)	Ex-Post-Prioritarian ($\gamma = 2$)
Uniform Risk Reduction						
Uniform Cost Incidence	$96	$96	$100	$50	$65	$94
Proportional Cost Incidence	$96	$96	$100	$73	$105	$165
Risk Reduction for Youngest						
Uniform Cost Incidence	$55	$96	$145	$72	$118	$223
Proportional Cost Incidence	$55	$96	$145	$105	$191	$393
Risk Reduction for Oldest						
Uniform Cost Incidence	$64	$96	$56	$27	$24	$20
Proportional Cost Incidence	$64	$96	$56	$39	$40	$37
Risk Reduction for Poorest						
Uniform Cost Incidence	$23	$96	$91	$36	$63	$118
Proportional Cost Incidence	$23	$96	$91	$53	$102	$208
Risk Reduction for Richest						
Uniform Cost Incidence	$270	$96	$108	$68	$66	$67
Proportional Cost Incidence	$270	$96	$108	$99	$107	$118

Population-average CBA is insensitive both to changes in the locus of risk reduction and to changes in cost incidence. It has the very same breakeven, \$96, for all ten policy types. It is thus quite dissimilar both to the SWFs (which respond to both types of changes), and to textbook CBA (which responds to the first).

VSLY-based CBA is also significantly different from all the SWFs. On the cost side (as is true for the other CBA variants), VSLY-based CBA is insensitive to changes in incidence. On the risk side, VSLY breakevens are at \$100 with a uniform risk reduction; this increases substantially (to \$145) if the reduction is concentrated on the youngest, decreases substantially (to \$56) if on the oldest, decreases slightly (to \$91) if on the poorest, and increases slightly (to \$108) if on the richest. The pattern of variation here is distinct from that of utilitarianism (the utilitarian breakevens change more substantially as risk reduction is shifted to the poorest or richest), let alone ex post prioritarianism ($\gamma = 2$). It is closest to that of ex post prioritarianism ($\gamma = 1$).

Yet this similarity should not be overstated. First, the VSLY-based breakeven increases by 45% if risk reduction is concentrated on the young and decreases by 44% if concentrated on the old; the corresponding changes for ex post prioritarianism ($\gamma = 1$) are larger (82% and 63%), reflecting its extra priority for the young. Moreover, as between VSLY-based CBA and ex post prioritarianism ($\gamma = 1$), the magnitudes of the breakevens are often quite different. Thus, while the *pattern of change* in the breakevens with a change in risk incidence is roughly similar as between the two approaches, the actual policy recommendations are not.

6.4 Justification

The aim of this chapter has been to show that the SWF framework, as applied to risk-regulation policies, differs substantially from the dominant methodology for assessing such policies in current governmental practice and applied economics: CBA. Although both approaches grow out of economics, they are quite distinct—in how they assign social value to the reduction of a given individual's risk (SVRR vs. VSL), and in their all-things-considered policy recommendations.

The sheer fact of substantial divergence between the two methodologies is, of course, neutral with respect to the issue of *justification*. That fact means that the two cannot be viewed as approximations for each other. The choice between the two is an ethically significant one. But knowing that a choice between methodologies is ethically significant tells us nothing about which methodology *ought* to be selected—about which one is justified.

In other writings, I have argued at length in favor of the SWF framework as against CBA.[35] That normative analysis will not be recapitulated in detail here. Rather, I'll briefly sketch the welfarist case against CBA—and in so doing will selectively draw upon the much fuller analysis presented in those writings.

6.4.1 Textbook CBA

CBA is rooted, historically, in an intellectual tradition within economics that is skeptical about interpersonal well-being comparisons. This tradition developed in the late nineteenth and early twentieth centuries and was given expression in Lionel Robbins' famous and influential critique of interpersonal comparisons in his 1932 book, *An Essay on the Nature and Significance of Economic Science*.[36] Working in the same intellectual milieu as Robbins, Nicholas Kaldor and John Hicks sought to develop policy-evaluation criteria that would eschew interpersonal comparisons.[37] Their efforts resulted in the concept of "Kaldor-Hicks" efficiency, as it's now known.[38] CBA, in turn, came to prominence in economics in the wake of Robbins', Kaldor's, and Hicks' work. A standard defense of CBA is that it implements the Kaldor-Hicks criterion.[39]

It is important to understand that the Pareto axioms, themselves, do not presuppose interpersonal comparisons. Kaldor and Hicks *endorsed* the Strong Pareto axiom and saw the Kaldor-Hicks criterion as an extension thereof—one that also required no such comparisons.

Consider, then, an ethical view that is consequentialist; that adopts the Pareto axioms (Strong Pareto and Pareto Indifference); but that rejects interpersonal well-being comparisons. For short, call this view IP-skeptical Paretian consequentialism. Should the proponent of such a view espouse CBA? Is CBA a well-justified policy evaluation methodology in light of it?

This is, no doubt, an interesting question, but it is not one that I need to address here. This book works within *welfarism*. Welfarism (as I mean it) is a species of consequentialism that is *not* skeptical about interpersonal comparisons. Such skepticism has never been influential in philosophy—certainly not in the

[35] Adler (2012, ch. 2; 2017; 2019a; 2019b). See also Adler and Posner (2006), criticizing Kaldor-Hicks defense of CBA and arguing that CBA is a rough proxy for overall well-being. Since the utilitarian SWF directly implements the criterion of overall well-being, the position of Adler and Posner (2006) does not support a preference for CBA over the SWF framework.

[36] Robbins (1935); second edition, first published in 1932.

[37] See Hicks (1939); Kaldor (1939).

[38] See sources cited in Adler (2012, p. 98, n. 75).

[39] See, e.g., Boardman, Greenberg, Vining, and Weimer (2018, ch. 2); Just, Hueth, and Schmitz (2004, ch. 1).

writings of utilitarians over the last 250 years beginning with Bentham, and not in the work of contemporary philosophers who have explored non-utilitarian versions of welfarism.[40] Welfarism, as stated in Chapter 1, includes a key axiom—Anonymity—that presupposes interpersonal comparisons.[41] And the major welfarist world-rankings described in Chapter 1—utilitarianism, prioritarianism, sufficientism, egalitarianism, and leximin—also presuppose them.[42]

The strategy of working within welfarism makes the project of this book a feasible one. A book that aimed *both* to defend welfarism *and* to develop a welfarist account of risk regulation would be unduly ambitious—and very long. Given this strategy, a defense of CBA that *departs* from welfarism by denying interpersonal comparability can be ignored.

That said, it is worth mentioning in passing that IP-skeptical Paretian consequentialism seems to be a highly problematic version of non-welfarism. Plausible challenges to welfarism can be mounted from various directions; but rejecting interpersonal comparability is not one of them. Such comparisons are a matter of common sense. And theories for measuring well-being that incorporate such comparisons, e.g., the theory set forth in Chapter 4, are available.

More to the point, here, are *welfarist* defenses of CBA. Can such defenses be mounted? Indeed they can. I'll briefly describe and respond to the two most important such defenses. I'll call the first the *"well-being-measure" defense* and the second the *"tax system" defense.*

The linchpin of CBA is the monetary equivalent. According to the well-being-measure defense, the monetary equivalent is *itself* the correct preference-based measure of individual well-being. Consider the CBA rule for ranking outcomes: x at least as good as y iff $\Sigma ME_i(x) \geq \Sigma ME_i(y)$. Let $w(\cdot)$ be our well-being measure. Assume, now, that $w_i(x) = ME_i(x)$: The number measuring individual i's well-being in outcome x, $w_i(x)$, is exactly equal to their monetary equivalent. If so, the utilitarian ranking of outcomes—x at least as good as y iff $\Sigma w_i(x) \geq \Sigma w_i(y)$—coincides perfectly with the CBA ranking.

[40] See sources cited Introduction, notes 3, 7–9.

[41] Anonymity was set forth in Section 1.3 (see also Section 1.A.3) under the more precise label "Lifetime Anonymity," since the well-being at issue is lifetime well-being. Here is what it requires. *Anonymity*: Let $\pi(\cdot)$ be a one-to-one, onto function that maps I (the set of individuals) onto itself. If the well-being level of i in world d is the same as that of $\pi(i)$ in world d^*, for all i in I, then the two worlds are equally good.

Absent interpersonal well-being comparisons, Anonymity is equivalent to Pareto Indifference (since, absent such comparisons, it is not possible for two distinct persons i and j to have the same well-being level). Thus Anonymity, stated as a constraint on the world-ranking distinct from Pareto Indifference, presupposes interpersonal well-being comparability.

[42] See Adler (2019b, ch. 2).

Generalizing, the well-being-measure defense argues that CBA's ranking of policies—assigning each policy a score $\Sigma ME_i(P)$, and ranking policies according to these scores—actually coincides perfectly with the utilitarian ranking.

In short, the well-being-measure defense of CBA denies any divergence between CBA and utilitarianism. The policy analyst implements utilitarianism *via* CBA—or so the argument goes.

The account of preference-based well-being measurement developed in Chapter 4 rejects any such coincidence between utilitarianism and CBA. Let $u_i(\cdot)$ denote the rescaled vNM utility function of individual i. Then, according to the Chapter 4 account, the utilitarian rule for ranking outcomes is by summing utilities and for ranking policies is by summing expected utilities. That is, x at least as good as y iff $\Sigma u_i(x) \geq \Sigma u_i(y)$; and P at least as good as P^* iff $\sum_x \pi_P(x)u_i(x) \geq \sum_x \pi_{P^*}(x)u_i(x)$. These rules need *not* coincide with the CBA rules. This is shown in detail in Section 6.2 of the current chapter. That section demonstrates a significant divergence between utilitarianism and CBA *given* the vNM measure of well-being.

I believe that there are variety of good reasons for denying that $w_i(x) = ME_i(x)$ and positing instead that $w_i(x) = u_i(x)$. (1) *Axiomatic*. Section 4.3 shows that the KLST and vNM axioms, together with the Bernoulli and Sovereignty axioms, lead to a well-being measure based on vNM utility functions. If there are good reasons to adopt those axioms given a preference-based view of well-being (as I believe there are),[43] then it follows that $w_i(x) = u_i(x)$ and therefore not that $w_i(x) = ME_i(x)$. (2) *Diminishing marginal well-being impact*. Setting $w_i(x) = u_i(x)$ is consistent with the truism that income has diminishing marginal impact on well-being.[44] Ceteris paribus, a given increment in the income of a richer person yields a smaller increase in their well-being than the same increment in the income of a poorer person. Setting $w_i(x) = ME_i(x)$ is inconsistent with this truism. (3) *Ethical benefits of redistribution*. A closely related truism is that equalizing the distribution of a fixed total of income is ethically beneficial. A world in which half the population has an income of \$10,000 and half an income of \$100,000 is worse, ceteris paribus, than one in which income is equalized at \$55,000. But if $w_i(x) = ME_i(x)$, equalizing income is ethically neutral; the two outcomes are equally good.

[43] I believe that there are good reasons independent of the specific theory of well-being to adopt the KLST axioms, the vNM axioms, and Bernoulli. Sovereignty reflects a preference-based account of well-being.

[44] Setting $w_i(x) = u_i(x)$ is consistent with this truism insofar as money has diminishing marginal utility with respect to $u_i(\cdot)$—which is commonly posited and observed.

The tax-system defense of CBA does not posit that the monetary equivalent is itself the measure of well-being. This defense is fully consistent with the view, adopted here, that $w_i(x) = u_i(x)$. Instead, the defense argues that CBA serves to identify policies that, if coupled with changes to the tax system, are universally beneficial.[45] Consider any case in which CBA favors policy P^*, while an alternative policy-evaluation methodology favors P. Then there is a change ("tweak") to the tax system ΔT such that ΔT together with P^* increases everyone's expected well-being as compared to P.

The tax-system defense has more argumentative power as leveled against utilitarianism than against prioritarianism.[46] So let's consider how the proponent of simple utilitarianism can respond to the tax-system defense.

Assume that P^* is ranked above P by CBA: $\Sigma ME_i(P^*) > \Sigma ME_i(P)$. Let's divide the population into three groups: those who prefer P^* (Group 1), those who prefer P (Group 2), and those who are indifferent (Group 3). Those in Group 1 have *larger* monetary equivalents for P^* than for P; those in Group 2 have *smaller* monetary equivalents for P^* than for P; those in Group 3 have *equal* monetary equivalents. Shifting from P to P^* *increases* the sum total of Group 1 monetary equivalents and *decreases* the sum total of Group 2 monetary equivalents. Because $\Sigma ME_i(P^*) > \Sigma ME_i(P)$, it must be the case that the increase in the sum total of Group 1 monetary equivalents is larger than the decrease in the sum total of Group 2 monetary equivalents. Thus, if we put in place P^* and, at the same time, shift income in appropriate amounts from Group 1 members to Group 2 and 3 members, it should be possible to increase *everyone's* expected well-being as compared to P.

In a nutshell, $\Sigma ME_i(P^*) > \Sigma ME_i(P)$ signals a surplus in monetary equivalents, which can be spread around so as to increase *everyone*'s expected well-being with P^*. This is the idea behind the tax-system defense of CBA.

This idea can be illustrated with the simulation model employed earlier in this chapter. Recall, specifically, that Section 6.2.3 considered policies coupling an average 1-in-100,000 risk reduction with income costs spread uniformly among the population or in proportion to income. In particular, as per the top row of Table 6.4, the simple-utilitarian breakeven cost for a uniform risk reduction coupled with uniform cost incidence was \$50. By contrast, the CBA breakeven was \$96. Consider, then a policy that reduces everyone's risk by 1-in-100,000 but at a uniform cost in between \$50 and \$96. Simple utilitarianism will see the

[45] See generally Kaplow (1996, 2004, 2008).

[46] The most attractive utilitarian uncertainty module (simple utilitarianism) satisfies the ex ante Pareto principle, while the most attractive prioritarian uncertainty module (ex post prioritarianism) does not. See Sections 7.1–7.2. As a consequence, if P^* together with ΔT indeed increases everyone's expected well-being as compared to P, simple utilitarianism will necessarily favor P^* together with ΔT over P, while ex post prioritarianism need not.

policy as worse than the status quo, while CBA will see the policy as an improvement over the status quo.

To illustrate, let P^* be a policy that combines a uniform 1-in-100,000 risk reduction with a uniform cost of $70. Table 6.9 shows how P^* changes each group's expected well-being as compared to the status quo. The sum of these changes is negative; simple utilitarianism prefers the status quo.

Table 6.10 displays each group's monetary equivalent for P^*. The groups that are worse off with P^* have negative monetary equivalents; the groups that are better off with P^* have positive monetary equivalents. The sum total of monetary equivalents is positive: CBA prefers P^* to the status quo.

Assume that there are M individuals in each of the 25 groups (assumed to be of equal size). Summing across the cells in Table 6.10, the CBA surplus for

Table 6.9 A Policy Favored by CBA and Disfavored by Simple Utilitarianism: Impacts on Expected Lifetime Well-Being

	Income: Low	Moderate	Middle	High	Top
Age 20	−11.7	−7.3	−4.0	−1.4	2.8
30	−3.0	−1.1	0.3	1.5	3.6
40	−2.3	−0.8	0.4	1.3	3.0
50	−2.7	−1.3	−0.2	0.6	2.1
60	−3.8	−2.3	−1.1	−0.2	1.3

Explanation: This table shows the change in each group's expected lifetime well-being from policy P^* relative to the status quo, normalized so that 1 indicates the change in expected lifetime well-being from a 1-in-100,000 risk reduction to a 60-year-old, Low income person. The results are rounded to one decimal place. Sum total across groups: −26.4.

Table 6.10 A Policy Favored by CBA and Disfavored by Simple Utilitarianism: Monetary Equivalents

	Income: Low	Moderate	Middle	High	Top
Age 20	−$56	−$48	−$36	−$18	$84
30	−$38	−$20	$8	$50	$282
40	−$37	−$18	$11	$56	$301
50	−$46	−$31	−$8	$27	$220
60	−$55	−$46	−$31	−$9	$115

Explanation: This table shows each group's monetary equivalent for policy P^*, rounded to zero decimal places. The sum total across all the groups is $657.

Table 6.11 A Policy Favored by CBA and Disfavored by Simple Utilitarianism: Tweaks to Income that Make Everyone Better Off

	Income: Low	Moderate	Middle	High	Top
Age 20	$82	$74	$62	$44	–$57
30	$65	$46	$18	–$24	–$256
40	$64	$44	$15	–$30	–$275
50	$72	$57	$34	–$1	–$194
60	$82	$72	$58	$35	–$88

Explanation: This table shows the tweak to income for each group that, if combined with policy P^*, will give each group the same, positive, monetary equivalent for P^* plus tweak.

Table 6.12 A Policy Favored by CBA and Disfavored by Simple Utilitarianism: Impacts on Expected Lifetime Well-Being after the Tweaks to Income

	Income: Low	Moderate	Middle	High	Top
Age 20	5.4	4.0	2.9	2.1	0.9
30	2.0	1.5	1.1	0.8	0.3
40	1.6	1.2	0.8	0.6	0.3
50	1.6	1.1	0.8	0.6	0.3
60	1.8	1.3	1.0	0.7	0.3

Explanation: This table shows the change in each group's expected lifetime well-being resulting from P^* plus the tweaks in Table 6.11, relative to the status quo, normalized so that 1 indicates the change in expected lifetime well-being from a 1-in-100,000 risk reduction to a 60-year-old, Low income person. Rounded to one decimal place. Note that every entry is positive, and hence the change in the sum of expected well-being across the groups is positive.

P^* as compared to the status quo is \$657*M*. Table 6.11 illustrates a scheme of "tweaks" to the income of group members that—if combined with P^*—makes all the groups better off than with the status quo. The sum of the tweaks is zero; we are simply redistributing income from those better off with P^* to those worse off. Specifically, the tweaks were calculated so as to evenly spread the surplus—meaning that each group's monetary equivalent for P^* plus the tweak is the same, positive monetary amount.

Finally, Table 6.12 shows the expected well-being of each group with P^* together with the tweaks to income in Table 6.11. As seen in Table 6.12, these expected well-being numbers are positive for all groups. Hence simple utilitarianism prefers P^* with the tweaks to the status quo—even though it preferred the status quo to P^* itself (Table 6.9).

How should the proponent of utilitarianism respond to the tax-system defense of CBA? One response points to the limitations of the actual tax system. In the example immediately above, income was costlessly transferred between groups—with no loss in the sum total of income across groups or other well-being losses. Such costless transfers may well be unachievable with actual tax systems. Thus, the fact that P^* is preferred by CBA to P—$\Sigma ME_i(P^*) > \Sigma ME_i(P)$—does not *necessarily* mean that there exists a tweak ΔT to the tax system such that P^* plus ΔT increases everyone's expected well-being relative to P.

Still, CBA might be taken as a *rough indicator* of the existence of the tax tweak. If CBA prefers P^* to P, then there's a reasonable chance that a tweak ΔT exists. But does this undermine the use of simple-utilitarianism as a policy evaluation tool? It does not. CBA may be useful in *signaling* the existence of additional policy options, which can be added to the set of available policies **P**; but the tax-system argument doesn't undercut simple utilitarianism, or justify CBA, as the methodology for *evaluating* the policies in **P**. (1) Assume that the policymaker evaluating **P** also controls the tax system. They have the power to implement ΔT. If so, they can add the policy option of P^* plus ΔT to the policy set. Simple utilitarianism, now, *prefers* P^* plus ΔT over P (as does CBA). A universally beneficial tax change, if implemented, will be approved by simple utilitarianism. (2) Assume, instead, that the policymaker evaluating **P** does not control the tax system. In this case, the policymaker might predict that P^* if chosen *will not* be accompanied by ΔT. If so, there are no grounds to favor P^* over P. CBA prefers P^* but this is the wrong result by the lights of simple utilitarianism. Alternatively, the policymaker might predict that P^* if chosen *will* be accompanied by ΔT. If so, P^* should be evaluated as if it were P^* plus ΔT: It should be seen as giving rise to the same probability distribution over outcomes (and thus the same array of individual lotteries over bundles) that P^* plus ΔT does. Simple utilitarianism prefers P^* plus ΔT to P (as does CBA).

In short, using simple utilitarianism produces the correct result in all cases, while CBA does not do so in cases where a *possible* universally beneficial tax change will not in fact be implemented.

6.4.2 Population-Average CBA and VSLY-Based CBA

It is very hard to see how population-average CBA can be defended on welfarist grounds. The well-being-measure defense of *textbook* CBA argues that $ME_i(P)$, rather than individual *i*'s expected utility with P, is the correct measure of the individual's well-being with policy P. This line of argument is a complete non-starter with respect to population-average CBA. If we calculate monetary equivalents with a population-average VSL, then an individual's monetary equivalent for a risk change is independent of their income, age, health, and other attributes, and also independent of their preferences. But it is exceedingly implausible that the well-being impact of the risk change is independent of all these characteristics.

The tax-system defense of textbook CBA is also a non-starter with respect to population-average CBA. Consider a case in which population-average CBA favors P^* over P. Population-average CBA *deviates* from textbook CBA—indeed, the simulation exercise demonstrated a substantial deviation. Thus, there is no reason to believe that $\Sigma ME_i(P^*) > \Sigma ME_i(P)$. Hence, there is no reason to believe that there exists some tweak ΔT which, together with P^*, would make everyone better off than with P.

Population-average CBA is defensible, if at all, in light of some non-welfarist ethical view—specifically one incorporating an "equal value of life" premise, namely, that the ethical value of saving a life or reducing a fatality risk is the same for all persons.[47] Evaluating the plausibility of such a view (as compared to welfarism or to non-welfarist accounts that deny the equal value of life) is beyond the scope of this book.

VSLY-based CBA, too, cannot be defended on welfarist grounds. The well-being-measure defense does not apply here. In valuing a risk reduction, VSLY-based CBA ignores everything about the individual except the magnitude of the reduction *and* life expectancy remaining. Other determinants of the well-being impact of the risk change (income, health, preferences, etc.) are ignored.[48] The tax-system defense also does not apply. VSLY-based CBA deviates substantially from textbook CBA—just as population-average CBA does. The fact that this methodology prefers P^* to P provides no reason to believe that there exists some tweak ΔT to the tax system which, together with P^*, would make everyone better off than with P.

The absence of welfarist backing for VSLY-based CBA should not be obscured by its similarity, in *one* respect, to ex post prioritarianism (a welfarist methodology) with an Atkinson SWF and $\gamma = 1$. Under VSLY-based CBA, the value of risk reduction is independent of individuals' period utility. Two individuals of the same age and facing the same survival curve have the same life expectancy remaining; thus VSLY-based CBA values risk reductions to the two equally, even

[47] See Section 5.4.3.

[48] Cf. Franklin (2022), offering an account of interpersonal comparisons based on VSLY. Engaging the details of Franklin's interesting account is not attempted here; suffice it to say that it differs quite substantially from the approach to constructing an interpersonally comparable welfare metric defended in Chapter 4, which is in turn the basis for the simulation model described in Chapter 5 and the current chapter.

if the two are at different levels of period utility. This will also be true with ex post prioritarianism using an Atkinson SWF and $\gamma = 1$, *if* the ratio between the two individuals' period utilities is fixed (the same ratio in all periods).[49]

But the similarity between VSLY-based CBA and $\gamma = 1$ ex post Atkinson prioritarianism should not be overstated. The latter will deviate from the former in valuing risk-reductions to individuals of the same age and facing the same survival curves if this ratio condition is not met. Moreover, as was evident in the simulation exercise, (1) $\gamma = 1$ ex post Atkinson prioritarianism accords more weight to the young than VSLY-based CBA, and (2) on the cost side, VSLY-based CBA ignores cost incidence while $\gamma = 1$ ex post Atkinson prioritarianism is quite sensitive to cost incidence.[50]

The justification for VSLY-based CBA, if there is one, lies in non-welfarism—specifically, in a non-welfarism that denies "equal value of life" and instead asserts "equal value of life expectancy." Appraising the ethical attractiveness of such a view is, again, beyond this book's scope.

[49] See Section 5.4.3.
[50] See Section 6.3.

7

Simple Utilitarianism and Ex Post Prioritarianism

A Defense, and Alternatives

This chapter has three aims. The first is to present a defense of simple utilitarianism and ex post prioritarianism—the uncertainty modules for utilitarianism and prioritarianism, respectively, that are the foundations of this book's account of risk regulation.[1] Chapter 5 showed, in great detail, how ex post prioritarianism and simple utilitarianism could be deployed to evaluate governmental policies that reduce fatality risks. But a *defense* of those modules was delayed until this chapter.

The second is to describe how the prioritarian uncertainty modules that are the leading competitors to ex post prioritarianism—namely, ex ante prioritarianism and expected EDE prioritarianism—would be used to evaluate risk-regulation policies.

The third is to move beyond utilitarianism and prioritarianism and to consider risk regulation through the lens of egalitarianism, sufficientism, and leximin.

Section 7.1 defends simple utilitarianism. Section 7.2 defends ex post prioritarianism. Section 7.3 discusses the application of ex ante prioritarianism and expected EDE prioritarianism to risk policies. Section 7.4 discusses, in turn, egalitarianism, sufficientism, and leximin.

This chapter will be concise, given the range of topics covered. Sections 7.1 and 7.2 are not novel; they draw upon a well-established literature on utilitarianism and prioritarianism under uncertainty. Interested readers are referred to that literature for a fuller treatment. Section 7.4 is concise for a different reason. Welfarist scholars who endorse egalitarianism, sufficientism, or leximin have not yet attended to the topic of fatality risk. This section therefore consists in brief and somewhat speculative sketches of how a proponent of each of these ethical views (not this author, who endorses prioritarianism) might tackle that topic.

Throughout, "well-being" is shorthand for "lifetime well-being."

[1] The construct of an SWF's uncertainty module is discussed in Section 1.4 and Adler (2019b, ch. 3; 2022b).

Risk, Death, and Well-Being. Matthew D. Adler, Oxford University Press. © Oxford University Press 2025.
DOI: 10.1093/9780197505984.003.0007

7.1 Simple Utilitarianism: A Defense

Simple utilitarianism, which assigns each policy a score equaling the expected sum of individual well-being and ranks policies according to these scores, is the dominant approach to applying utilitarianism under uncertainty.[2] Although the utilitarian SWF certainly does have other modules,[3] none of these are widely discussed, or robustly defended, in the literature. This is by way of contrast with scholarship about prioritarianism, where one sees a real debate about the best approach to handling uncertainty—in particular, between ex post, ex ante, and expected EDE prioritarianism.

So there is a sense in which simple utilitarianism needs no defense. Still, it is useful to highlight the features of simple utilitarianism in light of which it is so widely acclaimed. This can be done by way of uncertainty axioms: constraints that, it might be proposed, an uncertainty module should satisfy. The following uncertainty axioms are all quite plausible: Expected Value Ethical Decisionmaking; Dominance; ex ante Pareto (meaning the combination of ex ante Pareto Indifference and ex ante Strong Pareto); and two tractability axioms, Decomposability and Policy Separability (these last two already discussed in Chapter 5).

The axioms are as follows. See chapter appendix, Section 7.A.1, for a formal statement.

> Expected Value Ethical Decisionmaking: There is some mathematical function, assigning scores (real numbers) to well-being vectors, such that (a) the SWF's ranking of vectors is in the order of these scores, and (b) the uncertainty module for that SWF calculates the expected score of each policy and ranks policies according to these expected scores.
> Dominance: Assume that P and P^* are such that the well-being vector for each outcome with a non-zero probability given P is ranked better by the SWF than the well-being vector for each outcome with a non-zero probability given P^*. Then the uncertainty module for that SWF should be such that P is ranked better than P^*.

[2] For general treatments of SWFs under uncertainty, including utilitarianism, see Fleurbaey (2010, 2018); Mongin and Pivato (2016).

[3] Adler, Hammitt, and Treich (2014) discusses "catastrophe-averse" utilitarianism. Catastrophe-averse utilitarianism ranks policies according to the following score: $\sum_x \pi_P(x) H\left(\sum_{i=1}^{N} w_i(x)\right)$, $H(\cdot)$ strictly increasing and strictly concave. This module satisfies neither ex ante Pareto nor the tractability axioms. In violating Policy Separability despite the fact that the utilitarian SWF satisfies Separability, catastrophe-averse utilitarianism can be criticized for violating the fully-informed-adviser maxim in the same way that expected EDE prioritarianism can. See Section 7.2.

Ex Ante Pareto. (1) Ex Ante Pareto Indifference: If each person's expected well-being with policy P is equal to their expected well-being with policy P^*, the two policies are equally good. (2) Ex Ante Strong Pareto: If each person's expected well-being with policy P is greater than or equal to their expected well-being with policy P^*, and at least one person has strictly greater expected well-being with P, then P is better than P^*.

Tractability Axioms. (1) Decomposability: Let P and P^* be such that for each individual i, i's lottery over well-being levels is the same with P as with P^*. Then P is equally good as P^*. (2) Policy Separability: Let P, P^*, P^+ and P^{++} be as follows. There is a subset **M** of the population $\mathbf{I}^{\mathbf{Mod}}$ such that for each individual in **M**, their well-being lottery with P is the same as their well-being lottery with P^*, and their well-being lottery with P^+ is the same as their well-being lottery with P^{++}. Policies P^+ and P^{++} are the same as P and P^*, respectively, as regards the well-being lotteries faced by individuals who do not belong to **M.** If so, the uncertainty module's ranking of P^+ as compared to P^{++} should be the same as its ranking of P as compared to P^*.

Why are these plausible axioms? Expected Value Ethical Decisionmaking flows from normative decision theory. Many defend *expected utility theory* as a normative account of choice.[4] If an individual is rational, their preferences over outcomes will be represented by a utility function, and their preferences over choices will be according to *expected utility*: the expected value of this utility function. The axiom Expected Value Ethical Decisionmaking simply applies expected utility theory to the domain of welfarist ethics. The decisionmaker's "preferences" over outcomes, now, are the ethical preferences encoded by an SWF. Expected utility theory, applied to *those* preferences, says that the SWF should be representable by a utility function and that the ranking of choices (policies) should be according to the choices' expected utilities as calculated using that utility function. This is exactly what Expected Value Ethical Decisionmaking says.

Expected utility theory is hardly uncontested. Although often accepted, this normative account of choice also has critics.[5] Dominance is a much weaker axiom for an uncertainty module—and one whose normative force I take to be yet more compelling. Dominance actually comes in various flavors.[6] Dominance as stated here is the weakest version I'm aware of and the hardest to contest. If

[4] For a review of the defenses, see Briggs (2023); Thoma (2019b). A standard defense is to endorse a package of axioms leading to an expected utility representation of the choices. On the various axiomatic setups that do so, see Kreps (1988; 2013, chs. 1–2, 5–6); Gilboa (2009); Mas-Colell, Whinston, and Green (1995, ch. 6).

[5] See, e.g., Buchak (2013).

[6] See Adler (2012, p. 495), discussing "Ordinary Stochastic Dominance"; and Adler (2019b, chs. 3–4), discussing statewise dominance.

an uncertainty module satisfies Expected Value Ethical Decisionmaking, it will necessarily satisfy Dominance—but the converse is not true.

The case for Dominance flows directly from consequentialism. Consequentialists posit that the ethical status of *choices* (here, governmental choices: "policies") is grounded in the goodness of the *consequences* of those choices ("consequences" meaning possible worlds, modeled within the SWF framework as outcomes). Consider a pair of policies, each of which has probability 1 of yielding some outcome: P yields x with probability 1 and P^* yields x^* with probability 1. Then consequentialists should surely accept that policy P is better than policy P^* iff x is better than x^*. Call this proposition "Dominance for Known-Outcome Policies." Consequentialists, surely, should endorse it.[7]

But it seems very hard to justify rejecting Dominance while accepting Dominance for Known-Outcome Policies. Faced with a pair of known-outcome policies, the decisionmaker knows for sure what the outcome of each policy will be. By contrast, the Dominance axiom is not limited in scope to pairs of known-outcome policies. Still, if two policies P and P^* meet the antecedent condition of the Dominance axiom, the decisionmaker can be sure of the following: *Whatever* the outcome that would occur were P to be chosen, and *whatever* the outcome that would occur were P^* to be chosen, the first outcome is better than the second. In short, if Dominance applies, the decisionmaker *is* certain about the betterness ranking of the outcomes of the two policies, albeit perhaps uncertain about the specific features of the outcomes. It's very hard to see why the consequentialist decisionmaker would invariably prefer one policy to a second if the decisionmaker knows (a) that the first policy will produce a better outcome and (b) knows the details of the two policies' outcomes but would *not* invariably prefer one policy to a second if they know (a) without knowing (b).

The ex ante Pareto axioms are uncertainty axioms, which are distinct from the Pareto axioms at the level of worlds[8] or at the level of well-being vectors. The vector-level Pareto axioms are as follows:

> <u>Pareto Indifference (for well-being vectors)</u>: If each person's well-being level with vector **w** is equal to their well-being level with vector **v**, the two vectors are equally good.
>
> <u>Strong Pareto (for well-being vectors):</u> If each person's well-being level with vector **w** is greater than or equal to their well-being level with vector **v**, and at least one person has a strictly greater well-being level with **w**, then **w** is better than **v**.

[7] Indeed, Dominance for Known-Outcome Policies is built into uncertainty modules. See Section 1.A.6, discussing "Module Consistency," which implies Dominance for Known-Outcome Policies.

[8] The Pareto axioms at the level of worlds (under the more precise labels "Lifetime Pareto Indifference" and "Lifetime Strong Pareto," since the well-being at issue is lifetime well-being) were set forth in Section 1.3.1.

If an SWF is meant to implement lifetime welfarism, it surely must satisfy these vector-level Pareto axioms. All of the SWFs considered in this book—utilitarian, prioritarian, egalitarian, sufficientist, and leximin—do satisfy the vector-level Pareto axioms.[9]

The *ex ante* Pareto axioms extrapolate from the world- and vector-level axioms. Note that each policy is associated with a vector of *expected well-being* numbers, one for each person in the population. While the world-level and vector-level Pareto axioms constrain the ranking of a pair of worlds and a pair of vectors, respectively, in light of the pattern of individual well-being, the ex ante Pareto axioms impose a (seemingly) isomorphic constraint on the ranking of a pair of policies in light of the pattern of individuals' expected well-being numbers arising from the two policies.

Note: the ex ante Pareto axioms as stated here, and as discussed throughout the chapter, presuppose the "Bernoulli" axiom for well-being measurement presented in Chapter 4.[10]

At first blush, the ex ante Pareto axioms seem highly plausible. The Pareto axioms at the level of worlds embody the core commitments of lifetime welfarism: that only a difference in someone's well-being makes an ethical difference between worlds (Lifetime Pareto Indifference) and that well-being makes a positive, not negative, contribution to ethical goodness (Lifetime Strong Pareto). How could a decisionmaker endorse these constraints, and the corresponding vector-level constraints, yet reject ex ante Pareto? In truth, I believe that the ex ante Pareto axioms are *far* less compelling than their world-level or vector-level counterparts—and will argue to this effect below. See Section 7.2. But this position is, clearly, contestable and probably a minority view among SWF theorists. A long-standing strand of the SWF literature, going back to John Harsanyi's aggregation theorem, uses the ex ante Pareto axioms as part of an axiomatic case in favor of utilitarianism.[11]

Turning finally to the tractability axioms, I'll recapitulate what was said in Chapter 5: If an uncertainty module satisfies both Decomposability and Policy

[9] SWFs automatically satisfy Pareto Indifference for well-being vectors. Strong Pareto for well-being vectors is not automatic but *is* satisfied by these five types of SWF; see Adler (2019b, ch. 3). One can also define Pareto axioms at the level of outcomes, see Chapter 6, note 11; these five types of SWF satisfy the outcome-level axioms (which follows immediately from their satisfying the vector-level Pareto axioms, since the SWF framework ranks outcomes in light of the outcomes' well-being vectors).

[10] An implication of Bernoulli is that the goodness of possible lotteries over well-being levels for a given individual, with the levels numerically measured by $w(\cdot)$, is tracked by the individuals' expected $w(\cdot)$ numbers with the lotteries. (Note that the ex ante Pareto axioms as stated here are framed in terms of individuals' expected well-being.) Chapter 4 defended Bernoulli. Analyzing how uncertainty modules for utilitarian, prioritarian, and other SWFs fare with respect to the ex ante Pareto axioms absent Bernoulli is beyond the scope of this chapter.

[11] On Harsanyi's aggregation theorem, see Adler (2019b, pp. 282–83); Mongin and Pivato (2016). Scholarship relying on the ex ante Pareto axioms to argue for utilitarianism is cited in Adler (2012, p. 497, n. 41) and Adler and Holtug (2019).

Table 7.1 Simple Utilitarianism and the Uncertainty Axioms

	Expected Value Ethical Decisionmaking	Dominance	Ex Ante Pareto Indifference	Ex Ante Strong Pareto	Decomposability	Policy Separability
Simple Utilitarianism	Yes	Yes	Yes	Yes	Yes	Yes

Separability, the analyst has a very useful decisional shortcut for characterizing the policies in **P**. Policies need not be explicitly characterized as probability distributions over whole outcomes or even as probability distributions over whole outcomes dropping the bundles of the unaffected. Instead, each policy can be characterized as an array of bundle lotteries, one for each *affected* individual. (Recall that an individual is "unaffected" if they face the same lottery over bundles regardless of which policy in **P** is chosen; otherwise they are "affected.")

Simple utilitarianism satisfies all of these axioms. See Table 7.1 To see why, consider the following rule for assigning scores to well-being vectors: $e(\mathbf{w}) = \sum_{i=1}^{N} \mathbf{w}_i$. (The score of a vector is the sum of its component well-being numbers.) This scoring rule represents the utilitarian SWF's vector ranking, *and* simple utilitarianism ranks policies according to the expected value of scores thus assigned. Thus, simple utilitarianism satisfies Expected Value Ethical Decisionmaking, and that in turn implies that it satisfies Dominance. As noted in Chapter 5, the expected sum of individual well-being is equal to the sum of individuals' expected well-being.[12] It's not difficult to see that ranking policies according to the sum of individuals' expected well-being will satisfy ex ante Pareto.[13] Finally, if individual i has the same lottery over well-being with P that they do with P^*, then their expected well-being is the same with both policies. If this true for all individuals (so that the antecedent condition for Decomposability obtains), the two policies have the same sum of individual expected well-being. Hence Decomposability holds true of simple utilitarianism. Finally, because simple utilitarianism scores policies according to the *sum* of individual expected well-being, unaffected individuals can be dropped from the score without affecting the policy ranking—hence Policy Separability also holds true.

[12] See Section 5.A.2.1.

[13] If each individual's expected well-being is the same with policy P as with P^*, then the sums will be the same, hence the two policies will be ranked equal (as required by ex ante Pareto Indifference); and if each person's expected well-being with P is at least as large as their expected well-being with P^*, and strictly greater for at least one person, then the sum of individual expected well-being with P will be strictly greater (as required by ex ante Strong Pareto).

7.2 Prioritarianism under Uncertainty

Ex post prioritarianism, ex ante prioritarianism, and expected EDE prioritarianism are the three most widely discussed prioritarian uncertainty modules.[14] Their formulas were provided in Section 1.4. The reader who has engaged with Chapter 5 will now be quite familiar with ex post prioritarianism: Its formula ranks policies according to the expected sum of individuals' transformed well-being or, equivalently, according to the sum of individuals' expected transformed well-being. By contrast, ex ante prioritarianism is the sum, across individuals, of the transformation function applied to expected well-being. Both approaches assign a score to a given policy *P* by summing an individual value—expected transformed well-being or transformed expected well-being—but these values are calculated in distinct ways. Ex post prioritarianism first applies the transformation function to the individual's final well-being in each of the possible outcomes of *P* and then calculates the expectation of transformed well-being; ex ante prioritarianism first calculates the individual's expected well-being and then applies the transformation function to this expected well-being value. This mathematical difference between the two modules—first transformation and then expectation, or vice versa—has profound axiomatic consequences.

Expected EDE prioritarianism works as follows. A given prioritarian SWF associates each well-being vector with an "equally distributed equivalent" (EDE). The equally distributed equivalent for vector $\mathbf{w} = (\mathbf{w}_1, \ldots, \mathbf{w}_N)$ is that single number w^* such that a vector in which everyone has w^* is ranked equally good by the SWF as $\mathbf{w}$. (For example, if the prioritarian transformation function is the square root function, the EDE for well-being vector (9, 25, 100) is 36.)[15] Expected EDE prioritarianism assigns a score to each policy *P* as follows: For each possible outcome, determine the EDE of the outcome's well-being vector and then calculate the expected value of these EDEs.

Table 7.2 is the counterpart to Table 7.1. It shows how ex post prioritarianism, ex ante prioritarianism, and expected EDE prioritarianism fare with respect to our suite of axioms. While simple utilitarianism satisfies all of these axioms, none of the prioritarian uncertainty modules satisfy all of them.

[14] On prioritarianism under uncertainty, see sources cited note 2 and also Adler (2012, ch. 7; 2019b, chs. 3–4; 2022b); Adler and Holtug (2019); Adler, Hammitt, and Treich (2014). Adler, Hammitt, and Treich (2014) discuss the application to fatality risk regulation of "catastrophe-averse prioritarianism," parallel to catastrophe-averse utilitarianism (see note 3). Catastrophe-averse prioritarianism ranks policies according to the following score: $\sum_x \pi_P(x) H\left(\sum_{i=1}^{N} g(\mathbf{w}_i(x))\right)$, $H(\cdot)$ strictly increasing and strictly concave. This module satisfies Expected Value Ethical Decisionmaking and Dominance; it fails the tractability axioms (thus, like expected EDE prioritarianism, it can be criticized for violating the fully-informed-adviser maxim, as discussed in this section); and, unlike expected EDE prioritarianism, does not satisfy the ex ante Pareto axioms even when individuals are identically situated.

[15] $\sqrt{9} + \sqrt{25} + \sqrt{100} = \sqrt{36} + \sqrt{36} + \sqrt{36}$.

Table 7.2 Prioritarian Uncertainty Modules and the Uncertainty Axioms

	Expected Value Ethical Decision-making	Dominance	Ex Ante Pareto Indifference	Ex Ante Strong Pareto	Decom-posability	Policy Separ-ability
Ex Post Prioritar-ianism	Yes	Yes	No	No	Yes	Yes
Ex Ante Prioritar-ianism	No	No	Yes	Yes	Yes	Yes
Expected EDE Prioritar-ianism	Yes	Yes	No (yes if individuals identically situated)	No (yes if individuals identically situated)	No	No

Does this checkered pattern reveal a lack of imagination on the part of SWF theorists? Might there be some "Theory X" for prioritarianism under uncertainty[16]—some magic module that will satisfy Expected Value Ethical Decisionmaking (hence Dominance) *and* ex ante Pareto *and* the tractability axioms, as simple utilitarianism does?

No. There is no such magic module. As Table 7.3 shows, it is impossible for a prioritarian uncertainty module to satisfy *both* Dominance *and* ex ante Pareto. (Hence it is also impossible for a prioritarian uncertainty module to satisfy both Expected Value Ethical Decisionmaking and ex ante Pareto.)[17]

The reader may be puzzled by the statement that no prioritarian uncertainty module can satisfy both Dominance and ex ante Pareto. Didn't we establish above that simple utilitarianism satisfies both?

It is critical to understand that what Dominance demands *depends upon the SWF*. Assume that P has a probability 0.5 of yielding an outcome with well-being vector $\mathbf{w} = (25, 81)$ and probability 0.5 of yielding an outcome with well-being vector $\mathbf{w}^+ = (81, 25)$, while policy P^* has probability 1 of yielding an outcome with well-being vector $\mathbf{v} = (50, 50)$. Consider the prioritarian SWF using a square-root transformation function. Dominance requires that the uncertainty module for this SWF prefer P^* to P; according to *this* SWF, $\mathbf{v}$ is better than both

[16] In *Reasons and Persons*, Parfit (1987, pt. 4) famously challenged the field of population ethics to produce a "Theory X" that would avoid the problematic axiomatic features of extant theories.

[17] Because Expected Value Ethical Decisionmaking implies Dominance, the proposition that no prioritarian uncertainty module can satisfy the combination of Dominance and either ex ante Pareto Indifference or ex ante Strong Pareto (as Table 7.3 shows) implies that no prioritarian uncertainty module can satisfy Expected Value Ethical Decisionmaking combined with either of these axioms.

Table 7.3 Prioritarian Uncertainty Modules, Dominance, and Ex Ante Pareto

	Policy P			Policy P+		
	$\pi = .5$	$\pi = .5$	expected well-being	$\pi = .5$	$\pi = .5$	expected well-being
Lillian	70	30	50	$50 - \varepsilon$	$50 - \varepsilon$	$50 - \varepsilon$
Maya	30	70	50	$50 - \varepsilon$	$50 - \varepsilon$	$50 - \varepsilon$
	Policy P*			Policy P**		
	$\pi = .5$	$\pi = .5$	expected well-being	$\pi = .5$	$\pi = .5$	expected well-being
Lillian	70	30	50	50	50	50
Maya	30	70	50	50	50	50

Explanation: Each of the policies (P, P^+, P^*, and P^{**}) leads to some outcome with probability .5 and some other outcome with probability .5. The table displays the well-being vectors corresponding to the outcomes.

In the top part of the table, for any prioritarian SWF, there is some cutoff value $c > 0$ (which depends on the transformation function) such that the well-being vector $(50 - \varepsilon\ 50 - \varepsilon)$ is preferred by the SWF to (70, 30) and (30, 70) for every ε, $0 < \varepsilon < c$. Dominance requires that the module for that SWF rank P^+ over P. But note that ex ante Strong Pareto requires that P be ranked above P^+. Ex ante prioritarianism ranks P over P^+; ex post prioritarianism and expected EDE prioritarianism rank P^+ over P.

In the bottom part of the table, Dominance requires that the module for any prioritarian SWF rank P^{**} over P^*, since any prioritarian SWF prefers the well-being vector (50, 50) to (70, 30) and (30, 70). However, ex ante Pareto Indifference requires that P^{**} and P^* be ranked equally good. Ex ante prioritarianism ranks P^* and P^{**} equally good. Ex post prioritarianism and expected EDE prioritarianism rank P^{**} over P^*.

w and **w**$^+$. By contrast, Dominance requires that the uncertainty module for the *utilitarian* SWF prefer P to P^*; according to *that* SWF, both **w** and **w**$^+$ are better than **v**.[18]

Turning to Table 7.3: there is no conflict in this table between what Dominance requires of a utilitarian uncertainty module, and ex ante Pareto.[19]

The fact that utilitarianism involves no conflict between Dominance and ex ante Pareto, while prioritarianism does, might well be seen as an argument *against* prioritarianism. This and related issues have been extensively discussed

[18] $\sqrt{25} + \sqrt{81} < \sqrt{50} + \sqrt{50}$; but $25 + 81 > 50 + 50$.

[19] In the top part of the table, Dominance for a utilitarian uncertainty module requires that P be ranked above P^+ (consistent with ex ante Strong Pareto), because the utilitarian SWF ranks (70, 30) and (30, 70) above $(50 - \varepsilon, 50 - \varepsilon)$ for any $\varepsilon > 0$. Dominance for a utilitarian module does not apply in the bottom part of the table, because the utilitarian is indifferent between (30, 70) or (70, 30) and (50, 50).

in the scholarly literature.[20] Suffice it to say that utilitarianism's capacity to jointly satisfy Dominance and ex ante Pareto—and indeed to jointly satisfy Expected Value Ethical Decisionmaking and ex ante Pareto—is purchased at a significant cost. The prioritarian SWF is sensitive to the distribution of well-being, as expressed in the Pigou-Dalton axiom; the utilitarian SWF is not. It can be shown that *any* SWF that satisfies Pigou-Dalton (not merely prioritarian SWFs) lacks an uncertainty module that conforms both to Dominance and to ex ante Pareto.[21]

Consider, then, how the proponent of prioritarianism—alive to the dilemma illustrated by Table 7.3—might weigh the pros and cons of its three main modules. In my own view, ex post prioritarianism has decisive advantages over its two competitors. Let's compare it, first, to ex ante prioritarianism and, second, to expected EDE prioritarianism.

For proponents of expected utility theory as a normative account of choice (such as this author), the failure of ex ante prioritarianism to satisfy Expected Value Ethical Decisionmaking is a significant flaw. But expected utility theory itself is contested, and thus the argument against ex ante prioritarianism would *not* be especially strong if it relied merely upon Expected Value Ethical Decisionmaking. That ex ante prioritarianism violates Dominance is a much more serious flaw. To repeat: Rejecting Dominance seems flatly inconsistent with consequentialism. The consequentialist surely must accept Dominance for Known-Outcome Policies; but endorsing that axiom, while rejecting Dominance, seems wholly arbitrary.

Dominance is also supported by a powerful maxim of rational choice, namely, act as you know your fully informed adviser would recommend.[22] (A fully informed adviser is someone who shares the decisionmaker's aims, i.e., outcome ranking, and has full information as to what the outcome of each choice would be.)[23] Consider a decisionmaker choosing between two policies, P and P^*, that

[20] See Adler (2012, ch. 7; 2019b, ch. 4); Adler and Holtug (2019), and sources cited therein.

[21] More precisely, any Pigou-Dalton respecting SWF lacks an uncertainty module that satisfies both Dominance and ex ante Pareto Indifference (as can be seen by the bottom part of Table 7.3); and any Pigou-Dalton respecting SWF that is minimally leak tolerant lacks an uncertainty module that satisfies both Dominance and ex ante Strong Pareto (Adler 2019b, pp. 140–44, 284–85).

[22] See Fleurbaey and Voorhoeve (2013).

[23] This is a rough description of the fully informed adviser. A better description needs to take account of the SWF framework—specifically, to be sensitive to the fact that outcomes are simplified representations of worlds and that decisionmaker probabilities are notional rather than actual epistemic probabilities. See Sections 1.4, 5.1.2. Consider some decisionmaker ("Audrey") using the SWF framework with outcome set **O** to decide among a set of policies **P**. Audrey's notional probabilities are based upon actual data regarding the linkage between policy choices and the types of individual attributes included in the outcomes in **O**. A fully informed adviser is someone who reasons about Audrey's decision using the same mental model that she does—the same outcome set—and shares Audrey's outcome ranking but is fully informed about the actual data. Thus, the adviser's notional probabilities are either 1 or 0: every choice P is a "degenerate" probability distribution over outcomes such that one outcome is assigned probability 1 given P, and all others are assigned probability 0.

meet the antecedent conditions of the Dominance axiom. P assigns non-zero probabilities to L outcomes $x_1, \ldots, x_L$; P^* assigns non-zero probabilities to M outcomes $x_1^*, \ldots, x_M^*$. The well-being vector for each of the outcomes $x_1, \ldots, x_L$ is ranked better, by the SWF, than the well-being vector for each of the outcomes $x_1^*, \ldots, x_M^*$. Felicia (say) is the decisionmaker considering whether P or P^* is the better choice. Felicia is *not* fully informed: she does not know what the outcome of P would be, and she does not know what the outcome of P^* would be. But, remarkably, she *is* in a position to know what her fully informed adviser would recommend. Namely, Felicia *does* know that her fully informed adviser would recommend P over P^*. Felicia can reason as follows: her fully informed adviser would know which one of the outcomes $x_1, \ldots, x_L$ would in fact result from P, and which one of the outcomes $x_1^*, \ldots, x_M^*$ would in fact result from P^*; whichever those two outcomes are, the adviser would rank the first policy over the second, since *every one* of the outcomes $x_1, \ldots, x_L$ is better than *every one* of the outcomes $x_1^*, \ldots, x_M^*$.[24]

Ex ante prioritarianism satisfies the ex ante Pareto axioms; this is its key axiomatic advantage over ex post prioritarianism.[25] But the ethical case in favor of these axioms (in my view) is much weaker than the case for the Pareto axioms at the level of worlds or well-being vectors. There is a *seeming* isomorphism between the world- and vector-level Pareto axioms and the ex ante Pareto axioms, which works as follows.[26] (1) Pareto Indifference. If each person is equally well off with world d as d^*, there is no well-being difference for anyone between the two worlds, and so (if we are welfarists) we should count the two worlds as equally good. Similarly, if each person's expected well-being is the same with P as with P^*, the policies are equally good from the perspective of each person's welfare, and thus the two *policies* should be counted equally good. (2) Strong Pareto. If each person is at least as well off in world d as compared to d^*, and at least one person is strictly better off, we can be sure that at least one person's well-being counts in favor of d, and no one's well-being counts against. Similarly, if each person's expected well-being with P is at least as large as their expected well-being with P^*, and at least one person's expected well-being with P is strictly greater, we can be sure that the expected well-being of at least one person counts in favor of P, and no one's counts against.

[24] Note that this assumes Felicia is not so poorly informed as to assign probability 0 to the outcome to which the adviser assigns probability 1.

[25] Some take a second advantage to be that ex ante prioritarianism satisfies an ex ante version of the Pigou-Dalton axiom. However, endorsing this axiom yields the same conflict with Dominance that endorsing ex ante Pareto does. No prioritarian uncertainty module can satisfy both ex ante Pigou-Dalton and Dominance. See Adler (2012, ch. 7).

[26] In the remainder of this paragraph, I spell out the apparent isomorphism between the Pareto axioms for worlds and the ex ante Pareto axioms. The apparent isomorphism between the vector-level Pareto axioms and the ex ante Pareto axioms is essentially the same.

However (in my view) this *seeming* isomorphism between the ex ante Pareto axioms and their world/vector counterparts is illusory. The ex ante Pareto axioms are infected by uncertainty; they constrain the ranking of a given pair of policies, P and P^*, above and beyond the vector-level Pareto axioms, *only* in light of the decisionmaker's uncertainty about how individuals will be affected.[27] In particular, the ex ante Pareto Indifference axiom can require that P be ranked equally good as P^* even though (given how the outcome probabilities line up) it is certain that at least one of the individuals will not be equally well off with the two policies. (In other words, it is certain that, whatever the actual outcomes of the two policies will be, the vector-level Pareto Indifference axiom will *not* apply to that pair of outcomes.) And the ex ante Strong Pareto axiom can require that P be ranked above P^* even though (given how the outcome probabilities line up) it is certain that at least one individual will be worse off with P and another worse off with P^*. (In other words, it is certain that, whatever the actual outcomes of the two policies, the vector-level Strong Pareto axiom will *not* apply to that pair of outcomes.) These points are illustrated by Table 7.3.

Here is a different way to see why the ex ante Pareto axioms are plausibly rejected. Let vectors **v** and **w** be such that some individuals are worse off with **v**, some worse off with **w**, but with the well-being levels and differences of the affected individuals such that any prioritarian SWF would prefer **w** to **v**. Now consider permutations of **v**. If the prioritarian decisionmaker prefers **w** to **v**, then they prefer **w** to any permutation of **v**. Finally, imagine that P yields **w** for certain, as compared to a policy P^* that assigns non-zero probability both to **v** and to some of its permutations. It is quite possible that ex ante Pareto Indifference requires indifference between the two policies. (Table 7.4 shows how.) Alternatively, it is quite possible that ex ante Strong Pareto requires a preference for P^* over a policy P^+ certain to yield a vector **w′** sufficiently close to **w** that it is also preferred by the prioritarian SWF to **v**. (Table 7.4 also shows how.) But surely, in these cases, the prioritarian decisionmaker should prefer P to P^* and P^+ to P^*. Although they are uncertain as to which specific individuals will be worse off with P^* as compared to the alternative policy (P or P^+) and which specific individuals will be better off, the decisionmaker *can* be sure that the losses to the first group will morally outweigh the gains to the second.

Let's turn to the comparison of ex post prioritarianism with expected EDE prioritarianism. The axiomatic advantage of the latter module, if there is one, concerns ex ante Pareto. It is critical to understand that expected EDE prioritarianism does *not* satisfy the ex ante Pareto axioms as stated above.

[27] If each of two policies involves no uncertainty with respect to individuals' well-being (i.e., each yields some particular well-being vector for certain), then the ex ante Pareto axioms will never constrain the policy ranking if the vector-level axioms do not.

Table 7.4 Why Prioritarians Might Reject Ex Ante Pareto

	Policy P	Policy P*			
	Outcome x	Outcome y	Outcome z	Outcome zz	
	$\pi_P(x) = 1$	$\pi_{P^*}(y) = 1/3$	$\pi_{P^*}(z) = 1/3$	$\pi_{P^*}(zz) = 1/3$	expected well-being
Ariella	50	70	30	50	50
Brianna	50	50	70	30	50
Caleb	50	30	50	70	50

	Policy P⁺
	Outcome x^*
	$\pi_{P+}(x^*) = 1$
Ariella	$50 - \varepsilon$
Brianna	$50 - \varepsilon$
Caleb	$50 - \varepsilon$

Explanation: Vector w = (50, 50, 50) is such that Ariella, Brianna, and Caleb each have a well-being level of 50. Vector v = (70, 50, 30) is such that Ariella gets 70, Brianna 50, and Caleb 30. Any prioritarian SWF will prefer w to v and, thus, to any permutation of v. In the top half of the table, policy *P* yields w for certain, while policy *P** yields v and two permutations—(70, 50, 30), (30, 70, 50) and (50, 30, 70)—each with probability 1/3. Note that ex ante Pareto Indifference requires that *P** and *P* be ranked equally good.

Any prioritarian SWF will prefer w′ = (50 − ε, 50 − ε, 50 − ε) to v = (70, 50, 30) for ε > 0 sufficiently small. (The specific range of ε values for which this holds true depends upon the transformation function.) In the bottom half of the table, policy *P*⁺ yields w′ for certain. Ex ante Strong Pareto requires that *P** be ranked above *P*⁺.

(Table 7.3 demonstrates that it does not.) Rather, it satisfies a restricted version of those axioms, which apply only if individuals are identically situated.[28]

Expected EDE prioritarianism has significant costs with respect to tractability. It violates both of the tractability axioms. For a simple illustration of why this module violates Decomposability, consider the following. The prioritarian SWF at hand uses the square root transformation function. There are two persons in the population, Ava and Barry. With policy *P*, there is a 0.5 probability of an outcome x in which the well-being vector of the two individuals is (25, 81) and a 0.5 probability of an outcome y in which the well-being vector is (81,

[28] Individuals are identically situated in *P* if, in each of the outcomes of *P* with non-zero probability, everyone has the same well-being. The ex ante Pareto axioms restricted to identically situated individuals require what the normal ex ante Pareto axioms do, but only as applied to a pair of policies *P* and *P** such that individuals are identically situated in both.

25). With policy P^*, there is a 0.5 probability of an outcome x^* in which the well-being vector of the two individuals is (25, 25) and a 0.5 probability of an outcome y^* in which the well-being vector of the two individuals is (81, 81). Note that each individual faces the same lottery with P as with P^*, namely, a 0.5 chance of well-being level 25 and a 0.5 chance of well-being level 81. But the expected EDE prioritarian module ranks P^* better than P.

To see why, note that the EDE for the vector (25, 25) is just 25, and the EDE for the vector (81, 81) is just 81. So the expected EDE for policy P^* is $(25+81)/2 = 53$. However, the EDE for the vector (25, 81) and (81, 25) is 49.[29] Thus the expected EDE for policy P is less than for P^*.

Because expected EDE prioritarianism violates Decomposability, it must also violate Policy Separability.[30] If a module satisfies Decomposability, each policy can be characterized as an array of bundle lotteries for the entire population. If a module satisfies Decomposability *and* Policy Separability, each policy can be characterized as an array of bundle lotteries for affected persons; the unaffected can be dropped from the analysis. With expected EDE prioritarianism, however, neither of these shortcuts is available. Each policy must be explicitly characterized as a probability distribution over whole outcomes, each outcome listing the lifetime bundles of unaffected and affected persons alike.[31] (Insofar as the unaffected include past generations—the already dead—modeling policies in this way can turn out to be quite onerous.) Section 7.3 below, specifically discussing risk assessment with expected EDE prioritarianism, will illustrate the added decisional costs that flow from using this module.

It might be argued that the ethical case for the ex ante Pareto axioms restricted to identically situated individuals is very strong, much stronger than the ethical case for the unrestricted axioms. If one takes this view while also endorsing Dominance, the reasonable conclusion could be that expected EDE prioritarianism is the best of the three modules. But it's not clear why the ethical case for the ex ante Pareto axioms restricted to identically situated individuals is sufficiently strong to warrant the costs of dropping the tractability axioms.[32]

[29] $\sqrt{25} + \sqrt{81} = 14$. The well-being level which, equally distributed, has the same prioritarian score (14) is 49, since $\sqrt{49} + \sqrt{49} = 14$.

[30] Because Policy Separability implies Decomposability, violating the latter implies violating the former. Table 7.5 below illustrates how expected EDE prioritarianism violates Policy Separability.

[31] The reader might wonder about an intermediate shortcut: characterizing each policy as a probability distribution over truncated outcomes that drop the bundles of the unaffected. This shortcut, too, is not available. The expected-EDE-prioritarian ranking of policies understood as probability distributions over whole outcomes is not necessarily the same as its ranking of policies understood as probability distributions over thus-truncated outcomes. Table 7.5 illustrates why. Expected EDE prioritarianism, considering whole outcomes, ranks policy P over P^* but P^{++} over P^+. Using truncated outcomes that drop the bundles of Ernie, who is unaffected, would constrain the P/P^* ranking to be the same as the P^+/P^{++} ranking.

[32] The ex ante Pareto axioms restricted to identically situated individuals are infected by uncertainty, just as the ordinary ex ante Pareto axioms are. (1) Assume that individuals are identically situated in P and P^* and ex ante Pareto Indifference applies. Given how the outcome probabilities

If this were the final state of play with respect to the debate between ex post prioritarianism and expected EDE prioritarianism—the pragmatic benefits of the first in light of the tractability axioms, balanced against restricted ex ante Pareto—it might seem that neither module is a decisive winner. But there is a further consideration, one that *does* decisively tip the balance—or so I believe. The prioritarian SWF satisfies the Separability axiom,[33] and yet expected EDE prioritarianism violates Policy Separability. This combination—an SWF that conforms to Separability, a module for that SWF that violates Policy Separability—runs afoul of the principle, "act as you know your fully informed adviser would recommend."

To see why endorsing Separability but denying Policy Separability is a problematic combination, I'll need to introduce the decision-theoretic concept of a "state-of-nature." Consider a decisionmaker selecting among some set of choices in light of some set of outcomes. Rational choice theory stipulates that if the decisionmaker is rational, there will be epistemic probabilities (probabilities measuring the decisionmaker's degrees of belief) that tie each possible choice to each possible outcome: the probability of that outcome given that choice. Indeed, the SWF framework adopts this basic premise of rational choice theory: the decisionmaker is, specifically, someone selecting among a set of policies **P**, in light of a set of outcomes **O** (each outcome x an allocation of bundles of welfare-relevant attributes to everyone in the population), and each policy P is associated with a probability distribution over the outcomes.

But what, more precisely, is the content of these probabilities? According to so-called causal decision theory,[34] the answer is as follows. There is a set of mutually

line up, it may well be certain that none of the individuals will be equally well off with the two policies (i.e., it may well be certain that Pareto Indifference for well-being vectors will not apply to the pair of actual outcomes of the two policies, whatever they may be.) Consider a case in which P has a .5 probability of an outcome in which everyone has well-being 90, and .5 probability of an outcome in which everyone has well-being 10, while P^* with probability 1 yields an outcome in which everyone has well-being 50. (2) Assume that individuals are identically situated in P and P^* and ex ante Strong Pareto applies, requiring that P be ranked better than P^*. It may well be *virtually certain* that, in fact, everyone well be better off with P^* (i.e., virtually certain that Strong Pareto for well-being vectors will rank the outcome of P^* better than that of P). Consider a case in which P has probability π of an outcome in which everyone gets w and $(1 - \pi)$ of an outcome in which everyone gets well-being 10, while P^* gives everyone 50 for certain. Pick π arbitrarily close to 0. Then, if $w > (40/\pi) + 10$, ex ante Strong Pareto requires that P be ranked better even though the probability is $(1 - \pi)$, arbitrarily close to 1, that P^* will have the better outcome for everyone.

[33] More precisely, the prioritarian SWF satisfies Outcome Separability, which is the outcome-level counterpart to Separability (an axiom at the level of worlds). See Section 5.A.1.2. In what follows, so as to simplify terminology, I use "Separability" as shorthand for "Outcome Separability."

[34] See Joyce (1999); Joyce and Gibbard (1988).

exclusive "states-of-nature." One or another of these is the actual state-of-nature; the decisionmaker doesn't know which. Each state-of-nature is causally independent of the choices in the choice set. Every possible combination of a state-of-nature and a choice results in some outcome. If the decisionmaker is rational, each state-of-nature will have a probability, measuring the decisionmaker's degree of belief that this is the actual state-of-nature. And the probability of some outcome, given some choice, is just the cumulative probability of those states-of-nature that, in combination with the choice, lead to the outcome.

Causal decision theory is controverted by a different version of rational choice theory, so called evidential decision theory. For most of this book, I have remained agnostic about this dispute.[35] It generally suffices for my purposes to stipulate that the probabilities assigned by the decisionmaker to outcomes or individual bundles (as in Chapter 5) are epistemic probabilities of some sort—whether constructed in the manner posited by causal decision theory or instead as per evidential decision theory. But *if* causal decision theory is the correct account (as in fact I believe), expected EDE prioritarianism comes into conflict with the fully-informed-adviser principle.

Table 7.5 illustrates how this happens. There are four policies, P, P^*, P^+, and P^{++}. Let $x^s(P)$, $x^s(P^*)$, $x^s(P^+)$, and $x^s(P^{++})$ be the outcomes of policies P, P^*, P^+, and P^{++}, respectively, in a given state-of-nature s. Assume that, in each state-of-nature, the Separability axiom applies to the outcomes in that state. Policy Separability therefore applies and requires that the P/P^* ranking be the same as the P^+/P^{++} ranking: P at least as good as P^* iff P^+ at least as good as P^{++}.

Suppose that the decisionmaker is using an SWF that satisfies the Separability axiom (as is true of the prioritarian SWF). Let *s-act* denote the actual state-of-nature. The fully informed adviser, using that SWF, would *know* what the actual state-of-nature is and would rank the policies according to the SWF's ranking of the outcomes in *s-act*. Since the Separability axiom applies to the four outcomes in every state of nature, including *s-act*, it follows that the fully informed adviser would rank the outcomes in *s-act* as follows: $x^{s\text{-}act}(P)$ at least as good as $x^{s\text{-}act}(P^*)$ iff $x^{s\text{-}act}(P^+)$ at least as good as $x^{s\text{-}act}(P^{++})$. Moreover, since the fully informed adviser ranks the four *policies* according to their outcomes in the actual state-of-nature, *s-act*, the adviser ranks the policies as Policy Separability requires: P at least as good as P^* iff P^+ at least as good as P^{++}.

Suppose now that the decisionmaker is using an uncertainty module for the SWF that violates Policy Separability (as is true of expected EDE prioritarianism).[36] For example, they rank P better than P^* but P^+ worse than P^{++}. The decisionmaker

[35] Adler (2012, pp. 481–90) was also agnostic on this dispute; while Adler (2019b, chs. 3–4) and Adler (2022b) adopted causal decision theory.

[36] The argument here presupposes that expected EDE prioritarianism violates not merely Policy Separability as stated in this book but also a logically weaker version thereof—namely, that if some

Table 7.5 Expected EDE Prioritarianism and Policy Separability

	Policy P			Policy P*		
	State s	State s'		State s	State s'	
	$\pi(s) = .5$	$\pi(s') = .5$		$\pi(s) = .5$	$\pi(s') = .5$	
Charles	1	2		4	4	
Deb	10	12		5	8	
Ernie	12	100		12	100	
Sum of √	7.63	14.88		7.70	14.83	
			expected EDE			expected EDE
EDE	6.46	24.60	15.53	6.59	24.43	15.51
	Policy P$^+$			Policy P^{++}		
	State s	State s'		State s	State s'	
	$\pi(s) = .5$	$\pi(s') = .5$		$\pi(s) = .5$	$\pi(s') = .5$	
Charles	1	2		4	4	
Deb	10	12		5	8	
Ernie	5	6		5	6	
Sum of √	6.40	7.33		6.47	7.28	
			expected EDE			expected EDE
EDE	4.55	5.97	5.26	4.65	5.89	5.27

Explanation: This example uses the prioritarian SWF with a square root transformation function. Policy Separability applies to these four policies, requiring that P is ranked at least as good as P^* iff P^+ is ranked at least as good as P^{++}. Expected EDE prioritarianism, in violation of Policy Separability, ranks P better than P^*, but P^{++} better than P^+. The decisionmaker is uncertain what the actual state-of-nature is; they assign probability .5 to s and probability .5 to s'. The ideal adviser will know what the actual state is. If the state is s, the adviser will rank P^* better than P and P^{++} better than P^+ in light of the prioritarian ranking of the well-being vectors produced by the four policies in state s (note the prioritarian scores for the four well-being vectors in state s). If the state is s', the adviser will rank P better than P^* and P^+ better than P^{++} in light of the prioritarian ranking of the well-being vectors produced by the four policies in state s'.

Note that, in either case, the ideal adviser does not rank P better than P^* but P^{++} better than P^+. The decisionmaker does not know what the actual state is, but can infer that the adviser would not rank the four policies as the decisionmaker does.

individuals have the same well-being levels in each state-of-nature with P as with P^*, the policy ranking is invariant to what those state-by-state well-being levels are. (This logically weaker axiom is referred to by Adler (2019b, p. 285) and Adler (2022b) as "Policy Separability.") Table 7.5 illustrates that expected EDE prioritarianism does indeed violate this logically weaker axiom.

is not themselves fully informed, but—by the structure of the setup—they can infer that the fully informed adviser will disapprove their policy evaluation. *Whatever* the actual state-of-nature, the fully informed adviser *would* conform to the constraint, P at least as good as P^* iff P^+ at least as good as P^{++}.

One objection to the line of argumentation pressed in the preceding paragraphs is that outcomes for purposes of the SWF are *models* of possible worlds (not genuinely possible worlds or sets of worlds) and probabilities are notional (not real) epistemic probabilities.[37] Thus the fully-informed-adviser maxim does not apply. I believe that this objection can be parried, for reasons elaborated in the notes.[38]

7.3 Evaluating Risk-Regulation Policies: Ex Ante Prioritarianism and Expected EDE Prioritarianism

7.3.1 Ex Ante Prioritarianism

Like simple utilitarianism and ex post prioritarianism, ex ante prioritarianism satisfies the tractability axioms. Thus, the apparatus for evaluating risk-regulation policies that was set forth in Chapter 5, Section 5.2.1, for the first two modules also applies to ex ante prioritarianism.[39] This is the risk-and-attribute-profile apparatus. An individual life is divided into periods, with T the maximum lifespan (number of periods). Each individual has an age (the number of periods that they have survived as of the present time); a policy-specific risk profile (a list of period survival probabilities—the probability of surviving to the end of the period conditional on being alive at its start—from the current period in the individual's life through

[37] See Sections 1.4, 5.1.2.

[38] As in note 23, consider a decisionmaker, Audrey, using the SWF framework with outcome set **O** to decide among a set of policies **P**. Just as outcomes are simplified models of worlds, so the states-of-nature that Audrey employs are simplified representations of genuine states-of-nature (simplified representations of the background causal factors that, together with policies, cause worlds to obtain). Audrey's notional probabilities assigned to states-of-nature are based upon actual data regarding how policy choices interact with background causal factors to yield the types of attributes included in the outcomes in **O**. A fully informed adviser is someone who reasons about Audrey's decision using the same mental model that she does (outcome set **O** *and* set of notional states-of-nature) and shares Audrey's outcome ranking, but is fully informed about the actual data—thus assigns probability 1 to one state-of-nature and 0 to all others. It seems very plausible that Audrey should defer to the policy ranking of this idealized counterpart, i.e., would be unjustified in knowingly departing from that ranking: the counterpart is similarly situated to Audrey in aims and modeling framework but has better information.

[39] On the application of ex ante prioritarianism to fatality risk regulation, see Adler, Ferranna, Hammitt, and Treich (2021); Adler, Hammitt, and Treich (2014); Ferranna, Hammitt, and Adler (2023); Ferranna, Sevilla, and Bloom (2022); Hammitt and Treich (2022).

period T); and a policy-specific attribute profile (a list of period bundles received in each period conditional on surviving to its end rather than being Dead).

This information is sufficient to ascertain each individual's lottery over lifetime bundles with any given policy P. That is, from individual i's risk and attribute profile for P, we can derive $\rho_{P,i}(b)$ for any bundle b: the probability that i receives b with P. Moreover, unaffected individuals (those who have the same risk profile and attribute profile for every policy in **P**) can be dropped from the analysis. Let $E^{EAP}(P)$ be the sum of affected individuals' transformed expected well-being for a given policy P. That is, $E^{EAP}(P) = \sum_i g\left(\sum_b \rho_{P,i}(b)w(b)\right)$, summing over affected individuals. Ex ante prioritarianism can be restated as ranking policies according to the rule: P at least as good as P^* iff $E^{EAP}(P) \geq E^{EAP}(P^*)$.[40]

Further, we can calculate an ex-ante-prioritarian social value of risk reduction, $\text{SVRR}_i^{\text{EAP}}$, just as we can for simple utilitarianism and ex post prioritarianism. $\text{SVRR}_i^{\text{EAP}}$ is the partial derivative of E^{EAP} with respect to i's current survival probability, with this partial derivative evaluated at i's baseline risk and attribute profile. Less formally, $\text{SVRR}_i^{\text{EAP}}$ is the change in ex-ante-prioritarian value per unit of current risk reduction for individual i, as evaluated for a marginal such reduction.

As in Section 5.4, let p_i^t denote individual i's baseline survival probability for period t; μ_i^t their baseline probability of living exactly t periods; and W_i^t their lifetime well-being if they live exactly t periods with their baseline attribute profile. The formulas for all three SVRRs are as follows.

$$SVRR_i^{SU} = -W_i^{A_i} + \sum_{t=A_i+1}^{T} \frac{\mu_i^t}{p_i^{A_i+1}} W_i^t$$

[40] Ex ante prioritarianism assigns each policy a score $\sum_{i=1}^{N} g\left(\sum_x \pi_P(x)\mathbf{w}_i(x)\right)$. Restated in terms of bundle probabilities, this score equals: $\sum_{i=1}^{N} g\left(\sum_b \rho_{P,i}(b)w(b)\right)$. See Section 5.A.2.1. Let **A(P)** denote the subset of affected individuals for a given policy set **P**. (An individual is "unaffected" relative to **P** if they face the same lottery over bundles for every policy in **P**, and otherwise is "affected.") If j is not a member of **A(P)**, then $g\left(\sum_b \rho_{P,j}(b)w(b)\right) = g\left(\sum_b \rho_{P^*,j}(b)w(b)\right)$ for every P, P^* in **P**. Let $E^{EAP}(P) = \sum_{i \in \mathbf{A(P)}} g\left(\sum_b \rho_{P,i}(b)w(b)\right)$.

Thus, for every P, P^* in **P**, $\sum_{i=1}^{N} g\left(\sum_b \rho_{P,i}(b)w(b)\right) \geq \sum_{i=1}^{N} g\left(\sum_b \rho_{P^*,i}(b)w(b)\right)$ iff $E^{EAP}(P) \geq E^{EAP}(P^*)$.

$$SVRR_i^{EPP} = -g(W_i^{A_i}) + \sum_{t=A_i+1}^{T} \frac{\mu_i^t}{p_i^{A_i+1}} g(W_i^t)$$

$$SVRR_i^{EAP} = g'\left(\sum_{t=A_i}^{T} \mu_i^t W_i^t\right) SVRR_i^{SU}$$

$SVRR_i^{SU}$ is the difference between *i*'s expected lifetime well-being, conditional on surviving the period, and their lifetime well-being if they die now. Both of the prioritarian SVRRs modify the simple-utilitarian formula, but in different ways. $SVRR_i^{EPP}$ is the difference between *i*'s expected transformed lifetime well-being, conditional on surviving the period, and their transformed lifetime well-being if they die now. By contrast, $SVRR_i^{EAP}$ is the simple-utilitarian SVRR multiplied by an extra term, which equals the slope of the transformation function calculated at the individual's expected lifetime well-being.

Table 5.13 summarized analytic results regarding the comparative statics of $SVRR_i^{SU}$ and $SVRR_i^{EPP}$ with respect to a single-period change in period well-being or survival probability. Table 7.6 expands this table to include the same results for $SVRR_i^{EAP}$.[41] This table shows significant differences[42] not merely between $SVRR_i^{EAP}$ and $SVRR_i^{SU}$—which is not very surprising, since what we have here is a shift from utilitarianism to prioritarianism—but between the two prioritarian SVRRs.

In short, despite both being *tractable* uncertainty modules for a prioritarian SWF, ex ante prioritarianism and ex post prioritarianism are different not only with respect to foundational uncertainty axioms (Dominance and ex ante Pareto) but—more concretely—with respect to the valuation of changes in fatality risk (the SVRR).

That said, $SVRR_i^{EAP}$ and $SVRR_i^{EPP}$ do also share some important similarities. First, both give more relative priority to risk reduction for the young than $SVRR_i^{SU}$. The "Extra Priority for the Young" property of $SVRR_i^{EPP}$ also holds true of $SVRR_i^{EAP}$.[43] Second, both can neutralize the simple-utilitarian skew toward better-off individuals in the case of permanent differences in period well-being.[44]

[41] This table, like Table 5.13, is based upon Adler, Ferranna, Hammitt, and Treich (2021).

[42] In Table 7.6, the "ambiguous" entries in certain instances for $SVRR^{EAP}$ means that $SVRR^{EAP}$ may be increasing, decreasing, or unchanged—depending upon the transformation function, the individuals' risk profiles, and the time path of their period well-being.

[43] Section 5.4.1 stated Extra Priority for the Young in the case of $SVRR_i^{EPP}$. The same result holds for $SVRR_i^{EAP}$. Let *i* and *j* be two individuals with the same risk profile and attribute profile, *i* older than *j*. Then $SVRR_j^{EAP}/SVRR_i^{EAP} > SVRR_j^{SU}/SVRR_i^{SU}$. See Adler, Ferranna, Hammitt, and Treich (2021).

[44] The result stated in Section 5.4.3 and proved in Section 5.A.2.4, regarding $SVRR^{SU}$ and $SVRR^{EPP}$ with permanent, proportional differences in well-being, also holds true of $SVRR^{EAP}$. Ellie's $SVRR^{EAP}$ is greater than/equal to/less than Frank's depending on whether the priority parameter is less than/equal to/greater than 1.

Table 7.6 Simple-Utilitarian, Ex-Post-Prioritarian, and Ex-Ante-Prioritarian SVRRs: Comparative Statics

	Period Well-Being: Single-Period Difference	Survival Probability: Single-Period Difference
$SVRR^{SU}$	Past period: *Unchanged* Current period: *Increasing* Future period: *Increasing*	 Current period: *Unchanged* Future period: *Increasing*
$SVRR^{EPP}$	Past period: *Decreasing* Current period: *Increasing* Future period: *Increasing*	 Current period: *Unchanged* Future period: *Increasing*
$SVRR^{EAP}$	Past period: *Decreasing* Current period: *Ambiguous* Future period: *Ambiguous*	 Current period: *Decreasing* Future period: *Ambiguous*

Explanation: This table shows the comparative statics of $SVRR^{SU}$, $SVRR^{EPP}$, and $SVRR^{EAP}$ with respect to a single-period change in period well-being or survival probability.

7.3.2 Expected EDE Prioritarianism

It is critical to understand that the risk-and-attribute-profile apparatus of Chapter 5, Section 5.2.1 tells us *nothing* about how individuals' lifetime well-being levels correlate. In knowing the policy-*P* risk profile and attribute profile for individual 1, individual 2, . . . , individual *N*, we can determine the policy-*P* lottery over lifetime well-being for individual 1, individual 2, . . . , individual *N*. But this individual-by-individual information does *not* tell us about the probability of a given population-wide distribution of lifetime well-being.

If a module satisfies Decomposability, it doesn't *need* information about the probability of population-wide well-being distributions. Two policies with the same individual-by-individual well-being lotteries are equally good, regardless of how they differ with respect to the probabilities of different possible population-wide well-being distributions. The risk-and-attribute-profile apparatus thus meshes perfectly with simple utilitarianism, ex post prioritarianism, and ex ante prioritarianism. All of these modules satisfy Decomposability; thus, none require the information about the probabilities of population-wide well-being distributions that the apparatus lacks.

Because expected EDE prioritarianism fails Decomposability, it cannot be applied to risk-regulation policies via the risk-and-attribute-profile apparatus—at least absent additional stipulations. Table 7.7 illustrates why not. Three policies involve different probabilities of population-wide distributions of longevity and, thereby, lifetime well-being; but each individual's lottery over lifespans and

Table 7.7 Expected EDE Prioritarianism, Decomposability, and Risk-Regulation Policies

	Outcome *x*	Outcome *y*	Outcome *z*	Outcome *zz*
	Raj and Sadie survive	Raj dies, Sadie survives	Raj survives, Sadie dies	Raj and Sadie die
Raj	100	36	100	36
Sadie	144	144	64	64
EDE (√)	121	81	81	49
Outcome Probabilities				
Policy P (correlated survival)	.5	0	0	.5
*Policy P** (independent survival)	.25	.25	.25	.25
*Policy P*** (anti-correlated survival)	0	.5	.5	0
	Expected EDE Prioritarian	**Simple Utilitarian**	**Ex Post Prioritarian**	**Ex Ante Prioritarian**
Policy Scores				
Policy *P*	85	172	18	18.44
Policy *P**	83	172	18	18.44
Policy *P***	81	172	18	18.44

Explanation: There are two individuals in the population, Raj and Sadie. Each can survive the current period and live a long lifespan, or die now and live a short lifespan. Raj's lifetime well-being numbers with a long and short lifespan are, respectively, 100 and 36, while Sadie's are 144 and 64. There are four possible outcomes, depending on whether Raj and Sadie both survive; one survives while the other dies now; or both die now. The four outcomes, their well-being vectors, and EDEs (using a square root transformation function) are shown in the top part of the table.

Three policies involve different probability distributions over the four outcomes. The example is constructed so that, with each of the three policies, both Raj and Sadie have a .5 chance of surviving the period. Thus each faces the same lottery over lifetime well-being with the three policies: Raj, a .5 chance of well-being 100, a .5 chance of 36; Sadie, a .5 chance of well-being 144, a .5 chance of 64.

However, the policies allocate the individuals' survival probabilities over the four outcomes in different ways. Policy *P*, correlated survival, assigns .5 probability to the individuals both surviving and .5 to them both dying. With Policy *P**, independent survival, whether each individual survives is independent of whether the other does. Policy *P*** is anti-correlated survival: .5 is assigned to each of the two outcomes in which one individual survives while the other dies.

The bottom part of the table shows policy scores. The expected EDE prioritarian score is different as between the three policies (a violation of Decomposability), while simple-utilitarian, ex-post-prioritarian, and ex-ante-prioritarian scores are the same.

lifetime well-being is the same with the three policies. Simple utilitarianism, ex post prioritarianism, and ex ante prioritarianism each give the same score to the three policies (consistent with Decomposability); expected EDE prioritarianism does not.

One route around the difficulty for expected EDE prioritarianism illustrated by Table 7.7 is to employ the risk-and-attribute-profile apparatus together with a stipulation about the correlation of individual longevities. (In what follows, risk and attribute profiles are for everyone in the population, not merely affected individuals.) Most simply, one might assume that individuals' longevities are probabilistically independent with any given policy *P*. Let *L* be a longevity distribution: a combination of possible lifespans for each person in the population. $L = (l_1, \ldots, l_N)$, with l_i the lifespan of individual *i*. From each individual's risk profile for *P*, we can calculate that individual's lifespan probabilities. Assume that, with policy *P*, individual 1 has a probability p_1 of lifespan l_1, individual 2 has a probability p_2 of lifespan $l_2, \ldots$, individual *N* has a probability p_N of lifespan l_N. *If* longevities are assumed to be probabilistically independent (with any policy and thus with *P*), then the probability with *P* of *L* is $p_1 \times p_2 \times \cdots \times p_N$. *L*, together with the policy-*P* array of individual attribute profiles, determines a specific outcome, the probability of which is just $p_1 \times p_2 \times \cdots \times p_N$.

The assumption of probabilistic independence, however, is quite strong. Individuals' event-specific fatality probabilities (their probabilities of dying as a result of some event) will often *not* be independent. To see this, imagine that Nestor and Mia both live near some factory, which might malfunction and release a toxin. Or they both use some infrastructure, which might collapse and cause fatalities. Or they both purchase consumer products from some manufacturer, which might design the products in a dangerous manner. Nestor's and Mia's event-specific fatality probabilities are independent if Nestor's probability of dying from the event (toxic release, infrastructure collapse, dangerous product design) equals his probability of dying from it, conditional on Mia dying from it, and vice versa. But note that each person's probability of dying from the event is discounted by the chance that the event doesn't occur; while each person's probability of dying from it, conditional on the other dying from it, presupposes (in the condition) that the event does occur. So typically these probabilities will not be equal.

Fatality-risk-regulation policies operate by eliminating or mitigating specific types of events that cause death. It is possible that, notwithstanding the non-independence of event-specific fatality probabilities, these interactions "cancel out" so that longevity probabilities *are* independent in the manner described two paragraphs above. Still, this seems like a quite special case rather than a defensible default assumption for policy analysis.

A different apparatus for applying expected EDE prioritarianism to risk policies, one that is flexible with respect to the correlation of individual longevities, is as follows. Each policy *P* is associated with a "longevity profile," which directly assigns a probability π to each possible *L*. Each policy is also associated with a population-wide array of individual attribute profiles. For each *L*, the corresponding outcome *x* (given *P*) is determined by this array of individual attribute profiles. The policy-*P* probability of *x* is π; and the EDE for *x* can be calculated using the well-being measure and prioritarian transformation function. Knowing outcome probabilities and EDEs, we can calculate the policy's expected EDE score.

Let's call this the "longevity and attribute profile" apparatus. It has not yet been investigated (as far as I'm aware). Doing so, and in particular defining a concept analogous to the SVRR within it, are topics for future research.

Also to be investigated is how already-dead individuals ("prior generations") should figure in expected-EDE-prioritarian analysis. Using the Chapter 5, Section 5.2.1 apparatus, already-dead individuals *can* be assigned a risk profile and attribute profile. Amit, if already dead, has a risk profile with a survival probability of 1 for each period of his life that he survived and 0 for the periods when he was Dead. Thus, the information in Amit's risk profile is equivalent to his realized lifespan. Amit's attribute profile records the bundle he receives each period, conditional on surviving to its end. But since he has probability 1 of living in each period through his realized lifespan, and 0 thereafter, Amit's attribute profile is equivalent to his realized lifetime bundle.

However, ex-post-prioritarian, simple-utilitarian, and ex-ante-prioritarian policy evaluation using the Section 5.2.1 apparatus does not in fact *need* to assign already-dead individuals a risk profile and attribute profile. Because Amit is unaffected—specifically, his risk profile (realized lifespan) and attribute profile (realized lifetime bundle) are the same for every policy in P—he can be dropped from ex-post-prioritarian, simple-utilitarian, and ex-ante-prioritarian policy assessment. Since those modules satisfy Policy Separability and Decomposability, including him and others already dead makes no difference to how the modules rank policies.

What to do about the already-dead is a more challenging topic for expected EDE prioritarianism. One possibility is to include the already-dead in the analysis. (1) If the expected EDE prioritarian is employing the risk-and-attribute-profile apparatus with an assumption of probabilistic independence, including the already-dead would work as follows. Realized lifespans and realized lifetime bundles are ascertained for the already-dead. A given policy *P* endows those not already dead with policy-specific risk and attribute profiles. From that information, we can calculate the policy-*P* probability π^* of "compressed" longevity distribution L^*, listing the lifespans of those not already dead. The corresponding "full" longevity distribution L, listing the lifespans of the entire population, is just L combined with the realized lifespans of the already-dead. The probability of L is just π^*. The outcome x corresponding to L can be determined from the realized bundles of the already-dead plus the policy-P attribute profiles of those not already dead. (2) If the expected EDE prioritarian is instead employing the longevity-and-attribute-profile apparatus, including the already-dead works the same way—except that the array of policy-specific risk profiles for those not already dead is replaced with a policy-specific "compressed" longevity profile, which specifies the probability of each possible "compressed" longevity distribution L^*.

A more streamlined approach is to drop the already-dead from expected EDE prioritarian analysis. That is, the population of interest depends on the time of policy choice; it is stipulated to include *only* those who are currently alive or will be alive in the future, at that time. This avoids the analytic burden of determining realized longevities and realized bundles for the already-dead. However, excluding the already-dead is ethically questionable. In the case of simple utilitarianism, ex post prioritarianism, and ex ante prioritarianism, the already-dead are *not* excluded on the grounds that they lack ethical standing. Rather, they are excluded because including them makes no difference to the policy ranking. The expected EDE prioritarian cannot give *that* rationale for excluding the already-dead; this module is sensitive to the well-being levels of the unaffected, including the already-dead. So what is the ethical argument for excluding them, while not excluding the unaffected who are currently alive or will be alive in the future?

Note further that excluding the already-dead from expected-EDE-prioritarian analysis can create a problem of time-consistency.[45]

7.4 Egalitarianism, Sufficientism, and Leximin under Uncertainty

7.4.1 Egalitarianism

The egalitarian SWFs that are most widely discussed in the SWF literature are the "rank-weighted SWFs." This is a class of SWFs, each of which is defined by a list of N positive and strictly decreasing weights: $k_1, k_2, \ldots, k_N,$

[45] Time-consistency is a principle of dynamic rationality which says that if a decisionmaker adopts a plan to take some action at a future time if the future unfolds in a certain way, then (absent unforeseen events) the decisionmaker should follow through on the plan if the future does unfold in that way. On the expected EDE approach, separability, and time-consistency, see Ferranna and Fleurbaey (2022); Fleurbaey (2010, 2018).

with $k_1 > k_2 > \cdots > k_N > 0$. A score is assigned to a given well-being vector **w** as follows: k_1 times the lowest well-being number in **w** plus k_2 times the second-lowest well-being number in **w** $\cdots$ plus k_N times the highest well-being number in **w**. Vectors are ranked according to these scores.[46] (Rank-weighted SWFs are also referred to as "generalized Gini" SWFs.)

Rank-weighted SWFs, like both the utilitarian SWF and prioritarian SWFs, satisfy the Pareto axioms for well-being vectors. Like prioritarian SWFs (but not the utilitarian SWF), they satisfy the Pigou-Dalton axiom. By contrast with both the utilitarian SWF and prioritarian SWFs, rank-weighted SWFs violate the Separability axiom.

Rank-weighted SWFs, because they respect Pigou-Dalton, confront the very same axiomatic trade-off under uncertainty that prioritarian SWFS do—namely, no uncertainty module for a rank-weighted SWF can satisfy both Dominance and ex ante Pareto.[47] Two modules are salient. *Ex post rank-weightism* assigns each policy a score equaling the expected sum of individuals' rank-weighted well-being. *Ex ante rank-weightism* assigns each policy a score equaling the sum of individuals' rank-weighted expected well-being. The first is similar to ex post prioritarianism and expected EDE prioritarianism in that it satisfies Expected Value Ethical Decisionmaking and thus Dominance, at the cost of ex ante Pareto. The second is similar to ex ante prioritarianism—in applying the SWF's scoring method to individuals' expected well-being numbers, thereby satisfying ex ante Pareto but violating Dominance. There is no distinct module that corresponds to expected EDE prioritarianism.[48]

See Table 7.8 for a summary of how ex post and ex ante rank-weightism fare with respect to the uncertainty axioms.

The argument against ex ante rank-weightism is the same as that against ex ante prioritarianism: violating Dominance is deeply problematic. I will therefore focus on ex post rank-weightism in these brief comments.

Ex post rank-weightism violates Decomposability, as illustrated in Table 7.9. It therefore also violates Policy Separability.[49]

Ex post rank-weightism thus has the same tractability properties as expected EDE prioritarianism. However, the justifiability of these properties is not the same. The proponent of ex post prioritarianism has *two* arguments against expected EDE prioritarianism: first, that giving up Policy Separability

[46] See chapter appendix, Section 7.A.2, for a precise statement. On rank-weighted SWFs, see, e.g., Adler (2019b, ch. 3–4); Blackorby, Bossert, and Donaldson (2005, ch. 4); Fleurbaey (2010). Rank-weighted SWFs are "egalitarian" in satisfying the definition of "egalitarianism" in Section 1.3, 1.A.4. (Note that since a rank-weighted SWF meets the conditions of the "Decomposition Theorem" set forth in Adler [2019b, p. 276], it has a corresponding inequality metric.)

[47] See Adler (2019b, pp. 140–44, 284–85).

[48] See chapter appendix, Section 7.A.2, for an explanation.

[49] See Adler (2022b, p. 68, table 2.6) for an explicit illustration.

Table 7.8 Uncertainty Modules for Rank-Weighted SWFs and the Uncertainty Axioms

	Expected Value Ethical Decision-making	Dominance	Ex Ante Pareto Indifference	Ex Ante Strong Pareto	Decompo-sability	Policy Separability
Ex Post Rank Weightism	Yes	Yes	No (yes if individuals identically situated)	No (yes if individuals identically situated)	No	No
Ex Ante Rank Weightism	No	No	Yes	Yes	Yes	No

Table 7.9 Ex Post Rank-Weightism and Decomposability

	Policy P				Policy P*			
	Outcome x		Outcome x^*		Outcome y		Outcome y^*	
	$\pi_p(x)=.5$		$\pi_p(x^*)=.5$		$\pi_{p^*}(y)=.5$		$\pi_{p^*}(y^*)=.5$	
	well-being	weight	well-being	weight	well-being	weight	well-being	weight
Arif	40	2	90	1	90	1	40	2
Bev	80	1	50	2	80	2	50	1
Cady	10	3	10	3	10	3	10	3
Sum of rank-weighted well-being	190		220		280		160	
Ex post rank weightism score (expected sum of rank-weighted well-being)	205				220			

Explanation: Policy P leads to outcomes x and x^*, each with probability .5, while policy P^* leads to outcomes y and y^*, each with probability .5. The table shows the well-being numbers of the three individuals and the weights applied to those well-being numbers. (The weights being used are these: the worst-off individual in an outcome gets weight 3, the second-worst-off 2, the best-off 1.) Decomposability applies, because each individual has the same well-being lottery with the two policies; but ex post rank weightism assign the policies different scores.

and Decomposability has large pragmatic disadvantages; and second, that combining an SWF that satisfies Separability (prioritarianism) with an uncertainty module that violates Policy Separability runs afoul of the principle, "act as you know your fully informed adviser would recommend."[50] In making the case against ex post rank-weightism, the proponent of ex post prioritarianism still has the first argument, but the second is not available.

Applying ex post rank-weightism to fatality risk policies is very similar to applying expected EDE prioritarianism. Because ex post rank-weightism violates Decomposability, the risk-and-attribute-profile apparatus of Chapter 5, Section 5.2.1 cannot be employed without further stipulation. As with expected EDE prioritarianism, one possibility is to employ that apparatus together with a stipulation about the correlation of individual longevities (most simply, that longevities are probabilistically independent). With that stipulation in hand, from the population-wide array of individual risk profiles, we arrive at a policy-specific probability of a given longevity distribution *L*. Another approach is to associate each policy with a "longevity profile," which directly specifies the probability of each longevity distribution *L*.

In either case, the outcome x corresponding to L is determined by the population-wide array of individual attribute profiles. With well-being measure $w(\cdot)$ and the rank weights $k_1, k_2, \ldots, k_N$ in hand, that outcome is assigned a rank-weighted score. Combining the outcome scores and probabilities, we arrive at the policy's expected rank-weighted score.[51]

7.4.2 Sufficientism

Sufficientism is a family of SWFs. Each such SWF is defined by a threshold level of lifetime well-being w^{Thresh} and a continuous, strictly increasing, and strictly concave transformation function $g(\cdot)$. A sufficientist SWF is prioritarian in making trade-offs below the threshold, utilitarian in making trade-offs above the threshold, and gives absolute priority to those below the threshold over those above. It does so by assigning each well-being vector **w** two scores: first, the sum of transformed individual lifetime well-being, but with these well-being numbers capped at the threshold level; and, second, the sum of individual lifetime well-being, but with well-being numbers below the threshold replaced by the threshold level. For short, let's call the first score assigned to **w** the "sum of transformed capped lifetime well-being"; and the second score "the sum of

[50] See Section 7.2.

[51] The discussion in Section 7.3.2 of how expected EDE prioritarianism should take account of the already-dead also applies to ex post rank weightism.

bottomed lifetime well-being." Vectors are compared using a two-step rule: If the first scores (sums of transformed capped lifetime well-being) are unequal, the vector with the higher first score is better; if those scores are equal and the second scores (sums of bottomed lifetime well-being) are unequal, the vector with the higher second score is better; and if both scores are equal, the vectors are equally good.[52]

Sufficientist SWFs, like prioritarian and rank-weighted SWFs, lack uncertainty modules that respect both Dominance and ex ante Pareto.[53] One possibility, *ex ante sufficientism*, is analogous to ex ante prioritarianism and ex ante rank-weightism. This approach takes the sufficientist vector-ranking rule and applies it to the vector of individuals' expected well-being numbers associated with each policy. Ex ante sufficientism violates Dominance and, in my view, should for this reason be rejected.

Sufficientism has no uncertainty module that satisfies Expected Value Ethical Decisionmaking. This is because a sufficient SWF's ranking of well-being vectors cannot be represented by a score assigned to each vector.[54]

However, recent scholarship has identified a sufficientist module that is otherwise quite similar to ex post prioritarianism. This module, *ex post sufficientism*,[55] satisfies Dominance and the tractability axioms. It assigns a given policy *two* scores: first, the expected sum of transformed capped lifetime well-being; and second, the expected sum of bottomed lifetime well-being. Policies are ranked in light of these two scores using a two-step rule isomorphic to the rule for ranking vectors.[56]

See Table 7.10 for the axiomatic properties of ex ante and ex post sufficientism.

Note that policy *P*'s first score (the expected sum of transformed capped lifetime well-being) is equal to the sum of individuals' expected transformed capped lifetime well-being. And the second score (the expected sum of bottomed lifetime well-being) is equal to the sum of individuals' expected bottomed lifetime well-being. That is, for a given policy *P*, each individual has two scores: first, the individual's expected transformed capped lifetime well-being; and second, the individual's expected bottomed lifetime well-being. Ex post

[52] The formal definition of a sufficientist SWF is provided in Adler (2019b, p. 273) and corresponds exactly to the sufficientist world-ranking as defined in Sections 1.3.2, 1.A.4.1.

[53] See Adler (2019b, pp. 140–44, 284–85). This can be seen simply from Table 7.3. Consider a sufficientist SWF with a given $g(\cdot)$ function and a threshold value above 70. Then Dominance for that SWF ranks the two policies in the top part and the two policies in the bottom part of the table the same way as a prioritarian SWF using $g(\cdot)$, in conflict with ex ante Pareto. A similar example can, of course, be constructed for any threshold value.

[54] See Adler (2019b, p. 262, n. 6).

[55] See chapter appendix, Section 7.A.3. Ex post sufficientism as stated there is based upon the "ex post sufficientarian" rule for ranking prospects set forth in Adler, Bossert, Cato, and Kamaga (forthcoming).

[56] The sufficientist SWF lacks an expected EDE module. If a well-being vector has entries both below and above the threshold, there is no EDE for that vector.

Table 7.10 Sufficientist Uncertainty Modules and the Uncertainty Axioms

	Expected Value Ethical Decision-making	Dominance	Ex Ante Pareto Indifference	Ex Ante Strong Pareto	Decompo-sability	Policy Separability
Ex Post Sufficientism	No	Yes	No	No	Yes	Yes
Ex Ante Sufficientism	No	No	Yes	Yes	Yes	Yes

sufficientism can be restated as assigning each policy two scores and applying the two-step rule to these scores. The first policy score is the sum of individuals' first scores (expected transformed capped lifetime well-being); the second policy score is the sum of individuals' second scores (expected bottomed lifetime well-being).

This restatement of ex post sufficientism (analogous to a similar restatement of ex post prioritarianism) makes clear why this module satisfies both Decomposability and Policy Separability. From an individual's policy-*P* lottery over lifetime well-being, we can calculate both the individual's first score and their second score. Thus, if each individual has the same lottery over lifetime well-being with *P* that they do with *P**, each individual's first scores with the two policies are the same *and* each individual's second scores are the same—and so the policy scores must be the same (Decomposability).

Moreover, the formula for calculating first and second policy scores is a simple summation of individuals' first and second scores, respectively. If an individual has the very same well-being lottery with two policies, the policy ranking is invariant to what that lottery is (Policy Separability)—since their first scores and second scores are just constants added to the summations.

Because the tractability axioms are satisfied, ex post sufficientism can be applied to risk-regulation policies via the risk-and-attribute-profile apparatus of Chapter 5, Section 5.2.1. A policy endows each individual with a risk profile and attribute profile. These fully determine the individual's lottery over lifetime bundles with the policy. As with simple utilitarianism, ex post prioritarianism, and ex ante prioritarianism, unaffected individuals—those with the same risk profile and attribute profile for every policy in **P**—can be dropped from the analysis.

Rather than employing the information in an affected individual's risk and attribute profile to calculate their expected lifetime well-being (simple utilitarianism), expected transformed lifetime well-being (ex post prioritarianism), or transformed expected lifetime well-being (ex ante prioritarianism), we use it to calculate the two individual scores: expected transformed capped lifetime well-being, and expected bottomed lifetime well-being. These are summed across the affected population to arrive at the two policy scores.

One difference between the risk-and-attribute-profile apparatus as applied to the utilitarian and prioritarian modules, and that apparatus applied to ex post sufficientism, is that the policies are ranked in light of *two* scores—not a single one. Thus, the SVRR concept is not directly applicable. The natural way to modify that concept for purposes of ex post sufficientism is to consider the marginal impact of a change to an individual's baseline current survival probability on each of the two scores. This is a topic for future research that sufficientists may wish to pursue.

7.4.3 Leximin

The leximin SWF[57] is similar to prioritarian, rank-weighted, and sufficientist SWFs in that it lacks an uncertainty module which satisfies both Dominance and ex ante Pareto.[58] Moreover, one of its uncertainty modules—*ex ante leximin*—is directly analogous to ex ante prioritarianism, ex ante rank weightism, and ex ante sufficientism. Ex ante leximin applies the leximin rule to the vector of expected well-being numbers associated with each policy. It satisfies ex ante Pareto but fails Dominance.[59]

On the "ex post" side, however, leximin is quite distinctive. The ranking of well-being vectors by the leximin SWF, like the ranking by sufficientist SWFs, cannot be represented by a score assigned to vectors.[60] Thus the leximin SWF, like sufficientist SWFs, lacks an uncertainty module that satisfies Expected Value Ethical Decisionmaking.

Still, ex post sufficientism comes "close" to Expected Value Ethical Decisionmaking in assigning each policy two scores, each of which is calculated by taking the expected value of outcome scores: the expected value of the sum of transformed well-being numbers capped at the threshold level,

[57] The formal definition of a leximin SWF is provided in Adler (2019b, p. 273) and corresponds exactly to the leximin world-ranking as defined in Sections 1.3.2, 1.A.4.1.

[58] See Adler (2019b, pp. 140–44, 284–85). The conflict can be seen directly from Table 7.3. Dominance for the leximin SWF requires that P^{**} be ranked above P^* in the bottom part of the table, in conflict with ex ante Pareto Indifference; and that P^+ be ranked above P in the top part of table as long as $(50 - \varepsilon) > 30$, in conflict with ex ante Strong Pareto.

[59] There is no expected EDE leximin. If a well-being vector has unequal entries, it lacks a leximin EDE.

[60] See Adler (2019b, p. 262, n. 6).

Table 7.11 Ex Post Leximin and Decomposability

	Policy P			Policy P*		
	<u>Outcome *x*</u>	<u>Outcome *y*</u>		<u>Outcome *x**</u>	<u>Outcome *y**</u>	
	$\pi_P(x)=.5$	$\pi_P(y)=.5$		$\pi_{P^*}(x^*)=.5$	$\pi_{P^*}(y^*)=.5$	
Ally	2	8		2	8	
Baia	4	1		1	4	
Cat	9	11		9	11	
			<u>expected well-being</u>			<u>expected well-being</u>
Worst-off	2	1	1.5	1	4	2.5
Second-worst-off	4	8	6	2	8	5
Best-off	9	11	10	9	11	10

Explanation: The top part of the table shows individuals' well-being numbers with the two policies. Note that each individual faces the same lottery over well-being with *P* as with *P**. The bottom part reorders the well-being numbers in each outcome from worst-off to best-off and calculates expected well-being at each position. Ex post leximin ranks the policies by applying the leximin rule to these vectors of expected well-being. It is not indifferent between the policies (in violation of Decomposability), preferring policy *P** because the lowest expected well-being with *P** (2.5) is greater than the lowest expected well-being with *P* (1.5).

Table 7.12 Leximin Uncertainty Modules and the Uncertainty Axioms

	Expected Value Ethical Decision-making	Dominance	Ex Ante Pareto Indifference	Ex Ante Strong Pareto	Decomposability	Policy Separability
Ex Post Leximin	No	Yes	No (yes if individuals identically situated)	No (yes if individuals identically situated)	No	No
Ex Ante Leximin	No	No	Yes	Yes	Yes	Yes

and the expected value of the sum of well-being numbers "bottomed" by the threshold level. No such expedient is available for leximin, which doesn't employ a threshold but instead gives absolute priority to every worse-off person over every better-off person. *Ex post leximin*, as proposed by Marc Fleurbaey,[61]

[61] Fleurbaey (2010).

employs a policy-ranking algorithm that is dissimilar to that of any of the other Dominance-respecting modules discussed in this chapter. A given policy is assigned a vector of *N* expected well-being numbers equaling the expected value of the well-being of the worst-off individual in each of the policy outcomes; the expected value of the well-being of the second-worst-off individual in each of the policy outcomes; . . . ; the expected value of the well-being of the best-off individual in each of the policy outcomes. Policies are then ranked by applying the leximin rule to their vectors of expected well-being numbers calculated this way.

Note that different individuals may occupy the worst-off, second-worst-off, etc. positions in different outcomes. Thus, in general, the vector of expected well-being numbers for a policy calculated as per ex post leximin is not the same as the vector of each individual's expected well-being, which is the input to ex ante leximin's policy-ranking formula.

Notably, ex post leximin *fails* Decomposability (see Table 7.11) and therefore fails Policy Separability. Thus, it is vulnerable to the same critique that I set forth above as regards expected EDE prioritarianism.[62] The leximin SWF satisfies the Separability axiom, and yet ex post leximin violates Policy Separability. As with expected EDE prioritarianism, this combination runs afoul of the principle, "act as you know your fully informed adviser would recommend."

See Table 7.12, summarizing the axiomatic properties of ex ante and ex post leximin.

Because ex post leximin fails Decomposability and Policy Separability, it would not be applied to risk-regulation policies via the risk-and-attribute-profile apparatus of Section 5.2.1, but instead via the less tractable methodology described above for expected EDE prioritarianism and ex post rank weightism.

Chapter 7: Appendix

7.A.1 Uncertainty Axioms

All of these axioms are requirements governing the uncertainty module for some SWF $\succcurlyeq^E$. Recall that an uncertainty module for this SWF is a formula for arriving at a ranking $\succcurlyeq^{E\text{-}P}$ of the policy set, in light of the SWF, the well-being measure $w(\cdot)$, and the probability distribution over outcomes associated with each policy P. $\mathbf{w}(x)$ is the well-being vector associated with outcome x.

Expected Value Ethical Decisionmaking: There exists $e(\cdot)$, a real-valued function on well-being vectors, such that (a) $\mathbf{w} \succcurlyeq^E \mathbf{v}$ iff $e(\mathbf{w}) \geq e(\mathbf{v})$; and (b) $P \succcurlyeq^{E\text{-}P} P^*$ iff $\sum_x \pi_P(x) e(\mathbf{w}(x)) \geq \sum_x \pi_{P^*}(x) e(\mathbf{w}(x))$.

[62] See Section 7.2.

Dominance: Let P, P^* be such that: for every pair of x, x^* such that $\pi_P(x) > 0$ and $\pi_{P^*}(x^*) > 0$, $\mathbf{w}(x) \succ^E \mathbf{w}(x^*)$. Then $P \succ^{E\text{-}P} P^*$.

Ex Ante Pareto. (1) Ex Ante Pareto Indifference: Let P, P^* be such that for each individual i, $\sum_x \pi_P(x)\mathbf{w}_i(x) = \sum_x \pi_{P^*}(x)\mathbf{w}_i(x)$. Then $P \sim^{E\text{-}P} P^*$.

(2) Ex Ante Strong Pareto: Let P, P^* be such that for each individual i, $\sum_x \pi_P(x)\mathbf{w}_i(x) \geq \sum_x \pi_{P^*}(x)\mathbf{w}_i(x)$, and for at least one individual j, $\sum_x \pi_P(x)\mathbf{w}_j(x) > \sum_x \pi_{P^*}(x)\mathbf{w}_j(x)$. Then $P \succ^{E\text{-}P} P^*$.

The tractability axioms (Decomposability and Policy Separability) are stated formally in Section 5.A.1.1.

7.A.2 Uncertainty Modules for Rank-Weighted SWFs

Let $\hat{\mathbf{w}}$ be a vector ordering the elements of $\mathbf{w}$ from smallest to largest.[63] A rank-weighted SWF is defined by a list of N weights $k_1, k_2, \ldots, k_N$, with $k_1 > k_2 > \ldots > k_N > 0$. Well-being vectors are ordered as follows: $\mathbf{w} \succcurlyeq^E \mathbf{v}$ iff $\sum_{i=1}^{N} k_i \hat{\mathbf{w}}_i \geq \sum_{i=1}^{N} k_i \hat{\mathbf{v}}_i$.

Ex post rank weightism orders policies as follows: $P \succcurlyeq^{E\text{-}P} P^*$ iff $\sum_x \pi_P(x) \sum_{i=1}^{N} k_i \hat{\mathbf{w}}_i(x) \geq \sum_x \pi_{P^*}(x) \sum_{i=1}^{N} k_i \hat{\mathbf{w}}_i(x)$.

Let $\mathbf{w}_i(P)$ denote i's expected well-being with policy P: $\mathbf{w}_i(P) = \sum_x \pi_P(x)\mathbf{w}_i(x)$. $\mathbf{w}(P)$ is the vector of these expected well-being numbers, and $\hat{\mathbf{w}}(P)$ is that vector reordered from smallest to largest. Then *ex ante rank weightism* orders policies as follows: $P \succcurlyeq^{E\text{-}P} P^*$ iff $\sum_{i=1}^{N} k_i \hat{\mathbf{w}}_i(P) \geq \sum_{i=1}^{N} k_i \hat{\mathbf{w}}_i(P^*)$.

As noted in the text, there is no distinct module for a rank-weighted SWF that corresponds to expected EDE prioritarianism. Note that the EDE for well-being vector $\mathbf{w}$ is just $w^* = \left(\sum_{i=1}^{N} k_i \hat{\mathbf{w}}_i\right) / \left(\sum_{i=1}^{N} k_i\right)$. Because $1 / \left(\sum_{i=1}^{N} k_i\right)$ is a positive constant, ranking policies according to the expected value of EDE values yields the same ranking as ex post rank weightism.

7.A.3 Uncertainty Modules for Sufficientist SWFs

A sufficientist SWF is defined by a threshold level of well-being w^{Thresh} and a strictly increasing, strictly concave, and continuous function $g(\cdot)$. The SWF's

[63] That is: the elements of $\hat{\mathbf{w}}$ are a permutation of those in $\mathbf{w}$, and $\hat{\mathbf{w}}_i \leq \hat{\mathbf{w}}_{i+1}$ for all $i = 1$ to $(N - 1)$.

rule for ranking well-being vectors, given w^{Thresh} and $g(\cdot)$, is stated in Section 1.A.4. In what follows, let $\succcurlyeq^E$ denote that rule. As in Section 1.A.4, let $\overline{\mathbf{w}}$ denote the elements of vector $\mathbf{w}$ truncated above ("capped") at w^{Thresh} and $\underline{\mathbf{w}}$ denote its elements truncated below ("bottomed") at w^{Thresh}.

Ex post sufficientism ranks policies as follows. (1) If $\sum_x \pi_P(x) \sum_{i=1}^N g(\overline{\mathbf{w}}_i(x)) > \sum_x \pi_{P^*}(x) \sum_{i=1}^N g(\overline{\mathbf{w}}_i(x))$, then $P \succ^{E\text{-}P} P^*$. (2) If $\sum_x \pi_P(x) \sum_{i=1}^N g(\overline{\mathbf{w}}_i(x)) = \sum_x \pi_{P^*}(x) \sum_{i=1}^N g(\overline{\mathbf{w}}_i(x))$ and

$\sum_x \pi_P(x) \sum_{i=1}^N \underline{\mathbf{w}}_i(x) > \sum_x \pi_{P^*}(x) \sum_{i=1}^N \underline{\mathbf{w}}_i(x)$,

then $P \succ^{E\text{-}P} P^*$. (3) If $\sum_x \pi_P(x) \sum_{i=1}^N g(\overline{\mathbf{w}}_i(x)) = \sum_x \pi_{P^*}(x) \sum_{i=1}^N g(\overline{\mathbf{w}}_i(x))$ and $\sum_x \pi_P(x) \sum_{i=1}^N \underline{\mathbf{w}}_i(x) = \sum_x \pi_{P^*}(x) \sum_{i=1}^N \underline{\mathbf{w}}_i(x)$ then $P \sim^{E\text{-}P} P^*$.

As stated in the text, $\sum_x \pi_P(x) \sum_{i=1}^N g(\overline{\mathbf{w}}_i(x)) = \sum_{i=1}^N \sum_x \pi_P(x) g(\overline{\mathbf{w}}_i(x))$: the expected sum of transformed capped well-being equals the sum of individuals' expected transformed capped well-being. And $\sum_x \pi_P(x) \sum_{i=1}^N \underline{\mathbf{w}}_i(x) = \sum_{i=1}^N \sum_x \pi_P(x) \underline{\mathbf{w}}_i(x)$: the expected sum of bottomed well-being equals the sum of individuals' expected bottomed well-being.

Ex ante sufficientism works as follows: $P \succcurlyeq^{E\text{-}P} P^*$ iff $\mathbf{w}(P) \succcurlyeq^E \mathbf{w}(P^*)$.[64]

7.A.4 Uncertainty Modules for the Leximin SWF

In what follows, $\succcurlyeq^E$ denotes the leximin vector-ranking rule as stated in Section 1.A.4. *Ex ante leximin* ranks policies as follows: $P \succcurlyeq^{E\text{-}P} P^*$ iff $\mathbf{w}(P) \succcurlyeq^E \mathbf{w}(P^*)$.

Let $\mathbf{w}^+(P)$ be defined as follows: $\mathbf{w}_i^+(P) = \sum_x \pi_P(x) \hat{\mathbf{w}}_i(x)$, with $\hat{\mathbf{w}}(x)$, as above, the vector of well-being numbers for x reordered from smallest to largest. *Ex post leximin* ranks policies as follows: $P \succcurlyeq^{E\text{-}P} P^*$ iff $\mathbf{w}^+(P) \succcurlyeq^E \mathbf{w}^+(P^*)$.

64 Section 1.A.4.1 stated conditions for $\succ^E$ and $\sim^E$ for a sufficientist SWF. $\mathbf{w} \succcurlyeq^E \mathbf{w}^*$ iff ($\mathbf{w} \succ^E \mathbf{w}^*$ or $\mathbf{w} \sim^E \mathbf{w}^*$).

8
Beyond the Focal Case
Variable Population, Infant Deaths, and Psychological Impairments and Breaks

This book has presented a welfarist account of fatality risk regulation. The account, thus far, has been limited to the Focal Case: the population of ethical concern, those beings whose welfare is accorded ethical weight, consists of a fixed and finite population of OHPs (ordinary human persons).

Limiting the analysis to the Focal Case has enabled me to avoid the many complications and puzzles that arise when we move beyond that setup, and thereby to present a less tentative, more detailed analysis. But an account of fatality risk regulation for the Focal Case is hardly a *complete* account. First, the exclusion of non-human animals is substantively unwarranted—as I stated squarely in Chapter 1. How to integrate the lifetime well-being of OHPs with the well-being of non-human animals, in light of a utilitarian maximand or a prioritarian maximand, is an underexplored, vitally important, and difficult research question—one that this book doesn't attempt to address but that beyond doubt needs to be tackled.

Second, even with the ethical population limited to human beings, the Focal Case imposes further constraints. An OHP, recall, is a human being who lives long enough to acquire the array of psychological characteristics set forth in Section 1.1.2 (characteristics of typical adult humans that are jointly sufficient for personhood); after acquiring these characteristics, retains them until they (the being) dies; and does not suffer a break in intertemporal psychological continuity. The Focal Case posits that the set of worlds D being ranked is such that the human beings who exist in these worlds—the ethical population—consists of a fixed and finite population of OHPs.[1]

In this chapter, I consider how to relax the assumptions regarding the human population built into the Focal Case. Section 8.1 allows for a *variable* rather than fixed population of OHPs. The field of "population ethics," which engages the ethical questions that arise with respect to decisions that change

[1] See Section 1.1.5 for a more precise statement.

Risk, Death, and Well-Being. Matthew D. Adler, Oxford University Press. © Oxford University Press 2025.
DOI: 10.1093/9780197505984.003.0008

the number or identity of existing humans, is a thriving area of research within contemporary moral philosophy and welfare economics. The question addressed in Section 8.1 is how the account of risk regulation for the Focal Case should be developed once the fixed-population assumption is dropped—in other words, how that account should be extended so as to link up with the literature on population ethics.

Section 8.2 considers the problem of infant deaths. A fatality-risk-regulation policy might well be predicted to prevent some infant deaths. But if Rodney, a human being, dies in world *d* as an infant, Rodney in *d* is not an OHP. Assume that Rodney in *d* has no health conditions that would have prevented his becoming an OHP, had he survived. Still, Rodney in *d* is not an OHP (not at death and, a fortiori, not before). He either wholly lacks, or possesses only in rudimentary form, some of the personhood-conferring attributes of typical adult humans set out in Section 1.1.2. Imagine that Rodney, in some other world *d**, survives to adulthood. How should we compare the two worlds, in light of Rodney's well-being and that of other humans? Does *lifetime welfarism*—the applicable ethical framework for the Focal Case, or so I have argued—still apply here? Or is it Rodney's momentary well-being that matters in world *d*—since in that world he lacks the capacity to conceive of himself as existing over a whole lifetime and also lacks other psychological attributes that support lifetime rather than momentary welfarism in the case of OHPs?

Section 8.3 considers departures from the OHP premise that arise, not by virtue of infant deaths, but by virtue of psychological impairments or breaks. For example, some humans will experience dementia in old age. Others may be mildly psychologically disabled throughout their lives; others, profoundly disabled. In such cases, the human beings either for some portion of their lives or for their entire lifetimes may lack or not fully possess some of the psychological attributes of OHPs. In other cases (admittedly less frequent), e.g., a profound amnesia caused by an accident, intertemporal psychological continuity may be breached. Although fatality risk regulation policies are not designed to cure or ameliorate psychological impairments, let alone breaks in psychological continuity, it doesn't follow that an account of risk regulation can ignore impairments or breaks. Some of those whose lives are extended by risk-regulation policies will have these conditions—and we'll need to determine whether lifetime welfarism should be applied unmodified to value the risk-reduction benefit for these individuals, or should instead be modified in some way.

This chapter does *not* aspire to provide a detailed and fully defended analysis of the problems of variable population, infant deaths, and psychological impairments and breaks. Its aim is more modest: namely, to sketch out how the full-fledged, lifetime-welfarist account of risk regulation for the Focal Case that *has* been set forth in previous chapters is *plausibly extended* to cover these cases.

In sketching these extensions, I hope to allay a worry that readers of the first seven chapters of this book might have: the worry that limiting attention there to the Focal Case has distorted the analysis, in ways that emerge only once we attempt to generalize that analysis. No such distortion has occurred—or so this chapter hopes to show. How to fill in the many gaps in these sketches—like the problem of expanding the ethical population to include non-humans—is a task for future research.

8.1 Variable Population

In this section, I continue to assume that all humans are OHPs. (I'll therefore, as in earlier chapters, refer to these humans as "persons.") Moreover, I continue to assume that the population of existing humans in any given world is *finite*.[2] But the fixed-population premise is now dropped. **D**, our set of worlds to be ranked, is now such that there are persons who exist in some but not all of the worlds in **D**. Moreover, the size of the population may not be constant. There may be N individuals who exist in d but N^* in d^*, with $N \neq N^*$. These twin possibilities—variation in the identity of the individuals who exist and variation in population size—are the staples of contemporary scholarship on population ethics.[3] I'll use the term "variable-population," the title for this section, to cover both possibilities.

Well-being, throughout this section, is shorthand for "lifetime well-being."

I, the ethical population, now consists of everyone who exists in at least one of the worlds in **D**. Each person in **I** is denoted with a unique natural number. $\mathbf{I} = \{1, 2, \ldots\}$. **I** might be infinite, in which case it is the set of all natural numbers; or **I** might be finite, with N members. What follows covers both cases.

For simplicity, both in this section and in subsequent sections of this chapter, I'll assume that the lifetime well-being comparison structure is measurable and that the world-ranking is complete.[4] If so, each world corresponds to a vector, with the first slot for individual 1, the second for individual 2, etc. These vectors have an infinite number of slots (if **I** is infinite) or a finite number (if **I** is finite). I'll use the symbol "Ω" to indicate that an individual doesn't exist in a particular

[2] Ranking worlds with infinite populations poses many puzzles, which have generated a special subliterature. See Adler (2009, pp. 1511–19), citing sources. Scholarship on population ethics often circumvents these puzzles—as I will here—by positing a finite number of existing persons in any given world.

[3] That literature is vast. For a useful overview, see Greaves (2017). Major books and handbooks include Arrhenius (forthcoming); Arrhenius, Bykvist, Campbell, and Finneron-Burns (2022); Blackorby, Bossert, and Donaldson (2005); Broome (2004); and the foundational text in this field, Parfit (1987, pt. 4).

[4] These are the same assumptions adopted in the text of Chapter 1; see Section 1.3.2.

world; and "$w_i(d)$" to denote the well-being number of individual *i* in world *d*, if they exist there. Thus, the entry in the slot for individual *i* in the vector corresponding to world *d* is either $w_i(d)$ or Ω. To illustrate, suppose that I has 5 members. Let world *d* be such that individuals 1, 4, and 5 exist in *d*, at well-being levels 67, 30, and 100, respectively. Then the well-being vector corresponding to *d* is (67, Ω, Ω, 30, 100).

I'll discuss how the utilitarian and prioritarian world-rankings might be extended to the variable-population case; and how these variable-population extensions might be implemented in the SWF framework. Consider, first, utilitarianism. The fixed-population utilitarian world-ranking is the sum of well-being numbers. A variable-population extension of utilitarianism should be such that in ranking any two worlds in which the very same number of individuals exist, this is done according to the fixed-population rule (calculating the sum of well-being in each world by summing across the individuals who exist in that world). Call this the "basic constraint" on variable-population utilitarianism.

For example, assume that *d* corresponds to the vector (67, Ω, Ω, 30, 100) and d^* to the vector (50, Ω, Ω, 40, 100). The two vectors have the same number of individuals; thus, the basic constraint applies to the d/d^* ranking and in this case requires that *d* be ranked above d^*. The sum of well-being in *d* equals 67 + 30 + 100 = 197, while the sum of well-being in d^* equals 50 + 40 + 100 = 190; 197 > 190, and thus the basic constraint requires that *d* be ranked better than d^*. Similarly, if d^+ corresponds to (Ω, 50, 40, Ω, 100), the basic constraint applies to the d/d^+ ranking—although the same particular individuals do not exist in the two worlds, the same number of individuals do—and requires that *d* be ranked above d^+.

There are *many* variable-population extensions of utilitarianism. These use different formulas for ranking worlds; all the formulas satisfy the basic constraint, but they diverge in comparing worlds with different population sizes. A leading text on population ethics lists nine different possibilities, including four that are widely discussed—total utilitarianism, critical-level utilitarianism, average utilitarianism, and number-dampened utilitarianism—as well as others.[5]

Total utilitarianism and critical-level utilitarianism have a common structure. They are *summative*: Each world is assigned a score equaling the sum total of the well-being of each person who exists in that world, subtracting a constant each time. In the case of total utilitarianism, this constant is w^{NE}, the well-being number of a life equally good for well-being as non-existence; in the case of critical-level utilitarianism, this constant is w^{crit}, the well-being number of the critical-level life.[6] That is, the total-utilitarian world-ranking is as follows:

[5] Blackorby, Bossert, and Donaldson (2005, chs. 5–6).
[6] See Section 4.5.

$$\underline{\text{Total Utilitarian}}: d \succcurlyeq^E d^* \text{ iff } \sum_{i \in \mathbf{I}(d)} (\mathbf{w}_i(d) - w^{NE}) \geq \sum_{i \in \mathbf{I}(d^*)} (\mathbf{w}_i(d^*) - w^{NE})$$

The critical-level utilitarian world-ranking is as follows:

$$\underline{\text{Critical-level Utilitarian}}: d \succcurlyeq^E d^* \text{ iff } \sum_{i \in \mathbf{I}(d)} (\mathbf{w}_i(d) - w^{crit}) \geq \sum_{i \in \mathbf{I}(d^*)} (\mathbf{w}_i(d^*) - w^{crit})$$

In these formulas, $\succcurlyeq^E$ denotes the world-ranking (as in Section 1.3). "$d \succcurlyeq^E d^*$" should be read: "world d is at least as good as world d^*." $\mathbf{I}(d)$ is the set of individuals who exist in world d.

I'll use the novel term "summative variable-population utilitarianism" as the family of world-rankings that take the summative form of which total and critical-level utilitarianism are specific instances.[7]

Utilitarianism in the fixed-population context satisfies the Separability axiom. That axiom, generalized to the variable-population context, states the following:

> Variable Population Separability: Let d and d^* be such that one or more individuals has the same level of lifetime well-being in the two worlds. Then the d/d^* ranking is invariant to the well-being levels of these individuals and to their existence.[8]

Interestingly, and importantly, a variable-population extension of utilitarianism need not satisfy Variable Population Separability. Indeed, the summative variable-population utilitarian rankings are the *only* variable-population extensions of utilitarianism that do so.[9]

To see how a variable-population extension of utilitarianism can lack this feature, consider the average-utilitarian rule—ranking worlds according to the average level of well-being. As Table 8.1 illustrates, average utilitarianism fails Variable Population Separability.

There are very good reasons, I believe, that a variable-population extension of utilitarianism *should* satisfy Variable Population Separability. To see why, let

[7] Summative variable-population utilitarianism: $d \succcurlyeq^E d^*$ iff $\sum_{i \in \mathbf{I}(d)} (\mathbf{w}_i(d) - w^+) \geq \sum_{i \in \mathbf{I}(d^*)} (\mathbf{w}_i(d^*) - w^+)$, with w^+ some constant.

[8] Variable Population Separability is what Blackorby, Bossert, and Donaldson (2005, ch. 5) term "existence independence." See chapter appendix, Section 8.A.1, for a precise statement.

[9] This is a consequence of Bossert's (2022) theorem 3, in turn based on Blackorby, Bossert, and Donaldson (2005, ch. 6). The theorem assumes Variable-Population Separability (existence independence) plus anonymity, strong Pareto, and continuity (which would be true of any variable-population extension of utilitarianism) plus a very weak condition, "existence of at least one critical level."

Table 8.1 Average Utilitarianism and Variable Population Separability

	World d	World d^*	World d^+	World d^{++}	World d'	World d''
Antonio	Ω	30	Ω	30	Ω	30
Brayden	40	40	100	100	50	50
Cindy	10	10	60	60	Ω	Ω
average well-being	25	80/3	80	190/3	50	40

Explanation: In each of the world pairs (d/d^*, d^+/d^{++}, and d'/d''), Brayden and Cindy each have the same well-being levels in the two worlds or don't exist in both, while Antonio doesn't exist in the first world and is at level 30 in the second. Variable Population Separability therefore applies and requires that the d/d^* ranking be the same as the d^+/d^{++} and d'/d'' rankings. Average utilitarianism, however, ranks d^* over d but d^+ over d^{++} and d' over d''.

us return for a moment to the utilitarian uncertainty module for a fixed population set forth in Chapter 5. Recall that this module, the "simple-utilitarian" module, satisfied an axiom of Policy Separability (which in turn implied an axiom of Decomposability). These *tractability* axioms greatly eased the assessment of risk-regulation policies. The tractability axioms can be generalized to the variable-population case; I'll refer to the axioms thus generalized as Variable Population Policy Separability and Variable Population Decomposability;[10] the former implies the latter.

The utilitarian uncertainty module extended to the variable-population case should satisfy these tractability axioms. The argument for such axioms is just as strong in the variable-population case as in the fixed-population case. Instead of characterizing policies as probability distributions over whole outcomes, each policy can instead be characterized (much more simply) as a list of lotteries over attribute bundles—one such lottery for each affected person. Unaffected persons can be dropped from the analysis. (In the fixed-population case, recall, an individual is "unaffected" if they face the same lottery over bundles for all policies in the set of policies **P** being considered and is "affected" otherwise. In the variable-population case, a person is "unaffected" if they have the same probability of existence and same lottery over bundles conditional on existence for each policy in **P**; otherwise, the person is "affected.")[11]

Moreover, conforming to the tractability axioms in the fixed- but not variable-population case injects a jarring kind of discontinuity into a policy-assessment framework. Consider the following example, which illustrates what it would

[10] See chapter appendix, Section 8.A.2.
[11] See chapter appendix, Section 8.A.2.

mean for a utilitarian module to satisfy Policy Separability but not Variable Population Policy Separability. First, we evaluate policies that are modeled as having well-being impacts on the present generation and future generations but not as changing the number or identity of future individuals (thus, this is a fixed-population case). Past generations are unaffected; we may be uncertain what the well-being levels of dead individuals were, but we can be certain that our policy choice won't change those well-being levels. Policy Separability kicks in—allowing us to make our policy choice without needing to estimate the well-being levels of past generations. We can conceptualize each policy as a list of lotteries over bundles, one for each present and future individual. Past generations can be dropped from the analysis.

Second, we evaluate policies that are modeled *both* as having well-being impacts on the present and future generations, *and* as possibly changing the number or identity of future individuals (thus this is now a variable-population case). If Variable Population Policy Separability is now, *not* satisfied, we will need to take account of past generations; we will need to estimate their well-being levels. But past generations are unaffected in both the fixed- and the variable-population cases. Why would we adopt a policy-assessment methodology that permits us to ignore the well-being levels of dead individuals (past generations) if, but only if, we do not expect to affect the number or identity of future individuals?

The previous three paragraphs argued that the uncertainty module for a variable-population utilitarian world-ranking should satisfy the tractability axioms. But this in turn provides an argument for why the world-ranking itself should satisfy Variable Population Separability. A variable-population utilitarian world-ranking can't be implemented via an uncertainty module that satisfies the axiom of Variable Population Policy Separability unless the world-ranking conforms to the axiom of Variable Population Separability.[12]

The foregoing considerations, to my mind, constitute a strong argument for summative variable-population utilitarianism, since these are the *only* variable-population extensions of utilitarianism that satisfy Variable Population Separability. A counterargument could arise if the summative rules had unappealing implications on other fronts. The literature on population ethics has intensively discussed the desirable properties of variable-population world-rankings. (The literature demonstrates that no world-ranking has all of the

[12] The analysis here is isomorphic to that in the fixed-population case. See Section 5.A.1.2. If the ranking of policies satisfies Variable Population Policy Separability, then that will be true, specifically, for the ranking of degenerate policies. But to stipulate that the ranking of degenerate policies must conform to Variable Population Policy Separability entails that the ranking of outcomes must conform to an axiom of Variable Population Separability (the same as the world-level axiom, but stated at the level of outcomes). This in turn would be justified only if the world-ranking satisfies Variable Population Separability.

desirable properties—and so choices among them will need to be made.) Major candidates for the desirable properties include avoiding the "repugnant conclusion," avoiding the "sadistic conclusion," "negative mere addition," "mere addition," and "priority for lives worth living," as well as others.

However, it is not the case that the summative rules do significantly worse with respect to these properties than non-summative variable-population extensions of utilitarianism.[13] Thus the prima facie argument for the summative approach, grounded on Variable Population Separability, is not (to my mind) overcome by countervailing considerations.

We've been discussing variable-population extensions of the utilitarian world-ranking. A closely parallel analysis applies to variable-population extensions of *prioritarian* world-rankings. A fixed-population prioritarian world-ranking is the sum of *transformed* well-being numbers—transformed by some strictly increasing, strictly concave, and continuous function $g(\cdot)$. A variable-population extension of prioritarianism should satisfy the basic constraint: In ranking any two worlds in which the very same number of individuals exist, it should do so according to the fixed-population prioritarian rule (calculating the sum of transformed well-being in each world by summing across the individuals who exist in that world). There are many extensions that satisfy this constraint, each analogous to a variable-population extension of utilitarianism. The *summative* variable-population prioritarian rankings include total prioritarianism (the prioritarian counterpart to total utilitarianism) and critical-level prioritarianism (the counterpart to critical-level utilitarianism).[14] These rankings are as follows:

Total Prioritarian: $d \succcurlyeq^E d^*$ iff

$$\sum_{i \in \mathbf{I}(d)} (g(\mathbf{w}_i(d)) - g(w^{NE})) \geq \sum_{i \in \mathbf{I}(d^*)} (g(\mathbf{w}_i(d^*)) - g(w^{NE}))$$

Critical-level Prioritarian: $d \succcurlyeq^E d^*$ iff

$$\sum_{i \in \mathbf{I}(d)} (g(\mathbf{w}_i(d)) - g(w^{crit})) \geq \sum_{i \in \mathbf{I}(d^*)} (g(\mathbf{w}_i(d^*)) - g(w^{crit}))$$

Each world is assigned a score equaling the sum total of the transformed well-being of each person who exists in that world, subtracting a constant each time (either the transformed value of w^{NE} or the transformed value of w^{crit}).

[13] See Blackorby, Bossert, and Donaldson (2005, chs. 5–6).

[14] Summative variable-population prioritarianism: $d \succcurlyeq^E d^*$ iff $\sum_{i \in \mathbf{I}(d)} (g(\mathbf{w}_i(d)) - g(w^+)) \geq \sum_{i \in \mathbf{I}(d^*)} (g(\mathbf{w}_i(d^*)) - g(w^+))$, with w^+ some constant.

The summative rankings are the only variable-population extensions of prioritarianism that satisfy Variable Population Separability. The case set out above for summative variable-population utilitarianism, grounded on Variable Population Separability, therefore carries over mutatis mutandis to summative variable-population prioritarianism.

What about the choice *within* the class of summative rules—more specifically, the choice between *total* utilitarianism/prioritarianism, on the one hand, and *critical-level* utilitarianism/prioritarianism, on the other?[15] This choice is a significant and contested one, to be sure—but I will remain agnostic regarding it here. *Both* approaches can be implemented, via an SWF and uncertainty module, in a manner that smoothly generalizes the fixed-population account of utilitarianism and prioritarianism under uncertainty set forth in Chapter 5.

Let's turn, then, to that implementation. In the fixed-population context, I argued that utilitarianism and prioritarianism should be applied under uncertainty via the "simple utilitarian" and "ex post prioritarian" modules, respectively. These modules satisfy both the Dominance axiom[16] and the tractability axioms. The simple-utilitarian rule (the expected sum of individual well-being) can be restated as assigning a given policy P the following score, summing across affected individuals: $E^{SU}(P)=\sum_i\sum_b \rho_{P,i}(b)w(b)$—with $\rho_{P,i}(b)$ denoting the probability given P that individual i receives bundle b. The ex-post-prioritarian rule (the expected sum of individual transformed well-being) can be restated as assigning a given policy P the following score, summing across affected individuals: $E^{EPP}(P)=\sum_i\sum_b \rho_{P,i}(b)g(w(b))$. $E^{SU}(P)$ is the sum of affected individuals' expected well-being; $E^{EPP}(P)$, the sum of affected individuals' expected transformed well-being.

In the variable-population context, we can generalize the definitions as follows. Simple utilitarianism corresponds to a module for total utilitarianism, the *simple total-utilitarian* module, and a module for critical-level utilitarianism, the *simple critical-level-utilitarian* module. These rank policies according to the expected sum of individual well-being subtracting the well-being level of a life equally good as non-existence or the critical-level life, respectively. These modules have desirable axiomatic properties corresponding to those of simple utilitarianism in the fixed-population context—in particular, satisfying both Dominance and the tractability axioms. They can be restated as follows. The simple total-utilitarian module assigns each P the score

[15] Although other summative approaches exist (with w^+ as per notes 7 and 14 equaling some value other than either w^{NE} or w^{crit}), such approaches have little if any support within the literature on population ethics.

[16] See Sections 7.1–7.2, 7.A.1.

$E^{SU/T}(P)=\sum_i\sum_b \rho_{P,i}(b)[w(b)-w^{NE}]$, and the simple critical-level-utilitarian module assigns each P the score $E^{SU/C}(P)=\sum_i\sum_b \rho_{P,i}(b)[w(b)-w^{crit}]$, in each case summing over affected individuals.[17] $\rho_{P,i}(b)$ now denotes the probability that the individual exists and receives bundle b. Intuitively, the total formula is the sum of each affected individual's existence-adjusted expected well-being (expected well-being conditional on existence, discounted by the probability of not existing), as normalized by w^{NE}, the well-being of a bundle equally good as non-existence. The critical level formula is the same, except that we are now normalizing by w^{crit}, the well-being of the critical-level bundle.

Ex post prioritarianism corresponds to a module for total prioritarianism, the *ex post total-prioritarian* module, and a module for critical-level prioritarianism, the *ex post critical-level-prioritarian* module. These rank policies according to the expected sum of individual transformed well-being subtracting the transformed well-being level of a life equally good as non-existence or the critical-level life, respectively. These modules have desirable axiomatic properties corresponding to those of ex post prioritarianism in the fixed-population context—in particular, satisfying Dominance and the tractability axioms. The modules can be restated as follows. The *ex post total-prioritarian module* assigns each P the score $E^{EPP/T}(P)=\sum_i\sum_b \rho_{P,i}(b)[g(w(b))-g(w^{NE})]$, and the *ex post critical-level-prioritarian module* assigns each P the score $E^{EPP/C}(P)=\sum_i\sum_b \rho_{P,i}(b)[g(w(b))-g(w^{crit})]$, again summing over affected individuals. Intuitively, the total prioritarian formula is the sum of each affected individual's existence-adjusted expected *transformed* well-being, as normalized by $g(w^{NE})$, the transformed well-being of a bundle equally good as non-existence; and the critical-level prioritarian formula is the same, except that we are now normalizing by $g(w^{crit})$, the transformed well-being of the critical-level bundle.

The four variable-population modules I have been describing—simple total and critical-level utilitarianism, and ex post total and critical-level prioritarianism—can each be applied to fatality risk policies via an apparatus that generalizes the apparatus set out in Chapter 5, Section 5.2.1: assigning each currently existing individual an age, policy-specific risk profile, and policy-specific attribute profile (as in Chapter 5); and now assigning each currently

[17] So as to avoid complications that might arise with infinite sums, I'll assume that P is finite. Because each policy in P assigns a non-zero probability only to a finite number of outcomes, the total number of individuals who exist in at least one such outcome is finite. The affected individuals are a subset (proper or improper) of those. How to generalize this formula to allow for an infinite policy set is not something I'll address here.

non-existing individual a policy-specific existence-and-risk profile (a policy-specific probability of existence and, contingent on existence, risk profile) and policy-specific attribute profile. If *i* currently exists, this information determines *i*'s lottery over lifetime bundles with the policy; if *i* doesn't currently exist, it determines their probability of existence and, conditional on existence, lottery over lifetime bundles with the policy. Such information, in turn, suffices to determine the policy's values as per the four modules.

8.2 Infant Deaths

Within the literature regarding the "badness" of death, some philosophers have argued that the death of an infant is not as bad as the death of an older child. Jeff McMahan has been the leading expositor of this view, as per the "time-relative interest" account of the badness of death that McMahan originally set forth in *The Ethics of Killing* (2002).[18] As McMahan explains in a recent restatement:

> [The Time-Relative Interest Account] is based . . . on Derek Parfit's argument that the fact that an individual at an earlier time and an individual at a later time are the same individual (that is, that they are *identical*) is *not* what makes it rational for the former to care in an egoistic way about what may happen to the latter. The basis of such rational egoistic concern is instead the *relations* that are constitutive of our identity over time. [These are] psychological relations grounded in physical, functional, and organizational continuities in the brain, such as continuities of memory, character, desire, belief, and intention. Whereas identity is all-or-nothing, the relevant relations are matters of degree. . . .
>
> According to the account I have defended, the extent to which death is a misfortune at time *t* is a function primarily of two variables: (1) the amount of good life lost (which is the sole factor recognized by the Life Comparative Account) and (2) the strength of the relevant relations that would have held between the individual at *t* and himself at those later times at which the good things in his life would have occurred. . . . Because there would be virtually no psychological relations between a barely conscious 28-week-old fetus and itself as a child or adult, the misfortune it suffers in dying at 28 weeks may be negligible even though the amount of good life it loses is great. . . . Even though the fetus would have a much better life if it were not to die, its interest at the time (or "time-relative interest") in avoiding death is very weak.[19]

[18] McMahan (2002, pp. 165–88).
[19] McMahan (2019, pp. 117–18).

Others, especially the bioethicist Joseph Millum, have proposed similar views.[20] Millum defines "gradualism" as the family of accounts of the badness of death, exemplified by McMahan's views, "according to which how bad it is to die is a function of both the future goods of which the decedent is deprived and her cognitive development when she dies."[21] For a "gradualist," the badness of an individual's death for her can be calculated as follows:

> First, take the quantity of valuable life of which she is deprived by dying. Then multiply that amount by a fraction representing the degree to which she is connected to the future life she loses. This will be 1.0 for most adults and adolescents but less than 1.0 for fetuses and very young children.[22]

Gradualism gains support from common intuitions about the badness of death and about the appropriate allocation of lifesaving resources. As Millum and collaborators note: "People tend to think that it is more tragic for older children and young adults to die than for fetuses and infants to die. Many fewer social resources are invested into preventing fetal deaths than into preventing the deaths of people who have been born."[23]

The concept of the badness of death plays no role in lifetime welfarism, for reasons explained in Chapter 3. Still, in specifying lifetime welfarism for the case of infant deaths (the topic of this section), we should be sensitive to what motivates gradualism: to intuitions about the badness of infant versus child versus adult deaths, and to the psychological facts regarding the infant's development and connections to later stages of life that are the factual underpinnings of McMahan's and Millum's views.

In order to clarify how lifetime welfarism might accommodate a priority for older children over infants, it's useful to consider a highly stylized case. An infant (Ike) and older child (Ollie) face identical life paths conditional on survival. That is, in each given year of life (year 1, year 2, etc.), Ike's welfare-relevant characteristics if he is alive will be the same as Ollie's if *he* is alive. Further, the common life-path is such that lifetime well-being is increasing in longevity. Living 2 years on this path is better than living 1, 3 better than 2, and so forth. Finally, the common life path is good enough that lifetime well-being of any duration is above the well-being level of non-existence.

[20] See Millum (2015, 2019); Millum, Gamlund, Ngamasana, and Solberg (2020). Gamlund and Solberg (2019) is an edited volume on the topic of gradualism.
[21] Millum (2015, p. 279).
[22] Millum, Gamlund, Ngamasana, and Solberg (2020, p. 245).
[23] Millum, Gamlund, Ngamasana, and Solberg (2020, p. 245).

Ike and Ollie each now face certain death in the immediate future unless government intervenes, and it can save only one. Consider three, increasingly robust, versions of priority for the older child in the situation just described.

> Weak Priority for Ollie. Assume that both Ike and Ollie, if saved, will live for *Y* additional years (the same number in both cases) and will then die. If so, government should save Ollie.

For example, if Ike is 1 and Ollie is 10, Weak Priority for Ollie says that government should extend Ollie's life by 30 years so that he dies at age 40 rather than extending Ike's life by 30 years so that he dies at age 31.

> Moderate Priority for Ollie. Suppose that Ike and Ollie's common life path is such that annual well-being in each year of life, conditional on surviving that year, is constant. Assume that both Ike and Ollie, if saved, will live for *Y* additional years (the same number in both cases) and will then die. If so, government should save Ollie.

For example, if Ike is 1 and Ollie is 10, Moderate Priority for Ollie says that government should extend Ollie's life by 30 years rather than extending Ike's life by 30 years *even if* the annual well-being that each of the two reaps in every year of life is the very same value.

> Robust Priority for Ollie. Assume that both Ike and Ollie, if saved, will die at the same age *A*. If so, government should save Ollie.

For example, if Ike is 1 and Ollie is 10, and government's life-saving intervention would extend Ike's life to age 70 or Ollie's life to age 70, Robust Priority for Ollie says that government should save Ollie: it should extend Ollie's life by 60 years rather than extending Ike's by 69 years.

As discussed in Section 2.5, lifetime welfarism is most straightforwardly defined on the premise that the "age of integration" is zero. Any event during a human's life is incorporated into their lifetime well-being.

If the age of integration is zero, then the rules for ranking worlds in the case of a fixed and finite population of OHPs (the Focal Case)—the rules discussed in Chapter 1—apply unchanged to a fixed and finite population that includes some humans who die in infancy in some worlds. A human who dies in infancy is assigned a lifetime well-being value that takes account of everything that affects their well-being from birth until death (just like the OHP, who dies later in life) and figures into the ranking of worlds by virtue of this lifetime well-being.

Positing a zero age of integration, thus, has the advantage of simplicity—but has downsides with respect to a robust priority for saving older children and adults over infants, as can now be seen with reference to the Ike/Ollie case.

Lifetime welfarism with a zero age of integration is consistent with Weak Priority for Ollie. It is possible for such priority to hold true, in the stylized case under discussion, if we make appropriate assumptions about the common life-path; about how lifetime well-being depends upon the individual's characteristics when alive; and about the nature of the lifetime-welfarist world-ranking (i.e., whether it is utilitarian, prioritarian, etc.). In particular, assume that lifetime well-being is additive in annual well-being and that characteristics on the common life-path are such that annual well-being is increasing over the entire lifetime. Then lifetime utilitarianism with a zero age of integration endorses extending Ollie's life by a given number of years rather than Ike's.

Lifetime welfarism with a zero age of integration is also consistent with Moderate Priority for Ollie. It is possible for such priority to hold true with appropriate assumptions about the functional form of lifetime well-being and the world-ranking. In particular, assume that lifetime well-being is additive in age-weighted annual well-being. Annual well-being in a given year of life is multiplied by a weighting factor for that year; these values are then summed to determine lifetime well-being.[24] If the age weights are specified appropriately, then lifetime utilitarianism with a zero age of integration endorses extending Ollie's life by a given number of years rather than Ike's.

In short, neither Weak Priority for Ollie nor Moderate Priority for Ollie presents a challenge to lifetime welfarism with a zero age of integration. Both can be endorsed, within the confines of that view. By contrast, Robust Priority for Ollie *does* constitute a challenge to lifetime welfarism with a zero age of integration. Regardless of the shape of the common life path, functional form of lifetime well-being, and nature of the world-ranking (utilitarian, prioritarian, etc.), lifetime welfarism with a zero age of integration endorses saving Ike and thereby extending his life to age *A* rather than saving Ollie and thereby extending his life to the same age.[25] And this is exactly where gradualism enters

[24] The approach here is similar to the (now-discontinued) use of age-weighted DALYs (disability adjusted life years) in the Global Burden of Disease study, as described in Norheim (2019).

[25] Let d be the world in which Ike and Ollie each die now. Ike's lifetime well-being level in d is w, and Ollie's is w^*; w^* is a higher well-being level than w (by the assumption that lifetime well-being on the common life-path is increasing in longevity). Let w^+ be the lifetime well-being level of living on the common life-path to age A. w^+ is a higher well-being level than w^* (by the same assumption). Let d' be the world in which Ike dies now and Ollie lives to age A, and d'' the world in which Ollie dies now and Ike lives to age A. In d', Ike has lifetime well-being level w and Ollie w^+; in d'', Ike has lifetime well-being level w^+ and Ollie w^*; every other person has the same well-being level in d'' that they do in d' and d. By Lifetime Anonymity and Lifetime Strong Pareto, d'' is better than d', which in turn by Lifetime Strong Pareto is better than d.

the stage. Some will have the intuition that it *would* be better to extend the older child's life by fewer years rather than extending the infant's life by more. The gradualist accounts set forth by McMahan and Millum would recommend doing just this.

However, one can imagine a variation on lifetime welfarism that adopts a non-zero age of integration. In particular, as I'll now explain, critical-level utilitarianism or prioritarianism with a non-zero age of integration is consistent with Robust Priority for Ollie. Strong intuitions about priority for children or adults over infants in lifesaving can be accommodated by modifying lifetime welfarism without departing from welfarism; the modification remains a consequentialist view and, more specifically, a welfarist one.

Let $\mathbf{I}(d)$ denote the set of all human beings who exist in a given world d; and let $\mathbf{I}'(d)$, a subset thereof, denote all the humans who live long enough to reach the age of integration in d. In what follows, I use the term "individual" to denote a human being (who may or may not live long enough to acquire the characteristics of a person). For each individual who reaches the age of integration in d, let $\mathbf{w}_i(d)$ denote the lifetime well-being of the individual in that world, as calculated starting with the age of integration. (As discussed in Section 2.5, lifetime well-being defined to start at the age of integration might more accurately be termed "long-term well-being" if the age of integration is non-zero; but to avoid proliferating terminology I will refer to this value as "lifetime well-being.") For *every* individual who exists in d, let $\mathbf{h}_i(d)$ denote the pre-integration hedonic well-being of the individual. This term will be needed in the formulas below, because we will want to take account of pre-integration events that produce pains and pleasures for the human, even if those events are not incorporated into their lifetime well-being. The suffering of infant Rhonda at age 3 months surely matters for welfarists, even if we stipulate that Rhonda's lifetime well-being is determined only by events in her life starting at age 5. Most plausibly, $\mathbf{h}_i(d)$ is the sum total of the individual's momentary hedonic well-being over all pre-integration moments.

The following formulas take the formulas for critical-level utilitarianism and critical-level prioritarianism, set forth in Section 8.1, and generalize them to allow for a non-zero age of integration.

<u>Critical-level utilitarianism allowing for a non-zero age of integration</u>: $d \succsim^E d^*$ iff

$$\alpha \sum_{i \in \mathbf{I}'(d)} (\mathbf{w}_i(d) - w^{crit}) + (1-\alpha) \sum_{i \in \mathbf{I}(d)} \mathbf{h}_i(d) \geq \alpha \sum_{i \in \mathbf{I}'(d^*)} (\mathbf{w}_i(d^*) - w^{crit}) + (1-\alpha) \sum_{i \in \mathbf{I}(d^*)} \mathbf{h}_i(d^*)$$

Critical-level prioritarianism allowing for a non-zero age of integration: $d \succcurlyeq^E d^*$ iff

$$\alpha \sum_{i \in \mathbf{I}'(d)} (g(\mathbf{w}_i(d)) - g(w^{crit})) + (1-\alpha) \sum_{i \in \mathbf{I}(d)} \mathbf{h}_i(d)$$
$$\geq \alpha \sum_{i \in \mathbf{I}'(d^*)} (g(\mathbf{w}_i(d^*)) - g(w^{crit})) + (1-\alpha) \sum_{i \in \mathbf{I}(d^*)} \mathbf{h}_i(d^*)$$

In a nutshell, the formulas rank worlds according to scores equaling the weighted average of either critical-level-utilitarian or critical-level-prioritarian value (here taking account of individuals who survive past the age of integration) and total pre-integration hedonic well-being.

Some clarifications regarding these formulas are in order. (1) The formulas apply in both the fixed-population and the variable-population contexts. **D**, the set of worlds being ranked, may be such that the very same humans exist in all the worlds (fixed-population context); or, instead, **D** may be such that there are humans who exist in some but not all of the worlds (variable-population context). The crucial point is this: In either context, we sum up lifetime well-being or transformed lifetime well-being numbers, subtracting a constant each time for the critical-level life, *only* for the humans in **I**′(d)—the humans who live long enough to reach the age of integration. (2) The weighting factor α, 0 < α < 1, reflects the relative contribution of lifetime well-being and pre-integration hedonic well-being to the overall ethical value of a given world. (3) The formulas are agnostic about the nature of lifetime well-being. Although pre-integration well-being is hedonic, post-integration lifetime well-being, as throughout this book, can be understood in terms of hedonic states, other experiential states, objective goods, or preferences.[26] (4) In the prioritarian formula, prioritarian considerations come into play with respect to lifetime well-being but not with respect to pre-integration hedonic well-being. (5) The formulas allow for, but do not require, a non-zero age of integration. If the age of integration is zero, the second term in the formulas (adding up individuals' pre-integration hedonic well-being) becomes zero. (6) The formulas are *generalizations* of those given earlier. If the age of integration is zero, they rank worlds the same way as per the formulas in Section 8.1 for critical-level utilitarianism and prioritarianism; if the age of integration is zero *and* the same humans exist in all world (fixed-population context), the formulas rank worlds the same way as per the utilitarian and prioritarian formulas from Chapter 1.

As Table 8.2 shows, critical-level utilitarianism and critical-level prioritarianism with a non-zero age of integration are consistent with Robust Priority for Ollie.

[26] See Section 1.2.

Table 8.2 Robust Priority for Ollie: Critical-Level Utilitarianism and Prioritarianism

	Status Quo			
	Age of death	Pre-integration hedonic well-being	Post-integration lifetime well-being	Critical-level utilitarian score
Ike	1	1	___	
Ollie	10	5	5 × 3 = 15	
				$\alpha(15 - w^{crit}) + (1-\alpha)6$
	Save Ike			
	Age of death	Pre-integration hedonic well-being	Post-integration lifetime well-being	Critical-level utilitarian score
Ike	70	5	65 × 3 = 195	
Ollie	10	5	5 × 3 = 15	
				$\alpha(210 - 2w^{crit}) + (1-\alpha)10$
	Save Ollie			
	Age of death	Pre-integration hedonic well-being	Post-integration lifetime well-being	Critical-level utilitarian score
Ike	1	1	___	
Ollie	70	5	65 × 3 = 195	
				$\alpha(195 - w^{crit}) + (1-\alpha)6$

Explanation: Assume that the age of integration is 5. Each year of life pre-integration adds 1 unit of hedonic well-being. Each year of life post-integration adds 3 units to lifetime well-being. Being dead during a year adds 0 to hedonic well-being (if pre-integration) and lifetime well-being (if post-integration). The critical-level utilitarian score for Save Ike is $\alpha(210 - 2w^{crit}) + (1 - \alpha)10$, while the critical-level utilitarian score for Save Ollie is $\alpha(195 - w^{crit}) + (1 - \alpha)6$. The latter score is higher as long as $\alpha(195 - w^{crit}) + (1-\alpha)6 > \alpha(210 - 2w^{crit}) + (1-\alpha)10$. This is true if $\alpha(w^{crit} - 15) + (\alpha-1)4 > 0$, which will be true if $w^{crit} > 15$ and α is sufficiently close to 1.

In the case of critical-level prioritarianism (formulas not shown in table), Save Ollie will be preferred to Save Ike if $\alpha(g(w^{crit}) - g(15)) + (\alpha-1)4 > 0$ —so again if $w^{crit} > 15$ and α sufficiently close to 1.

We should also now note another possibility: total utilitarianism and total prioritarianism with a non-zero age of integration. These approaches do *not* endorse Robust Priority for Ollie.[27] However, they might be justified on other grounds. The welfarist who (a) holds a view of lifetime well-being that argues for a non-zero age of integration, (b) rejects the critical-level approach to population ethics, and (c) rejects Robust Priority for Ollie might endorse one of these formulas.

<u>Total utilitarianism allowing for a non-zero age of integration</u>: $d \succcurlyeq^E d^*$ iff

$$\alpha \sum_{i \in \mathbf{I}'(d)} (\mathbf{w}_i(d) - w^{NE}) + (1-\alpha) \sum_{i \in \mathbf{I}(d)} \mathbf{h}_i(d) \geq \alpha \sum_{i \in \mathbf{I}'(d^*)} (\mathbf{w}_i(d^*) - w^{NE}) + (1-\alpha) \sum_{i \in \mathbf{I}(d^*)} \mathbf{h}_i(d^*)$$

<u>Total prioritarianism allowing for a non-zero age of integration</u>: $d \succcurlyeq^E d^*$ iff

$$\alpha \sum_{i \in \mathbf{I}'(d)} (g(\mathbf{w}_i(d)) - g(w^{NE})) + (1-\alpha) \sum_{i \in \mathbf{I}(d)} \mathbf{h}_i(d) \geq \alpha \sum_{i \in \mathbf{I}'(d^*)} (g(\mathbf{w}_i(d^*)) - g(w^{NE})) + (1-\alpha) \sum_{i \in \mathbf{I}(d^*)} \mathbf{h}_i(d^*)$$

To summarize: Lifetime welfarism with a zero age of integration draws no distinction between the deaths of human infants and the deaths of older individuals. However, lifetime welfarism can, instead, be coupled with a non-zero age of integration. I've, specifically, written down four formulas that do so: critical-level utilitarianism, critical-level prioritarianism, total prioritarianism, and total utilitarianism, all allowing for a non-zero age of integration.[28]

Which approach should be adopted? I won't take a stand on that issue here. Both a zero and a non-zero age of integration are plausible routes for the lifetime

[27] Consider total utilitarianism with a non-zero age of integration (the analysis translates to total prioritarianism). Clearly, if Ike and Ollie are both above or both below the age of integration, Robust Priority for Ollie will not be satisfied. So let's assume (as in Table 8.2) that Ollie's current age is above the age of integration, while Ike's is below. Let w_A denote the lifetime well-being of a life that ends at age A on Ike's and Ollie's common life-path, and w_O the lifetime well-being of a life that ends at Ollie's current age, in each case calculated starting at the age of integration. Let Δh be the increase in pre-integration hedonic well-being from extending Ike's life to the age of integration. According to total utilitarianism with a non-zero age of integration, the increase in ethical value from extending Ollie's life to A is $\alpha(w_A - w_O)$, while the increase in ethical value from extending Ike's life to A is $\alpha(w_A - w^{NE}) + (1-\alpha)\Delta h$. We are assuming that the common life-path is such that lifetime well-being of any duration is better than non-existence. Thus $w_O > w^{NE}$. Leaving aside the possibility of a life path so bad that pre-integration hedonic well-being is negative, we have also that $\Delta h > 0$. Thus, the increase in ethical value from extending Ollie's life is less than the increase in ethical value from extending Ike's.

[28] See chapter appendix, Section 8.A.4, for discussion of a different kind of modification to lifetime welfarism that can endorse Robust Priority for Ollie, one that hews more closely in formal structure to Millum's gradualist analysis of the badness of death, rather than employing the age-of-integration concept.

welfarist to follow when we move beyond the Focal Case and confront the issue of infant deaths. The chief aim of this section has been to show that both routes are available to the lifetime welfarist.

Weighing in favor of a zero age of integration would be a well-being account that sees no qualitative welfare-relevant difference between the psychology of infants and older humans. In particular, adopting a hedonic account of the lifetime well-being of an OHP would weigh in favor of a zero age of integration. On such an account, what determines the lifetime well-being of a human who dies at any age is that individual's pains and pleasures over their lifetime; but infants have pains and pleasures too; and so there is nothing in the account of well-being that identifies a developmental break-point separating infants from older humans.

Weighing in favor of a non-zero age of integration would be a number of factors. (1) The Well-Being Account. Adopting a well-being account that *does* see a qualitative welfare-relevant distinction between the psychology of infants and older humans would suggest a non-zero age of integration. An objective-good account may well include goods that infants are unable to realize. A preference account (specifically one that sees well-being as the realization of global preferences)[29] would also tend to see infants and older humans as differently situated: infants don't have the psychology to have global preferences, let alone to act on such preferences or to refine global preferences through a process of deliberation (as some preference theories require).

(2) Prioritarianism and Compensation. According to lifetime prioritarianism, the ethical weight of an increment to an adult human's well-being depends on their level of lifetime well-being. This level, in turn, is determined by *everything* that occurs in their life after the age of integration. But it seems counterintuitive that events during infancy can affect the ethical weight of an increment to adult well-being. Imagine that Max and Dahlia are each now 50 years old and have had equally good lives since the age of two. Max suffered from various acute health conditions during his first two years of life, which caused him much pain and distress. Dahlia had a relatively pain-free infancy. Lifetime prioritarianism with a zero age of integration implies that someone in a position to deliver a well-being benefit now to Dahlia or Max should choose Max. Dahlia has been *compensated* for the non-receipt of the benefit now by her less painful infancy. This is counterintuitive because Max and Dahlia now, as adults, have no memory of their infancies. They have no memory of the events that give Max a stronger claim to the current benefit. And this lack of memory isn't happenstance; infant psychology and human development are such that adults don't remember infancy.[30]

[29] See Section 1.2.1.
[30] See Bremner and Wachs (2010, p. 289).

To be sure, the prioritarian intuitions here against a zero age of integration might be rejected. While Dahlia can't remember the events in her infancy that compensate her for the non-receipt of the benefit, she *can* learn about those events (her parents or other adults who knew her in infancy can tell her about them); she can perceive those events as part of her life (Dahlia now has autonoetic consciousness)[31]; and so she can perceive the events as compensatory.

(3) Priority for Saving Older Children. Intuitions in favor of a robust priority for older children over infants with respect to lifesaving (as crystallized by the Ike/Ollie case) would weigh in favor of a non-zero age of integration.[32]

If the age of integration isn't zero, what number should it be? That cutoff age would need to be specified by working through the various rationales for a non-zero cutoff just described. Millum, Gamlund, Ngamasana, and Solberg (discussing gradualism) argue that the facts of child development make it difficult to justify a discount for the badness of children's death past the age of five.

> By age 5 a normally developing child understands the past, present, and future; has permanent memories; can distinguish fantasy from reality (and

[31] See Section 1.1.2.

[32] Two objections might be leveled against using critical-level utilitarianism or prioritarianism with a non-zero age of integration to account for a robust priority for saving older children. First, this approach will in some cases recommend against extending the life of an infant from pre-integration age l to post-integration age l^*, even if the time from l to the age of integration would have positive hedonic value and the lifetime well-being that accrues from the age of integration until l^* would be better than non-existence. (Let w^* denote the infant's lifetime well-being if their life is extended to age l^*, with $w^* > w^{NE}$; and let $\Delta h > 0$ denote their increase in pre-integration hedonic value from living past l to the age of integration. Then, as per the formulas in the text, life-extension reduces overall ethical value if $w^* + \frac{1-\alpha}{\alpha}\Delta h < w^{crit}$ in the utilitarian case and $g(w^*) + \frac{1-\alpha}{\alpha}\Delta h < g(w^{crit})$ in the prioritarian case.)

As the chapter appendix shows, a competing account of robust priority that sticks closer to Millum's gradualist analysis of the harm of death has a similar implication. See Section 8.A.4. Moreover, although proponents of critical-level approaches to population ethics *might* find this implication counterintuitive, the implication doesn't seem *more* counterintuitive than the core feature of critical-level approaches—namely, that they recommend against expanding the population by adding individuals whose lives would be worth living (above w^{NE}) but would be below the critical level (w^{crit}). Theorists willing to accept that core feature should accept the implication.

Second, the aim of critical-level approaches is to avoid the repugnant conclusion. But using the formulas $\alpha \sum_{i \in \mathbf{I}'(d)} (\mathbf{w}_i(d) - w^{crit}) + (1-\alpha) \sum_{i \in \mathbf{I}(d)} \mathbf{h}_i(d)$ or $\alpha \sum_{i \in \mathbf{I}'(d)} (g(\mathbf{w}_i(d)) - g(w^{crit})) + (1-\alpha) \sum_{i \in \mathbf{I}(d)} \mathbf{h}_i(d)$ to rank worlds is vulnerable to a *kind* of repugnant conclusion: that for every world in which there are N humans each of whom lives beyond the age of integration and achieves a high level of lifetime well-being, there is some sufficiently large number $M > N$ such that this world is *worse* than one in which M humans live short lives with barely positive hedonic value and die before the age of integration. Here, I would respond that a similar problem arises once welfarism is expanded (as it surely should be) to take account of the hedonic states of sentient non-human animals. A solution to *that* problem, if there is one, would also warrant modifications to the formulas above; this is a matter for future research.

> tell both true and fantastical stories); can form close friendships; may have interests that last for the rest of her life (such as music or sports); may be afraid of death; and can feel guilt, pride, and empathy. It is hard to see what the average 5-year-old lacks but the average adult has that could be relevant to how bad it is to die.[33]

These same developmental facts would tend to suggest that the age of integration is not plausibly set above five years.

How would utilitarianism and prioritarianism with a non-zero age of integration be implemented, via the SWF framework, to yield a procedure for ranking policies? The policy-ranking formulas are smooth generalizations of the formulas I presented earlier with a zero age of integration, namely, simple utilitarianism and ex post prioritarianism. Dominance and the tractability axioms continue to be satisfied.[34]

Before concluding the discussion of infant deaths, let me return to the issue of "animalism" versus "personalism" covered in Chapter 1, Section 1.1.4. Animalists and personalists disagree about the essential characteristics of human persons: the characteristics that each such being possesses from the very beginning of its existence, and cannot lose without ceasing to exist. Animalists posit that human persons are essentially a certain kind of animal (a human animal) and only contingently persons; personalists posit that human persons are essentially persons.

This book adopts the animalist view. In justifying that choice, in Chapter 1, I observed that the appropriate individuation of beings depends upon our purposes. The purpose of *this* book is to elaborate an ethical theory grounded upon the welfare of human beings. Animalism is better suited for these purposes because it is both simpler and more flexible than personalism.

Animalism is simpler than personalism (for purposes of this book) because it involves fewer types of beings. A human animal, when it comes into existence at birth (which I use as shorthand for the point somewhere between conception and live birth at which the animal's existence starts), does not yet have psychological characteristics sufficient for personhood. Let's call the "age of personhood" the age when a human acquires those characteristics. Consider a given world *d*, with a population of humans some or all of whom live long enough to reach the age of personhood. According to the personalist approach, a given human who dies in world *d* at age *A*, above the age of personhood, falls into two

[33] Millum, Gamlund, Ngamasana, and Solberg (2020, p. 250).
[34] See chapter appendix, Section 8.A.3.

categories of beings. That human is both a particular human animal, who exists from birth to age *A*; and a particular human person, who comes into being when the animal reaches the age of personhood and ceases to exist when the animal dies, at age *A*. By contrast, according to animalists, there is but a single type of being in this scenario: the human animal.[35]

The personalist *could* simplify their typology of beings by ignoring what happens to humans before the age of personhood. The personalist could say that the only being of relevance in the case of a human animal who dies above the age of personhood is the human person. But welfarists can hardly follow *this* strategy. Although humans below the age of personhood lack some of the attributes that OHPs eventually acquire, they are still sentient and still have a welfare.

Animalism is also more flexible than personalism—and now, having fully discussed the age of integration, we are in a good position to see why. Animalism leaves open the choice between a zero and non-zero age of integration. In the first case, each being (human animal) is associated with a particular type of welfare characteristic that in turn is directly, ethically, relevant to the world-ranking: a lifetime well-being, encompassing everything that occurs from the birth of the animal until its death. In the latter case, each being is associated with either one or two types of welfare characteristics that are directly, ethically, relevant to the world-ranking: first, a pre-integration hedonic well-being; and second, if the being survives past the age of integration, a lifetime well-being that extends from integration until death.

Both approaches are fully consistent with animalism. Animalism is agnostic regarding the nature and number of the ethically relevant welfare attributes that arise as the human animal develops.

By contrast, personalism fits very awkwardly both with a zero age of integration and with a non-zero age of integration that is below the age of personhood. Abe, the human animal, lives until he dies at age *A*; at the age of personhood, a new being, Pete, pops into existence. Events in the life of Abe before the age of personhood are not events that occur in Pete's life. The personalist who nonetheless wishes to have those events included among the determinants of Pete's well-being will have seriously difficulty explaining how they can be.

[35] The discussion in the text assumes *perdurantist* personalism. By contrast, according to *endurantist* personalism, there would also be two beings, but in a different way: the human animal who exists from birth to the age of personhood, and the person who exists from the age of personhood until age *A*. Both perdurantist and endurantist animalism identify a single being. See Chapter 1, notes 18–19.

8.3 Psychological Impairments and Breaks

8.3.1 Psychological Impairments: Alzheimer's Disease

In what follows, I use the term "psychological impairment" (shortened to "impairment") as a term of art: to mean the absence of one or more of the psychological characteristics of typical adult humans that are jointly sufficient for personhood (the characteristics in Section 1.1.2), or having one or more of these characteristics in a diminished form. Impairments can, of course, arise in many different ways, with many different psychological profiles. I'll illustrate how an account of fatality risk regulation can be extended beyond OHPs by focusing on a particular impairment: Alzheimer's disease.

Alzheimer's disease is, unfortunately, quite common. In the United States, roughly 10% of the population above 65 has the disease.[36] Alzheimer's disease leads to dementia, which becomes increasingly severe as the illness progress. One overview describes four clinical stages of Alzheimer's disease, as follows.[37] Mild cognitive impairment due to Alzheimer's disease. At this stage, individuals experience "subtle symptoms such as problems with memory, language and thinking" which "may not interfere with the individual's ability to carry out everyday activities." Mild Alzheimer's dementia. At this stage, "most individuals are able to function independently in many areas but are likely to require assistance with some activities. . . . Declines in executive function can play out as difficulty planning, organizing and carrying out tasks, as well as poor judgment, socially inappropriate behavior, and inability to understand how one's behavior or choices affect others." Moderate Alzheimer's dementia. "In the moderate stage of Alzheimer's dementia, which is often the longest stage, individuals experience more problems with memory and language, are more likely to become confused, and find it harder to complete multistep tasks such as bathing and dressing. They may become incontinent at times, begin to have problems recognizing loved ones, and start showing personality and behavioral changes, including suspiciousness and agitation." Severe Alzheimer's dementia. "In the severe stage of Alzheimer's dementia, individuals' ability to communicate verbally is greatly diminished, and they are likely to require around-the-clock care. Because of damage to areas of the brain involved in movement, individuals may be unable to walk. . . . Damage to areas of the brain that control swallowing makes it difficult to eat and drink."

Alzheimer's patients in all stages are *sentient*. This is obviously true in earlier stages, but also (as far as we know) in the most severe stage.[38] At that stage, the

[36] Alzheimer's Association (2024, p. 3722).
[37] Alzheimer's Association (2024, pp. 3713–14).
[38] Huntley et al. (2021).

individual with Alzheimer's may lack an "I" concept but still is conscious, has perceptions, and feels pains and pleasures.

An account of fatality risk regulation clearly needs to grapple with Alzheimer's disease. A risk-regulation policy, by improving the annual survival probabilities of a given cohort of individuals, increases their chances of surviving to ages at which the prevalence of Alzheimer's is substantial. Those years lived at older ages may be years in which the individual's psychological attributes are unimpaired; but there is also a significant chance (given the prevalence of this condition) that the individual in those years will experience Alzheimer's disease and its associated impairments. We therefore need to grapple with how to value the welfare impact of those shortfalls.

The strategy I suggest for extending the analysis so as to take account of Alzheimer's disease is isomorphic to that for handling infancy. This is *not* to say that the loss of psychological capacities as the disease progresses tracks the gain of capacities as infants mature. The disease is not a mirror image of infant development; there is no isomorphism in that sense. What is isomorphic is the structure by which lifetime welfarism can take account of the disease—and of psychological impairments more generally.

The suggestion, specifically, is that the lifetime welfarist posit an impairment *threshold*, identifying cutoffs with respect to some or all of the psychological attributes set forth in Section 1.1.2. If the Alzheimer's patient is at a sufficiently severe stage of the disease that their characteristics lie below the threshold, events in their life are not integrated into their lifetime well-being but instead are accounted for by means of a separate hedonic value. This impairment threshold—demarcating between the final portion of an Alzheimer patient's life, which counts hedonically but not toward their lifetime well-being, and the earlier portions that do contribute to lifetime well-being—is analogous to the age of integration, which effects a parallel demarcation. A very low threshold would be *sentience*, which Alzheimer's patients would tend to reach only upon death; higher impairment thresholds would involve cutoffs with respect to sentience *and* some of the other Section 1.1.2 characteristics.

To be concrete, consider individual *i* ("Claudia"), who in a particular world *d* incurs Alzheimer's and dies at age 70. Consider four possibilities. (1) A zero age of integration and an impairment threshold set at sentience. If Claudia in *d* remains sentient until death, then she is assigned a lifetime well-being in *d*, $\mathbf{w}_i(d)$, which incorporates everything that occurs in her life from birth until death. (2) A non-zero age of integration equal to age 3, and an impairment threshold set above sentience, which Claudia reaches at age 68. Claudia's lifetime well-being in *d*, $\mathbf{w}_i(d)$, incorporates events in her life between the ages of 3 and 68. She is also assigned a hedonic well-being term, $\mathbf{h}_i(d)$, which is the sum of hedonic well-being over all moments before age 3 and starting again at age 68. (3) A zero age of integration, and an impairment threshold set above sentience, which Claudia reaches at age 68. Now, $\mathbf{w}_i(d)$ incorporates everything in Claudia's life until age 68, and $\mathbf{h}_i(d)$ sums hedonic well-being in Claudia's life starting at age 68. (4) A non-zero age of integration equal to 3, and an impairment threshold set at sentience. Now, $\mathbf{w}_i(d)$ incorporates everything in Claudia's life after she hits the age of integration, and $\mathbf{h}_i(d)$ sums hedonic well-being before that age.

The utilitarian and prioritarian world-ranking formulas remain the same as in the previous section. The only difference is that the $\mathbf{h}_i(d)$ term in these formulas for a given individual *i* includes *both* the hedonic well-being in their life before the age of integration (if that is non-zero), *and* the hedonic well-being in their life during later times when they are below the impairment threshold (if they hit that threshold before death). Application under uncertainty also remains the same.

The considerations weighing in favor of an impairment threshold set at sentience and countervailing considerations pointing to a higher threshold are similar, respectively, to those arguing for a zero versus a non-zero age of integration. Similar, but not identical. A hedonic account of the lifetime well-being of an OHP would weigh in favor of a sentience threshold (just as it weighs in favor of a zero age of integration). An objective-good account would weigh in favor of a higher threshold (since the goods posited by such accounts require a suite of capacities beyond sentience).

Considerations regarding prioritarianism and compensation would also cut in favor of a higher threshold. Assume that Daniel and Imani are the same age, and are both well into the moderately severe stage of the dementia caused by Alzheimer's disease. Both are sentient, but their autonoetic consciousness and memory are impaired. They intermittently have a sense of themselves as existing over time but remember little and are confused about the past. Prior to incurring the disease, Imani had a better life than Daniel. If the lifetime well-being term for each individual, $\mathbf{w}_i(d)$ for individual *i*, includes what happens to Daniel and Imani *now*, then (according to the prioritarian formula) Daniel takes priority over Imani with respect to a current well-being improvement. For example, if only one spot is open in a care home, Daniel should receive the spot. But Imani can't perceive herself as compensated for the loss of the spot by her past, since her sense of the past (let alone grasp of the concept of "compensation") is diminished.

Two important differences between the considerations regarding the age of integration and those regarding the impairment threshold should be noted. First, many people, deliberating about the possibility of Alzheimer's disease, have strong preferences regarding their care if the disease occurs. These preferences are reflected in individuals' advance directives (stipulating, for example, that life support be provided or not provided at the most severe stage of the disease), and in informal instructions to family members. These preferences are self-regarding. Rashid's pre-Alzheimer's preference regarding the care he should receive if he has the disease is about himself (the human animal Rashid) and motivated by a concern for his well-being. Rashid, pre-Alzheimer's, can act on this preference (by signing an advance directive, putting aside money for his care, etc.). These observations suggest that a preference account of well-being should set a low impairment threshold. What happens to someone during severe Alzheimer's can advance or frustrate the life plan that the individual formulated for that contingency and thereby promote or hinder their lifetime well-being—even though the individual at the severe Alzheimer's stage no longer has the preference or the capacity to act upon it.[39]

There is no parallel with respect to infancy. Adults *can* formulate retrospective preferences regarding what occurred in infancy. But they can't act on these preferences, nor can anyone else. Thus, a preference view seems to have a weaker rationale for a zero age of integration than for a low impairment threshold.

A second difference is that there seem to be widespread intuitions regarding the priority that older children should take over infants with respect to lifesaving efforts. These intuitions, animating the "gradualism" literature,[40] would also weigh in favor of a non-zero age of integration—as I noted earlier. There are not (as far as I'm aware) comparably widespread and firm intuitions regarding the relative priority of Alzheimer's patients and non-impaired persons of the same age with respect to lifesaving.

The strategy sketched here for reworking lifetime welfarism in light of Alzheimer's disease generalizes to any type of psychological impairment. A particular condition was chosen so as to add detail to the analysis; I selected Alzheimer's as that condition because of its prevalence and because its progressive nature encourages reflection about where the impairment threshold should be set.

8.3.2 Psychological Breaks: The Amnesiac

By a "break," I mean a radical interruption in intertemporal psychological continuity. Such breaks are unusual but can occur. Moreover, they pose special intellectual interest for any ethical theory grounded on human well-being over a lifetime—since psychological continuity over a lifetime is much discussed in the philosophical literature on personal identity.

39 Philosophical treatments of this topic include DeGrazia (2005, ch. 5); Dworkin (1993, ch. 8); Hawkins (2014); McMahan (2002, ch. 5).

40 See Section 8.2.

To orient the discussion, let's consider a specific, and extreme, case. Andy at age 50 has a serious car accident. He wakes up from a coma with relatively unimpaired capacities, but with no memories of his life before the accident, and with a very different personality, beliefs, and preferences.

Recall that OHPs are psychologically *continuous* in a manner famously conceptualized by Derek Parfit. A human at one time is "strongly connected" to themselves at another time if there are a sufficient number of direct connections between their mental states at the two times. (Examples of direct connections include having the same belief at both times; having the same preference at both times; having a memory at the later time of an event that was experienced at the earlier time.) A human at one time is psychologically continuous with themselves at an earlier time if there is an overlapping chain of strong connections between the two times.[41]

Andy, unlike an OHP, has experienced a break in day-to-day strong connectedness and, thus, a break in psychological continuity. There is no overlapping chain of strong connections linking Andy at any time after the accident to Andy at any time before.

Earlier, discussing the age of integration, I noted that an animalist account of the identity of humans was simpler and more flexible than a personalist account.[42] Andy's case also illustrates the relative flexibility of animalism, in a different way. Why? According to personalism, Andy before the accident and Andy afterward are two, distinct persons: two beings, each a person, and distinct from each other in virtue of the absence of psychological continuity. The personalist will therefore be impelled to incorporate events that occur to Andy before the accident into one well-being quantity (the lifetime welfare of one being, pre-accident Andy), and events that occur to Andy afterward into a different well-being quantity (the lifetime welfare of a different being, post-accident Andy).

By contrast, animalists see the relevant being as the human animal, Andy, who remains the same being from birth to death notwithstanding the psychological break. Animalists have the flexibility to handle Andy's case in a number of different ways—the two most salient alternatives being as follows. First, animalists can treat Andy the very same way as an OHP: assigning him a lifetime well-being that covers everything in his life from birth to death (leaving aside pre-integration events if the age of integration is non-zero). Second, and alternatively, animalists might handle Andy's case via *stage welfarism*. Stage welfarism separates a human life into temporal stages—each assigned its own well-being. Andy's life, if divided into stages, would consist of two (leaving aside

[41] See Section 1.1.3.
[42] See Section 8.2.

pre-integration events if the age of integration is non-zero): the pre-accident stage and the post-accident stage.

While personalism *mandates* stage welfarism in Andy's case, animalism *allows* but does not require it.

In Section 2.3, I criticized stage welfarism—meaning, there, the kind of stage welfarism that attempts to divide the life of an OHP into multiple stages. There is no non-arbitrary way to do this. But in Andy's case there *is* a non-arbitrary way; we can say, non-arbitrarily, that a break in psychological continuity starts a new stage. In the current discussion, by "stage welfarism" I mean the version of stage welfarism that uses psychological breaks to identify stages. Stage welfarism (thus defined) sees the entire lifetime of an OHP as a single stage. Stage welfarism reduces to lifetime welfarism for a population of OHPs, but diverges from lifetime welfarism once the population includes humans like Andy.

Critical-level and total utilitarianism and prioritarianism, applied to lifetime well-being numbers, have stage well-being counterparts. To illustrate, consider how critical-level *stage* utilitarianism with a zero age of integration and no impairment threshold would rank outcomes. It does so via the following formula:

Critical-level stage utilitarianism:

$$d \succcurlyeq^E d^* \text{ iff } \sum_{i \in \mathbf{I}(d)} \sum_{s=1}^{S_i(d)} (\mathbf{w}_i^s(d) - w^{s\text{-}crit}) \geq \sum_{i \in \mathbf{I}(d^*)} \sum_{s=1}^{S_i(d^*)} (\mathbf{w}_i^s(d^*) - w^{s\text{-}crit})$$

$\mathbf{I}(d)$ is the set of individuals who exist in world d; $S_i(d)$ is the total number of stages of individual i in outcome d; $\mathbf{w}_i^s(d)$ is individual i's stage well-being in d during stage s. This formula sums up stage well-being (across existing individuals and, for each individual, across all stages), subtracting the critical level of stage well-being, $w^{s\text{-}crit}$, each time. There are parallel formulas for critical-level stage prioritarianism, total stage utilitarianism, and total stage prioritarianism.

These formulas reduce to lifetime approaches in the case of a population of OHPs. (Again, for an OHP, a stage is a whole lifetime.) Extending the formulas to allow for a non-zero age of integration and/or an impairment threshold means adding a second term that accounts for pre-integration and/or sub-threshold hedonic well-being.

While stage welfarism is a *possible* way to handle Andy's case, I believe there are powerful arguments against it—favoring instead the lifetime approach whereby pre- and post-accident events are both absorbed into a single lifetime welfare value. Such an approach is supported by a hedonic account of well-being: pre- and post-accident pains and pleasures are the pains and pleasures of a single being, Andy (the human animal). They are arguably supported, too, by an objective-good account of well-being, on parallel grounds: the goods realized both pre- and post-accident are those of a single being, Andy.

It might seem that prioritarianism cuts in the other direction. Lifetime prioritarianism means that in deciding whether to confer a benefit upon Andy after the accident, or instead upon a different human (Balin), we take account of how well Andy's life was going before the accident. Yet Andy has no memory of that life. The inability of adults to remember infancy suggested that prioritarians should support a non-zero age of integration; if so, shouldn't prioritarians also support stage welfarism in Andy's case?

But stage prioritarianism has quite counterintuitive consequences. Imagine that Andy and Balin are now age 60. Assume that the decisionmaker is certain that each will die at age 80. Moreover, Andy's well-being in each year of life has been and will be roughly constant; the same is true for Balin; and this constant level is the same for the two individuals. (The difference between them is that Andy experienced a psychological break at age 50, while Balin is an OHP who has not and will not experience breaks.) Finally, there is Cleopatra, who is currently age 10 and will live until age 30, at the same year-to-year well-being level as the other two.

If lifetime and stage well-being are additive in annual well-being, stage prioritarianism will accord *substantial* priority to Andy over Balin with respect to a benefit that government is considering conferring upon one of the three individuals. He'll have the same priority vis-à-vis Balin as Cleopatra.[43] This seems problematic. Andy will live a much longer life than Cleopatra and with equally good years. Although the psychological break that Andy has suffered should perhaps result in *some* ethical priority for Andy over Balin, it shouldn't accord him the same priority as Cleopatra. In short: stage prioritarianism inflates the ethical significance of psychological breaks.

It might also seem that a preference view of well-being would support stage welfarism. After all, pre-accident and post-accident Andy have different preferences. But compare Andy to a counterpart, Andy*, who changes preferences at age 50 without a psychological break. The proponent of the preference view *could* take the position that a substantial change in preferences triggers a new stage even without a psychological break. Yet that position, combined with prioritarianism, has the problematic upshot that the occurrence of preference change confers *significant* ethical priority. Andy* would have the same priority vis-à-vis Balin (whose preferences don't change, let's assume) as Cleopatra.

If preference change without a psychological break doesn't trigger stage welfarism—as surely is the case—then it's not clear why stage welfarism should come into play with a break. Andy (who suffers the break) and Andy* may do equally well in acting on their preferences both before the age of 50, and

[43] This assumes stage prioritarianism with a zero age of integration. If the age of integration is non-zero, the example should be modified so that Cleopatra has currently lived 10 years past the age of integration and will die 30 years after that age.

thereafter. If Andy* doesn't take Cleopatra-like priority vis-à-vis Balin, why should Andy?

In short, I believe that lifetime welfarism is the best format for handling human populations of all kinds—both a population of OHPs (the Focal Case) and human populations that take us beyond the Focal Case. In the latter instance, we may need to modify lifetime welfarism by including a non-zero age of integration and/or an impairment threshold, but we shouldn't handle psychological breaks (let alone milder alterations in psychology over time, such as preference change) via stage welfarism.

That said, the summary critique of stage welfarism articulated in the last few paragraphs is hardly a decisive rebuttal. Animalism allows for both stage and lifetime welfarism; their respective pros and cons merit deeper analysis.

Chapter 8: Appendix

8.A.1 World-Rankings in the Variable-Population Case

See Section 1.A.4 for world-rankings in the fixed-population case. That analysis can be extended to the variable-population case as follows.

Let **D** be a set of worlds. d and variations (d^*, d^+, etc.) denote a member of **D**. **D** is such that for each d in **D**, every human who exists in d is an OHP in d, and there are a finite number of such individuals. **I**(d) is the set of individuals (OHPs) who exist in d; and **I**, the population, which may be finite or infinite, is the set of individuals (OHPs) each of whom exists in at least one of the worlds in **D**. The lifetime well-being comparison structure is defined essentially the same way as in the fixed-population case. **H** is the set of histories. $\mathbf{H} = \{(d; i): d \in \mathbf{D} \text{ and } i \in \mathbf{I}(d)\}$. The lifetime well-being comparison structure consists of a quasiordering on **H**, the well-being level quasiordering, denoted $\succcurlyeq^{L\text{-}\mathbf{D}}$; and a quasiordering on **H**×**H**, the well-being difference quasiordering, denoted $\succcurlyeq^{D\text{-}\mathbf{D}}$. (As in the fixed-population case, the structure also includes a ranking of history lotteries, but that will not figure here.)

$\succcurlyeq^{L\text{-}\mathbf{D}}$ and $\succcurlyeq^{D\text{-}\mathbf{D}}$ satisfy the same axioms as in the fixed-population case.[44] The "measurability" of the lifetime well-being comparison structure is also defined the same way as in the fixed-population case.[45] Given measurability, d has a corresponding well-being vector $\mathbf{w}(d)$. I'll use "$\mathbf{w}_i(d)$" to denote the entry in this vector for i if i exists in d, which in that case is equal to $w(d; i)$, i's well-being

[44] Namely, Linkage, Reversal, Difference Separability, Neutrality, and Concatenation.

[45] There exists a well-being measure (a real-valued function $w(\cdot)$ on the set of histories **H** associated with **D**) such that $w(h) \geq w(h^*)$ iff $h \succcurlyeq^{L\text{-}\mathbf{D}} h^*$; and $w(h) - w(h^*) \geq w(h^+) - w(h^{++})$ iff $(h, h^*) \succcurlyeq^{D\text{-}\mathbf{D}} (h^+, h^{++})$.

number in d. If i does not exist in d, the entry for i in $\mathbf{w}(d)$ is Ω, indicating i's non-existence.

$\succcurlyeq^{E\text{-}\mathrm{D}}$, the world-ranking, is a quasiordering on $\mathbf{D}$. (In the main text, $\succcurlyeq^{E\text{-}\mathrm{D}}$ is abbreviated as "$\succcurlyeq^{E}$".)

The axiom of Variable Population Separability is as follows.

Variable Population Separability: Let $\mathbf{M}$ be a subset of $\mathbf{I}$, and let $\mathbf{M}^+ = \mathbf{I} \setminus \mathbf{M}$ (all individuals not in $\mathbf{M}$). Assume d, d^*, d^+, d^{++} are as follows. For all $i \in \mathbf{M}$, $(d; i) \sim^{L\text{-}\mathrm{D}} (d^*; i)$ and either (a) $(d^+; i) \sim^{L\text{-}\mathrm{D}} (d^{++}; i)$ or (*b*) i exists in neither d^+ nor d^{++}. For all $j \in \mathbf{M}^+$: (1) j exists in d iff they exist in d^+, and if so $(d; j) \sim^{L\text{-}\mathrm{D}} (d^+; j)$; and (2) j exists in d^* iff they exist in d^{++}, and if so $(d^*; j) \sim^{L\text{-}\mathrm{D}} (d^{++}; j)$.

Then $d \succcurlyeq^{E\text{-}\mathrm{D}} d^*$ iff $d^+ \succcurlyeq^{E\text{-}\mathrm{D}} d^{++}$.

Variable Population Separability essentially corresponds to what Blackorby, Bossert, and Donaldson (2005, pp. 159–60) term "existence independence."[46]

With well-being measurability, Variable Population Separability can be stated thus:

Variable Population Separability: Let $\mathbf{M}$ be a subset of $\mathbf{I}$, and let $\mathbf{M}^+ = \mathbf{I} \setminus \mathbf{M}$ (all individuals not in $\mathbf{M}$). Assume d, d^*, d^+, d^{++} are as follows. For all $i \in \mathbf{M}$, $\mathbf{w}_i(d) = \mathbf{w}_i(d^*)$ and either (a) $\mathbf{w}_i(d^+) = \mathbf{w}_i(d^{++})$ or (*b*) i exists in neither d^+ nor d^{++}. For all $j \in \mathbf{M}^+$: (1) j exists in d iff they exist in d^+, and if so $\mathbf{w}_j(d) = \mathbf{w}_j(d^+)$; and (2) j exists in d^* iff they exist in d^{++}, and if so $\mathbf{w}_j(d^*) = \mathbf{w}_j(d^{++})$.

Then $d \succcurlyeq^{E\text{-}\mathrm{D}} d^*$ iff $d^+ \succcurlyeq^{E\text{-}\mathrm{D}} d^{++}$.

If the lifetime well-being comparison structure is measurable and $\succcurlyeq^{E\text{-}\mathrm{D}}$ is complete, $\succcurlyeq^{E\text{-}\mathrm{D}}$ can be expressed as follows (analogously to the fixed-population case). If $\mathbf{I}$ is finite, with N individuals, let $\mathbf{W}$ be the set of all N-entry vectors with either a real number[47] or Ω in each slot.[48] If $\mathbf{I}$ is infinite, $\mathbf{W}$ is the set of all such infinite vectors. Let $\succcurlyeq^{E}$ denote a complete quasiordering of $\mathbf{W}$. Then $\succcurlyeq^{E\text{-}\mathrm{D}}$ conforms to $\succcurlyeq^{E}$ as follows: $d \succcurlyeq^{E\text{-}\mathrm{D}} d^*$ iff $\mathbf{w}(d) \succcurlyeq^{E} \mathbf{w}(d^*)$.

The functional forms of $\succcurlyeq^{E\text{-}\mathrm{D}}$ for summative variable-population utilitarianism and prioritarianism—assuming well-being measurability and a complete

[46] Strictly, the axiom limited to prong (a) of the third sentence corresponds to what they call "utility independence," and the axiom limited to prong (b) corresponds to what they term "existence independence." However, existence independence implies utility independence with a sufficiently rich set of worlds. Blackorby, Bossert, and Donaldson (2005, pp. 159–60) demonstrate as much.

[47] Chosen from the real line or restricted to the positive, non-negative, negative, or non-positive real line.

[48] Excluding the vector with only Ω in every slot.

world-ranking—are given in the main text. It is clear that these rankings satisfy Variable Population Separability. The generalizations of these rankings to the case in which well-being is not measurable and/or the world-ranking is not complete will also do so.[49]

8.A.2 The SWF Framework in the Variable-Population Case

The SWF framework in the variable-population case has the same components as in the fixed-population case (see Section 1.4, 1.A.6), except as follows. $\mathbf{I}^{\text{Mod}}$, the set of notional individuals, is the finite or infinite set of individuals each of whom exists in at least one of the outcomes. $\mathbf{w}(x)$, the well-being vector corresponding to outcome x, is the finite vector (if $\mathbf{I}^{\text{Mod}}$ is finite) or infinite vector (if $\mathbf{I}^{\text{Mod}}$ is infinite) with Ω in the slot for i if i does not exist in x, and $\mathbf{w}_i(x) = w(b_i(x))$ if i exists in x. (Note that I'll use "$\mathbf{w}_i(x)$" to denote i's entry in $\mathbf{w}(x)$ only if i exists in x.) If $\mathbf{I}^{\text{Mod}}$ is finite, let N be its cardinality; if so, $\mathbf{W}$ is the set of all N-entry vectors with either a real number[50] or Ω in each slot.[51] If $\mathbf{I}^{\text{Mod}}$ is infinite, $\mathbf{W}$ is the set of all such infinite vectors. Finally, to simplify the mathematics, I assume that the policy set $\mathbf{P}$ is finite.

The SWF proper, $\succcurlyeq^E$, is a complete quasiordering of $\mathbf{W}$. An uncertainty module for $\succcurlyeq^E$ is a formula for arriving at a ranking of the policy set, $\succcurlyeq^{E\text{-}\mathbf{P}}$, as a function of the well-being vector associated with each outcome and the outcome probabilities.

For a given outcome x, let $\mathbf{I}(x)$ be the set of individuals who exist in x. $\mathbf{I}(\mathbf{P})$ is the set of individuals each of whom exists in at least one outcome to which some policy in $\mathbf{P}$ assigns non-zero probability.[52] $\mathbf{I}(x)$ is finite, because only a finite number of individuals exist in a given outcome; and $\mathbf{I}(\mathbf{P})$ is finite, because $\mathbf{P}$ is finite and each policy P is a finite probability distribution over possible outcomes.[53]

The Dominance axiom is the same as in the fixed-population case (see Section 7.A.1). The tractability axioms are as follows.

Let $L_{P,i}$ denote the lottery for individual i that results from policy P, giving i some probability of existence and, if in existence, probabilities of well-being levels. $L_{P,i}(\Omega)$ is i's probability of non-existence with P: $L_{P,i}(\Omega) = \sum_{x: i \notin \mathbf{I}(x)} \pi_P(x)$.

[49] Such generalizations should satisfy the constraints described in Section 1.A.4.2.
[50] Chosen from the real line or restricted to the positive, non-negative, negative, or non-positive real line.
[51] Excluding the vector with only Ω in every slot.
[52] Equivalently, if $\mathbf{O}(\mathbf{P})$ is the subset of the outcome set consisting of outcomes assigned a non-zero probability by at least one policy in $\mathbf{P}$, $\mathbf{I}(\mathbf{P})$ is the union of $\mathbf{I}(x)$ for every outcome x in $\mathbf{O}(\mathbf{P})$.
[53] On complications that arise in the variable-population context with infinite probability distributions, see Goodsell (2021).

Their probability of existence is, of course, just $1 - L_{P,i}(\Omega) = \sum_{x:i\in \mathbf{I}(x)} \pi_P(x)$. With v a real number, $L_{P,i}(v) = \sum_{x:\mathbf{w}_i(x)=v} \pi_P(x)$, i.e., $L_{P,i}(v)$ is the probability with policy P that individual i exists and attains well-being level v. $L_{P,i} = L_{P^*,i}$ indicates that i faces the same lottery with policies P and P^*, that is: $L_{P,i}(\Omega) = L_{P^*,i}(\Omega)$ and, for every real number v, $L_{P,i}(v) = L_{P^*,i}(v)$.

I can now state the tractability axioms for the variable-population case.[54]

Variable Population Decomposability: If $L_{P,i} = L_{P^*,i}$ for all i, then $P \sim^{E\text{-}P} P^*$.

Variable Population Policy Separability: Let $\mathbf{M}$ be a subset of $\mathbf{I}^{\text{Mod}}$, and let $\mathbf{M}^+ = \mathbf{I}^{\text{Mod}} \setminus \mathbf{M}$ (all individuals not in $\mathbf{M}$). Assume P, P^*, P^+, P^{++} are as follows. For all $i \in \mathbf{M}$, $L_{P,i} = L_{P^*,i}$ and $L_{P+,i} = L_{P++,i}$. For all $j \in \mathbf{M}^+$, $L_{P,j} = L_{P+,j}$ and $L_{P^*,j} = L_{P++,j}$. Then $P \succcurlyeq^{E\text{-}P} P^*$ iff $P^+ \succcurlyeq^{E\text{-}P} P^{++}$.

Variable Population Policy Separability implies Variable Population Decomposability (same proof strategy as in the fixed-population case), but not vice versa.

Finally, here are formulas for the four uncertainty modules mentioned in the text. Each assigns a given policy P a score using this formula and ranks policies in the order of these scores.

Simple Total Utilitarianism: $\sum_x \pi_P(x) \sum_{i\in \mathbf{I}(x)} (\mathbf{w}_i(x) - w^{NE})$

Simple Critical-Level Utilitarianism: $\sum_x \pi_P(x) \sum_{i\in \mathbf{I}(x)} (\mathbf{w}_i(x) - w^{crit})$

Ex Post Total Prioritarianism: $\sum_x \pi_P(x) \sum_{i\in \mathbf{I}(x)} (g(\mathbf{w}_i(x)) - g(w^{NE}))$

Ex Post Critical-Level Prioritarianism: $\sum_x \pi_P(x) \sum_{i\in \mathbf{I}(x)} (g(\mathbf{w}_i(x)) - g(w^{crit}))$

[54] The reader will note that these axioms are expressed using the very same words and symbols as their fixed-population counterparts (Decomposability and Policy Separability; see Section 5.A.1.1), but the content has changed—since "L" is now defined as above, to mean a lottery over existence and, if in existence, well-being.

Each of these formulas satisfies Expected Value Ethical Decisionmaking (see Section 7.A.1), and so it is immediate that the four modules satisfy Dominance.

In what follows, I show that simple total utilitarianism satisfies the tractability axioms; and that it can be restated as summing, across affected individuals, the expected value of each individual's bundle (as per the bundle formula given in the main text). This demonstration extrapolates straightforwardly to the other three modules.

The simple total-utilitarian score as given immediately above can be expressed as a summation across individuals. $\sum_x \pi_P(x) \sum_{i \in \mathbf{I}(x)} (\mathbf{w}_i(x) - w^{NE}) = \sum_{i \in \mathbf{I}(\mathbf{P})} \sum_{x: i \in \mathbf{I}(x)} \pi_P(x)(\mathbf{w}_i(x) - w^{NE})$. In turn, $\sum_{i \in \mathbf{I}(\mathbf{P})} \sum_{x: i \in \mathbf{I}(x)} \pi_P(x)(\mathbf{w}_i(x) - w^{NE}) = \sum_{i \in \mathbf{I}(\mathbf{P})} \sum_v L_{P,i}(v)(v - w^{NE})$. Thus simple total utilitarianism ranks policies according to the rule: $P \succcurlyeq^{E\text{-}\mathrm{P}} P^*$ iff $\sum_{i \in \mathbf{I}(\mathbf{P})} \sum_v L_{P,i}(v)(v - w^{NE}) \geq \sum_{i \in \mathbf{I}(\mathbf{P})} \sum_v L_{P^*,i}(v)(v - w^{NE})$. This reformulation makes it clear why simple total utilitarianism satisfies Variable Population Policy Separability (and hence Variable Population Decomposability).

Let $\rho_{P,i}(b)$ denote the probability that individual i exists and receives bundle b. $\rho_{P,i}(b) = \sum_{x: b_i(x) = b} \pi_P(x)$. ("$b_i(x)$" is the bundle of i in x if i exists there.). Then the simple total-utilitarian score assigned to each policy can be restated, once more, as follows: $\sum_{i \in \mathbf{I}(\mathbf{P})} \sum_b \rho_{P,i}(b)[w(b) - w^{NE}]$.

Finally, let **A(P)**, a subset of **I(P)**, denote the subset of *affected* individuals. An individual in **I(P)** is "unaffected" relative to **P** if they face the same probability of existence and same lottery over bundles conditional on existence for every policy in **P**; and they are "affected" if this is not the case. Let $E^{SU/T}(P) = \sum_{i \in \mathbf{A}(\mathbf{P})} \sum_b \rho_{P,i}(b)[w(b) - w^{NE}]$. The simple total-utilitarian module can be restated a final time as ranking policies according to $E^{SU/T}$ scores. $\sum_{i \in \mathbf{I}(\mathbf{P})} \sum_b \rho_{P,i}(b)[w(b) - w^{NE}] \geq \sum_{i \in \mathbf{I}(\mathbf{P})} \sum_b \rho_{P^*,i}(b)[w(b) - w^{NE}]$ iff $E^{SU/T}(P) \geq E^{SU/T}(P^*)$.[55]

[55] This is because $\sum_b \rho_{P,i}(b)(w(b) - w^{NE}) = \sum_b \rho_{P^*,i}(b)(w(b) - w^{NE})$ for any P and P^* if $i \notin \mathbf{A}(\mathbf{P})$.

Note that $\sum_b \rho_{P,i}(b)[w(b) - w^{NE}] = (1 - L_{P,i}(\Omega))\sum_b \left(\frac{\rho_{P,i}(b)}{(1 - L_{P,i}(\Omega))} \right)[w(b) - w^{NE}]$.[56]
Thus, as stated in the main text, $E^{SU/T}$ is the sum of affected individuals' existence-adjusted expected well-being (expected well-being conditional on existence, discounted by the probability of nonexistence), as normalized by w^{NE}.

8.A.3 The SWF Framework with a Non-Zero Age of Integration

In this portion of the appendix, I show how the simple total-utilitarian module generalizes to allow for a non-zero age of integration. (Parallel analyses apply to simple critical-level utilitarianism, ex post total prioritarianism, and ex post critical-level prioritarianism.)

I use the apparatus for the variable-population case set forth above in 8.A.2, modified as follows. Let $\mathbf{I}'(x)$, a subset of $\mathbf{I}(x)$, denote the individuals who exist in x and live long enough to reach the age of integration in x. In what follows, an individual's "bundle" means a combined bundle including all of their attributes, both pre- and post-integration; this simplifies the presentation. Let $h(b)$ denote the pre-integration hedonic well-being of the individual with bundle b; and let $\mathbf{h}_i(x) = h(b_i(x))$. Let $w(b)$ denote lifetime well-being with bundle b (defined only if the individual with bundle b reaches the age of integration, and if so calculated beginning at that age), and $\mathbf{w}_i(x) = w(b_i(x))$.

The simple total-utilitarian module with a non-zero age of integration assigns each policy P a score equaling $\sum_x \pi_P(x)\left(\alpha \sum_{i \in \mathbf{I}'(x)} (\mathbf{w}_i(x) - w^{NE}) + (1-\alpha) \sum_{i \in \mathbf{I}(x)} \mathbf{h}_i(x) \right)$.

This score is equal to: $\sum_{i \in \mathbf{I}(\mathbf{P})} \left(\alpha \sum_b \rho_{P,i}(b)[v(b)] + (1-\alpha) \sum_b \rho_{P,i}(b) h(b) \right)$, with $v(b) = 0$ if the individual with b does not reach the age of integration, and otherwise $v(b) = w(b) - w^{NE}$. This is the sum, across the individuals in $\mathbf{I}(\mathbf{P})$, of the weighted average of expected post-integration lifetime well-being (as normalized by w^{NE}) and expected pre-integration hedonic well-being.

[56] The formula $\sum_b \rho_{P,i}(b)[w(b) - w^{NE}]$ is defined if and only if $(1 - L_{P,i}(\Omega)) \neq 0$, i.e., i has a non-zero probability of existence with P—in which case dividing by $(1 - L_{P,i}(\Omega))$ is well-defined.

The Dominance axiom remains the same as in the fixed-population case. In order to restate the tractability axioms (Variable Population Decomposability and Variable Population Policy Separability) for this case, the concept of $L_{P,i}$ (the lottery for individual *i* that results from policy *P*) needs to be changed. $L_{P,i}$ is now a lottery that gives *i* a probability of existence and, if in existence, probabilities of *pairs* of lifetime well-being levels and pre-integration hedonic well-being levels. The tractability axioms are restated using lotteries thus conceived. It can be shown (although I will not do so here) that the simple total-utilitarian module with a non-zero age of integration, and the corresponding formulas for simple critical-level utilitarianism, ex post total prioritarianism, and ex post critical-level prioritarianism, satisfy the tractability axioms and Dominance.

8.A.4 The Multiplier Model for Gradualism

The gradualist intuition (as illustrated by "Robust Priority for Ollie" in the main text) is that it may be morally better to save an older child or adult from death, as opposed to an infant, even if the older child/adult and infant face identical life paths conditional on survival; life extension is beneficial; and the older/child adult and infant would live the same total lifespan if saved.

The text proposes an age-of-integration model for accommodating the gradualist intuition within lifetime welfarism. A different model sticks more closely to Joseph Millum's proposal (alone and with collaborators) that the badness of death for some individual is their loss of lifetime well-being from death multiplied by a number (the "multiplier") that is an increasing function of the age of death—increasing from 0 at birth to 1 at some age in childhood and remaining at 1 thereafter.[57] For short, call this the "multiplier model" for modifying lifetime welfarism, as contrasted with the age-of-integration model.

I'll illustrate the multiplier model using lifetime utilitarianism. It also applies in parallel fashion to lifetime prioritarianism.

Unlike the age-of-integration approach, which accommodates the gradualist intuition by endorsing a specific variable-population extension of utilitarianism (namely, critical-level utilitarianism), the multiplier approach is agnostic about variable-population questions. It can therefore be presented in a fixed-population framework.

[57] See Millum (2019); Millum, Gamlund, Ngamasana, and Solberg (2020). "Birth," for purposes of this book, is the point between conception and live birth when the human animal comes into existence. The specific proposal of Millum and collaborators is that the multiplier be set to 0 at 28 weeks gestational age.

Lifetime utilitarianism ranks worlds as follows: d at least as good as d^* iff $\sum_{i=1}^{N} \mathbf{w}_i(d) \geq \sum_{i=1}^{N} \mathbf{w}_i(d^*)$. Let v denote some benchmark level of lifetime well-being (which can be thought of as the lifetime well-being associated with a long lifespan at a high level of period well-being). The utilitarian rule can be restated as follows: d at least as good as d^* iff $\sum_{i=1}^{N}\left(v - \mathbf{w}_i(d)\right) \leq \sum_{i=1}^{N}(v - \mathbf{w}_i(d^*))$. In short, lifetime utilitarianism ranks worlds in inverse relation to the sum of the losses of individuals' lifetime well-being relative to a benchmark level. Note that the choice of benchmark level doesn't matter—yet. The world-ranking achieved by the formula above is invariant to the choice of v. It *will* matter once we modify the formula to include a multiplier.

Let $l_i(d)$ denote i's lifespan in world d. And let $\alpha(l)$ be a multiplier that behaves as Millum suggests. Multiplier-modified lifetime utilitarianism ranks worlds as follows: d at least as good as d^* iff $\sum_{i=1}^{N}\left(v - \mathbf{w}_i(d)\right)\alpha(l_i(d)) \leq \sum_{i=1}^{N}(v - \mathbf{w}_i(d^*))\alpha(l_i(d^*))$. It ranks worlds in inverse relation to the sum of *adjusted* losses of individuals' lifetime well-being relative to a benchmark level. Let k be the cutoff age above which the multiplier becomes 1. If individual i dies at or above age k in world d, their adjusted loss is equal to their loss. But if individual i dies below age k in d, their adjusted loss is *less* than their loss, since $\alpha(l) < 1$ for $l < k$. The loss of well-being from dying before the cutoff is adjusted downward for those who die sufficiently young.

As I'll show momentarily, the multiplier model, like the age-of-integration model, does indeed accommodate the gradualist intuition. One advantage of the multiplier model is that (as already mentioned) it is agnostic about variable-population questions. Conversely, an advantage of the age-of-integration model is its breadth: by positing that some stages of the life of a human being are channeled not into a lifetime well-being value but into a separate hedonic value, the model accounts not only for the gradualist intuition but also for the prioritarian intuition that events within infancy should not affect the ethical weight of an increment to adult well-being; and it offers a framework for handling psychological impairments to adults. The multiplier model lacks this breadth.

Let's turn to the implications of the multiplier model for lifesaving. To see them, imagine that two individuals face identical life paths conditional on survival. $w(l)$ is each individual's lifetime well-being if their longevity is l. Further, lifetime well-being is increasing in longevity: $w(\cdot)$ is strictly increasing.

One individual, the "infant," has longevity $l_c < k$ in the status quo; the second individual, the "adult," has longevity $l_a > k$ in the status quo. Imagine that we can extend the lifespan of either individual to $l^* > l_a > l_c$. The ethical value of extending the adult's life (the reduction in loss: the loss of dying at l_a minus the loss of dying at l^*) equals: $(v - w(l_a)) - (v - w(l^*)) = w(l^*) - w(l_a)$. The ethical value of extending the infant's lifespan (the reduction in *adjusted* loss: the adjusted loss of dying at l_c minus the loss of dying at l^*) equals: $\alpha(l_c)(v - w(l_c)) - (v - w(l^*)) = w(l^*) - \alpha(l_c)w(l_c) - v(1 - \alpha(l_c))$. Note that the ethical value of saving the infant may be less than saving the adult; thus the gradualist intuition is accommodated. This will be the case if $w(l_a) - \alpha(l_c)w(l_c) < v(1 - \alpha(l_c))$.

The multiplier model shares a counterintuitive feature with the age-of-integration model: extending the life of an infant to adulthood can have ethical disvalue. Consider extending the infant's longevity l_c to l^* in the case at hand. The ethical value of doing so will be negative if $w(l^*) - \alpha(l_c)w(l_c) < v(1 - \alpha(l_c))$.

But the multiplier model has an *additional* counterintuitive feature that doesn't affect the age-of-integration model: namely, extending the life of an infant so that they die at a later age in infancy can also have ethical disvalue. Imagine that the infant's life is extended to $l' < k$. The ethical value of doing so (the reduction in adjusted loss) equals: $(v - w(l_c))\alpha(l_c) - (v - w(l'))\alpha(l')$. This value is *negative* if $(v - w(l'))\alpha(l') > (v - w(l_c))\alpha(l_c)$. What is happening here is that the *smaller* loss that occurs in dying at an older age in infancy is multiplied by a *larger* adjustment factor, so that life extension has negative ethical value.

References

Adler, Matthew D. 2003. "Risk, Death and Harm: The Normative Foundations of Risk Regulation." *Minnesota Law Review* 87: 1293–1445.

Adler, Matthew D. 2009. "Future Generations: A Prioritarian View." *George Washington Law Review* 77: 1478–1520.

Adler, Matthew D. 2012. *Well-Being and Fair Distribution: Beyond Cost-Benefit Analysis*. New York: Oxford University Press.

Adler, Matthew D. 2013. "Happiness Surveys and Public Policy: What's the Use?" *Duke Law Journal* 62: 1509–1601.

Adler, Matthew D. 2016a. "Benefit-Cost Analysis and Distributional Weights: An Overview." *Review of Environmental Economics and Policy* 10: 264–285.

Adler, Matthew D. 2016b. "Extended Preferences." In Matthew D. Adler and Marc Fleurbaey, eds., *The Oxford Handbook of Well-Being and Public Policy*, pp. 476–517. New York: Oxford University Press.

Adler, Matthew D. 2017. "A Better Calculus for Regulators: From Cost-Benefit Analysis to the Social Welfare Function." Working paper, Duke Law School Public Law and Legal Theory Series No. 2017-19. https://papers.ssrn.com/sol3/papers.cfm?abstract_id=2923829.

Adler, Matthew D. 2018. "Prioritarianism: Room for Desert?" *Utilitas* 30: 172–197.

Adler, Matthew D. 2019a. "Cost-Benefit Analysis and Social Welfare Functions." In Mark D. White, ed., *The Oxford Handbook of Ethics and Economics*, pp. 399–422. Oxford: Oxford University Press.

Adler, Matthew D. 2019b. *Measuring Social Welfare: An Introduction*. New York: Oxford University Press.

Adler, Matthew D. 2020a. "Social Welfare Functions." In Ole F. Norheim, Ezekiel J. Emanuel, and Joseph Millum, eds., *Global Health Priority-Setting: Beyond Cost-Effectiveness*, pp. 123–141. New York: Oxford University Press.

Adler, Matthew D. 2020b. "What Should We Spend to Save Lives in a Pandemic? A Critique of the Value of Statistical Life." *CovidEconomics* 33: 1–45.

Adler, Matthew D. 2022a. "Claims across Outcomes and Population Ethics." In Gustaf Arrhenius, Krister Bykvist, Tim Campbell, and Elizabeth Finneron-Burns, eds., *The Oxford Handbook of Population Ethics*, pp. 320–349. New York: Oxford University Press.

Adler, Matthew D. 2022b. "Theory of Prioritarianism." In Matthew D. Adler and Ole Norheim, eds., *Prioritarianism in Practice*, pp. 37–127. Cambridge: Cambridge University Press.

Adler, Matthew D. 2025. "Narrowly Person-Affecting Axiology: A Reconsideration." *Economics and Philosophy* 41: 119–160.

Adler, Matthew D., Walter Bossert, Susumu Cato, and Kohei Kamaga. Forthcoming. "Ex-post Approaches to Prioritarianism and Sufficientarianism." *Theoretical Economics*.

Adler, Matthew D., and Koen Decancq. 2022. "Well-Being Measurement." In Matthew D. Adler and Ole Norheim, eds., *Prioritarianism in Practice*, pp. 128–171. Cambridge: Cambridge University Press.

Adler, Matthew D., Maddalena Ferranna, James K. Hammitt, and Nicolas Treich. 2021. "Fair Innings? The Utilitarian and Prioritarian Value of Risk Reduction over a Whole Lifetime." *Journal of Health Economics* 75: 102412.

Adler, Matthew D., and Marc Fleurbaey, eds. 2016. *The Oxford Handbook of Well-Being and Public Policy*. New York: Oxford University Press.

Adler, Matthew D., James K. Hammitt, and Nicolas Treich. 2014. "The Social Value of Mortality Risk Reduction: VSL versus the Social Welfare Function Approach." *Journal of Health Economics* 35: 82–93.

Adler, Matthew D., and Nils Holtug. 2019. "Prioritarianism: A Response to Critics." *Politics, Philosophy & Economics* 18: 101–144.

Adler, Matthew D., and Ole Norheim, eds. 2022. *Prioritarianism in Practice.* Cambridge: Cambridge University Press.

Adler, Matthew D., and Eric A. Posner. 2006. *New Foundations of Cost-Benefit Analysis.* Cambridge, MA: Harvard University Press.

Adler, Matthew D., and Nicolas Treich. 2015. "Prioritarianism and Climate Change." *Environmental and Resource Economics* 62: 279–308.

Aldy, Joseph E., and W. Kip Viscusi. 2007. "Age Differences in the Value of Statistical Life: Revealed Preference Evidence." *Review of Environmental Economics and Policy* 1: 241–260.

Al-Najjar, Nabil I., and Jonathan Weinstein. 2009. "The Ambiguity Aversion Literature: A Critical Assessment." *Economics and Philosophy* 25: 249–284.

Alzheimer's Association. 2024. "2024 Alzheimer's Disease Facts and Figures." *Alzheimer's and Dementia* 20: 3708–3821.

Andrić, Vuko, and Anders Herlitz. 2021. "Prioritarianism, Timeslices and Prudential Value." *Australasian Journal of Philosophy* 100: 595–604.

Arneson, Richard J. 1999. "Human Flourishing versus Desire Satisfaction." In Ellen Frankel Paul, Fred D. Miller, and Jeffrey Paul, eds., *Human Flourishing*, pp. 113–142. Cambridge: Cambridge University Press.

Arneson, Richard J. 2000. "Luck Egalitarianism and Prioritarianism." *Ethics* 110: 339–349.

Arneson, Richard J. 2006. "Desire Formation and Human Good." In Serena Olsaretti, ed., *Preferences and Well-Being*, pp. 9–32. Cambridge: Cambridge University Press.

Arneson, Richard J. 2007. "Desert and Equality." In Nils Holtug and Kasper Lippert-Rasmussen, eds., *Egalitarianism: New Essays on the Nature and Value of Equality*, pp. 262–293. Oxford: Oxford University Press.

Arrhenius, Gustaf. Forthcoming. *Population Ethics: The Challenge of Future Generations.* Oxford: Oxford University Press.

Arrhenius, Gustaf, Krister Bykvist, Tim Campbell, and Elizabeth Finneron-Burns, eds. 2022. *The Oxford Handbook of Population Ethics.* New York: Oxford University Press.

Baker, Lynne Rudder. 2000. *Persons and Bodies: A Constitution View.* Cambridge: Cambridge University Press.

Belshaw, Christopher. 2009. *Annihilation: The Sense and Significance of Death.* Durham: Acumen.

Berger, Loïc. 2022. "What Is Partial Ambiguity?" *Economics and Philosophy* 38: 206–220.

Bidadanure, Juliana Uhuru. 2021. *Justice across Ages: Treating Young and Old as Equals.* Oxford: Oxford University Press.

Blackorby, Charles, Walter Bossert, and David Donaldson. 2002. "Utilitarianism and the Theory of Justice." In Kenneth J. Arrow, Amartya K. Sen, and Kotaro Suzumura, eds., *Handbook of Social Choice and Welfare*, vol. 1, pp. 543–596. Amsterdam: Elsevier.

Blackorby, Charles, Walter Bossert, and David Donaldson. 2005. *Population Issues in Social Choice Theory, Welfare Economics, and Ethics.* Cambridge: Cambridge University Press.

Blatti, Stephan, and Paul F. Snowdon, eds. 2016. *Animalism: New Essays on Persons, Animals, and Identity.* Oxford: Oxford University Press.

Bleichrodt, Han, and John Quiggin. 1999. "Life-Cycle Preferences over Consumption and Health: When Is Cost-Effectiveness Analysis Equivalent to Cost-Benefit Analysis?" *Journal of Health Economics* 18: 681–708.

Boadway, Robin. 2016. "Cost-Benefit Analysis." In Matthew D. Adler and Marc Fleurbaey, eds., *The Oxford Handbook of Well-Being and Public Policy*, pp. 47–81. New York: Oxford University Press.

Boadway, Robin, and Neil Bruce. 1984. *Welfare Economics*. Oxford: Basil Blackwell.

Boardman, Anthony E., David H. Greenberg, Aidan R. Vining, and David L. Weimer. 2018. *Cost-Benefit Analysis: Concepts and Practice*. Fifth edition. Cambridge: Cambridge University Press.

Bognar, Greg. 2015. "Fair Innings." *Bioethics* 29: 251–261.

Boonin, David. 2019. *Dead Wrong: The Ethics of Posthumous Harm*. New York: Oxford University Press.

Bossert, Walter. 2022. "Anonymous Welfarism, Critical-Level Principles, and the Repugnant and Sadistic Conclusions." In Gustaf Arrhenius, Krister Bykvist, Tim Campbell, and Elizabeth Finneron-Burns, eds., *The Oxford Handbook of Population Ethics*, pp. 63–85. New York: Oxford University Press.

Bossert, Walter, Susumu Cato, and Kohei Kamaga. 2022. "Critical-level Sufficientarianism." *Journal of Political Philosophy* 30: 434–461.

Bossert, Walter, and John A. Weymark. 2004. "Utility in Social Choice." In Salvador Barberà, Peter J. Hammond, and Christian Seidl, eds., *Handbook of Utility Theory*, vol. 2 (*Extensions*), pp. 1099–1177. Boston: Kluwer Academic.

Bou-Habib, Paul. 2011. "Distributive Justice, Dignity, and the Lifetime View." *Social Theory and Practice* 37: 285–310.

Bowen, Joseph. 2022. "'But You Could Have Hurt Me!': Risk and Harm." *Law and Philosophy* 41: 517–546.

Botzen, W. J. Wouter, and Jeroen C. J. M. van den Bergh. 2014. "Specifications of Social Welfare in Economic Studies of Climate Policy: Overview of Criteria and Related Policy Insights." *Environmental and Resource Economics* 58: 1–33.

Bradley, Ben. 2009. *Well-Being and Death*. New York: Oxford University Press.

Bradley, Ben. 2015. *Well-Being*. Cambridge: Polity Press.

Bradley, Ben. 2016. "Well-Being and Death." In Guy Fletcher, ed., *The Routledge Handbook of Philosophy of Well-Being*, pp. 320–328. Milton Park: Routledge.

Bradley, Ben, Fred Feldman, and Jens Johansson. 2013. *The Oxford Handbook of Philosophy of Death*. New York: Oxford University Press.

Bramble, Ben. 2018. *The Passing of Temporal Well-Being*. Milton Park: Routledge.

Brandt, Richard B. 1979. *A Theory of the Right and the Good*. Oxford: Oxford University Press.

Bremner, J. Gavin, and Theodore D. Wachs, eds. 2010. *The Wiley-Blackwell Handbook of Infant Development*, vol 1. (*Basic Research*). Second edition. Chichester: Wiley.

Briggs, R.A. 2023. "Normative Theories of Rational Choice: Expected Utility." *Stanford Encyclopedia of Philosophy*. https://plato.stanford.edu/entries/rationality-normative-utility/.

Brink, David O. 1997. "Rational Egoism and the Separateness of Persons." In Jonathan Dancy, ed., *Reading Parfit*, pp. 96–134. Oxford: Blackwell.

Broome, John. 1991. *Weighing Goods: Equality, Uncertainty and Time*. Oxford: Blackwell.

Broome, John. 1999. "Goodness Is Reducible to Betterness: The Evil of Death Is the Value of Life." In John Broome, *Ethics out of Economics*, pp. 162–173. Cambridge: Cambridge University Press.

Broome, John. 2004. *Weighing Lives*. Oxford: Oxford University Press.

Brown, James L.D. 2019. "Additive Value and the Shape of a Life." *Ethics* 130: 92–101.

Bruckner, Donald W. 2019. "The Shape of a Life and Desire Satisfaction." *Pacific Philosophical Quarterly* 100: 661–680.

Brueckner, Anthony L., and John Martin Fischer. 1986. "Why Is Death Bad?" *Philosophical Studies* 50: 213–221.

Buchak, Lara. 2013. *Risk and Rationality*. Oxford: Oxford University Press.

Burri, Susanne. 2021. "The Option Value of Life." *Economics and Philosophy* 37: 118–138.

Bykvist, Krister. 2016. "Preference-Based Views of Well-Being." In Matthew D. Adler and Marc Fleurbaey, eds., *The Oxford Handbook of Well-Being and Public Policy*, pp. 321–346. New York: Oxford University Press.

Bykvist, Krister. 2024. "Wellbeing and Changing Attitudes across Time." *Ethical Theory and Moral Practice* 27: 429–443.

Chetty, Raj, et al. 2016. "The Association between Income and Life Expectancy in the United States, 2001–2014." *JAMA (Journal of the American Medical Association)* 315: 1750–1766.

Clark, Samuel. 2018. "Narrative, Self-Realization, and the Shape of a Life." *Ethical Theory and Moral Practice* 21: 371–385.

Cookson, Richard, Ole F. Norheim, and Ieva Skarda. 2022. "Prioritarianism and Health Policy." In Matthew D. Adler and Ole F. Norheim, eds., *Prioritarianism in Practice*, pp. 260–316. Cambridge: Cambridge University Press.

Cookson, Richard, et al. 2021. "Quality Adjusted Life Years Based on Health and Consumption: A Summary Wellbeing Measure for Cross-Sectoral Economic Evaluation." *Health Economics* 30: 70–85.

Crisp, Roger. 2003. "Equality, Priority, and Compassion." *Ethics* 113: 745–763.

Cropper, Maureen, James K. Hammitt, and Lisa A. Robinson. 2011. "Valuing Mortality Risk Reductions: Progress and Challenges." *Annual Review of Resource Economics* 3: 313–336.

d'Aspremont, Claude, and Louis Gevers. 2002. "Social Welfare Functionals and Interpersonal Comparability." In Kenneth J. Arrow, Amartya K. Sen, and Kotaro Suzumura, eds., *Handbook of Social Choice and Welfare*, vol. 1, pp. 459–541. Amsterdam: Elsevier.

Debreu, Gerard. 1954. "Representation of a Preference Ordering by a Numerical Function." In R. M. Thrall, C. H. Coombs, and R. L. Davis, eds., *Decision Processes*, pp. 159–165. New York: Wiley.

DeGrazia, David. 1996. *Taking Animals Seriously: Mental Life and Moral Status.* Cambridge: Cambridge University Press.

DeGrazia, David. 2005. *Human Identity and Bioethics.* New York: Cambridge University Press.

DeGrazia, David. 2014. "The Nature of Human Death." In Steven Luper, ed., *The Cambridge Companion to Life and Death*, pp. 80–97. Cambridge: Cambridge University Press.

Dolan, Paul, Rebecca Shaw, Aki Tsuchiya, and Alan Williams. 2005. "QALY Maximisation and People's Preferences: A Methodological Review of the Literature." *Health Economics* 14: 197–208.

Dorsey, Dale. 2013. "Desire-satisfaction and Welfare as Temporal." *Ethical Theory and Moral Practice* 16: 151–171.

Dworkin, Ronald. 1993. *Life's Dominion: An Argument about Abortion, Euthanasia, and Individual Freedom.* New York: Penguin Random House.

Dyer, James S. 2005. "MAUT—Multiattribute Utility Theory." In José Figueira, Salvatore Greco, and Matthias Ehrgott, eds., *Multiple Criteria Decision Analysis: State of the Art Surveys*, pp. 265–295. New York: Springer.

Dyer, James S., and Rakesh K. Sarin. 1979. "Measurable Multiattribute Value Functions." *Operations Research* 27: 810–822.

Eeckhoudt, Louis R., and James K. Hammitt. 2001. "Background Risks and the Value of a Statistical Life." *Journal of Risk and Uncertainty* 23: 261–279.

Eggleston, Ben, and Dale E. Miller, eds. 2014. *The Cambridge Companion to Utilitarianism.* Cambridge: Cambridge University Press.

Emanuel, Ezekiel J., et al. 2020. "Fair Allocation of Scarce Medical Resources in the Time of Covid-19." *New England Journal of Medicine* 382: 2049–2055.

Evans, Mary F., and V. Kerry Smith. 2010. "Measuring How Risk Tradeoffs Adjust with Income." *Journal of Risk and Uncertainty* 40: 33–55.

Fei, Song. 2019. "Rights against High-Level Risk Impositions." *Ethical Theory and Moral Practice* 22: 763–778.

Feinberg, Joel. 1993. "Harm to Others." In John Martin Fischer, ed., *The Metaphysics of Death*, pp. 171–190. Stanford: Stanford University Press.

Feldman, Fred. 1991. "Some Puzzles about the Evil of Death." *Philosophical Review* 100: 205–227.

Feldman, Fred. 1992. *Confrontations with the Reaper: A Philosophical Study of the Nature and Value of Death*. New York: Oxford University Press.

Feldman, Fred. 1995. "Adjusting Utility for Justice: A Consequentialist Reply to the Objection from Justice." *Philosophy and Phenomenological Research* 55: 567–585.

Ferranna, Maddalena, and Marc Fleurbaey. 2022. "Prioritarianism and Climate Change." In Matthew D. Adler and Ole Norheim, eds., *Prioritarianism in Practice*, pp. 360–407. Cambridge: Cambridge University Press.

Ferranna, Maddalena, James K. Hammitt, and Matthew D. Adler. 2023. "Age and the Value of Life." In David E. Bloom, Alfonso Sousa-Poza, and Uwe Sunde, eds., *The Routledge Handbook of the Economics of Ageing*, pp. 566–577. New York: Routledge.

Ferranna, Maddalena, J. P. Sevilla, and David E. Bloom. 2022. "Prioritarianism and the COVID-19 Pandemic." In Matthew D. Adler and Ole Norheim, eds., *Prioritarianism in Practice*, pp. 572–650. Cambridge: Cambridge University Press.

Ferreira, Francisco H. G., and Vito Peragine. 2016. "Individual Responsibility and Equality of Opportunity." In Matthew D. Adler and Marc Fleurbaey, eds., *The Oxford Handbook of Well-Being and Public Policy*, pp. 746–784. New York: Oxford University Press.

Finkelstein, Claire. 2003. "Is Risk a Harm?" *University of Pennsylvania Law Review* 151: 963–1001.

Finnis, John. 1988. *Natural Law and Natural Rights*. Reprint, with corrections. Oxford: Clarendon Press. First published in 1980.

Fischer, John Martin. 2006. "Earlier Birth and Later Death: Symmetry through Thick and Thin." In Kris McDaniel, Jason R. Raibley, Richard Feldman, and Michael J. Zimmerman, eds., *The Good, the Right, Life and Death: Essays in Honor of Fred Feldman*, pp. 189–201. Aldershot: Ashgate.

Fishburn, Peter C. 1982. *The Foundations of Expected Utility*. Dordrecht: Reidel.

Fletcher, Guy. 2016a. "Objective List Theories." In Guy Fletcher, ed., *The Routledge Handbook of Philosophy of Well-Being*, pp. 148–160. Milton Park: Routledge.

Fletcher, Guy, ed. 2016b. *The Routledge Handbook of Philosophy of Well-Being*. Milton Park: Routledge.

Fleurbaey, Marc. 2010. "Assessing Risky Social Situations." *Journal of Political Economy* 118: 649–680.

Fleurbaey, Marc. 2016. "Equivalent Income." In Matthew D. Adler and Marc Fleurbaey, eds., *The Oxford Handbook of Well-Being and Public Policy*, pp. 453–475. New York: Oxford University Press.

Fleurbaey, Marc. 2018. "Welfare Economics, Risk, and Uncertainty." *Canadian Journal of Economics* 51: 5–40.

Fleurbaey, Marc, and Rossi Abi-Rafeh. 2016. "The Use of Distributional Weights in Benefit-Cost Analysis: Insights from Welfare Economics." *Review of Environmental Economics and Policy* 10: 286–307.

Fleurbaey, Marc, and Didier Blanchet. 2013. *Beyond GDP: Measuring Welfare and Assessing Sustainability*. Oxford: Oxford University Press.

Fleurbaey, Marc, and Gregory Ponthiere. 2022. "The Value of a Life-Year and the Intuition of Universality." *Journal of Ethics and Social Philosophy* 22: 355–381.

Fleurbaey, Marc, and Alex Voorhoeve. 2013. "Decide as You Would with Full Information! An Argument against *Ex Ante* Pareto." In Nir Eyal, Samia A. Hurst, Ole F. Norheim, and Daniel Wikler, eds., *Inequalities in Health: Concepts, Measures, and Ethics*, pp. 113–128. New York: Oxford University Press.

Fleurbaey, Marc, and Stéphane Zuber. 2021. "Fair Utilitarianism." *American Economic Journal: Microeconomics* 13: 370–401.

Forcehimes, Andrew T., and Luke Semrau. 2019. *Thinking Through Utilitarianism: A Guide to Contemporary Arguments*. Indianapolis: Hackett.

Frankfurt, Harry G. 1971. "Freedom of the Will and the Concept of a Person." *Journal of Philosophy* 68: 5–20.

Franklin, Donald. 2022. "Respecting Equality in Economic Option Appraisal: Valuing the Time of Your Life." *Economics and Philosophy* 38: 419–449.

Frederick, Shane, George Loewenstein, and Ted O'Donoghue. 2002. "Time Discounting and Time Preference: A Critical Review." *Journal of Economic Literature* 40: 351–401.

Freeman III, A. Myrick, Joseph A. Herriges, and Catherine L. Kling. 2014. *The Measurement of Environmental and Resource Values*. Third edition. Milton Park: Taylor & Francis.

Frick, Johann. 2015. "Contractualism and Social Risk." *Philosophy and Public Affairs* 43: 175–223.

Friedman, Daniel, R. Mark Isaac, Duncan James, and Shyam Sunder. 2014. *Risky Curves: On the Empirical Failure of Expected Utility*. New York: Routledge.

Gamlund, Espen, and Carl Tollef Solberg, eds. 2019. *Saving People from the Harm of Death*. New York: Oxford University Press.

Gilboa, Itzhak. 2009. *Theory of Decision under Uncertainty*. Cambridge: Cambridge University Press.

Gilboa, Itzhak, Andrew Postlewaite, Larry Samuelson, and David Schmeidler. 2014. "Economic Models as Analogies." *Economic Journal* 124: F513–F533.

Gollier, Christian. 2001. *The Economics of Risk and Time*. Cambridge, MA: MIT Press.

Goodin, Robert E. 1995. *Utilitarianism as a Public Philosophy*. Cambridge: Cambridge University Press.

Goodsell, Zachary. 2021. "A St Petersburg Paradox for Risky Welfare Aggregation." *Analysis* 81: 420–426.

Gosseries, Axel. 2003. "Intergenerational Justice." In Hugh LaFollette, ed., *The Oxford Handbook of Practical Ethics*, pp. 459–484. Oxford: Oxford University Press.

Graham, Carol. 2016. "Subjective Well-Being in Economics." In Matthew D. Adler and Marc Fleurbaey, eds., *The Oxford Handbook of Well-Being and Public Policy*, pp. 424–450. New York: Oxford University Press.

Greaves, Hilary. 2017. "Population Axiology." *Philosophy Compass* 12: e12442.

Griffin, James. 1986. *Well-Being: Its Meaning, Measurement, and Moral Importance*. Oxford: Clarendon Press.

Griffin, James. 1996. *Value Judgement: Improving Our Ethical Beliefs*. Oxford: Clarendon Press.

Hájek, Alan. 2023. "Interpretations of Probability." *Stanford Encyclopedia of Philosophy*. https://plato.stanford.edu/entries/probability-interpret/.

Hamermesh, Daniel S., and Neal M. Soss. 1974. "An Economic Theory of Suicide." *Journal of Political Economy* 82: 83–98.

Hammerton, Matthew. 2020. "Relativized Rankings." In Douglas W. Portmore, ed., *The Oxford Handbook of Consequentialism*, pp. 46–66. New York: Oxford University Press.

Hammitt, James K. 2000. "Valuing Mortality Risk: Theory and Practice." *Environmental Science and Technology* 34: 1396–1400.

Hammitt, James K. 2007. "Valuing Changes in Mortality Risk: Lives Saved versus Life Years Saved." *Review of Environmental Economics and Policy* 1: 228–240.

Hammitt, James K. 2023. "Consistent Valuation of a Reduction in Mortality Risk Using Values per Life, Life Year, and Quality-Adjusted Life Year." *Health Economics* 32: 1964–1981.

Hammitt, James K., Peter Morfeld, Jouni T. Tuomisto and Thomas C. Erren. 2020. "Premature Deaths, Statistical Lives, and Years of Life Lost: Identification, Quantification, and Valuation of Mortality Risks." *Risk Analysis* 40: 674–695.

Hammitt, James K., and Nicolas Treich. 2022. "Prioritarianism and Fatality Risk Regulation." In Matthew D. Adler and Ole F. Norheim, eds., *Prioritarianism in Practice*, pp. 317–359. Cambridge: Cambridge University Press.

Hare, Richard M. 1981. *Moral Thinking: Its Levels, Method, and Point*. Oxford: Clarendon Press.

Harsanyi, John C. 1977. *Rational Behavior and Bargaining Equilibrium in Games and Social Situations*. Cambridge: Cambridge University Press.

Harsanyi, John C. 1982. "Morality and the Theory of Rational Behaviour." In Amartya Sen and Bernard Williams, eds., *Utilitarianism and Beyond*, pp. 39–62. Cambridge: Cambridge University Press.

Hasman, Andreas, and Lars Peter Østerdal. 2004. "Equal Value of Life and the Pareto Principle." *Economics and Philosophy* 20: 19–33.

Hausman, Daniel M. 2012. *Preference, Value, Choice, and Welfare*. New York: Cambridge University Press.

Hawkins, Jennifer. 2014. "Well-Being, Time, and Dementia." *Ethics* 124: 507–542.

Hawley, Katherine. 2014. "Persistence and Time." In Steven Luper, ed., *The Cambridge Companion to Life and Death*, pp. 47–63. Cambridge: Cambridge University Press.

Haybron, Daniel M. 2016. "Mental State Approaches to Well-Being." In Matthew D. Adler and Marc Fleurbaey, eds., *The Oxford Handbook of Well-Being and Public Policy*, pp. 347–378. New York: Oxford University Press.

Heathwood, Chris. 2016. "Desire-Fulfillment Theory." In Guy Fletcher, ed., *The Routledge Handbook of Philosophy of Well-Being*, pp. 135–147. Milton Park: Routledge.

Hemel, Daniel. 2022. "Regulation and Redistribution with Lives in the Balance." *University of Chicago Law Review* 89: 649–734.

Hicks, John R. 1939. "The Foundations of Welfare Economics." *Economic Journal* 49: 696–712.

Hirose, Iwao. 2005. "Intertemporal Distributive Judgment." *Ethical Theory and Moral Practice* 8: 371–386.

Hirose, Iwao. 2014. *Egalitarianism*. New York: Routledge.

HM Treasury. 2022. *The Green Book: Central Government Guidance on Appraisal and Evaluation*. www.gov.uk/official-documents.

Hoefer, Carl. 2007. "The Third Way on Objective Probability: A Sceptic's Guide to Objective Chance." *Mind* 116: 549–596.

Holtug, Nils. 2007. "Animals: Equality for Animals." In Jesper Ryberg, Thomas S. Petersen, and Clark Wolf, eds., *New Waves in Applied Ethics*, pp. 1–24. Houndmills: Palgrave Macmillan.

Holtug, Nils. 2010. *Persons, Interests, and Justice*. Oxford: Oxford University Press.

Holtug, Nils. 2017. "Prioritarianism." *Oxford Research Encyclopedia of Politics*. Oxford University Press.

Holtug, Nils. 2019. "Prioritarianism: Ex Ante, Ex Post, or Factualist Criterion of Rightness?" *Journal of Political Philosophy* 27: 207–228.

Horta, Oscar, Gary David O'Brien, and Dayron Teran. 2022. "The Definition of Consequentialism: A Survey." *Utilitas* 34: 368–385.

Horton, Joe. 2020. "Aggregation, Risk, and Reductio." *Ethics* 130: 514–529.

Huntley, Jonathan D., et al. 2021. "Understanding Alzheimer's Disease as a Disorder of Conciousness." *Alzheimer's and Dementia: Translational Research and Clinical Interventions* 7: e12203.

Hurka, Thomas. 2016. "Objective Goods." In Matthew D. Adler and Marc Fleurbaey, eds., *The Oxford Handbook of Well-Being and Public Policy*, pp. 379–402. New York: Oxford University Press.

Huseby, Robert. 2010. "Sufficiency: Restated and Defended." *Journal of Political Philosophy* 18: 178–197.

Huseynov, Samir, Marco A. Palma, and Rodolfo M. Nayga, Jr. 2020. "General Public Preferences for Allocating Scarce Medical Resources during COVID-19." *Frontiers in Public Health* 8: 587423.

Jeffrey, Richard C. 1990. *The Logic of Decision*. Second edition. Chicago: University of Chicago Press.

Johansson, Jens. 2013. "The Timing Problem." In Ben Bradley, Fred Feldman, and Jens Johansson, eds., *The Oxford Handbook of Philosophy of Death*, pp. 255–273. New York: Oxford University Press.

Johansson, Per-Olov. 2002. "On the Definition and Age-Dependency of the Value of a Statistical Life." *Journal of Risk and Uncertainty* 25: 251–263.

Jones-Lee, Michael, Susan Chilton, Hugh Metcalf, and Jytte Seested Nielsen. 2015. "Valuing Gains in Life Expectancy: Clarifying Some Ambiguities." *Journal of Risk and Uncertainty* 51: 1–21.

Joyce, James M. 1999. *The Foundations of Causal Decision Theory*. Cambridge: Cambridge University Press.

Joyce, James M., and Allan Gibbard. 1998. "Causal Decision Theory." In Salvador Barberà, Peter J. Hammond, and Christian Seidl, eds., *Handbook of Utility Theory*, vol. 1 (*Principles*), pp. 627–666. Dordrecht: Kluwer Academic.

Just, Richard E., Darrell L. Hueth, and Andrew Schmitz. 2004. *The Welfare Economics of Public Policy: A Practical Approach to Project and Policy Evaluation*. Cheltenham: Edward Elgar.

Kagan, Shelly. 1998. *Normative Ethics*. Boulder, CO: Westview Press.

Kagan, Shelly. 2012a. *Death*. New Haven: Yale University Press.

Kagan, Shelly. 2012b. *The Geometry of Desert*. Oxford: Oxford University Press.

Kagan, Shelly. 2019. *How to Count Animals, More or Less*. Oxford: Oxford University Press.

Kaldor, Nicholas. 1939. "Welfare Propositions of Economics and Interpersonal Comparisons of Utility." *Economic Journal* 49: 549–552.

Kamm, F. M. 1993. *Morality, Mortality*, vol. 1 (*Death and Whom to Save from It*). New York: Oxford University Press.

Kamm, F. M. 1996. *Morality, Mortality*, vol. 2 (*Rights, Duties, and Status*). New York: Oxford University Press.

Kaplow, Louis. 1996. "The Optimal Supply of Public Goods and the Distortionary Cost of Taxation." *National Tax Journal* 49: 513–533.

Kaplow, Louis. 2004. "On the (Ir)Relevance of Distribution and Labor Supply Distortion to Government Policy." *Journal of Economic Perspectives* 18: 159–175.

Kaplow, Louis. 2008. *The Theory of Taxation and Public Economics*. Princeton: Princeton University Press.

Kaplow, Louis, and Steven Shavell. 2002. *Fairness versus Welfare*. Cambridge, MA: Harvard University Press.

Kappel, Klemens. 1997. "Equality, Priority, and Time." *Utilitas* 9: 203–225.

Keller, Simon. 2014. "Posthumous Harm." In Steven Luper, ed., *The Cambridge Companion to Life and Death*, pp. 181–197. Cambridge: Cambridge University Press.

Keeney, Ralph L., and Howard Raiffa. 1993. *Decisions with Multiple Objectives: Preferences and Value Tradeoffs*. Cambridge: Cambridge University Press.

Killingsworth, Matthew A., Daniel Kahneman, and Barbara Mellers. 2023. "Income and Emotional Well-Being: A Conflict Resolved." *Proceedings of the National Academy of Science* 120: e2208661120.

King, Owen C. 2020. "The Good of Today Depends Not on the Good of Tomorrow: A Constraint on Theories of Well-Being." *Philosophical Studies* 177: 2365–2380.

Kniesner, Thomas J., and W. Kip Viscusi. 2019. "The Value of a Statistical Life." *Oxford Research Encyclopedia of Economics and Finance*. Oxford University Press.

Köbberling, Veronika. 2006. "Strength of Preference and Cardinal Utility." *Economic Theory* 27: 375–391.

Korsgaard, Chrstine M. 2018. *Fellow Creatures: Our Obligations to the Other Animals*. Oxford: Oxford University Press.

Krantz, David H., R. Duncan Luce, Patrick Suppes, and Amos Tversky. 2007. *Foundations of Measurement*, vol. 1 (*Additive and Polynomial Representations*). Mineola, NY: Dover. [First published in 1971 by Academic Press.]

Kraut, Richard. 2007. *What Is Good and Why: The Ethics of Well-Being*. Cambridge, MA: Harvard University Press.

Kreps, David M. 1988. *Notes on the Theory of Choice*. Boulder: Westview Press.

Kreps, David M. 2013. *Microeconomic Foundations I: Choice and Competitive Markets*. Princeton: Princeton University Press.

Krupnick, Alan. 2007. "Mortality-risk Valuation and Age: Stated Preference Evidence." *Review of Environmental Economics and Policy* 1: 261–282.

Kumar, Rahul. 2015. "Risking and Wronging." *Philosophy and Public Affairs* 43: 27–51.

Lenman, James. 2008. "Contractualism and Risk Imposition." *Politics, Philosophy & Economics* 7: 99–122.

Lazar, Seth. 2019. "Risky Killing: How Risks Worsen Violations of Objective Rights." *Journal of Moral Philosophy* 16: 1–26.

Lin, Eden. 2022a. "Well-Being, Part 1: The Concept of Well-Being." *Philosophy Compass* 17: e12812.

Lin, Eden. 2022b. "Well-Being, Part 2: Theories of Well-Being." *Philosophy Compass* 17: e12813.

Lippert-Rasmussen, Kasper. 2003. "Measuring the Disvalue of Inequality over Time." *Theoria* 69: 32–45.

Luper, Steven. 2009. *The Philosophy of Death*. Cambridge: Cambridge University Press.

Luper, Steven, ed. 2014. *The Cambridge Companion to Life and Death*. Cambridge: Cambridge University Press.

Luper, Steven. 2021. "Death." *Stanford Encyclopedia of Philosophy*. Available at https://plato.stanford.edu/entries/death/.

Maheshwari, Kritika. 2021. "On the Harm of Imposing Risk of Harm." *Ethical Theory and Moral Practice* 24: 965–980.

Marino, Lori, and Kristin Allen. 2017. "The Psychology of Cows." *Animal Behavior and Cognition* 4: 474–498.

Mas-Colell, Andreu, Michael D. Whinston, and Jerry R. Green. 1995. *Microeconomic Theory*. New York: Oxford University Press.

McCarthy, David. 2017. "The Priority View." *Economics and Philosophy* 33: 215–257.

McCarthy, David, Kalle Mikkola, and Teruji Thomas. 2020. "Utilitarianism with and without Expected Utility." *Journal of Mathematical Economics* 87: 77–113.

McKerlie, Dennis. 1989. "Equality and Time." *Ethics* 99: 475–491.

McKerlie, Dennis. 1992. "Equality between Age-Groups." *Philosophy and Public Affairs* 21: 275–295.

McKerlie, Dennis. 1997. "Priority and Time." *Canadian Journal of Philosophy* 27: 287–309.

McKerlie, Dennis. 2001a. "Dimensions of Equality." *Utilitas* 13: 263–288.

McKerlie, Dennis. 2001b. "Justice between the Young and the Old." *Philosophy and Public Affairs* 30: 152–177.

McKerlie, Dennis. 2007. "Egalitarianism and the Difference between Interpersonal and Intrapersonal Judgments." In Nils Holtug and Kasper Lippert-Rasmussen, eds., *Egalitarianism: New Essays on the Nature and Value of Equality*, pp. 157–173. Oxford: Clarendon Press.

McKerlie, Dennis. 2013. *Justice between the Young and the Old*. New York: Oxford University Press.

McMahan, Jeff. 2002. *The Ethics of Killing: Problems at the Margins of Life*. New York: Oxford University Press.

McMahan, Jeff. 2019. "Early Death and Later Suffering." In Espen Gamlund and Carl Tollef Solberg, eds., *Saving People from the Harm of Death*, pp. 116–133. New York: Oxford University Press.

Millum, Joseph. 2015. "Age and Death: A Defence of Gradualism." *Utilitas* 27: 279–297.

Millum, Joseph. 2019. "Putting a Number on the Harm of Death." In Espen Gamlund and Carl Tollef Solberg, eds., *Saving People from the Harm of Death*, pp. 61–75. New York: Oxford University Press.

Millum, Joseph, Espen Gamlund, Emery Ngamasana, and Carl Tollef Solberg. 2020. "Age and the Disvalue of Death." In Ole F. Norheim, Ezekiel J. Emanuel, and Joseph Millum, eds., *Global Health Priority-Setting: Beyond Cost-Effectiveness*, pp. 239–261. New York: Oxford University Press.

Mongin, Philippe, and Claude d'Aspremont. 1998. "Utility Theory and Ethics." In Salvador Barberà, Peter J. Hammond, and Christian Seidl, eds., *Handbook of Utility Theory*, vol. 1 (*Principles*), pp. 371–481. Dordrecht: Kluwer Academic.

Mongin, Philippe, and Marcus Pivato. 2016. "Social Evaluation under Risk and Uncertainty." In Matthew D. Adler and Marc Fleurbaey, eds., *The Oxford Handbook of Well-Being and Public Policy*, pp. 711–745. New York: Oxford University Press

Moreno-Ternero, Juan D., and Lars Peter Østerdal. 2023. "Entitlements to Continued Life and the Evaluation of Population Health." *Review of Economic Design* 27: 561–579.

Nagel, Thomas. 1979a. "Death." In *Mortal Questions*, pp. 1–10. Cambridge: Cambridge University Press.

Nagel, Thomas. 1979b. "Equality." In *Mortal Questions*, pp. 106–127. Cambridge: Cambridge University Press.

Nagel, Thomas. 1991. *Equality and Partiality*. New York: Oxford University Press.

Norheim, Ole F. 2019. "The Badness of Death: Implications for Summary Measures and Fair Priority Setting in Health Care." In Espen Gamlund and Carl Tollef Solberg, eds., *Saving People from the Harm of Death*, pp. 33–47. New York: Oxford University Press

Nurmi, Väinö, and Heini Ahtiainen. 2018. "Distributional Weights in Environmental Valuation and Cost-Benefit Analysis: Theory and Practice." *Ecological Economics* 150: 217–228.

O'Brien, David. 2019. "The Unit and Currency of Egalitarian Concern." *Journal of Moral Philosophy* 16: 613–643.

Oberdiek, John. 2017. *Imposing Risk: A Normative Framework*. Oxford: Oxford University Press.

OECD. 2012. *Mortality Risk Valuation in Environment, Health and Transport Policies*. Paris: OECD Publishing.

Olson, Eric T. 2007. *What Are We? A Study in Personal Ontology*. New York: Oxford University Press.

Olson, Eric T. 2014. "The Nature of People." In Steven Luper, ed., *The Cambridge Companion to Life and Death*, pp. 30–46. Cambridge: Cambridge University Press.

Olson, Eric T. 2023. "Personal Identity." Edward N. Zalta and Uri Nodelman, eds., *Stanford Encyclopedia of Philosophy*. https://plato.stanford.edu/entries/identity-personal/.

Otsuka, Michael. 2015. "Risking Life and Limb: How to Discount Harms by their Improbability." In I. Glenn Cohen, Norman Daniels, and Nir Eyal, eds., *Identified versus Statistical Lives: An Interdisciplinary Perspective*, pp. 77–93. New York: Oxford University Press.

Otsuka, Michael, and Alex Voorhoeve. 2009. "Why It Matters That Some Are Worse Off than Others: An Argument against the Priority View." *Philosophy and Public Affairs* 37: 171–199.

Otsuka, Michael, and Alex Voorhoeve. 2018. "Equality versus Priority." In Serena Olsaretti, ed., *The Oxford Handbook of Distributive Justice*, pp. 65–85. Oxford: Oxford University Press.

Parfit, Derek. 1986. "Comments." *Ethics* 96: 832–872.

Parfit, Derek. 1987. *Reasons and Persons*. Revised and corrected edition. Oxford: Oxford University Press. First published in 1984.

Parfit, Derek. 2000. "Equality or Priority?" In Matthew Clayton and Andrew Williams, eds., *The Ideal of Equality*, pp. 81–125. Houndmills: Palgrave. Delivered as the Lindley Lecture at the University of Kansas in 1991.

Parfit, Derek. 2012. "We Are Not Human Beings." *Philosophy* 87: 5–28.

Perry, Stephen R. 1995. "Risk, Harm, and Responsibility." In David G. Owen, ed., *Philosophical Foundations of Tort Law*, pp. 321–346. New York: Oxford University Press.

Perry, Stephen R. 2001. "Responsibility for Outcomes, Risk, and the Law of Torts." In Gerald J. Postema, ed., *Philosophy and the Law of Torts*, pp. 72–130. New York: Cambridge University Press.

Perry, Stephen. 2003. "Harm, History, and Counterfactuals." *San Diego Law Review* 40: 1283–1313.

Perry, Stephen. 2007. "Risk, Harm, Interests, and Rights." In Tim Lewens, ed., *Risk: Philosophical Perspectives*, pp. 190–209. New York: Routledge.

Perry, Stephen. 2014. "Torts, Rights, and Risk." In John Oberdiek, ed., *Philosophical Foundations of the Law of Torts*, pp. 38–64. Oxford: Oxford University Press.

Pinto-Prades, Jose-Luís, Carmen Herrero, and Jose María Abellán. 2016. "QALY-Based Cost-Effectiveness Analysis." In Matthew D. Adler and Marc Fleurbaey, eds., *The Oxford Handbook of Well-Being and Public Policy*, pp. 160–192. New York: Oxford University Press.

Placani, Adriana. 2017. "When the Risk of Harm Harms." *Law and Philosophy* 36: 77–100.

Portmore, Douglas W. 2007. "Welfare, Achievement, and Self-Sacrifice." *Journal of Ethics and Social Philosophy* 2 (2).

Portmore, Douglas W., ed. 2020. *The Oxford Handbook of Consequentialism*. New York: Oxford University Press.

Preston, Samuel H., Patrick Heuveline, and Michel Guillot. 2001. *Demography: Measuring and Modeling Population Processes*. Oxford: Blackwell.

Quinn, Warren. 1984. "Abortion: Identity and Loss." *Philosophy and Public Affairs* 13: 24–54.

Rawls, John. 1999. *A Theory of Justice*. Revised edition. Cambridge, MA: Harvard University Press. First published in 1971.

Reibetanz, Sophia. 1998. "Contractualism and Aggregation." *Ethics* 108: 296–311.

Renda, Andrea. 2011. *Law and Economics in the RIA World*. Cambridge: Intersentia.

Rimkeviciene, Jurgita, John O'Gorman, and Diego De Leo. 2015. "Impulsive Suicide Attempts: A Systematic Literature Review of Definitions, Characteristics, and Risk Factors." *Journal of Affective Disorders* 171: 93–104.

Robbins, Lionel. 1935. *An Essay on the Nature and Significance of Economic Science*. 2nd edition. London: Macmillan. First published in 1932.

Robeyns, Ingrid. 2017. *Well-Being, Freedom and Social Justice: The Capability Approach Reexamined*. Cambridge: Open Book Publishers.

Robinson, Lisa A., James K. Hammitt, and Lucy O'Keeffe. 2019. "Valuing Mortality Risk Reductions in Global Benefit-Cost Analysis." *Journal of Benefit-Cost Analysis* 10 (S1): 15–50.

Rosati, Connie S. 2013. "The Story of a Life." *Social Philosophy and Policy* 30: 21–50.

Roussos, Joe. 2022. "Modelling in Normative Ethics." *Ethical Theory and Moral Practice* 25: 865–889.

Rowe, Thomas. 2021. "Can a Risk of Harm Itself Be a Harm?" *Analysis* 81: 694–701.

Scanlon, T.M. 1998. *What We Owe to Each Other*. Cambridge, MA: Harvard University Press.

Segall, Shlomi. 2016. *Why Inequality Matters: Luck Egalitarianism, Its Meaning and Value*. Cambridge: Cambridge University Press.

Sharp, Daniel, and Joseph Millum. 2018. "Prioritarianism for Global Health Investments: Identifying the Worst Off." *Journal of Applied Philosophy* 35: 112–132.

Sher, George. 1997. *Beyond Neutrality: Perfectionism and Politics*. Cambridge: Cambridge University Press.

Shields, Liam. 2020. "Sufficientarianism." *Philosophy Compass* 15: e12704.

Shoemaker, Sydney. 2011. "On What We Are." In Shaun Gallagher, ed., *The Oxford Handbook of the Self*, pp. 352–371. Oxford: Oxford University Press.

Singer, Peter. 2011. *Practical Ethics*. Third edition. Cambridge: Cambridge University Press.

Sinnott-Armstrong, Walter. 2023. "Consequentialism." Edward N. Zalta and Uri Nodelman, eds., *Stanford Encyclopedia of Philosophy*. Available at https://plato.stanford.edu/entries/consequentialism/.

Song, Fei. 2019. "Rights against High-Level Risk Impositions." *Ethical Theory and Moral Practice* 22: 763–778.

Smart, J. J. C., and Bernard Williams. 1973. *Utilitarianism: For and Against*. Cambridge: Cambridge University Press.

Smith, James E., and James S. Dyer. 2021. "On (Measurable) Multiattribute Value Functions: An Expository Argument." *Decision Analysis* 18: 247–256.

Sugden, Robert. 2013. "How Fictional Accounts Can Explain." *Journal of Economic Methodology* 20: 237–243.

Sullivan, Meghan. 2018. *Time Biases: A Theory of Rational Planning and Personal Persistence.* Oxford: Oxford University Press.
Sumner, L. W. 1996. *Welfare, Happiness, and Ethics.* Oxford: Clarendon Press.
Tännsjö, Torbjörn. 1998. *Hedonistic Utilitarianism.* Edinburgh: Edinburgh University Press.
Tännsjö, Torbjörn. 2019. *Setting Health-Care Priorities: What Ethical Theories Tell Us.* New York: Oxford University Press.
Temkin, Larry. 1993. *Inequality.* New York: Oxford University Press.
Thoma, Johanna. 2019a. "Risk Aversion and the Long Run." *Ethics* 129: 230–253.
Thoma, Johanna. 2019b. "Decision Theory." In Richard Pettigrew and Jonathan Weisberg, eds., *The Open Handbook of Formal Epistemology*, pp. 57–106. The PhilPapers Foundation. https://jonathanweisberg.org/pdf/open-handbook-of-formal-epistemology.pdf.
Thoma, Johanna, and Jonathan Weisberg. 2017. "Risk Writ Large." *Philosophical Studies* 174: 2369–2384.
Timmerman, Travis. 2019. "A Dilemma for Epicureanism." *Philosophical Studies* 176: 241–257.
Timmerman, Travis. 2022. "Dissolving Death's Time-of-Harm Problem." *Australasian Journal of Philosophy* 100: 405–418.
Tuomala, Matti. 2016. *Optimal Redistributive Taxation.* Oxford: Oxford University Press.
US Office of Management and Budget. 2015. 2015 Report to Congress on the Benefits and Costs of Federal Regulations and Agency Compliance with the Unfunded Mandates Reform Act. https://obamawhitehouse.archives.gov/omb/inforeg_regpol_reports_congress/.
US Office of Management and Budget. 2016. 2016 Draft Report to Congress on the Benefits and Costs of Federal Regulations and Agency Compliance with the Unfunded Mandates Reform Act. https://obamawhitehouse.archives.gov/omb/inforeg_regpol_reports_congress/.
US Office of Management and Budget. 2017. 2017 Report to Congress on the Benefits and Costs of Federal Regulations and Agency Compliance with the Unfunded Mandates Reform Act. https://bidenwhitehouse.archives.gov/omb/information-regulatory-affairs/reports/.
US Office of Management and Budget. 2023. Circular No. A-4. https://bidenwhitehouse.archives.gov/wp-content/uploads/2023/11/CircularA-4.pdf.
Vallentyne, Peter. 2007. "Of Mice and Men: Equality and Animals." In Nils Holtug and Kasper Lippert-Rasmussen, eds., *Egalitarianism: New Essays on the Nature and Value of Equality*, pp. 211–237. Oxford: Oxford University Press.
Varner, Gary E. 2012. *Personhood, Ethics, and Animal Cognition: Situating Animals in Hare's Two-Level Utilitarianism.* New York: Oxford University Press.
Velleman, J. David. 1991. "Well-Being and Time." *Pacific Philosophical Quarterly* 72: 48–77.
Viscusi, W. Kip. 2018. *Pricing Lives: Guideposts for a Safer Society.* Princeton: Princeton University Press.
Viscusi, W. Kip, and Joseph E. Aldy. 2003. "The Value of a Statistical Life: A Critical Review of Market Estimates throughout the World." *Journal of Risk and Uncertainty* 27: 5–76.
von Neumann, John, and Oskar Morgenstern. 1944. *Theory of Games and Economic Behavior.* Princeton: Princeton University Press.
von Winterfeldt, Detlof, and Ward Edwards. 1986. *Decision Analysis and Behavioral Research.* Cambridge: Cambridge University Press.
Voorhoeve, Alex. 2014. "How Should We Aggregate Competing Claims?" *Ethics* 125: 64–87.
Walen, Alec. 2020. "Risks and Weak Aggregation: Why Different Models of Risk Suit Different Types of Cases." *Ethics* 131: 62–86.
Warren, Mary Anne. 1973. "On the Moral and Legal Status of Abortion." *Monist* 57: 43–61.
Warren, James. 2014. "The Symmetry Problem." In Steven Luper, ed., *The Cambridge Companion to Life and Death*, pp. 165–180. Cambridge: Cambridge University Press.
Weymark, John A. 2016. "Social Welfare Functions." In Matthew D. Adler and Marc Fleurbaey, eds., *The Oxford Handbook of Well-Being and Public Policy*, pp. 126–159. New York: Oxford University Press.

Weymark, John A. 2022. "Vaihinger's Fictionalism Meets Binmore's Knowledge-as-Commitment." *Homo Oeconomicus* 39: 199–217.

White House. 2025. Executive Order: "Unleashing Prosperity Through Deregulation". https://www.whitehouse.gov/presidential-actions/2025/01/unleashing-prosperity-through-deregulation/.

Wiener, Jonathan B. 2013. "The Diffusion of Regulatory Oversight." In Michael A. Livermore and Richard L. Revesz, eds., *The Globalization of Cost-Benefit Analysis in Environmental Policy*, pp. 123–141. Oxford: Oxford University Press.

Wiener, Jonathan B., and Alberto Alemanno. 2017. "Comparing Regulatory Oversight Bodies: the US Office of Information and Regulatory Affairs and the EU Regulatory Scrutiny Board." In Susan Rose-Ackerman, Peter L. Lindseth and Blake Emerson, eds., *Comparative Administrative Law*. Second edition, pp. 333–351. Cheltenham: Edward Elgar.

Woodard, Christopher. 2019. *Taking Utilitarianism Seriously*. Oxford: Oxford University Press.

World Bank. 2022. *Poverty and Shared Prosperity 2022: Correcting Course*. Washington, DC: World Bank.

Index

For the benefit of digital users, indexed terms that span two pages (e.g., 52–53) may, on occasion, appear on only one of those pages.